Critical Thinking Handbook:

K – 3

A Guide for Remodelling Lesson Plans in Language Arts, Social Studies, & Science

by
Richard Paul, A. J. A. Binker, and Daniel Weil

Foundation for Critical Thinking
Sonoma State University
Rohnert Park, CA 94928
707–664–2940
© 1990

Acknowledgments

We are deeply grateful to Trish Taylor and Renee Denise, for without their diligent and often brilliant rewriting and editing, the book, especially the strategy chapter and remodels, would have been significantly less clear, complete, and vivid. Furthermore, our thanks to Trish for her invaluable work in overseeing the staff and ensuring this book's timely publication. We would also like to thank Eric Brittenham for his apropos drawings of Nancy, Fran, and Sam; and Ron Lisky for his fine graphics work. Finally, we wish to acknowledge the help of Paige C. Binker, Cameron Marshall, Marla Charbonneau, Kenneth Adamson, Jane Kelsberg, and Niki Snowden.

Contents

6 Remodelling Social Studies Lessons

7 Remodelling Science Lessons

8 Remodelling Math Lessons

9 Remodelling Thematic Units

Part II: Achieving the Deeper Understandings

10 Thinking Critically About Teaching: From Didactic to Critical Teaching

11 Remodelling the Curriculum

12 Remodelling: A Foundation For Staff Development

13 The Greensboro Plan: A Sample Staff Development Plan

14 What Critical Thinking Means to Me: The Views of Teachers

15 Regarding a Definition of Critical Thinking

16 Glossary: An Educators' Guide to Critical Thinking Terms and Concepts

Appendices

Resources for Teaching Critical Thinking

Introduction

The Design of the Book

This handbook has one basic objective: to demonstrate that it is possible and practical to integrate instruction for critical thinking into the teaching of all subjects. We focus on language arts, social studies, and science, but we believe that the range of sample *before* and *after* lessons we provide will prove to any open-minded person that teaching so as to cultivate the critical thinking of students is eminently *practical*. We also believe that it should be given the highest priority, for it is *necessary* if we genuinely want to prepare our students for the real world which awaits them personally, politically, and vocationally.

Of course, to say that it is practical is not to say that it is simple and easy. To teach for critical thinking requires that teachers themselves think critically, and very often teachers have not been encouraged to do so. Furthermore, sometimes they do not feel competent to do so. Every teacher interested in fostering critical thinking must be prepared to undergo an evolutionary process over an extended period of time. Mistakes will be made along the way. Many didactic teaching habits have to be broken down, to be replaced by ones more like coaching than lecturing. In any case, there are many dimensions of critical thinking, and one needs to be patient to come to terms with them. Of course, since critical thinking is essential in the life of adults as well as children, teachers will find many uses for their emerging critical thinking abilities in their everyday life outside the classroom: as a consumer, citizen, lover, and person.

We have divided this handbook into two parts: "Putting Critical Thinking into Instruction," and "Achieving the Deeper Understandings." We have put a good deal of the theory of critical thinking instruction into "Part Two" because most teachers like to get a good look at application before they spend much time on theory. In a way this makes good sense. Why learn a theory if you're not happy with what the theory makes possible? On the other hand, it is sometimes hard to understand and appreciate the application if one is not clear about the theory that underlies it.

1

How and *why* are often deeply intertwined. We hope therefore that the reader will move back and forth between parts one and two, as needed. It would probably be a good idea to thumb through the book as a whole, familiarizing yourself with what's there, so that when you run into a problem you will be apt to remember sections of the book that are likely to shed light upon it. For example, notice that the glossary of critical thinking terms may be of use if you run across a term in critical thinking whose use and importance is not perfectly clear to you. In fact, reading randomly in the glossary is a good way to stimulate your sense of what critical thinking is.

Each of the chapters makes the transition from a didactic paradigm of education to a critical one a little easier. This chapter provides an introduction to critical thinking and its importance for education, an introduction to lesson remodelling, and some suggestions for using this book. Chapter 2, "Global Strategies", begins to delve more deeply into what education for critical thought requires of teachers. Chapter 3 describes the thirty-five remodelling strategies, explains their importance, and suggests how to teach for them. The rest of "Part One" consists primarily of remodelled lessons. The three main subject areas are introduced with chapters describing the relationship between the subject and critical thought, and some frequently encountered flaws in textbook approaches. The last chapter focuses on remodelling lessons into thematic units.

"Part II: Achieving the Deeper Understandings", opens with a comparison of didactic and critical views on education. Its purpose is to help teachers grasp the educational big picture, and distinguish what education is from what it is not. It includes a description of common features of texts that impede critical thought. Chapter 9 outlines the changes in curriculum required by a shift toward education for critical thought. Chapter 10 and 11 provide practical ideas for facilitating staff development in critical thinking. Chapter 12, "What Critical Thinking Means to Me", consists of short writings on critical thinking by Greensboro teachers after a workshop on critical thinking. In chapter 13 we consider the problem of defining critical thinking, and examine several definitions. Chapter 14 is an analytic glossary of words and phrases key to critical thinking and education.

Why Critical Thinking Is Essential to Education

If we consider some of the many complaints of classroom teachers concerning their pupils and then contrast them with what we look for in the ideal student, we will recognize that the fundamental missing element in schooling today is *thinking students* or, more precisely, *critically thinking* students.

Here are some of the many complaints we hear from teachers:

- ✓ "Most students aren't motivated; they don't want to study or work. They look for chances to goof off, clown around, or disrupt class. They'd rather talk about music, clothes, cars, ..."
- ✓ "Students forget what they've learned. We have to keep going over the same points, reminding them of what they've learned, rather than building on past learning. Each class begins at square one."
- ✓ "Most students are obsessed with grades and don't care about learning."
- ✓ "They're impatient. They want clear simple answers and they want them fast."
- ✓ "They make the same mistakes over and over again. They don't learn to correct their own mistakes."
- ✓ "They don't use what they've learned."
- ✓ "They need to be told every little thing. They don't even try to figure things out. They want us to do all of their thinking for them."

✓ "When I ask if there are questions, they don't have any; but they haven't understood the lesson."

✓ "When assigned position papers, many students just write facts. The rest simply state and repeat their feelings."

✓ "They hate to read. (It's boring.)"

✓ "They hate to write. (It's too hard.)"

✓ "Instead of explaining or developing their ideas, they just repeat themselves."

✓ "They can't seem to stay on topic for long without going off on tangents."

The kind of students teachers would like to have are equally easy to describe:

✓ Students who are motivated to learn, get excited by ideas, don't need to be reprimanded, and pay attention by choice.

✓ Students who remember what they learned yesterday, last month, last year; who don't have to be reminded over and over again what was covered before.

✓ Students who see grades as a by-product of learning; who put learning on a par with grades.

✓ Students who recognize that they can't completely understand everything at once, who are willing to delve; who are dissatisfied with pat answers.

✓ Students who learn from their mistakes, correct themselves.

✓ Students who *use* what they've learned.

✓ Students who can and will try to figure things out for themselves and don't expect me to do all of the thinking.

✓ Students who recognize when they don't understand something and can ask questions for clarification.

✓ Students who can get beyond the facts and the surface to explore deeper meaning; students who respond thoughtfully and go beyond knee-jerk reactions and first impressions.

✓ Students who like to read and talk about what they've read.

✓ Students who recognize the need to write in order to develop their ideas.

✓ Students who know the difference between explaining themselves and repeating themselves.

✓ Students who can and do stick to the point.

If we look closely at how teaching is typically structured, we will see that at the root of it are conceptions of knowledge, learning, and teaching that unwittingly take the motivation to *think* away from students. In most classes most of the time, teachers are talking and actively engaged, while students are listening passively. Most teachers' utterances are statements, not questions. When teachers ask questions, they typically wait only a couple of seconds before they answer their own questions. Knowledge is taken to be equivalent to recall, so that when students can repeat what the teacher or text said, they are thought to have knowledge. Attempt is continually made to reduce the complex to the simple, giving students formulas, procedures, short cuts, and algorithms to memorize and practice in hopes that understanding will emerge at the same time.

Schoenfeld reports on an experiment in which elementary students were asked questions like this: "There are 26 sheep and 10 goats on a ship. How old is the captain?" 76 of the 97 students "solved" the problem by adding, subtracting, multiplying or dividing. (Schoenfeld, 1989.) They felt they were expected to do so as quickly and "correctly" as possible. They did *not* feel they were expected to *make sense of* the problem. Instruction and practice had not emphasized *understanding* the problem.

Schoenfeld cites many similar cases, including a study that demonstrated that students tend to approach "word problems" in math by using the key word algorithm, that is, when

3

reading problems like, "John had eight apples. He gave three to Mary. How many does John have left?", they look for the words like 'left' to tell them what operation to perform. As Schoenfeld puts it, "... the situation was so extreme that many students chose to subtract in a problem that began 'Mr. Left ...'." (Schoenfeld, 1982.) Giving students such short cuts as indicator words, though it seems to make learning easier, actually interferes with learning in a deeper sense. Students are, in effect, taught that problems can be solved by circling data and going through steps practiced before ("I'm supposed to do this, then this, then this."); that they shouldn't slow down and think things through. They have had much more practice going through the steps than they have at thinking things through.

This tendency toward robotic, mindless responses becomes obsessive in many students. Hence, in their minds, history class becomes a place where they hear names, dates, events, and judgments about them, and then try to repeat what they have heard on tests. Literature becomes uninteresting stories to remember along with what the teacher said is important about them, such as foreshadowing.

Consider how students are generally taught factual detail. Students are continually presented with easily retainable facts (for example, foreign countries' main exports), and merely expected to reiterate them. They do not clearly understand *why* they should remember these facts. These collections of facts become merely sets of words in their heads, with no meaning, significance, or use. They *can* have meaning to students, can become *intelligible* to students, when they tell students something important, something students need to know. If students are trying to understand a country's economic problems, it may become important to know its chief exports. In such a context, that fact isn't just sitting there in the student's head as a bunch of words, it has meaning. It has a place in a broader picture; it has consequences; it helps that student understand that country's problem. It is *context*, not the mere fact itself, that gives it meaning, that makes it intelligible.

Values and principles tend to be treated as though they were facts. They are stated, and students are expected to reiterate them. This sort of process does not produce *understanding*. Principles (such as, "Write clearly!" and, "Stick to the point!") have their meaning and their justification in their application, in their *use*. I may know that I'm supposed to stick to the point, but this principle is little more than words to me if I don't know *how* to stick to the point, if I don't learn how to recognize *for myself* when I'm focused and when I stray. I can only learn how by practice, by *thinking* — by trying, sometimes succeeding, sometimes failing, by seeing for myself when I succeeded, when I failed, and by *understanding* the differences between the successes and failures.

A critical model of education reverses these patterns at every point. Students are continually asked to think about what they learn, to try to apply their new ideas, to compare their own ideas with those in their textbooks, to actively discuss what they are learning in small groups.

The underlying assumption in present education is that knowledge consists of bits of information, concepts, and skills which students can learn through lecture and rote memorization. Educators assume that students automatically replace ignorance with knowledge, misconception with truth. This assumption is unjustified.

One main consequence of this idea is that being told something, however clear the explanation, does not guarantee understanding. If you tell me something that contradicts or is incompatible with my present system of beliefs, I'm unlikely to replace my whole belief system with that new idea. I will often distort what you've said so that it fits my belief system. I may simply "tack it on" to my beliefs, ignoring the incompatibility between old and new, bouncing back and forth between them, sometimes using one, sometimes the other, willy-nilly; or I may simply fail to take it in at all. To really learn the new idea, I have to struggle through the problems the idea creates for me, *build* a new mental structure or system of beliefs. This process requires me to make my present beliefs explicit (figure out what I really think), and slowly reshape the old system into a new body of thought. Hence, to understand the new idea, concept, or principle, I have to think my way through to it, internalize it. One way to achieve this is through extended discussion, talking and listening to others as they internalize new knowledge. Consider how this conception of learning works.

When I state my thoughts aloud, I think again about what I'm saying, realize, perhaps, that my thinking is not clear. I may think of a new example; I may put the point in a slightly better way, or different way, and thus come to see new sense in it. When I have to convince others (such as classmates), I have to try to give convincing reasons for thinking as I do. The people I'm talking to respond: they understand some parts of what I've said better than others, forcing me to rephrase my point and so think it through again in a slightly different way, with the result that I understand it more clearly. My audience says things in response that had never occurred to me; they ask questions, raise objections, and so on. As I answer, I find myself saying things I hadn't realized I believed. Sometimes I say things I know are wrong, and so I have to change my original idea somewhat. My audience may suggest new examples, or expand on my ideas in a new way. In short, while I'm discussing things with my classmates *I am learning*. By listening to me, reacting, and hearing my replies, my classmates are learning. We're all thinking things through together. As a group, we know more, can figure out more, and have more and better ideas than any one of us has individually. Having done our own thinking and developed our own views, we understand more deeply; what we learn becomes part of us rather than mere words which we will soon forget.

This is at the heart of education for critical thought. Students learn to think by practicing thinking, learn to learn by practicing learning, learn to judge by practicing judging and by assessing those judgments. In this way, students come to use more of the full power of their minds.

When teachers begin to integrate critical thinking into their instructional practice, they have experiences like the following (taken from *The Greensboro Plan: Infusing Reasoning and Writing into the K-12 Curriculum*):

Beth:

I teach North Carolina History and 8th grade English, and I am always trying to bridge the gap and use an interdisciplinary approach. What critical thinking helps me do is go beyond the textbook and find things we can really discuss using the Socratic method — to go beyond just the facts and try to analyze the situation — to put ourselves in the other person's shoes — to look at a lot of different components.

Here is an article on slavery which I have copied and brought with me to show how you do not have to rewrite all your lesson plans to infuse critical thinking into your curriculum. Instead, you go further and bring in other things to enhance what you're teaching and give opportunities for discussion. This article is about slavery and slave trading. I have the students become one of the slaves on the ship and write a diary about how it would feel to be a slave. Later on in English, students write an essay on whether or not the ship captains should have been tried as criminals. This asks students to look at ideas from different viewpoints. For a final activity, I asked students to assume that they were a member of the English Parliament of 1807 and to write a persuasive essay on whether or not slavery should be banned and why.

Mandy:

Since I have taken part in this project, I have become a much more critical thinker. That's helped me tremendously in my classroom.

I always explain to my students how all our subjects are overlapping; this helps them in real life. One revised science lesson we used this year was building a rain forest in our room in a terrarium. We turned it into a vivarium by adding an anole, a small lizard.

The students decided they wanted to write a book about the anole, and the first thing they wanted to do was go to the library to *copy* information. Instead of this, we brainstormed to find out what we already knew and what we could learn just by observation. All my students became motivators for others while we worked with words.

After the pre-writing exercises, I took them to the media center for research. Again, they wanted to fall into the trap of copying from the encyclopedia. But I allowed them only to write down words — single words or maybe a phrase, rather than copying down sentences. It was difficult for them — it was difficult for me too.

They came back from the media center with ideas rather than with things they had copied. We talked about the ideas and categorized — and then I told them to write down ideas in their own words. It was amazing what happened! If I had given this assignment a year ago, a description of the anole would be only a few sentences long. My students this year wrote pages — they really did — and they were excited. This was their work; this was their description; it was not *World Book's* description. And it made it much more real to them — and of course more real to me, too.

In the first example, notice how students had to grapple again and again with the concept of slavery from different angles: What was it like? In what ways were different people partly responsible? What do I think of it? How can I convince others to agree with me? Each time students explored the issue, they were learning and using facts, probing and clarifying values, using principles, and each time they were putting these pieces together.

The second example above illustrates the difference between passive recall and active thought. Students first publicly shared their original beliefs, ideas, and suggestions. Then, when they consulted resources, they wrote only the barest bones of the information, and were thus forced to *reconstruct* the new knowledge. Furthermore, though this process was more difficult, the students wrote more and were more pleased with the results.

Finally, consider two more experiences of teaching students to learn deeply.

Sylvia

My involvement in the Reasoning and Writing project came about because I believe the following: *1)* students are faced with an explosion of information; *2)* given a limited time in which to learn, students must choose *what* information they need and learn *how* to acquire it; *3)* to make intelligent choices, students must exercise good judgment; *4)* successful living in today's world requires high order thinking and reasoning skills; *5)* writing can be used as a tool to improve thinking and reasoning skills in all curriculum areas ....

I have incorporated two new ideas this year: Socratic questioning and writing to aid concept development. I have worked primarily with one class, using questioning techniques to encourage students to think critically. The results have been encouraging: class discussions became more animated, students offered ideas freely, criticism was constructive, helpful, and resulted in better ideas. I believe that the entire class benefitted.

One high school teacher tried to focus on critical thinking in a sophomore English class. This teacher designed small group and paired discussions only to have the students complain, "You're supposed to use the grammar book. You're supposed to start on the first page and give us the sentences to do and then check them and then we do the next sentence ...."

The students insisted that "doing the sentences" was the top priority. One of the students said, in defense of this method, "We learned about prepositions." However, when the instructor asked the class *what* they had learned about prepositions, the class went silent. When asked, "Do you remember what prepositions are? Can you name some?" nobody could. Though this teacher continued her emphasis on critical thinking, she also gave students "sentences to do" for part of the class time. After the fourth day, no students objected when she neglected to assign more sentences. On their final exam, these students were asked, "Why is it better for a school to teach you how to find answers than to teach you the answers?" Among their responses were the following:

✓ So you can get in the habit of doing it yourself and not depend on someone else.
✓ When you teach people the answer, they will never try to find the answer thereself. They will look for somebody to give them the answer instead of looking for it because they don't know how to find it.
✓ When you get a job, they will expect you to find the answers yourself.
✓ Because it makes you feel good about yourself when you can look up something by yourself and get the answer correct. You feel more independent in school.
✓ School is not going to be with you all your life.
✓ So you can learn how to find the answers to *your* problems because one day you're going to have to find the answers yourself. Nobody is going to be able to give you the answers.
✓ Because it won't help you to know the answers and not know what they mean.
✓ Because in the future there won't be a teacher to hold your hand or to tell you everything you should know. You should learn on your own.

As you consider the rest of the material in this book, we ask you to apply these basic ideas to each facet of the task of incorporating critical thought into instructional practice. Just as students must struggle through a process of restructuring their thought to incorporate new facts, skills, and principles, so must teachers grapple with the problems of restructuring their conceptions of education and learn to apply the principles underlying it. We encourage you to work your way through our ideas — reading, explaining, listening, questioning, writing, applying, assessing — figuring out what you think about what we say.

Our Concept of Critical Thinking

Our basic concept of critical thinking is, at root, simple. We could define it as the art of taking charge of your own mind. Its value is also at root simple: if we can take charge of our own minds, we can take charge of our lives; we can improve them, bringing them under our self command and direction. Of course, this requires that we learn self-discipline and the art of self-examination. This involves becoming interested in how our minds work, how we can monitor, fine tune, and modify their operations for the better. It involves getting into the habit of reflectively examining our impulsive and accustomed ways of thinking and acting in every dimension of our lives.

All that we do, we do on the basis of some motivations or reasons. But we rarely examine our motivations to see if they make sense. We rarely scrutinize our reasons critically to see if they are rationally justified. As consumers we sometimes buy things impulsively and uncritically, without stopping to determine whether we really need what we are inclined to buy or whether we can afford it or whether it's good for our health or whether the price is competitive. As parents we often respond to our children impulsively and uncritically, without stopping to determine whether our actions are consistent with how we want to act as parents or whether we are contributing to their self esteem or whether we are discouraging them from thinking or from taking responsibility for their own behavior.

As citizens, too often we vote impulsively and uncritically, without taking the time to familiarize ourselves with the relevant issues and positions, without thinking about the long-run implications of what is being proposed, without paying attention to how politicians manipulate us by flattery or vague and empty promises. As friends, too often we become the victims of our own infantile needs, "getting involved" with people who bring out the worst in us or who stimulate us to act in ways that we have been trying to change. As husbands or wives, too often we think only of our own desires and points of view, uncritically ignoring the needs and perspectives of our mates, assuming that what we want and what we think is clearly justified and true, and that when they disagree with us they are being unreasonable and unfair.

As patients, too often we allow ourselves to become passive and uncritical in our health care, not establishing good habits of eating and exercise, not questioning what our doctor says, not designing or following good plans for our own well-ness. As teachers, too often we allow ourselves to uncritically teach as we have been taught, giving assignments that students can mindlessly do, inadvertently discouraging their initiative and independence, missing opportunities to culti-vate their self-discipline and thoughtfulness.

It is quite possible, and unfortunately quite "natural", to live an unexamined life, to live in a more or less automated, uncritical way. It is possible to live, in other words, without really taking charge of the persons we are becoming, without developing, or acting upon, the skills and insights we are capable of. However, if we allow ourselves to become unreflective persons, or rather, to the extent that we do, we are likely to do injury to ourselves and others, and to miss many opportuni-ties to make our own lives, and the lives of others, fuller, happier, and more productive.

On this view, as you can see, critical thinking is an eminently practical goal and value. It is focused on an ancient Greek ideal of "living an examined life". It is based on the skills, the insights, and the values essential to that end. It is a way of going about living and learning that empowers us and our students in quite practical ways. When taken seriously, it can transform every dimension of school life: how we formulate and promulgate rules, how we relate to our students, how we encourage them to relate to each other, how we cultivate their reading, writing, speaking, and listening, what we model for them in and outside the class-room, and how we do each of these things.

Of course, we are likely to make critical thinking a basic value in school only insofar as we make it a basic value in our lives. Therefore, to become adept at teaching so as to foster critical thinking, we must become committed to thinking critically and reflectively about our own lives and the lives of those around us. We must become active, daily, practitioners of critical thought. We must regularly model for our students what it is to reflectively examine, critically assess, and effectively improve the way we live.

Introduction to Remodelling: Components of Remodels and Their Functions

The basic idea behind lesson plan remodelling as a strategy for staff development in critical thinking is simple. Every practicing teacher works daily with lesson plans of one kind or another. To remodel lesson plans is to critique one or more lesson plans and formulate one or more new lesson plans based on that critical process. To help teachers generalize from specific remodelling moves, and so facilitate their grasp of strong sense critical thinking and how it can be taught, we have devised a list of teaching strategies. Each strategy highlights an aspect of critical thought. Each use of it illustrates how that aspect can be encouraged in students. In the chapter, "Strategies", we explain the thirty-five strategies illustrated in the remodels. Each strategy has two main parts: the "principle" and the "application". The principle links the strategy to the idea of strong sense critical thinking. In the application, we explain some ways the aspect of critical thought can be encouraged.

Complete remodelled lessons have three major components: an "Original Lesson", or statement of the "Standard Approach" (which describes the topic and how it is covered, including questions and activities); the "Critique" (which describes the significance of the topic and its value for the educated thinker, evaluates the original, and provides a general idea of how the lesson can be remodelled); and the "Remodelled Lesson" (which describes the new lesson, gives questions to be posed to students and student activities, and cites the critical thinking strategies by number). The strategy number generally follows the questions or activities it represents. When an entire remodel or section develops one dimension of critical thought in depth, the number appears at the top of the remodel or section. Complete remodel sets also include a list of "Objectives" which integrate the objectives of the original with the critical thinking goals; and the list of critical thinking "Strategies" applied in the remodel (listed in order of first appearance). Note the functions of these parts in the example below. Each component can serve some purpose for both the writer and the reader.

Advertising

Objectives of the remodelled lesson
The students will:
- practice listening critically by analyzing and evaluating T.V. commercials
- exercise fairmindedness by considering advertisements from a variety of perspectives
- analyze and evaluate the arguments given in ads
- practice using critical vocabulary to analyze and evaluate ads
- clarify key words
- distinguish relevant from irrelevant facts in ads
- examine assumptions in ads
- develop insight into egocentricity by exploring the ways in which ads appeal to unconscious desires

Standard Approach

> Very few texts actually address the issue of advertising. Those that do touch upon indicators to watch for which signal the use of some sort of reasoning — such indicators as "if ... then", "because", "since", "either ... or", and "therefore". Students are to decide if the reasoning presented is logical or illogical. Some lessons on ads focus on finding and decoding the factual information regarding sales. Students are often asked to write their own ads.

Critique

We chose this lesson for its subject: advertising. Ads are a natural tie-in to critical thinking, since many are designed to persuade the audience that it needs or wants a product. Ads provide innumerable clear-cut examples of irrelevance, distortion, suppressed evidence, and vague uses of language. Analysis of ads can teach students critical thinking micro-skills and show their use in context. Practice in analyzing and evaluating ads can help students develop

9

the ability to listen critically. The standard approach, however, is not done in a way which best achieves these results.

Such lessons often focus more on writing ads than critiquing them. They tend to treat neutral and advertising language as basically equivalent in meaning, though different in effect, rather than pointing out how differences in effect arise from differences in meaning. They down-play the emptiness, irrelevance, repetition, questionable claims, and distortion of language in most ads. Their examples bear little resemblance to real ads. By rarely addressing ads aimed at students, texts minimize useful transfer.

Since most students are exposed to more television commercials than other ads, we recommend that students discuss real commercials aimed at them. We also provide suggestions for using ads to practice use of critical vocabulary and to discuss the visual and audio aspects of commercials.

Strategies used to remodel

S–22 listening critically: the art of silent dialogue
S–9 developing confidence in reason
S–14 clarifying and analyzing the meanings of words or phrases
S–16 evaluating the credibility of sources of information
S–3 exercising fairmindedness
S–31 distinguishing relevant from irrelevant facts
S–18 analyzing or evaluating arguments, interpretations, beliefs, or theories
S–35 exploring implications and consequences
S–30 examining or evaluating assumptions
S–28 thinking precisely about thinking: using critical vocabulary
S–2 developing insight into egocentricity or sociocentricity
S–29 noting significant similarities and differences

Remodelled Lesson Plan S–22

Due to the number of ads to which students are exposed, and their degree of influence, we recommend that the class spend as much time as possible on the subject. As students learn to approach ads thoughtfully and analytically and practice applying critical insight to their lives, they develop faith in their reasoning powers and their ability to see through attempts to irrationally manipulate them. **S–9**

To focus on ads and language, begin by having students give complete descriptions of what is said in a variety of television commercials. Put the quotes on the board. For each commercial, the class can evaluate the arguments presented in ads by discussing the following questions: What ideas does it give you about the product (or service) and owning or using it? Does it give reasons for buying the product? If so, what reasons? Are they good reasons? What are the key words? Do they have a clear meaning? What? **S–14** What other words could have been chosen? Who made this ad? Why? Do they have reason to distort evidence about the worth of the product? **S–16** How might someone who wasn't trying to sell the product describe it? How might a competitor describe it? **S–3** What would you need to know in order to make a wise decision about whether to buy it? Does the commercial address these points? **S–31** Why or why not? Has anyone here had experience with the product? What? **S–18**

The teacher interested in developing students' critical vocabulary can have students practice while critiquing ads. Use questions like the following: What does the ad *imply*? **S-35** Does the ad make, or lead the audience to make, any *assumptions*? Are the *assumptions* true, *questionable*, or false? **S-30** Does the ad contain an *argument*? If so, what is the *conclusion*? Is the *conclusion* stated or *implied*? Does the ad misuse any *concepts* or ideas? To judge the product, what facts are *relevant*? Are the *relevant* facts presented? **S-31** Does it make any *irrelevant* claims? **S-28**

When the commercials have been discussed, have students group them by the nature of the ads (repetition, positive but empty language, etc.) or by the appeals made (to the desires to have fun, be popular, seem older, etc.) Have students fill out the groups by naming similar commercials not previously discussed. Students could discuss why these appeals are made. "How do ads work? Why do they work? Do they work on you? On whom? Why? What are slogans for? Jingles? Why are running stories and continuing characters used? Why are the various techniques effective?" **S-2**

The class could also compare different ads for the same product, aimed at different audiences (e.g., fast food ads aimed at children, and at adults). "How do these two differ? Why? To whom is each addressed? Why are they different?" **S-29** The class could compare ads for different brands of the same or similar products; compare ads to what can be read on ingredients labels; or design and conduct blind taste tests. **S-18**

To gain further insight into listening critically, the class could also discuss aspects of the ads other than use of language. "What does the ad show? What effect is it designed to achieve? How? Why? What is the music like? Why is it used? Do the actors and announcers use their tone of voice to persuade? Facial expression? How? Are these things relevant to judging or understanding the product?" **S-22**

The teacher may also have the class critique ads for any stereotyping (e.g., sexual stereotyping). **S-2**

For further practice, if a VCR is available, watch and discuss taped commercials. Students could jot notes on critical points and share their insights.

The "Standard Approach" (or "Original Lesson") describes how the subject is treated. As a summary, it provides focus for the critique and remodel. Teachers who share their work can better follow the remodel when the original is clearly described. The critical thinking infused is better highlighted — for both the writer and the reader — when the original is available for contrast with the remodel.

The "Critique" generally begins by explaining the use of having students study the subject, the role such study has in the life of the critical thinker, and how critical thinking applies to the topic. It then provides a critique of the original from the point of view of education for critical thinking. Given the reasons for studying the topic, and the role such study should have for the critical thinker, the ways the original fosters and fails to foster such understanding is explicated.

Thus, the analysis of the significance of the topic provides a focus for and basis of the evaluation. The evaluation, then, mentions parts of the original that can be kept, and parts that should be changed or dropped, and *why*. The critique often includes a general statement suggesting what must be added to raise deeper issues and develop insight into the material. In short, the critique *justifies* the changes made to produce the remodel.

The "Remodelled Lesson" then follows, based on the analysis and evaluation of the topic and its treatment in the original. It reflects the reasoning given in the critique. It includes teacher questions and student activities designed to overcome the problems in the original. Citing the strategy numbers helps make the critical thinking infused explicit, and offers cross-referencing for others to better see what is being done in the new lesson and why. Readers of the remodel can refer to the strategy descriptions given in the "Strategy" chapter, if the function of the strategy is unclear to them. Furthermore, citing the strategy provides a check for the writer, who, during the writing and revision process, can evaluate the questions and activities to make sure that they do in fact engage the students in that particular dimension of critical thought.

The list of "Strategies used to remodel" helps readers who want to better understand a particular strategy, or want ideas for applying it, to easily find examples. As the readers read the "Remodelled Plan", they can easily refer to this list for the names of the strategies cited.

The "Objectives" provide an opportunity for writers of remodels to summarize their work, and show the readers how the strategies apply to the content, that is, to show the relationship between the content and critical thought. Writing objectives, looking at what you've written, and making the goals explicit as a list of what students will do, helps the writer ensure that the remodel does achieve the goals as stated. If not, the goals should be added to the remodel or dropped from the objectives. (Does the activity as described *really* have students carefully and fairmindedly evaluate these assumptions?) Objectives can also show relationships between the strategies as they apply to that lesson; they make explicit that, in this case, this one strategy is (or these three strategies are) used in the service of this main strategy. For example, "Students will practice dialogical thinking by considering evidence and assumptions from multiple perspectives." Reading through the objectives of other people's remodels can make it easier to find ideas in them to use in one's own work. When confronted with a particular remodelling problem, reading the objectives of other remodels is an easy way of finding out which remodels can provide help or inspiration.

The finished form of the complete "remodel sets" and the separation and order of their elements is not intended to suggest the precise order in which the elements are developed or written. Generally, the three major components are begun in rough form: an initial statement of key parts of the original and their functions, its most obvious strengths and weaknesses, and provisional revisions are usually jotted down first.

The writer can then step back and evaluate these rough ideas and begin to analyze the situation more deeply. Does my critique really get at the heart of the matter? Is the evaluation fair, accurately stated, and properly justified? Does my remodel really address the flaws I've identified? Could I add something to take the lesson more deeply into the subject? Am I missing a good opportunity to encourage careful, honest thought? Are the main points of the remodel explained or justified by what I've said in the critique?

The remodeller may also want to review pertinent strategies, skim other remodels for ideas, and share their work with colleagues for comments before beginning a final rewrite. When the three main components are in relatively finished form, the writer can list the strategies used. The final version of the "objectives" is usually written last and checked to ensure that it reflects the remodel.

Although going through an extended process like this may seem like a lot of unnecessary work, and you needn't write up every instance of infusing critical thinking in polished form, we encourage you to put at least some of your work in this form for the following reasons:

- First impressions and initial ideas about what to do may be misleading and are rarely as valuable for either students or colleagues as a finished product which has been carefully evaluated and revised.

- The evaluation, revision, double-checking, and analysis provide crucial opportunities for teachers to develop the ability to engage in careful critical thought.

- Having to organize one's ideas and express them clearly helps the writer to more thoroughly probe those ideas, and discover other ideas.

- An extended process creates a finished product which is clearer and more helpful to colleagues with whom it is shared, than rough notes and scattered ideas would be.

- The objectives most worthwhile to pursue in the remodel will rarely be apparent until after the analysis and critique of the original lesson plan and the development of a remodelled lesson.

- Revision after further analysis can correct such mistakes as failing to include crucial points, or covering the material in a superficial or tangential way. It's remarkably easy to blast a critique for missing an important opportunity for developing critical thought, but then neglect to take advantage of the opportunity oneself. It's easy to miss the main point, purpose, or context of a topic, principle, or skill, when first considering it. It's easy to write fabulous-sounding objectives and then fail to fulfill them.

We therefore recommend a more extended process of producing remodels, with the elements given above, whether done in that order or not. (For example, the first step might be to confer with colleagues. With some lessons, one might have to review some strategies, remodels, or the subject introduction before being able to come up with remodel ideas.) Whatever process you use, we strongly encourage you to gain some experience in the careful and complete analysis and evaluation required to produce well written, complete remodel sets.

How to Use this Book

You may choose to read this book as you would any other book, but if you do, you will probably miss a good deal of the benefit that can be derived from it. There are no algorithms or recipes for understanding or teaching critical thinking. Although we separate aspects of critical thinking, the global concept of the truly reasonable person is behind each aspect, and each aspect relates both to it and to the other dimensions. Thus, to develop critical thought, one must continually move back and forth between the global ideal of the rational and fairminded thinker and the details describing such a thinker. Similarly, although we separate the aspects of staff development for integrating critical thinking into instruction (understanding the concept, critiquing present practice, formulating remodels), teachers must continually move back and forth between these activities.

If you are a K–3 teacher and you want to improve your ability to teach for critical thinking, this book can help you develop the ability to remodel your own lesson plans. Your own teaching strategies will progressively increase as your repertoire of critical thinking strategies grows. As you begin, try to develop a baseline sense of your present understanding of critical thinking and of your ability to critique and redesign lesson plans. The critiques and remodels that follow, and the principles and strategies that precede them, may provide an immediate catalyst for you to take your lesson plans and redesign them. But the longer critiques and remodels here might seem intimidating. Some of the strategies may seem unclear or confusing, and you may bog down as soon as you attempt to redesign your own lessons. Keep in mind that in some of our remodels, we put as many ideas as we could, in order to provide as many examples and varieties of applications as possible. Thus, some of the remodelled plans are longer and more elaborate than you might initially be willing to produce or teach. The purpose of this book is not to simply give you lesson ideas, but to encourage you to develop your own.

We therefore suggest alternative approaches and ways of conceiving the process:

- Read through the strategies and a couple of remodels, then write critiques and remodels of your own. After you have attempted a critique and remodel, read our critique and remodel of a similar lesson. By using this procedure, you will soon get a sense of the difficulties in the critique-remodel process. You will also have initiated the process of developing your own skills in this important activity.

- Another way of testing your understanding of the critical insights is to read the principle section of a strategy, and write your own application section.

- You could review a remodel of ours and find places where strategies were used but not cited and places where particular moves could be characterized by more than one strategy.

- You may want to take several strategies and write about their interrelationships.

- Or you might take a subject or topic and list significant questions about it. Share and discuss your lists with colleagues.

- If, when reviewing a remodel, you find a particular strategy confusing, review the principle and application in the strategy chapter. If, when reading the strategy chapter, you feel confused, review the critiques and remodels of the lessons listed below it. If you are still confused, do not use the strategy. Review it periodically until it becomes clear.

- When remodelling your own lessons, you will probably find that sometimes you can make more drastic changes or even completely rewrite a lesson, while at other times you may make only minor adjustments. Some of your remodels may make use of many strategies, say, two or more affective strategies, and a macro-ability requiring the coordinated use of several micro-skills. For other remodels, you may use only one strategy. It is better to use one clearly understood strategy than to attempt to use more than you clearly understand.

- You may want to begin remodelling by using only one or two strategies clearest to you. After remodelling some lessons, you will likely find yourself spontaneously using those strategies. You could then reread the strategy chapter and begin infusing additional strategies with which you feel comfortable. Thus, as the number of strategies you regularly use grows, your teaching can evolve at the pace most comfortable to you.

- If students don't grasp a critical idea or skill when you introduce it, don't give up. Critical insight must be developed over time. For instance, suppose the first attempt to get students to fairmindedly consider each other's views fails. It is likely that students are not in the habit of seriously considering each other's positions, and hence may not listen carefully to each other. If you make restating opposing views a routine part of discussion, students will eventually learn to prepare themselves by listening more carefully.

- Although the main purpose of this book is to help you remodel lesson plans, we have not limited our suggestions to the remodelling process. We strongly urge you to apply the insights embedded in the strategies to all aspects of the classroom (including discussions, conflicts, and untraditional lessons such as movies). You may also use our remodels or sections of them. Though many of our lessons are too long for one class period, we did not suggest where to break them up, nor did we provide follow-up questions. If you do experiment with any of our remodels, you will probably have to remodel them somewhat to take your students and text into account.

- We urge you to apply your growing critical insight to the task of analyzing and clarifying your concept of education and the educated person. Of each subject you teach, ask yourself what is most basic and crucial for an educated person to know or to be able to do. Highlight those aspects and teach them in a way that most fosters in-depth and useful understanding.

- Texts often have the same features — whether problems or opportunities for critical thought — occurring over and over again. Hence, remodelling a couple of lessons from a text can give you a basic structure to use many times over the course of the year.

- When comparing your work to ours, keep in mind that this is a flexible process; our remodel is not the only right one. Any changes which promote fairminded critical thought are improvements.

However you use what follows in this book, your understanding of the insights behind the strategies will determine the effectiveness of the remodels. Despite the detail with which we have delineated the strategies, they should not be translated into mechanistic, step-by-step procedures. Keep the goal of the well-educated, fairminded critical thinker continually in mind. Thinking critically involves insightful critical judgments at each step along the way. It is never done by recipe.

> *Lesson plan remodelling as a strategy for staff and curriculum development is not a simple one-shot approach. It requires patience and commitment. But it genuinely develops the critical thinking of teachers and puts them in a position to understand and help transform the curriculum into effective teaching and learning.*

Diagram 1

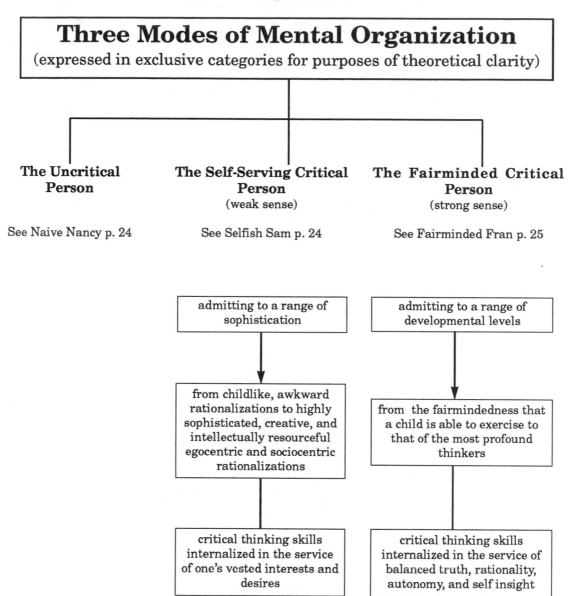

Three Modes of Mental Organization
(expressed in exclusive categories for purposes of theoretical clarity)

The Uncritical Person	The Self-Serving Critical Person (weak sense)	The Fairminded Critical Person (strong sense)
See Naive Nancy p. 24	See Selfish Sam p. 24	See Fairminded Fran p. 25

admitting to a range of sophistication	admitting to a range of developmental levels
from childlike, awkward rationalizations to highly sophisticated, creative, and intellectually resourceful egocentric and sociocentric rationalizations	from the fairmindedness that a child is able to exercise to that of the most profound thinkers
critical thinking skills internalized in the service of one's vested interests and desires	critical thinking skills internalized in the service of balanced truth, rationality, autonomy, and self insight

Note
Children enter school as fundamentally non-culpable, uncritical and self-serving thinkers. The educational task is to help them to become, as soon as possible and as fully as possible, responsible, fairminded, critical thinkers, empowered by intellectual skills and rational passions. Most people are some combination of the above three types; the proportions are the significant determinant of which of the three characterizations is most appropriate. For example, it is a common pattern for people to be capable of fairminded critical thought only when their vested interests or ego-attachments are not involved, hence the legal practice of excluding judges or jury members who can be shown to have such interests.

Diagram 2

Critical Thinking Lesson Plan Remodelling

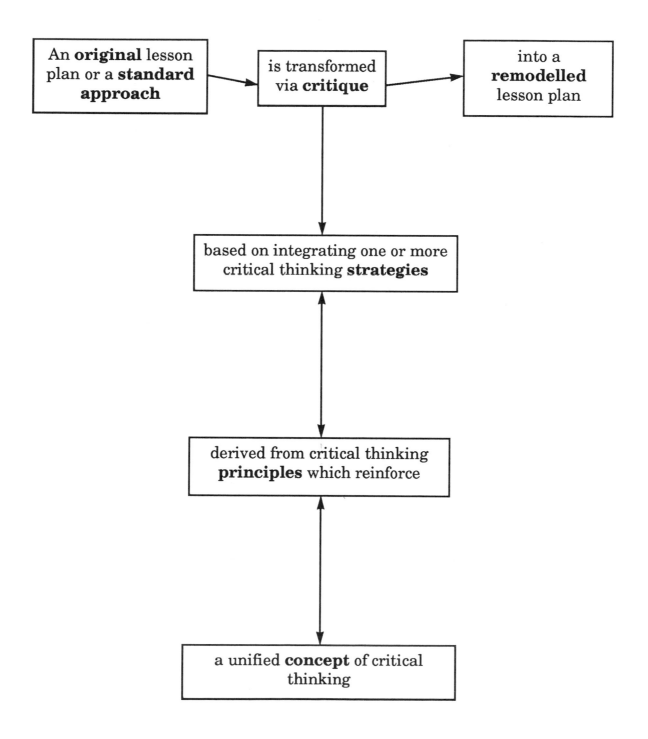

An **original** lesson plan or a **standard approach** → is transformed via **critique** → into a **remodelled** lesson plan

based on integrating one or more critical thinking **strategies**

derived from critical thinking **principles** which reinforce

a unified **concept** of critical thinking

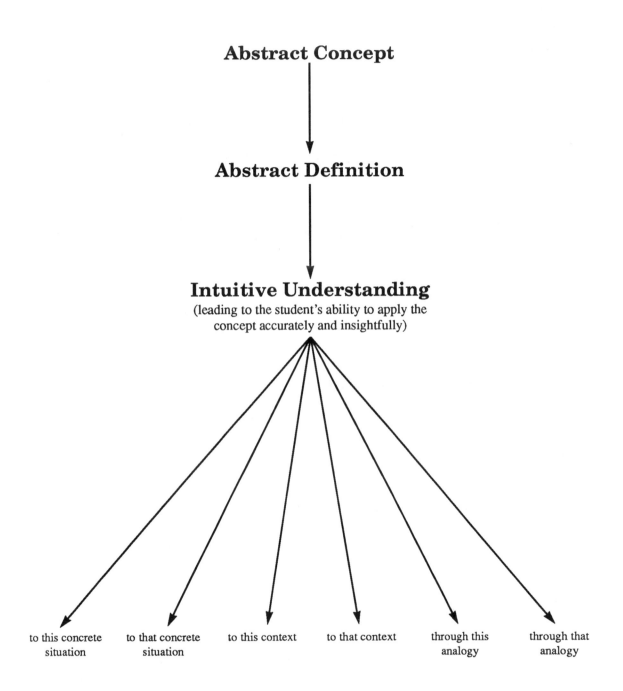

Abstract Concept

Abstract Definition

Intuitive Understanding
(leading to the student's ability to apply the
concept accurately and insightfully)

to this concrete
situation

to that concrete
situation

to this context

to that context

through this
analogy

through that
analogy

*Intuitive Understanding Enables Us
to Insightfully Bridge the Gap
Between Abstract Concept & Concrete Application*

This, is probably the fundamental reason why so much school learning is not effectively transferred to real life. It lacks the *intuitive* basis, the *insights,* for the translation. When we were students, our own teachers rarely took pains to ensure that we intuitively understood the basic concepts we were learning. Hence their teaching did not model for us teaching that fosters intuitive learning. As a result we are rarely sufficiently aware of the similar effect of our own teaching. As long as students are performing in certain standard ways, we often uncritically assume they "understand", that they are building a basis for using what they learn, that they will eventually be able to take what they learn and put it to use in the everyday world. This assumption is rarely justified.

As a first step toward preparing to help our students develop intuitive understandings of critical thinking concepts, we must make sure that the basic concepts that underlie critical thinking are intuitive to us. To help our students internalize the understandings essential to critical thought, we must ourselves gain practice in translating those same understandings into the context of our own lives. We must, in other words, internalize the basic concepts and principles of critical thinking so deeply that we habitually use them in all of the various dimensions of our own lives: as parents, consumers, teachers, and citizens, so that when we teach we teach in a way that helps our students translate all fundamental and root concepts and principles into the circumstances of their own day-to-day lives. (See the chart on the next page.)

Both we and our students, in other words, need to develop full-fledged *critical thinking intuitions*. This is, of course, a matter of long-term development. Neither we nor they can develop deep intuitions overnight. How, then, are we to proceed? What must we do to foster this long term development of critical thinking intuitions?

We must begin with an initial sense of what it is to develop intuitions. Then we must progressively deepen that sense as we explore a variety of ways of fostering critical thinking intuitions. The primary goal of this chapter is to lay a foundation for this understanding. The rest of the handbook will provide further examples to build upon as to the nature and importance of "intuitive" teaching.

To accomplish this end, we shall take a couple of the most fundamental distinctions that underlie critical thinking and illustrate how they can be made intuitive to children. At the same time, we will illustrate how these concepts can become more intuitive to us as teachers. Of course, we shall not attempt to cover all of the important distinctions but merely to illustrate the process of teaching for intuitive understanding. As you read, the kinds of essential "translations" required to help students ground basic concepts in basic insights should become progressively clearer.

We shall assume that you will pursue analogous strategies for the various other basic concepts in critical thinking on your own. Remember, the aim is an on-going commitment to the process of fostering an intuitive basis for all the principles of critical thinking, a commitment to the process of engaging students continually in translating back and forth between the abstract and the concrete, the general and the particular, the academic and the "real".

Using Dramatization to Foster Critical Thinking Intuitions

The Power of the Dramatic

The world that is most real to us is the world of actual persons dreaming, hoping, planning, acting out their lives, facing conflicts and problems, struggling to find happiness, success, and meaning. Abstract concepts become much more meaningful to us when we relate them directly to a dramatized world. That is why novels, plays, television programs, and movies typically have much more appeal to and impact on us than abstract treatises do. One reason for this is that there is a

Abstract Concept

(e.g., the concept of democracy)

We might have our students look up the word in a dictionary where they will find abstract characterizations (like "rule by the people")

Building Intuitive Understanding

(We might lead a class discussion Socratically focused on questions like "What does it mean to say that the people rule?", "What does it mean to say that the people decide?", "What if the people don't consider the issues, have they still decided?" "What if they don't get accurate information, are they still deciding?" "In what sorts of situations in your life is democratic decision-making used?" "When is non-democratic decision-making used?", "Is it sometimes better not to decide things democratically?"

Leading To

students' starting to apply the concept of democracy seriously to their daily lives.

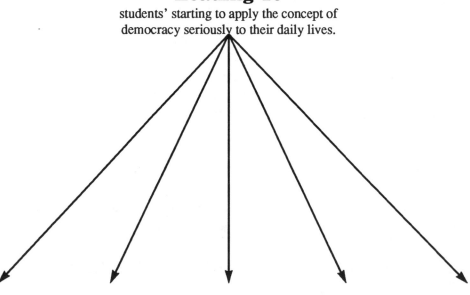

| Let's see, I guess there are a lot of decisions that are not *made* democratically. | At home we never vote on what to do. It seems like Dad decides some things and Mom decides others. | At school we don't decide many things democratically. The teacher makes most of the decisions. | We try to make decisions democratically on the playground, but usually some of the kids seem to do most of the deciding | Maybe democracy is not always a good way to decide things or maybe we need to change the way we do some things. |

direct relationship between stories and experiences. We learn about the world principally through our experiences of it and our experiences, from the beginning, are "story-like" in character.

When we talk about ourselves we tell others the story of our lives, as it were. Furthermore, most of our real beliefs are embodied in our actions and in what our actions "mean" to us. A powerful way to make the abstract more intuitive, is, therefore, to use stories and dramatized characters for that purpose. In this section, we will illustrate this point by the use of three fictional characters to illustrate three abstract concepts.

Uncritical, Selfish, and Fairminded Critical Thinkers

The distinctions between uncritical thinking and critical thinking, on the one hand, and between selfish and fairminded critical thinking on the other hand, underlie our whole approach to critical thinking. It highlights the danger of focusing on critical thinking skills alone, independent of critical thinking values. It continually calls to our attention the need to attend to the intellectual and moral standards our students are forming as a result of the way we are cultivating their learning.

A basic, though abstract, explanation for the differences between uncritical, selfish critical, and fairminded critical persons is given in the following brief characterizations:

1) *Uncritical persons* are those who have not developed intellectual skills, persons who are naive, conformist, easily manipulated, often inflexible, easily confused, typically unclear, narrowminded, and consistently ineffective in their use of language. They may have a good heart but they are not able to skillfully analyze the problems they face so as to effectively protect their own interests.

2) *Selfish critical persons* are skilled thinkers who do not genuinely accept the values of critical thinking, persons who use the intellectual skills of critical thinking selectively and self-deceptively to foster and serve their vested interests (at the expense of truth). They are typically able to identify flaws in the reasoning of others and refute them and to back up their own claims with plausible reasons, but they have not learned how to reason empathically within points of view with which they disagree.

3) *Fairminded critical persons* are skilled thinkers who do accept and honor the values of critical thinking, persons who use the intellectual skills of critical thinking to accurately reconstruct the strongest versions of points of view in conflict with their own and to question deeply their own framework of thought. They try to find and correct flaws in their own reasoning and to be scrupulously fair to those with whom they disagree.

This is fine as far as it goes, but how are we to make these abstractions more real to our students? And how are we and our students to see the significance of these distinctions in the everyday world?

It may seem to us that these theoretical discriminations are much beyond the grasp of our students. But whether they are or are not, is not a matter of the distinctions themselves, but of the way they are introduced to students. In fact, it is important for children to begin to grasp these differences as soon as possible. Let us now examine how we might use dramatization as a strategy for making these critical thinking concepts more intuitive.

Naive Nancy, Selfish Sam, and Fairminded Fran

One of the ways to aid students in developing critical thinking intuitions is to create characters whose dramatic personalities illustrate abstract distinctions. For example, we have created three imaginary children whose characters and personalities illustrate the contrast between the uncritical thinker, the selfish critical thinker, and the fairminded critical thinker. We can get some insight into the distinction by imagining what each of these characters might say about themselves if they had a clear sense of the person they were becoming and a willingness to be candid and forthright. Children who were actually developing these contrasting behavior patterns and traits would probably not, of course, have the insight suggested by these hypothetical self-descriptions.

First meet Naive Nancy. Here is what she might say of herself (if she could clearly see how she uses thinking to deal with the world):

Naive Nancy

"I don't need to think! I understand everything without thinking. I just do whatever occurs to me to do. I believe most of what I hear. I believe most of what I see on TV. I don't see why I should question either. And I don't need to waste a lot of time trying to figure things out. Why should I, when someone will figure things out for me if I wait long enough? It's a lot easier to say 'I can't!' than to do a lot of work. My parents and my teachers take care of me when I can't take care of myself. The other day I was having trouble with my math homework and started to cry, so my father did it for me. My parents give me a lot of help. It's easier that way. I do what I'm told, keep my mouth shut, and go along with whatever my friends decide. I don't like to make waves. Thinking gets you into trouble."

Next meet Selfish Sam. Here is what he might say (if he could clearly see how he uses thinking to deal with the world):

Selfish Sam

"I think a lot! It helps me trick people and get what I want. I believe whatever I want to believe, whatever gets me what I want. I question anyone who asks me to do what I don't want to do. I figure out how to get around my parents. I figure out how to get other kids to do what I want them to do. I even figure out how to avoid thinking if I want. Sometimes I say 'I can't!' when I know I could but don't want to. You can get what you want from people if you know how to manipulate them. Just the other night, I got to stay up till 11:00 by arguing with my mother about bedtime! It helps to tell people what they want to hear. Of course, sometimes what they want to hear isn't true, but that doesn't matter because you only get into trouble when you tell people what they don't want to hear. You can always trick people if you know how. Guess what, you can even trick yourself if you know how."

Next meet Fairminded Fran. Here is what she might say (if she could clearly see how she uses thinking to deal with the world):

Fairminded Fran

"I think a lot. It helps me to learn. It helps me to figure things out. I want to understand my parents and my playmates. In fact, I even want to understand myself and why I do things. Sometimes I do things that I don't understand. It's not easy trying to understand everyone and everything. Lots of people say one thing and do another. You can't always believe what people say. You can't believe a lot of what you see on TV. People often say things not because they mean them but because they want things and are trying to please you. I would like to make the world a better place. I want to make it better for everyone, not just for me and my friends. To understand other people you have to look at things as they do. You have to understand their situation and what you would feel like if you were them. You have to put yourself in their shoes. The other night I got mad at my sister because she wanted to watch a TV program that was on at the same time my favorite show was on. I didn't want to let her until I realized that she needed to watch her program to do some homework for school. I knew then that it wouldn't be fair of me to insist on my show, since she did have to do her homework for school. It isn't easy to be fair. It's a lot easier to be selfish and just think about yourself. But if I don't think about others, why should they think about me? I want to be fair to others because I expect everyone to be fair to me."

You may have noticed that we had each imaginary child introduce him or herself in terms of their attitudes toward thinking, how they go about thinking, and what they aim to achieve through their thinking. Each of these dimensions of character are important.

Naive Nancy does not see much reason to think at all. She takes things as they come. She believes what she hears. She usually goes along with whatever her peers say. She intends no harm but also assumes that no one else is going to harm her. She is a ready victim for more

sophisticated manipulators: adults or children. Naive Nancy will make a good student only insofar as thought is not required. She will literally, and thoughtlessly, do what she is told. She doesn't question or try to understand her own motives. She will make mistakes because she doesn't know how to listen closely and monitor what she hears for accuracy of interpretation. Wherever mindless obedience succeeds, she will get by. What is more, much of the time her innocent "helplessness" will enable her to get others to do things for her. Rather than try to think her way through a difficulty, she is learning to say "I can't do it!" after the first or second try. She is finding out that she can usually get by without much thinking. Her innocent likeability and perpetual "incompetence" is both her strength and her (ultimate) downfall. Her only real thinking skills are in the art of being helpless, in enticing others to do her thinking for her.

Selfish Sam contrasts well with Naive Nancy. Sam values thinking. And the more he does it, the more he values it. But only in a special sense. He thinks to gain advantage, to get what he wants, to successfully put his desires above the rights and needs of others. To put it briefly, Sam is discovering

the power of con-artistry. Sam is discovering that you can best get what you want by focusing clearly on your own desires, figuring out what is standing in the way of your interests, and manipulating others into acting in your interest. Selfish Sam is becoming an egocentric problem solver. He defines his problems so as to center them around getting what he wants for himself. Sometimes this means figuring out how to get out of work. But unlike Nancy, Sam is learning the power of figuring things out for himself. He is also learning how to impress both adults and kids by what he can do. Eventually Sam will come to appreciate the power there is in groups, the advantages one gains by becoming a leader and exercising control over others. He will use his thinking to win others to his side, to defeat his "enemies" (whoever he doesn't like), and extend his power and advantage over others. It isn't that he doesn't care at all about others, but rather that he cares only about those who serve him, those who are members of *his* group. Eventually, Sam could become an

effective promoter of a vested interest, an excellent sales person, a politician, or a lawyer ... any job that can "successfully" be performed without a well developed sense of fairmindedness.

Fairminded Fran contrasts well with both Nancy and Sam. Like Sam, Fran is learning the power of thought. She is learning the value of figuring things out for herself. Unlike Nancy, she is not learning the art of "helplessness" because she is experiencing the pleasure and deep satisfac-

tion that comes from successfully figuring things out for herself. She is discovering that she has a mind and can use it to solve problems, protect herself, do difficult jobs, learn complicated things, express herself well, and get along with others. But that is not all she's learning. She is also learning that other people have minds, other people have desires and needs, other people have rights, and other people have a different way of looking at things. She is learning how to enter into the thinking of others, how to see things from other people's point of view, how to learn from other people's perspective. She is beginning to notice the need to protect herself from the "Sams" of the world. She is learning to test for herself what people say. She is learning to protect her interests without violating the rights of others.

Fran's thinking is beginning to develop a richness that Sam's will never develop (as long as he thinks selfishly), for she is learning how much one can learn from others. Eventually, Fran will gain many insights from the art of thinking within the perspective of others. Fran's early thinking is laying the foundation for later breadth of vision. Fran's ability to think for herself in a skilled and fairminded way will enable her to pursue any career goal that she later takes on. She will be highly valued by those who value justice and fairplay. But she will also be treated with suspicion by the "true believers", by the people whose first allegiance is to a special group, to "our side". Those given to *group think* will come to recognize that you can't depend on Fran to always support the "right" side (our side). She sometimes agrees with the enemy, the opposition, the "other guys".

By introducing these characters, we can help make a basic distinction in critical thinking more alive and vivid to our students. We can breathe life into these important ideas and help our students build mental bridges between the abstract and the concrete, between the theoretical and the practical. There are, of course, a variety of ways that we might use these characters. We could, for example, develop stories about their adventures together, stories in which their interactions in a variety of situations further illuminate their contrasting modes of thinking and judging. We might make pictures and visuals which gave illustrated commentary from each of the characters about how to behave and act in various situations. We might have discussions with our students about which of these characters they thought they were most like *and why*, or what they liked or did not like about each of these characters. We could also ask if they ever acted like Naive Nancy or Selfish Sam, and then to explain, if some said yes, what it is that they did and why.

How many ways we find to make use of these dramatizations of contrasting modes of thinking entirely depends on the limits of our own imaginations. The important point is this: students learn deeply only those things they translate into their own experience and which make deep contact with their emerging values.

If you now review the above abstract definitions of the terms uncritical, selfishly critical, and fairmindedly critical and compare what you learned from Nancy, Sam, and Fran, you will have a basis for recognizing the importance of critical thinking intuitions. Students who gain an intuitive grasp of the differences between Nancy, Sam, and Fran will have the insights necessary to recognize similar patterns of behavior in themselves and others.

Now let's turn our attention to another important distinction in critical thinking and experiment with a somewhat different process of making ideas more intuitive.

Exemplification: Understanding Abstract Concepts Through Vivid Everyday Examples

The Power of Examples

Everything in the natural world is concrete and particular. Whatever is abstract must ultimately translate, therefore, into what is concrete and particular. Giving examples, is a powerful way to help students learn. Furthermore, one of the best ways to assess student learning is to determine the extent to which they can give examples of what they are learning. In this section, we will illustrate how examples can be used to make abstract concepts intuitive. We will focus on two concepts: inference and assumption.

Inferences and Assumptions

Learning to distinguish inferences from assumptions is another important distinction in critical thinking. It is therefore a good place to develop basic intuitions. In this case, we will not begin by developing characters who illustrate the concepts, we will instead explore alternative ways to make them vivid and practical, first to you the teacher, through a wide variety of everyday examples intelligible to adults. Then I will turn my attention more and more to the process by which we can help make these concepts more vivid to children. As before let us begin with a couple of abstract and general explanations of the concepts:

Inference: An inference is a step of the mind, an intellectual act by which one concludes that something is so in light of something else's being so, or seeming to be so. If you come at me with a knife in your hand, I would probably *infer* that you mean to do me harm. Inferences can be strong or weak, justified or unjustified.

Assumption: An assumption is something we take for granted or presuppose. All human thought and experience is based on assumptions. Assumptions can be unjustified or justified, depending upon whether we do or do not have good reasons for what we are assuming. For example, I heard a scratch at the door. I got up to let the cat in. I *assumed* that only the cat makes that noise, and that he makes it only when he wants to be let in.

We humans have no trouble actually making assumptions and inferences, for we make them, not only every day of our lives, we make them every moment of every day of our lives (at least, every *waking* moment of our lives). Assumptions and inferences permeate our lives precisely because we cannot act without them. Our lives are conducted almost exclusively on the basis of the judgments, the interpretations, and the beliefs we form. Each is the result of the mind's ability to come to conclusions, to give meanings to what we experience, in short, to *make inferences*. And the inferences we make depend on what we take for granted, what we *assume*, as we attempt to make sense of what is going on around us.

Put a human in any situation and he or she starts to give it some meaning or other. People automatically make inferences to gain a basis for understanding and action. So quickly and automatically do we make inferences that we do not, without training, learn to notice them as such. We see dark clouds and infer rain. We hear the door slam and infer someone has arrived. We see a frowning face and infer the person is angry. Our friend is late and we infer she is being inconsiderate. We meet a tall boy and infer he is good at basketball, an Asian and infer he will be good at math. We read a book, and infer what the various sentences and paragraphs, indeed what the whole book, is saying. We listen to what people say, and make a continual series of inferences as to what they mean. As we write we make inferences as to what others will make of what we are writing. We make inferences as to the clarity of what we are saying, as to what needs further explanation, as to what needs exemplification or illustration.

Many of our inferences are justified and reasonable. But many are not. One of the most important critical thinking skills is the skill of noticing and reconstructing the inferences we make, so that the various ways in which we inferentially shape our experiences become more and more apparent to us. This skill, this sensitivity or ability, enables us to separate our experiences into analyzed parts. We learn to distinguish the raw data of our experience from our interpretations of those data (in other words, from the inferences we are making about them). Eventually we realize that the inferences we make are heavily influenced by our point of view and the assumptions we have made about people and situations. This puts us in the position of being able to broaden the scope of our outlook, to see situations from more than one point of view, to become more open-minded. (See the chart on the following page.)

Abstract Concept
(e.g., the concept of inference)

Abstract Definition
(e.g., "to conclude or decide from something known or assumed; to derive by reasoning; to draw as a conclusion")

Building Intuitive Understanding
("Let's see, we're always having to make sense of what we experience, so that means, I guess, we have to draw conclusions about everything we give meaning to. In fact, that means that whenever I am making sense of *anything*, I must be making *inferences* about it, even though I never seem to notice myself doing this. I guess my mind works very quickly and silently and I often am unaware of what it is doing.")

Leading To
the ability to apply the concept accurately and insightfully to cases.

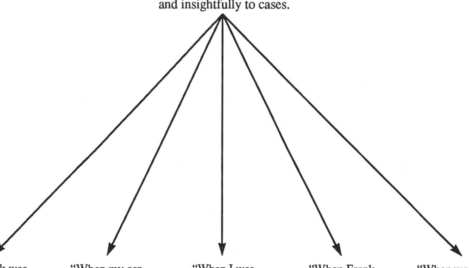

"When Jack was late and I decided he was being irresponsible, *that* was an inference"

"When my car didn't start and I concluded that the battery was dead, *that* was an inference"

"When I was about to put my red sweater on but decided it clashed with my brown pants, *that* was an inference"

"When Frank walked by without saying anything to me and I concluded that he was angry with me, *that* was an inference"

"Whenever I read a book and decide what it means, that must be the result of a whole lot of inferences"

Often, of course, different people make different inferences because they bring to situations a different point of view. They see the data differently. Or, to put it another way, they have different assumptions about what they see. For example, if two people see a man lying in a gutter, one might infer, "There's a drunken bum". The other might infer, "There's a man in need of help." These inferences are based on different assumptions about the conditions under which people end up in gutters and these assumptions are connected to the point of view about people that each has formed. The first person assumes: "Only drunks are to be found in gutters". The second person assumes: "People lying in the gutter are in need of help". The first person may have developed the point of view that people are fundamentally responsible for what happens to them and ought to be able to take care of themselves. The second may have developed the point of view that the problems people have are often caused by forces and events beyond their control.

In any case, as soon as possible, we want to help our students begin to notice the inferences they are making, the assumptions they are basing those inferences on, and the point of view about the world they are developing. To help our students do this we need to give them clear examples of simple cases, and lots and lots of practice analyzing and reconstructing them. For example, we could reconstruct the above inferences in the following way:

Person One

SITUATION: "A man is lying in the gutter."
ASSUMPTION: "Only bums lie in gutters."
INFERENCE: "That man's a bum."

Person Two

SITUATION: "A man is lying in the gutter."
ASSUMPTION: "Anyone lying in the gutter is in need of help."
INFERENCE: "That man is in need of help."

Our goal of sensitizing students to the inferences they make and to the assumptions that underlie their thinking enables them to begin to gain command over their thinking. Because all human thinking is inferential in nature, our command of our thinking depends on command of the inferences embedded in it and thus of the assumptions that underlie it.

Consider the way in which we plan and think our way through everyday events. We think of ourselves as washing up, eating our breakfast, getting ready for work, arriving on time, sitting down at our desk, making plans for lunch, paying bills, engaging in small talk, etc. Another way to put this is to say that we are continually interpreting our actions, giving them meanings, *making inferences* about what is going on in our lives. And this is to say that we must choose among a variety of possible meanings. For example, are we "relaxing" or "wasting time"? Am I being "determined" or "stubborn", or worse, "pig-headed". Am I "joining" a conversation or "butting in"? Is someone "laughing with me" or "laughing at me"? Am I "helping a friend" or "being taken advantage of"? Every time we interpret our actions, every time we give them a meaning, we are making one or more inferences on the basis of one or more assumptions.

As humans we continually make assumptions about ourselves, our jobs, our mates, our children, about the world in general. We take some things for granted, simply because we can't always be questioning everything. Sometimes we take the wrong things for granted. For example, I run off to the store (assuming that I have enough money with me) and arrive to find that I have left my money at home. I assume that I have enough gas in the car only to find that I have run out. I assume that an item marked-down in price is a good buy only to find that it was "marked up" before it was "marked down". I assume that it will not, or that it will, rain. I assume that my car will start when I turn on the key and press the starter. I assume that I mean well in my dealings with others. We make hundreds of assumptions without knowing it, that is, without thinking about it. Most of them are quite sound and justifiable. Some however are not.

The question then becomes: "How can we teach young children to begin to recognize the inferences they are making, the assumptions they are basing those inferences on, and the point of view, the perspective on the world that they are beginning to form?".

It seems to me that there are many ways to foster children's awareness of their inferences and assumptions. For one thing, all disciplined subject matter thinking requires that we learn to make correct assumptions about the content of what we are studying and that we become practiced in making justifiable inferences. For example, in doing math we make mathematical assumptions and mathematical inferences; in doing science we make scientific assumptions and scientific inferences; in constructing historical accounts we make historical assumptions and historical inferences.

Every subject we teach provides us with opportunities for facilitating student recognition of inferences and assumptions. When students mis-read a mathematical problem, for example, they make the wrong inferences about it, usually as the result of having made false assumptions about it. The difficulty for us is usually not because there aren't many opportunities to foster these skills and recognitions. It is usually because we ourselves are not practiced in this very art, hence we miss most of the opportunities inherent in the everyday classroom.

Here is one place to start. We can give students exercises which they can do in groups which help both them and us become more aware of inferences, assumptions, and points of view lurking behind them. We could start by asking the class collectively to identify common inferences. For example:

If it was 12:00 noon, what might you infer? .... (It's time for lunch.)

If there were black clouds in the sky? .... (It's probably going to rain.)

If Jack comes to school with a bump on his head? .... (He probably got hit.)

If there are webs in the corners of the ceiling? .... (Spiders made them.)

If Jill is in the 8th grade? .... (She is probably 13 or 14 years old.)

After an exercise of this sort, you could then switch to practice in small groups of the same sort. When you felt that the students were developing an intuitive grasp of inferences, you could then orchestrate some practice with assumptions, helping the students to see how the inferences they make are a result of the assumptions they bring to situations. For example:

If it was 12:00 noon and you inferred it was time for lunch, what did you assume?
(That everyone eats lunch at 12:00 noon.)

If there are black clouds in the sky and you infer that it's probably going to rain, what did you assume?
(That it usually rains whenever there are black clouds in the sky.)

31

If Jack comes to school with a bump on his head and you infer that he must have been hit, what did you assume?

(That the only time you develop a bump on the head is when you are hit.)

You could continue this exercise until students began to develop some skill in identifying the assumptions that accounted for their inferences. You could ask the students in each case to consider whether the assumptions made in each case were justified and why. For example, are we justified in assuming that everyone eats lunch at 12:00? Are we justified in assuming that it usually rains when there are black clouds in the sky? Are we justified in assuming that bumps on the head are only caused by blows?

The point would not be to get everyone to agree on which assumptions were justified but to begin to show students that we all make many assumptions as we go about our daily life and that we ought to be able to recognize and question them. As students develop these critical intuitions, they begin to notice more and more inferences made by themselves and others. They begin to recognize more and more what they and others are taking for granted. They begin to recognize more and more how their points of view shape their experiences.

Visualization: Using Visuals to Make Critical Thinking Principles More Intuitive

One of the most powerful ways to make abstractions more intuitive is through the process of visualization and imagination. We are sensual beings. Our senses play a powerful role in our learning. The power of sight, for example, sometimes enables us to grasp in a moment what would be very difficult otherwise — "A picture is worth a thousand words." (and there is no sense more powerful than sight).

Of course we must be careful in using images and pictures to represent abstract ideas. For one thing, pictures require interpretation and one picture can always be interpreted many ways. To put the point in other words, different people give different meanings to the same image or picture. We don't simply "see" what is there. We "read into", that is, make inferences about, what we see.

So though it is important to develop visuals that help our students develop critical intuition, we must be ever watchful of the interpretations that accompany visualization. We must be careful to distinguish, for example, "intuition" from "stereotype", simplification from oversimplification.

One principle of critical thinking in the strong sense is the principle of fairness to the views of others (See **S-3** in the Strategy Chapter). We have already dramatized this principle of thought in the character of Fairminded Fran, but suppose we try to use a visual to reinforce the concept. Consider what we might use. We might try a representation of the scales of justice (see figure 1, next page).

Some discussion would be necessary before the students could begin to use this image in a fruitful way. Since the scales appear tipped in favor of "Justice for Ourselves", a Socratic discussion would be necessary to facilitate the students' recognition of our common tendency to be more sensitive to injustice toward ourselves than we are of injustice toward others, especially if we happen to be the perpetrators of the injustice.

We might introduce a second image of the scales (see figure 2, next page).

We might have the students discuss the implications of the two different drawings. This would help make both images more intelligible. Our discussion should result in the students giving

figure 1

figure 2

examples of experiences of their own, both of the sort in which others failed to treat them justly and in which they failed to treat others justly. Sibling rivalries are a fruitful area to discuss here, for at the bottom of them is often a perceived sense of unequal treatment. Through a discussion rich in examples which we should draw out from the students, the visual would begin to link up with vivid experiences, strengthening both the meaningfulness of the visual and the perceived implications of the experiences. This combination of visual and analyzed experiences is an excellent way to build critical thinking intuitions.

Or consider the following image.

We all see the world differently

figure 3

We can use this to show students the need for insight into egocentricity as well as reciprocity. We could develop the analogy between different kinds of glasses and how we each develop a unique way of looking at the world, a unique point of view. We might also use an image of a mountain with different observers seeing different parts of it. Or we might use the parable of the six blind men examining different parts of an elephant, each of them coming to different conclusions about the shape of the elephant as a result. Or we might have the class discuss the folk adage of looking at the world through rose-colored glasses. We could foster some sense of the importance of reciprocity by helping the students to begin to recognize why they should strive to see the world through the eyes (in this case, "glasses") of others. Whatever analogies and images we use, it will be essential to translate them into clear examples and concrete experiences meaningful to our students.

Or consider this image of the Statue of Liberty. Though we can be sure that the image will engender common associations among most children raised in the United States, we cannot assume that the associations are based on an intuitive grasp of the principles of human rights and freedoms articulated in the Bill of Rights of the Constitution.

figure 4

The same would hold for virtually any other "patriotic" image or symbol, such as the flag, the White House, George Washington crossing the Delaware, Abraham Lincoln reading by the light of the fire in a one room cabin. In other words, just as pictures and images can be used to make an abstract idea more concrete and intuitive, they can also be used to obfuscate or obscure fundamental meanings and principles. Using an image as a tool for fostering critical intuitions must be understood to involve not only the grounding of abstract concepts in vivid case-by-case applications, but also the critique of associations that so often lead to a systematic misinterpretation of relevant ideals, concepts, and principles.

After all, what does the Statue of Liberty stand for? What does it imply? Were these implications true in all the days of our national past? And are they still true today? Today, for example, West Germany is the only country in the world that provides universal refuge to all children of every nationality who need shelter and protection. It provides free food, shelter, and education to all such children. The U.S. does not. Does this mean that we have abandoned the ideal that the Statue of Liberty stands for? Student discussion of these questions helps develop insight into the deeper meanings that underlie traditional ideals of the United States and the problems involved in living in accord with those ideals.

Imagination as a Form of Visualization

Critical thinking requires an extensive use of the student's imagination. Whenever we think about abstract meanings, whenever we try to understand or assess a statement or belief, whenever we attempt to predict a consequence, or determine the implications of an action, we need to use our imaginations effectively. Most students are not practiced in this use of their imaginations. They often find it difficult to conjure up circumstances that exemplify abstract meanings.

For example, suppose we ask students to describe a circumstance in which some person was behaving in an unquestionably honest way. Most students find it difficult to imagine a case when called upon to do so. Very few would say something like: "Well, if I found your wallet on the playground and nobody knew I found it, but I still returned it to you — that would be being honest." They recognize the case when *someone else* thinks it up, but they often have difficulty in thinking them up, imagining them, on their own.

One of the reasons for this deficiency is the failure at all levels of education to teach in a way that fosters intuitive learning. If we focused attention, as we should, on the ability of students to move back and forth comfortably and insightfully between the abstract and the concrete, they would soon develop and discipline their imaginations so as to be able to generate cases that exemplify abstractions. All students have, as a matter of fact, experienced hundreds of situations that exemplify any number of important abstract truths and principles. But they are virtually never asked to dig into their experience to find examples, to imagine cases, which illustrate this or that principle, this or that abstract concept.

The result is an undisciplined and underdeveloped imagination combined with vague, indeed muddled, concepts and principles. They are left with experiences that are blind, experiences from which they learn few truths, ideas that are empty, that they cannot relate perceptively to their experience. What is missing is the intuitive synthesis between concept and percept, between idea and experience, between image and reality.

Conclusion

Some people erroneously believe that critical thinking and intuitive thinking are incompatible opposites. If one means by intuitive thinking a form of inexplicable, non-rational thought, the claim is correct, for critical thinking is always both intelligible and rational. But if one means by intuition the process by which one translates the abstract into the concrete, based on insight into the principles upon the basis of which one is thinking, then not only are critical and intuitive thinking compatible, they are necessarily conjoined. Solid critical thinking always requires fundamental insights, fundamental intuitions, to guide it.

If this is true, then teachers committed to fostering the critical thinking of their students must interest themselves in the means by which critical thinking intuitions are formed and developed. The dramatic, the concrete, and the highly visual and imaginative, are crucial instrumentalities for this purpose. Properly used they inevitably foster reflective intuition and insight. Whatever we are teaching, we should therefore continually ask ourselves, "What are the intuitions and insights essential to this mode of knowledge and thought?" and "How can I most effectively foster them with these students?"

Global Strategies:
Socratic Questioning &
Role-Playing

The Role of the Teacher

A teacher committed to teaching for critical thinking must think beyond compartmentalized subject matter, teaching toward ends and objectives that transcend subject matter classification. To teach for critical thinking is, first of all, to create an environment in the class and in the school that is conducive to critical thinking. It is to help make the classroom and school environment a mini-critical society, a place where the values of critical thinking (truth, openmindedness, empathy, autonomy, rationality, and self-criticism) are encouraged and rewarded. In such an environment, students learn to believe in the power of their own minds to identify and solve problems. They learn to believe in the efficacy of their own thinking. Thinking for themselves is not something they fear. Authorities are not those who tell them the "right" answers, but those who encourage and help them to figure out answers for themselves, who encourage them to discover the powerful resources of their own minds.

The teacher is much more a questioner than a preacher in this model. The teacher learns how to ask questions that probe meanings, that request reasons and evidence, that facilitate elaboration, that keep discussions from becoming confusing, that provide incentive for listening to what others have to say, that lead to fruitful comparisons and contrasts, that highlight contradictions and inconsistencies, and that elicit implications and consequences. Teachers committed to critical thinking realize that the primary purpose of all education is to teach students how to learn. Since there are more details than can be taught and no way to predict which the student will use, teachers emphasize thinking about basic issues and problems. Thus, details are learned as a necessary part of the process of settling such questions, and so are functional and relevant.

The teacher who teaches students how to learn and think about many basic issues gives them knowledge they can use the rest of their lives. This teacher realizes that subject matter divisions are arbitrary and are a matter of convenience, that the most important problems of everyday life rarely fall neatly into subject matter divisions, that understanding a situation fully usually requires a synthesis of knowledge and insight from several subjects. An in-depth understanding of one subject requires an understanding of others. (One cannot answer questions in history, for example, without asking and answering related questions in psychology, sociology, etc.) Students must discover the value of knowledge, evidence, and reasoning by finding significant payoffs in dealing with their everyday life problems outside of school. Recognizing the universal problems we all face, the teacher should encourage each student to find personal solutions through self-reflective experiences and thought processes:

> Who am I? What is the world really like? What are my parents, my friends, and other people like? How have I become the way I am? What should I believe in? Why should I believe in it? What real options do I have? Who are my real friends? Whom should I trust? Who are my enemies? Need they be my enemies? How did the world become the way it is? How do people become the way they are? Are there any really bad people in the world? Are there any really good people in the world? What is good and bad? What is right and wrong? How should I decide? How can I decide what is fair and what is unfair? How can I be fair to others? Do I have to be fair to my enemies? How should I live my life? What rights do I have? What responsibilities?

The teacher who believes in personal freedom and thinking for oneself does not spoon-feed students with predigested answers to those questions. Nor should students be encouraged to believe that the answers to them are arbitrary and a matter of sheer opinion. Raising probing questions whenever they are natural to a subject under discussion, the teacher realizes that, in finding the way to answers, the student forges an overall perspective into which subject matter discoveries will be fit. Neither the discussion nor the student should be forced to conclusions that do not seem reasonable to the student.

Thus, such teachers reflect upon the subjects they teach, asking themselves, "What ideas and skills are the most basic and crucial in this subject? What do practitioners in this field do? How do they think? Why should students be familiar with this subject? What use does a well-educated person and citizen of a republic make of this subject? How can these uses be made apparent to and real for my students? Where do the various subject areas overlap? How should the tools and insights of each subject inform one's understanding of the others? Of one's place in the world?"

The teacher committed to teaching for critical thinking realizes that the child has two sources of belief: beliefs that the child forms as a result of personal experience, inward thinking, and interaction with peers and environment; and beliefs that the child learns through instruction by adults. The first could be called "real" or "operational" beliefs. They are what define the child's real world, the foundation for action, the source of acted-upon values. They are a result of the child making sense of or figuring out the world. They are heavily influenced by what has been called "pleasure-principle thinking". They are in large measure egocentric, unreflective, and unarticulated.

People believe in many things for egocentric, irrational reasons: because others hold the belief, because certain desires may be justified by the belief, because they feel more comfortable with the belief, because they are rewarded for the belief, because they ego-identify with the belief, because others reject them for not acting on the belief, because the belief helps to justify feelings of like or dislike toward others.

Students, of course, also have spontaneously formed reasonable beliefs. Some of those are inconsistent with the expressed beliefs of parents and teachers. As a result of this contradiction with authority, students rarely raise these beliefs to what Piaget calls "conscious realization".

Students have also developed their own theories about psychology, sociology, science, language, and so on, covering most subjects. The totality of these real beliefs is unsynthesized and contains many contradictions which students will discover only if encouraged to freely express them in an atmosphere that is mutually supportive and student-centered.

The other source of belief, didactic instruction from adult authority figures, is an authority's interpretation of reality, not the students'. The students learn to verbalize it but do not synthesize it with operational beliefs. Therefore, they rarely recognize contradictions between these two belief systems. A student's own theories and beliefs are not necessarily replaced with the knowledge offered in school.

The teacher concerned with this problem, then, provides an environment in which students can discover and explore their beliefs. Such teachers refrain from rushing students who are struggling to express their beliefs, allow time for thoughtful discussion, refuse to allow anyone to attack students for their beliefs, reward students for questioning their own beliefs, and support students when they consider many points of view.

Unless the teacher provides conditions in which students can discover operational beliefs through reflective thinking, these two systems of beliefs will exist in separate dimensions of their lives. The first will control their deeds, especially private deeds; the second will control their words, especially public words. The first will be used when acting for themselves; the second when performing for others. Neither, in a sense, will be taken seriously. Neither will be subjected to rational scrutiny: the first because it isn't openly expressed and challenged verbally; the second because it is not tested in the crucible of action and practical decision-making. This dichotomy, when embedded in an individual's life, creates a barrier to living an "examined life". Students lack the wherewithal to explore contradictions, double standards, and hypocrisies. They will use critical thinking skills, if at all, as weapons in a struggle to protect themselves from exposure, and to lay bare the contradictions of the "other", the "enemy". When they integrate critical thinking skills into this dichotomous thinking, they become self-serving, not fairminded, critical thinkers.

The role of the teacher could be summarized as follows:

- help break big questions or tasks into smaller, more manageable parts
- create meaningful contexts in which learning is valued by the students
- help students clarify their thoughts by rephrasing or asking questions
- pose thought-provoking questions
- help keep the discussion focussed
- encourage students to explain things to each other
- help students find what they need to know by suggesting and showing students how to use resources
- ensure that students do justice to each view, that no views are cut off, ignored, or unfairly dismissed

Socratic Questioning: Wondering Aloud About Meaning and Truth

Introduction

Socratic discussion, in which students' thought is elicited and probed, allows students to develop and evaluate their thinking by making it explicit. By encouraging students to slow their thinking down and elaborate on it, Socratic discussion gives students the opportunity to develop and test their ideas — the beliefs they have spontaneously formed and those they learn in school. Thus, students can synthesize their beliefs into a more coherent and better-developed perspective.

Socratic questioning requires teachers to take seriously and wonder about what students say and think: what they mean, its significance to them, its relationship to other beliefs, how it can be tested, to what extent and in what way it is true or makes sense. Teachers who wonder about the meaning and truth of students' statements can translate that curiosity into probing questions. By wondering aloud, teachers simultaneously convey interest in and respect for student thought, and model analytical moves for students. Fruitful Socratic discussion infects students with the same curiosity about the meaning of and truth of what they think, hear, and read and gives students the clear message that they are expected to think and to take everyone else's beliefs seriously.

Socratic questioning is based on the idea that all thinking has a logic or structure, that any one statement only partially reveals the thinking underlying it, expressing no more than a tiny piece of the system of interconnected beliefs of which it is a part. Its purpose is to expose the logic of someone's thought. Use of Socratic questioning presupposes the following points: All thinking has assumptions; makes claims or creates meaning; has implications and consequences; focuses on some things and throws others into the background; uses some concepts or ideas and not others; is defined by purposes, issues, or problems; uses or explains some facts and not others; is relatively clear or unclear; is relatively deep or superficial; is relatively critical or uncritical; is relatively elaborated or undeveloped; is relatively monological or multi-logical. Critical thinking is thinking done with an effective, self-monitoring awareness of these points.

Socratic instruction can take many forms. Socratic questions can come from the teacher or from students. They can be used in a large group discussion, in small groups, one-to-one, or even with oneself. They can have different purposes. What each form has in common is that someone's thought is developed as a result of the probing, stimulating questions asked. It requires questioners to "try on" others' beliefs, to imagine what it would mean to accept them, and to wonder what it would be like to believe otherwise. If a student says that people are selfish, the teacher may wonder aloud as to what it means to say that, or what the student thinks it means to say that an act or person was unselfish. The discussion which follows should help clarify the concepts of selfish and unselfish behavior, identify the kind of evidence required to determine whether or not someone is or is not acting selfishly, and explore the consequences of accepting or rejecting the original generalization. Such a discussion enables students to examine their own views on such concepts as generosity, motivation, obligation, human nature, and right and wrong.

Some people erroneously believe that holding a Socratic discussion is like conducting a chaotic free-for-all. In fact, Socratic discussion has distinctive goals and distinctive ways to achieve them. Indeed, any discussion — any thinking — guided by Socratic questioning is structured.

The discussion, the thinking, is structured to take student thought from the unclear to the clear, from the unreasoned to the reasoned, from the implicit to the explicit, from the unexamined to the examined, from the inconsistent to the consistent, from the unarticulated to the articulated. To learn how to participate in it, one has to learn how to listen carefully to what others say, to look for reasons and evidence, to recognize and reflect upon assumptions, to discover implications and consequences, to seek examples, analogies, and objections, to seek to discover, in short, what is really known and to distinguish it from what is merely believed.

Socratic Questioning

- raises basic issues
- probes beneath the surface of things
- pursues problematic areas of thought
- helps students to discover the *structure* of their own thought
- helps students develop sensitivity to clarity, accuracy, and relevance
- helps students arrive at judgment through their own reasoning
- helps students note claims, evidence, conclusions, questions-at-issue, assumptions, implications, consequences, concepts, interpretations, points of view — the elements of thought

---

Three Kinds of Socratic Discussion

We can loosely categorize three general forms of Socratic questioning and distinguish three basic kinds of preparation for each: the spontaneous, the exploratory, and the focused.

Spontaneous or unplanned

Every teacher's teaching should be imbued with the Socratic spirit. We should always keep our curiosity and wondering alive. If we do, there will be many occasions in which we will spontaneously ask students questions about what they mean and explore with them how we might find out if something is true. If one student says that a given angle will be the same as another angle in a geometrical figure, we may spontaneously wonder how we might go about proving or disproving that. If one student says Americans love freedom, we may spontaneously wonder about exactly what that means (Does that mean, for example, that we love freedom more than other people do? How could we find out?). If in a science class a student says that most space is empty, we may be spontaneously moved to raise some question on the spot as to what that might mean and how we might find out.

Such spontaneous discussions provide models of listening critically as well as exploring the beliefs expressed. If something said seems questionable, misleading, or false, Socratic questioning provides a way of helping students to become self-correcting, rather than relying on correction by the teacher. Spontaneous Socratic discussion can prove especially useful when students become interested in a topic, when they raise an important issue, when they are on the brink of grasping or integrating a new insight, when discussion becomes bogged down or confused or hostile. Socratic questioning provides specific moves which can fruitfully take advantage of the interest, effectively approach the issue, aid integration and expansion of the insight, move a troubled discussion forward, clarify or sort through what appears confusing, and diffuse frustration or anger.

Although by definition there can be no pre-planning for a particular spontaneous discussion, teachers can prepare themselves by becoming familiar and comfortable with generic Socratic questions, and developing the art of raising probing follow-up questions and giving encouraging and helpful responses. Ask for examples, evidence, or reasons, propose counter-examples, ask the rest of the class if they agree with a point made, suggest parallel or analogous cases, ask for a paraphrase of opposing views, rephrase student responses clearly and succinctly. These are among the most common moves.

Translating Wonderings into Questions

- If you see little or no relevance in a student comment, you may think, "I wonder why this student mentioned that now?" and ask, "What connection do you see between our discussion and your point that ...?" or "I'm not sure why you mentioned that now. Could you explain how it's related to this discussion?" or "What made you think of that?" Either the point is germane, and you can clarify the connection, or only marginally related, and you can rephrase it and say "A new issue has been raised." That new issue can be pursued then, tactfully postponed, or can generate an assignment.

- If a student says something vague or general, you may think, "I wonder about the role of that belief in this student's life, the consequences of that belief, how the student perceives the consequences, or if there are any practical consequences at all". You may ask, "How does that belief affect how you act? What, for example, do you do or refrain from doing because you believe that?" You might have several students respond and compare their understandings, or suggest an alternative view and have students compare its consequences.

To summarize: Because we begin to wonder more and more about meaning and truth, and so think aloud in front of our students by means of questions, Socratic exchanges will occur at many unplanned moments in our instruction. However, in addition to these unplanned wonderings we can also design or plan out at least two distinct kinds of Socratic discussion: one that explores a wide range of issues and one that focuses on one particular issue.

Exploratory

What we here call *exploratory* Socratic questioning is appropriate when teachers want to find out what students know or think and to probe into student thinking on a variety of issues. For example, you could use it to assess student thinking on a subject at the beginning of a semester or unit. You could use it to see what students value, or to uncover problematic areas or potential biases, or find out where your students are clearest and fuzziest in their thinking. You could use it to discover areas or issues of interest or controversy, or to find out where and how students have integrated school material into their belief systems. Such discussions can serve as preparation in a general way for later study or analysis of a topic, as an introduction, as review, to see what students understood from their study of a unit or topic before they take a test, to suggest where they should focus study for test, as a basis for or guide to future assignments, or to prepare for an assignment. Or, again, you might have students take (or pick) an issue raised in discussion and give their own views, or have students form groups to discuss the issue or topic.

With this type of Socratic questioning, we raise and explore a broad range of interrelated issues and concepts, not just one. It requires minimal pre-planning or pre-thinking. It has a relatively loose order or structure. You can prepare by having some general questions ready to raise when appropriate by considering the topic or issue, related issues and key concepts. You can also prepare by predicting students' likeliest responses and preparing some follow-up questions. Remember, however, that once students' thought is stimulated there is no predicting exactly where discussion will go.

Focused

Much of the time you will approach your instruction with specific areas and issues to cover. This is the time for focused Socratic questioning. To really probe an issue or concept in depth, to have students clarify, sort, analyze and evaluate thoughts and perspectives, distinguish the known from the unknown, synthesize relevant factors and knowledge, students can engage in an extended and focused discussion. This type of discussion offers students the chance to pursue perspectives to their most basic assumptions and through their furthest implications and consequences. These discussions give students experience in engaging in an extended, ordered, and integrated discussion in which they discover, develop, and share ideas and insights. It requires pre-planning or thinking through possible perspectives on the issue, grounds for conclusions, problematic concepts, implications, and consequences. You can further prepare by reflecting on those subjects relevant to the issue: their methods, standards, basic distinctions and concepts, and interrelationships — points of overlap or possible conflict. It is also helpful to be prepared by considering likeliest student answers. This is the type of Socratic questioning most often used in the lesson remodels themselves. Though we can't provide the crucial follow-up questions, we illustrate pre-planning for focused Socratic questioning in numerous remodels.

All three types of Socratic discussion require development of the art of questioning. They require the teacher to develop familiarity with a wide variety of intellectual moves and sensitivity to when to ask which kinds of questions, though there is rarely one best question at any particular time.

Some Topics for Socratic Discussion
- What are friends? Why do people have friends? Does having friends ever cause problems? When is it hard to be a good friend? What's the difference between friends and best friends?
- What's the difference between wanting something and needing it?
- What is good? What is bad? What's the difference between good and bad?
- What are rules? What are they for? What's the difference between good rules and bad rules?
- What are the differences between people and animals?

A Taxonomy of Socratic Questions

It is helpful to recognize, in light of the universal features in the logic of human thought, that there are identifiable categories of questions for the adept Socratic questioner to dip into: questions of clarification, questions that probe assumptions, questions that probe reasons and evidence, questions about viewpoints or perspectives, questions that probe implications and consequences, and questions about the question. Here are some examples of generic questions in each of these categories. Many of these questions may need to be modified to take the grade level into account.

Questions of Clarification

- What do you mean by _____?
- What is your main point?
- How does ____ relate to ___?
- Could you put that another way?
- What do you think is the main issue here?
- Is your basic point _____ or _____?
- Let me see if I understand you; do you mean _____ or _____?
- How does this relate to our discussion/ problem/ issue?
- What do you think John meant by his remark? What did you take John to mean?
- Jane, would you summarize in your own words what Richard has said? ... Richard, is that what you meant?

- Could you give me an example?
- Would this be an example: _____?
- Could you explain that further?
- Would you say more about that?
- Why do you say that?

Questions that Probe Assumptions

- What are you assuming?
- What is Karen assuming?
- What could we assume instead?
- You seem to be assuming _____. Do I understand you correctly?
- All of your reasoning depends on the idea that ____. Why have you based your reasoning on _____ rather than _____?
- You seem to be assuming ____. How would you justify taking this for granted?
- Is it always the case? Why do you think the assumption holds here?

Questions that Probe Reasons, Evidence, and Causes

- What would be an example?
- What are your reasons for saying that?
- What other information do we need to know?
- Could you explain your reasons to us?
- Is that good evidence for believing that?
- Are those reasons adequate?
- Is there reason to doubt that evidence?
- Who is in a position to know if that is the case?
- What would you say to someone who said ____?
- What do you think the cause is?
- By what reasoning did you come to that conclusion?
- How could we go about finding out whether that is true?
- Can someone else give evidence to support that response?

- How do you know?
- Why did you say that?
- Why do you think that is true?
- What led you to that belief?
- Do you have any evidence for that?
- How does that apply to this case?
- What difference does that make?
- What would convince you otherwise?
- What accounts for that?
- How did this come about?

Questions About Viewpoints or Perspectives

- You seem to be approaching this issue from ____ perspective. Why have you chosen this rather than that perspective?
- How would other groups/types of people respond? Why? What would influence them?
- How could you answer the objection that _____ would make?
- Can/did anyone see this another way?
- What would someone who disagrees say?
- What is an alternative?
- How are Ken's and Roxanne's ideas alike? Different?

Questions that Probe Implications and Consequences

- What are you implying by that?
- When you say _____, are you implying _____?
- But if that happened, what else would also happen as a result? Why?

- What effect would that have?
- Would that necessarily happen or only probably happen?
- What is an alternative?
- If this and this are the case, then what else must be true?

Questions About the Question
- How can we find out?
- How could someone settle this question?
- Is the question clear? Do we understand it?
- Is this question easy or hard to answer? Why?
- Would _____ put the question differently?
- Does this question ask us to evaluate something?
- Do we all agree that this is the question?
- Is this the same issue as _____?
- Can we break this question down at all?
- How would _____ put the issue?
- What does this question assume?
- Why is this question important?
- Do we need facts to answer this?
- To answer this question, what other questions would we have to answer first?
- I'm not sure I understand how you are interpreting the main question at issue.

There are Four Directions in which Thought Can Be Pursued

There is another way to classify, and so arrange in our minds, questions we can ask to help stimulate student thought. This second taxonomy emphasizes "four directions in which thought can be pursued". For some of our readers this additional way of thinking about the kinds of questions that help students develop and discipline their thought may make the categories above more *intuitive*. As you examine the diagram below, you will see that all of the categories above except two are accentuated.

This diagram, and the classifications implicit in it, helps accentuate the following important facts about thinking. All thinking has a history in the lives of particular persons. All thinking depends upon a substructure of reasons, evidence, and assumptions. All thinking leads us in some direction or other (has implications and consequences). And all thinking stands in relation to other possible ways to think (there is never just one way to think about something). This classificatory scheme highlights, therefore, four ways we can help students come to terms with their thought:

✔ We can help students reflect on how they have come to think the way they do on a given subject. (In doing this, we are helping them look into the *history* of their thinking on that subject, helping them find the source or origin of their thinking in their biographies.)

✔ We can help students reflect on how they do support or might support their thinking (in doing this, we are helping them to express the reasons, evidence, and assumptions that underlie what they think.)

✔ We can help students reflect on what "follows from" their thinking, what implications and consequences their thinking generates. (In doing this, we are helping them to realize that all thinking entails or involves "effects" or "results" that we are obliged to consider.)

✔ We can help students reflect on how it is that people with points of view different from theirs' might raise legitimate objections or propose alternative ways to think that they should take into account. (In doing this, we are helping them to think more broadly, more comprehensively, more fairmindedly).

One disadvantage of this four-fold classification is that it does not highlight the important categories of "questions of clarification" and "questioning the question", so, if we find this four-fold classification helpful, we should take pains not to forget these categories.

Socratic Discussion

There are *four directions* in which thought can be pursued.

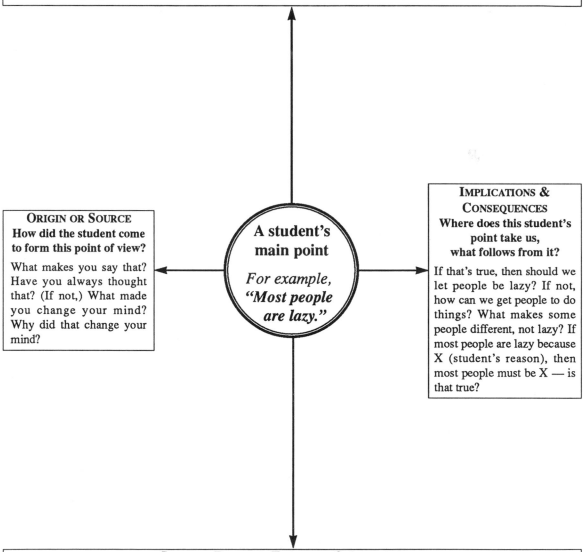

CONFLICTING VIEWS
How does this student's thinking conflict with other points of view?

What would you say to someone who said that people basically *want* to accomplish things and learn about things, that people *need* to work and keep busy and feel that they contribute? Could there be other reasons why people seem lazy, like maybe people are afraid of messing up, and that's why they don't go out there and do stuff? Your history book is full of people who did things, worked hard, fought, and so on — how do you explain that?

ORIGIN OR SOURCE
How did the student come to form this point of view?

What makes you say that? Have you always thought that? (If not,) What made you change your mind? Why did that change your mind?

A student's main point

For example, "Most people are lazy."

IMPLICATIONS & CONSEQUENCES
Where does this student's point take us, what follows from it?

If that's true, then should we let people be lazy? If not, how can we get people to do things? What makes some people different, not lazy? If most people are lazy because X (student's reason), then most people must be X — is that true?

SUPPORT, REASONS, EVIDENCE, & ASSUMPTIONS
Can the student support his or her view with reasons or evidence?

Why do you think so? Are there certain kinds or groups of people that *aren't* lazy? Why are most people lazy? How do you know? How could we find out if that might be so? Do people chose to be lazy, or decide that it doesn't matter if they are lazy, or are they just that way naturally? Do you think most people think of themselves as lazy? Why?

Wondering (And Wondering About Your Wonderings)

As a blossoming critical thinker, you will find yourself wondering in many directions. You will often, however, be unsure about how many of these wonderings to share with your students. You certainly don't want to overwhelm them. Neither do you want to confuse them or lead them in too many directions at once. So when do you make the wonderings explicit in the form of a question and when do you keep them in the privacy of your mind?

There is no pat formula or procedure for answering these questions, though there are some principles:

- *Test and find out.* There is nothing wrong with some of your questions misfiring. You won't always be able to predict what questions will stimulate students thought. So you must engage in some trial-and-error questioning.
- *Tie in to student experience and perceived needs.* You may think of numerous examples of ways students can apply what they learn, and formulate questions relating academic material to students' lives.
- *Don't give up too soon.* If students don't respond to a question, wait. If they still don't respond, you could rephrase the question or break it down into simpler questions.

The teacher must use care and caution in introducing students to Socratic questioning. The level of the questions should match the level of the students' thought. It should not be assumed that students will be fully successful with it, except over time. Nevertheless, properly used, it can be introduced in some form or other at virtually any grade level.

Transcript of a 4th Grade Socratic Discussion

The following is a transcript of a 4th grade exploratory Socratic discussion. The discussion leader was with these particular students for the first time. The purpose was to determine the status of the children's thinking on some of the abstract questions whose answers tend to define our broadest thinking. The students were eager to respond and often seemed to articulate responses that reflected potential insights into the character of the human mind, the forces that shape us, the influence of parents and peer group, the nature of morality and of ethnocentric bias. The insights are disjointed, of course, but the questions that elicited them and the responses that articulated them could be used as the basis of future discussions or simple assignments with these students.

While reading the transcript which follows, you may want to formulate questions that could have been asked but weren't: student responses that could have been followed up, or other directions the discussion could have taken. Other ways to approach the manuscript would include explaining the function of each question or categorizing the questions.

Transcript

➤ *How does your mind work?*
Where's your mind? **(A Foundational Question)**

Student: In your head. (numerous students point to their heads)

➤ *Does your mind do anything?* **(Question of Clarification)**

Student: It helps you remember and think.

Student: It helps, like, if you want to move your legs. It sends a message down to them.

Student: This side of your mind controls this side of your body and that side controls this other side.

Student: When you touch a hot oven it tells you whether to cry or say ouch!

➤ *Does it tell you when to be sad and when to be happy?*
How does your mind know when to be happy and when to be sad?
(Clarification and Probing Implications)

Student: When you're hurt it tells you to be sad.

Student: If something is happening around you is sad.

Student: If there is lightning and you are scared.

Student: If you get something you want.

Student: It makes your body operate. It's like a machine that operates your body.

➤ *Does it ever happen that two people are in the same circumstance but one is happy and the other is sad? Even though they are in exactly the same circumstance?*
(Exploring Viewpoints or Perspectives)

Student: You get the same toy. One person might like it. The other gets the same toy and he doesn't like the toy.

➤ *Why do you think that some people come to like some things and some people seem to like different things?*
(Exploring Viewpoints or Perspectives)

Student: Cause everybody is not the same. Everybody has different minds and is built different, made different.

Student: They have different personalities?

➤ *Where does personality come from?* **(Probing the Cause)**

Student: When you start doing stuff and you find that you like some stuff best.

➤ *Are you born with a personality or do you develop it as you grow up?* **(Probing the Cause)**

Student: You develop it as you grow up.

➤ *What makes you develop one rather than another?* **(Probing the Cause)**

Student: Like, your parents or something.

➤ *How can your parent's personality get into you?* **(Probing the Cause)**

Student: Because you're always around them and then the way they act, if they think they are good and they want you to act the same way, then they'll sort of teach you and you'll do it.

Student: Like, if you are in a tradition. They want you to carry on something that their parents started.

➤ *Does your mind come to think at all the way the children around you think? Can you think of any examples where the way you think is like the way children around you think? Do you think you behave like other American kids?*
(Exploring Viewpoints or Perspectives)

Student: Yes.

➤ *What would make you behave more like kids around you than like Eskimo kids?*
(Exploring Viewpoints or Perspectives)

Student: Because you're around them.

Student: Like, Eskimo kids probably don't even know what the word 'jump-rope' is. American kids know what it is.

➤ *And are there things that the Eskimo kids know that you don't know about?*
(Exploring Viewpoints or Perspectives)

Student: Yes.

Student: And also we don't have to dress like them or act like them, and they have to know when a storm is coming so they won't get trapped outside.

➤ *O.K., so if I understand you then, parents have some influence on how you behave and the kids around you have some influence on how you behave.... Do you have some influence on how you behave? Do you choose the kind of person you're going to be at all?*
(Probing Causes)

Student: Yes.

➤ *How do you do that do you think?* **(Probing Reasons and Causes)**

Student: Well if someone says to jump off a five-story building, you won't say O.K. You wouldn't want to do that ...

➤ *Do you ever sit around and say, "Let's see shall I be a smart person or a dumb one?"*
(Probing Implications)

Student: Yes.

➤ *But how do you decide?* **(Probing Causes)**

Student: Your grades.

➤ *But I thought your teacher decided your grades. How do you decide?* **(Probing Causes)**

Student: If you don't do your homework you get bad grades and become a dumb person but if you study real hard you'll get good grades.

➤ *So you decide that, right?* **(Probing Causes)**

Student: And if you like something at school, like computers, you work hard and you can get a good job when you grow up. But if you don't like anything at school you don't work hard.

Student: You can't just decide you want to be smart, you have to work for it.

Student: You got to work to be smart just like you got to work to get your allowance.

➤ *What about being good and being bad, do you decide whether you're good or you're bad? How many people have decided to be bad? (3 students raise their hands) [To first student:] Why have you decided to be bad?*
(Probing Causes)

Student: Well, I don't know. Sometimes I think I've been bad too long and I want to go to school and have a better reputation, but sometimes I feel like just making trouble and who cares.

➤ *Let's see, is there a difference between who you are and your reputation? What's your reputation? That's a pretty big word. What's your reputation?*
(Clarification)

Student: The way you act. If you had a bad reputation people wouldn't like to be around you and if you had a good reputation, people would like to be around you and be your friend.

➤ *Well, but I'm not sure of the difference between who you are and who people think you are. Could you be a good person and people think you bad? Is that possible?*
(Clarifying and Probing Implications)

Student: Yeah, because you could try to be good. I mean, a lot of people think this one person's really smart, but this other person doesn't have nice clothes, but she tries really hard and people don't want to be around her.

➤ *So sometimes people think somebody is real good and they're not and sometimes people think that somebody is real bad and they're not. Like if you were a crook, would you let everyone know you're a crook?*
(Probing Implications)

Students: [Chorus] NO!

➤ *So some people are really good at hiding what they are really like. Some people might have a good reputation and be bad; some people might have a bad reputation and be good.*
(Clarification)

Student: Like, everyone might think you were good, but you might be going on dope or something.

Student: Does reputation mean that if you have a good reputation you want to keep it just like that? Do you always want to be good for the rest of your life?

➤ *I'm not sure ...* **(Clarification)**

Student: So if you have a good reputation you try to be good all the time and don't mess up and don't do nothing?

➤ *Suppose somebody is trying to be good just to get a good reputation — why are they trying to be good?* **(Probing Causes)**

Student: So they can get something they want and they don't want other people to have?

Student: They might be shy and just want to be left alone.

Student: You can't tell a book by how it's covered.

➤ *Yes, some people are concerned more with their cover than their book. Now let me ask you another question. So, if its true that we all have a mind and our mind helps us to figure out the world, and we are influenced by our parents and the people around us, and sometimes we choose to do good things and sometimes we choose to do bad things, sometimes people say things about us and so forth and so on ... Let me ask you: Are there some bad people in this world?* **(Probing Causes)**

Student: Yeah.

Student: Terrorists and stuff.

Student: Night-stalker.

Student: The TWA hijackers.

Student: Robbers.

Student: Rapers.

Student: Bums.

➤ *Bums, are they bad?* **(Clarification)**

Student: Well, sometimes.

Student: The Klu Klux Klan.

Student: The Bums ... not really cause they might not look good but you can't judge them by how they look. They might be really nice and everything.

➤ *O.K., so they might have a bad reputation but be good, after you care to know them. There might be good bums and bad bums.* **(Clarification)**

Student: Libyan guys and Machine gun Kelly.

➤ *Let me ask you, do the bad people think they're bad?* **(Exploring Perspectives)**

Student: A lot of them don't think they're bad, but they are. They might be sick in the head.

➤ *Yes, some people are sick in their heads.* **(Clarification)**

Student: A lot of them (bad guys) don't think they're bad.

➤ *Why did you say Libyan people?* **(Probing Reasons)**

Student: Cause they have a lot o' terrorists and hate us and bomb us ...

➤ *If they hate us do they think we are bad or good?* **(Probing Implications)**

Student: They think we are bad.

➤ *And we think they are bad? And who is right?* **(Exploring Perspectives)**

Student: Usually both of them.

Student: None of us are really bad!

Student: Really, I don't know why our people and their people are fighting. Two wrongs don't make a right.

Student: It's like if there was a line between two countries, and they were both against each other, if a person from the first country crosses over the line, they'd be considered the bad guy. And if a person from the second country crossed over the line, he'd be considered the bad guy.

➤ *So it can depend on which country you're from who you consider right or wrong, is that right?* **(Exploring Perspectives)**

Student: Like a robber might steal things to support his family. He's doing good to his family but actually bad to another person.

➤ *And in his mind do you think he is doing something good or bad?* **(Exploring Perspectives and Implications)**

Student: It depends what his mind is like. He might think he is doing good for his family or he might think he is doing bad for the other person.

Student: It's like the underground railroad a long time ago. Some people thought it was bad and some people thought it was good.

➤ *But if lots of people think something is right and lots of people think something is wrong, how are you supposed to figure out the difference between right and wrong?* **(Probing Causes)**

Student: Go by what you think!

➤ *But how do you figure out what to think?* ***(Probing Causes)***

Student: Lots of people go by other people.

➤ *But somebody has to decide for themselves, don't they?* ***(Probing Implications)***

Student: Use your mind?

➤ *Yes, let's see, suppose I told you: "You are going to have a new classmate. Her name is Sally and she's bad." Now, you could either believe me or what could you do?*
(Probing Consequences)

Student: You could try to meet her and decide whether she was bad or good.

➤ *Suppose she came and said to you: "I'm going to give you a toy so you'll like me." And she gave you things so you would like her, but she also beat up on some other people, would you like her because she gave you things?* ***(Probing Consequences)***

Student: No, because she said I'll give you this so you'll like me. She wouldn't be very nice.

➤ *So why should you like people?* ***(Probing Reasons)***

Student: Because they act nice to you.

➤ *Only to you?* ***(Probing Implications)***

Student: To everybody!

Student: I wouldn't care what they gave me. I'd see what they're like inside.

➤ *But how do you find out what's on the inside of a person?* ***(Probing Causes and Reasons)***

Student: You could ask, but I would try to judge myself.

Socratic questioning is flexible. The questions asked at any given point will depend on what the students say, what ideas the teacher wants to pursue, and what questions occur to the teacher. Generally, Socratic questions raise basic issues, probe beneath the surface of things, and pursue problematic areas of thought.

The above discussion could have gone in a number of different directions. For instance, rather than focussing on the mind's relationship to emotions, the teacher could have pursued the concept 'mind' by asking for more examples of its functions, and having students analyze them. The teacher could have followed up the response of the student who asked, "Does reputation mean that if you have a good reputation you want to keep it just like that?" He might, for instance, have asked the student why she asked that, and asked the other students what they thought of the idea. Such a discussion may have developed into a dialogical exchange about reputation, different degrees of goodness, or reasons for being bad. Or the concept 'bad people' could have been pursued and clarified by asking students why the examples they gave were examples of bad people. Students may then have been able to suggest tentative generalizations which could have been tested and probed through further questioning. Rather than exploring the influence of perspective on evaluation, the teacher might have probed the idea, expressed by one student, that no one is "really bad". The student could have been asked to explain the remark, and other students could have been asked for their responses to the idea. In these cases and others, the teacher has a choice between any number of equally thought provoking questions. No one question is the 'right' question.

Excerpts from a First Grade Socratic Discussion

Consider the following transcript taken from "Instruction for Self-Regulated Reading", by Annemarie Sullivan Palincsar and Ann L. Brown.* Six children, five with language difficulties which made them at-risk, participated in a "Reciprocal Teaching" program.

(The teacher reads a text about bear cubs.) "Baby Bear was bigger than his sister and he began to play too rough. His sister jumped onto a tree trunk and climbed quickly upward."

Kendra interrupts for a clarification: "What's rough?"

Mara, one of the children, suggests, "Like you say rough texture."

The teacher interjects, "Well, that's one kind of rough."

Another child, Robert, adds, "The other one is like they beat you up."

The teacher turns their attention to the text for clarification. "That's another kind of rough. Let me read the sentence and see which one you think it is. If it's the way you feel the texture, or the beating up." (Rereads.) "Baby Bear was bigger than his sister and he began to play too rough."

Mara says, "It's the kind he means (referring to Robert)."

Teacher replies, "The punching and the hitting, playing too hard. Okay."

(The teacher continues reading and comes to a portion of the text where a prediction would be appropriate.) "His front paws caught hold on the branch, but he could not pull himself up. He hung there, swinging in midair. ... Now the limb bent lower, and lower, SNAP.... (Teacher stops reading.) Prediction?"

Children answer, "It fell."

The teacher replies, "That's your prediction. Let's see if it's true." (The teacher reads) "The limb broke and Baby Bear fell, splash into the cold stream. He squalled for his mother. Now the mother splashed into the water...."

Robert interrupts for another clarification, "What's squalled?"

(Teacher rereads) "He squalled for his mother. What do you think he did when he fell into the water?"

Robert answers, "Whining, whining and crying."

Teacher: "Good, Robert!"

The teacher then continued reading and asked the discussion leader, Margo, to begin by asking her question.

Margo asks, "What did he lay in?"

The group has been talking about the different kinds of questions that one can ask: questions that are about details in the story and questions that you have to think about to answer. Perhaps as a consequence of these discussions, Mara offers the following comment on Margo's question: "It's true you could get an answer for that question. But is that gonna get an answer from more than one people? Probably, it's just gonna get an answer from one, and there's better questions you could ask."

The teacher interjects at this point: "Well, let's go ahead and answer her and see if we can get *this* one."

The children then answer Margo's question and she asks another one, "What did the mother do after he squalled? Robert?"

Robert: "Licked him all over."

Margo: "Correct. Any more questions?"

* *Toward the Thinking Curriculum: Current Cognitive Research* 1989 ASCD Yearbook, Lauren B. Resnick and Leopold E. Klopfer editors, 1989, Association for Supervision and Curriculum Development, pp. 33–36.

Several children have additional questions which the group discussed.

The teacher then asks Margo to summarize:

Margo: "This part of the story told us about Baby Bear and sister bear are wrestling."

The teacher provides the following feedback regarding Margo's summary: "Tell us a little bit more. There's an important thing you left out. While they were wrestling, what happened?"

The children then complete the summary as a group, adding additional details about the events which occurred in that part of the story. Included in their summary is the observation that Baby Bear didn't get hurt."

"Why didn't he get hurt?"

Kinata: "Water is real soft, like you can jump on it like a mat. If you land on a rock you will hurt yourself."

Teacher: "A rock doesn't give way does it? It just stays hard; but the water will give way and come around you. Good point! We got some good discussion."

Mara: "You know what time of year it was when it told you he would splash, because if it was *this* time of year (February), I don't think he'd splash in the water. I think he'd crack!"

The teacher then reads on. The next portion of the text concerns the diet of the bear cubs. The teacher has earlier made the prediction that the bear cubs are no longer nursing, sharing her reasoning that they now go in search of stream water. In this portion of the text, it becomes clear that the cubs are indeed still nursing. The teacher corrects herself: "They are still nursing. They are still taking their mother's milk. Mine wasn't a very good prediction then, was it? I thought that when they said they were drinking water that they had finished drinking their mother's milk."

However, Kinata reassures the teacher: "Well, that was a good prediction. It just didn't come true."

When discussing this program, the authors mention that these students spontaneously engage their teachers in similar discussion during small-group reading time.

Role Playing and Reconstructing Opposing Views

A fundamental danger for human thought is narrowness. We do not naturally and spontaneously open our minds to the insights of those who think differently from us. We have a natural tendency to use our native intelligence and our cognitive skills to protect and maintain our system of beliefs rather than to modify and expand it, especially when ideas are suggested that have their origin in a very different way of thinking. We can never become fairminded unless we learn how to enter sympathetically into the thinking of others, to reason from their perspectives and eventually to try seeing things as they see them.

Learning how to accurately reconstruct the thinking of others and how to role play their thinking (once reconstructed) are fundamental goals of critical thinking instruction. Very little work has yet been done in giving students opportunities to role play the reasoning of others, so it is not now clear to what extent or in what forms role playing to enhance critical reciprocity is possible.

But imagine some possible experiments. Students could brainstorm two lists, one list of their reasons for being allowed to stay up late and one for the reasons their parents might give forbidding it. A role play might be devised in which two students would pretend that they were parents and were asked, in that role, to give their reasons why their children should not be allowed to stay up late. It would be interesting to see how accurately the students could reconstruct the reasoning of their parents. They will probably find this challenging and should be encouraged to be as clear as possible in their reasons. Socratically questioning them would reveal more about their thinking. Then one might experiment with a discussion between a student playing "parent" and another student playing "daughter" or "son". The class might subsequently discuss what the best reasons were on each side of the dispute and who seemed to have the stronger argument.

An interesting follow-up exercise might be to have the students, either in pairs or singly, compose a dialogue on a given issue or on a chosen one. Remind them to brainstorm lists of reasons for both sides of the issue, being sure to focus on the side they don't hold. Then have them write a short dialogue expressing the opposing viewpoints. Some of the pairs of students could present their dialogues to the class.

Teaching the Distinction Between Fact, Opinion, and Reasoned Judgment

Many texts claim to foster critical thinking by teaching students to divide all statements into facts and opinions. When they do so, students fail to grasp the significance of dialogical thinking and reasoned judgment. When an issue is fundamentally a matter of fact (for example, "What is the weight of this block of wood?" or "What are the dimensions of this figure?"), there is no reason to argue about the answer; one should carry out the process that yields the correct answer. Sometimes this might require following complex procedures. In any case, weighing and measuring, the processes needed for the questions above, are not typically matters of debate.

On the other hand, questions that raise matters of mere opinion, such as, "What sweater do you like better?" "What is your favorite color?" or "Where would you like to spend your vacation?" do not have any one correct answer since they ask us merely to express our personal *preferences*.

But most of the important issues we face in our lives are not exclusively matters of fact or matters of preference. Many require a new element: that we reason our way to conclusions while we take the reasoned perspectives of others into account. As teachers, we should be clear in encouraging students to distinguish these three different situations: the ones that call for facts alone, the ones that call for preference alone, and the ones that call for reasoned judgment. When, as members of a jury, we are called upon to come to a judgment of innocence or guilt, we do not settle questions of pure fact, and we are certainly not expected to express our subjective preferences.

Students definitely need to learn procedures for gathering facts, and they doubtless need to have opportunities to express their preferences, but their most important need is to develop their capacities for reasoned judgment. They need to know how to come to conclusions of their own based on evidence and reasoning of their own within the framework of their own perspectives. Their values and preferences will, of course, play a role in their perspectives and reasoning, but their perspectives should not be a matter of pure opinion or sheer preference. I should not believe in things or people just because I *want* to. I should have good reasons for my beliefs, except, of course, where it makes sense to have pure preferences. It does make sense to prefer butterscotch to chocolate pudding, but it does not make sense to prefer taking advantage of people rather than respecting their rights. Over time, students need to distinguish fact, opinion, and reasoned judgment, since they will never be good thinkers if they commonly confuse them as most students now do. (See the section on Text Treatment of Critical Thinking in "Thinking Critically about Teaching: From Didactic to Critical Teaching".)

In passing, be sure not to confuse this distinction with that of convergent and divergent questions. Questions of opinion and questions of reasoned judgment are both divergent, but the first does not involve the question of truth or accuracy (because it calls for expression of preference), while the second does (since reasoned judgment can be more or less reasonable, more or less prejudiced, more or less justified).

We have put this distinction into the "Global Strategies" chapter to underscore its importance as a pervasive emphasis in all instruction. In any event, we should always keep in mind global, as well as more specific, strategies for fostering critical thinking. When we habitually reflect on our role as teachers, play the role of Socratic questioner, seek opportunities to have students reconstruct and role play the thinking of others, and habitually encourage students to distinguish preference from reasoned judgment, we will discover new possibilities for critical thinking instruction and will develop global insights that help guide us in understanding and applying the strategies illustrated more specifically in the lesson remodels that follow.

> *"Be aware of the hidden curriculum in all schools. If teachers ask only factual questions that test memory and recall, students assume that this is the most important aspect of learning. If principals spend more time focusing on administrative concerns, discipline, or standardized test scores, teachers also assume these aspects of school are the most important."*
>
> *Greensboro Handbook,*
> *Greensboro Public Schools*
> *Reasoning and Writing Project*

Strategies

Introduction

The purpose of this chapter is to illustrate how the concept of the autonomous, precise, fairminded thinker can be translated into classroom activities and discussions. We have broken the global concept of critical thinking down into 35 aspects or instructional strategies. Each strategy section has three parts. The "principle" provides the theory of critical thinking on which the strategy is based and links the strategy to the ideal of the fairminded critical thinker. We could have labeled it "What the Critical Thinker Does, and Why". We included it because we are convinced that one cannot do or teach critical thinking well without understanding why one should honor principles of critical thought, and to help overcome the tendency in education to treat insights and skills in isolation from each other. The "application" provides examples of when and how the strategy can be used in the classroom. Our lists of possible questions are often larger and more detailed here than in the remodels, and sometimes our remarks are general. We tried to provide some idea of when the principle could apply, to describe ways texts and some standard instructional practices can undermine or interfere with students learning the principle, and some initial suggestions to further illustrate and clarify the principle and get you started developing your own techniques for teaching it. Each strategy description concludes with a list of lesson plans in which we use the strategy for reference. If you aren't sure you understand the principle and how it can be taught, or want more examples of teaching it, or want to see it taught in context, you could look up some of the lessons and read a use of the strategy and (in many cases) justification for that use.

Here is an example. The thirteenth strategy on our list, **S–13,** is called "Clarifying Issues, Conclusions, or Beliefs". The principle that underlies it is briefly characterized as follows:

Principle: The more completely, clearly, and accurately an issue or statement is formulated, the easier and more helpful the discussion of its settlement or verification. Given a clear statement of an issue, and prior to evaluating conclusions or solutions, it is important to recognize what is required to settle it. And before we can agree or disagree with a claim, we must understand it clearly. It makes no sense to say "I don't know what you mean, but I deny it, whatever it is." Critical thinkers make sure that understanding precedes judgment. They routinely distinguish facts from interpretations, opinions, judgments, or theories. They seek to express themselves clearly and precisely.

Following the principle is an explanation of some of the ways we might teach for it:

Application: Teachers should encourage children to slow down and reflect before coming to conclusions. When discussing an issue, the teacher can ask students first, *"How would you describe the problem?"* Children should be encouraged to continually re-formulate the issue in light of new information. They should be encouraged to see how the first statement of the issue or problem is rarely best (that is, most accurate, clear, and complete) and that they are in a better position to settle a question *after* they have developed as clear a formulation as possible.

When talking about an issue, teachers can have children discuss such questions as, *"Do we understand the issue? Do we know how to get an answer? Have we stated it fairly? Are the words clear? Are we evaluating anything? What? Why? How can we get the evidence we need?"*

When a statement is unclear, the class can discuss such questions as, *"How can we know whether or not this is it? Are any words or phrases unclear? Is there a clearer way to say this? Is there a more accurate way to say this? Can it be rephrased? Do the different ways of putting it say the same thing?"*

This strategy provides a way of remodelling lessons that focus on "Fact/ Opinion," or which have vague passages of text.

Immediately after the application we provide a list of lesson plans in which the strategy is used.

The reader should keep in mind the connection between the principles and applications on the one hand, and the character traits of a fairminded critical thinker on the other. Our aim is not a set of disjointed skills, but an integrated, committed, thinking person. The strategies and lessons should be used to illuminate each other. If puzzled by a remodel (ours or your own), see the strategies. If puzzled by a strategy, see the originals and our critiques and remodels for clarification. All of the pieces of the remodelling process — understanding what critical thinking is and why one should do it; breaking the concept into teachable components; inventing ways to help students learn and practice critical thought; evaluating lessons; and improving them — all fit together. These activities are interdependent. Figuring out how to teach a particular principle helps you better understand what critical thinking is (and isn't). Analyzing and evaluating a lesson helps you see how critical thinking applies to particular situations. Clarifying the global concept of critical thinking helps you keep your focus on its most important features, and suggests ways of understanding and teaching specific principles and skills.

The strategies listed below are divided into three categories — one for the affective and two for the cognitive. This of course is not to imply that the cognitive dimension of critical thinking should be given twice as much emphasis. Indeed, the affective dimension is every bit as important to critical thinking. No one learns to think critically who is not motivated to do so. In any case, whatever dimension is emphasized, the other dimension should be integrated. We want students to continually use their emerging critical thinking skills and abilities in keeping with the critical spirit, and the critical spirit can be nurtured only when actually practicing critical thinking in some (cognitive) way. One cannot develop one's fairmindedness, for example, without actually thinking fairmindedly. One cannot develop one's intellectual independence without actually thinking independently. This is true of all the essential critical thinking traits, values, or dispositions. They are developmentally embedded in thinking itself. In teaching for critical thinking in a strong sense, the affective dimension of thinking is fully as important as the cognitive.

Before we explore the interdependence of the affective strategies, we shall present three versions of our strategies. The first will formally name them, the second will reduce them to their simplest beginnings, the third will express them as they might be expressed by Fairminded Fran. We hope these formulations will help make these strategies more intuitive.

> *Do not to spend too much time on the general formulations of what critical thinking is before moving to the level of particular strategies, since people tend to have trouble assimilating general concepts unless they are made accessible by concrete examples.*

Strategy List: 35 Dimensions of Critical Thought
(Formally named)

A. Affective Strategies

S-1 thinking independently

S-2 developing insight into egocentricity or sociocentricity

S-3 exercising fairmindedness

S-4 exploring thoughts underlying feelings and feelings underlying thoughts

S-5 developing intellectual humility and suspending judgment

S-6 developing intellectual courage

S-7 developing intellectual good faith or integrity

S-8 developing intellectual perseverance

S-9 developing confidence in reason

B. Cognitive Strategies — Macro-Abilities

S-10 refining generalizations and avoiding oversimplifications

S-11 comparing analogous situations: transferring insights to new contexts

S-12 developing one's perspective: creating or exploring beliefs, arguments, or theories

S-13 clarifying issues, conclusions, or beliefs

S-14 clarifying and analyzing the meanings of words or phrases

S-15 developing criteria for evaluation: clarifying values and standards

S-16 evaluating the credibility of sources of information

S-17 questioning deeply: raising and pursuing root or significant questions

S-18 analyzing or evaluating arguments, interpretations, beliefs, or theories

S-19 generating or assessing solutions

S-20 analyzing or evaluating actions or policies

S-21 reading critically: clarifying or critiquing texts

S-22 listening critically: the art of silent dialogue

S-23 making interdisciplinary connections

S-24 practicing Socratic discussion: clarifying and questioning beliefs, theories, or perspectives

S-25 reasoning dialogically: comparing perspectives, interpretations, or theories

S-26 reasoning dialectically: evaluating perspectives, interpretations, or theories

C. Cognitive Strategies — Micro-Skills

S-27 comparing and contrasting ideals with actual practice

S-28 thinking precisely about thinking: using critical vocabulary

S-29 noting significant similarities and differences

S-30 examining or evaluating assumptions

S-31 distinguishing relevant from irrelevant facts

S-32 making plausible inferences, predictions, or interpretations

S-33 giving reasons and evaluating evidence and alleged facts

S-34 recognizing contradictions

S-35 exploring implications and consequences

Strategy List: 35 Dimensions of Critical Thought
(Informally characterized)

A.   We use teaching strategies that encourage our children to begin to develop the attitudes and values essential to critical thinking. As a result:

S-1   Our children begin to think for themselves.

S-2   Our children begin to notice when they are seeing things narrowly.
Our children begin to see when they are conforming to their peer group.

S-3   Our children begin to appreciate the point of view of others.

S-4   Our children begin to think about why they feel as they do.

S-5   Our children begin to notice when they really know something and when they merely believe without good reasons.

S-6   Our children begin to question what their peer group says and to speak up for what they believe.

S-7   Our children begin to live up to what they expect of others.

S-8   Our children begin to persevere in their tasks even when the work is difficult.

S-9   Our children begin to discover how powerful their minds are, how much they can figure out by thinking.

B.   We use teaching strategies that encourage our children to begin to develop large scale critical thinking skills and abilities. As a result:

S-10 Our children begin to be more precise in what they say and to notice complexity.

S-11 Our children begin to apply what they are learning to diverse situations.

S-12 Our children begin to discover and develop their own points of view.

S-13 Our children begin to clarify problems and questions.

S-14 Our children begin to clarify what words mean.

S-15 Our children begin to discover standards for measuring or judging things.

S-16 Our children begin to discover when it makes sense to believe what they hear.

S-17 Our children begin to ask deeper questions.

S-18 Our children begin to analyze what they say and do.

S-19 Our children begin to develop solutions to their problems.

S-20 Our children begin to evaluate rules, policies, and behavior.

S-21 Our children begin to learn how to question as they read.

S-22 Our children begin to listen attentively and to ask questions that clarify what is said.

S-23 Our children begin to make connections between what they are learning in different subjects.

S-24 Our children begin to discover and ask different kinds of questions.

S-25 Our children begin to learn from working and talking with each other.

S-26 Our children begin to learn how to discuss differences in a more reasoned way.

C. We use teaching strategies that encourage our children to begin to develop some of the fine-grained critical thinking skills. As a result:

S–27 Our children begin to distinguish ideals from actual practice.

S–28 Our children begin to use critical thinking terms in their work and discussion.

S–29 Our children begin to notice significant similarities and differences and use comparison to learn.

S–30 Our children begin to examine and evaluate what they usually assume.

S–31 Our children begin to figure out what facts they need to consider and notice when they are distracted by facts that have nothing to do with it.

S–32 Our children begin to fill in missing pieces, notice what things mean beyond what they say, make reasonable predictions.

S–33 Our children begin to give reasons for their beliefs and learn how to judge details, evidence, and facts.

S–34 Our children begin to notice when two statements or beliefs contradict each other.

S–35 Our children begin to explore implications and consequences.

> *It should not be assumed that there is a universal standard for how fast teachers should proceed with the task of remodelling their lesson plans. A slow but steady evolutionary process is much more desirable than a rush job across the board.*

Strategy List: 35 Dimensions of Critical Thought
(As They Might Be Explained by Fairminded Fran)

In the chapter "Making Critical Thinking Intuitive" we introduced three fictional characters whose way of thinking illustrated the distinction between uncritical thinking (Naive Nancy), weak sense critical thinking (Selfish Sam), and strong sense critical thinking (Fairminded Fran). Before you examine our more formal explanations of the 35 dimensions of critical thinking you might find it useful to examine the following summaries as they might be expressed by Fairminded Fran. It is our hope that students will begin to think in these ways as we foster their thinking and encourage them to become not only skilled but fairminded as well.

A. Affective Strategies

S-1 thinking independently: "I try to do my own thinking, to figure things out for myself. It's good to listen to others to find out what they're thinking, but you must always use your own thinking to decide who to believe and what to do."

S-2 developing insight into egocentricity or sociocentricity: "If I don't watch myself, I pay too much attention to what I want, and go along too quickly with what my friends say. I have to remember that everyone usually puts what they want first and believes what their friends believe. Just because I or my friends think something doesn't make it so."

S-3 exercising fairmindedness: "Whenever I disagree with someone I should try to look at things from their point of view. Maybe If I see why someone disagrees with me, I will find a reason to agree with at least part of what they are saying."

S-4 exploring thoughts underlying feelings and feelings underlying thoughts: "When I get angry or sad, I should think about why. Maybe I could change the way I am looking at things and then not be so angry or so sad after all."

S-5 developing intellectual humility and suspending judgment: "I shouldn't say things that I don't really know are true. Lots of things that people say aren't true. Even TV and books are sometimes wrong. I should always be willing to ask 'How do *you* know that? How do *I* know that?'"

S-6 developing intellectual courage: "I should be ready to speak up for what I think is right, even if it is not popular with my friends or the kids I am with. I should be courteous but I should not be afraid to think differently."

S-7 developing intellectual good faith or integrity: "I should be careful to practice what I preach. It is no good saying I believe in something if I don't really act on it."

S-8 **developing intellectual perseverance:** "It isn't always easy to solve problems. Sometimes you have to think for a long, long time to do it. Even though my mind gets tired, I must not give up too easily."

S-9 **developing confidence in reason:** "I know my head can figure things out, if I am willing to think logically, look for evidence, and accept only good reasons for things."

B. Cognitive Strategies — Macro-Abilities

S-10 **refining generalizations and avoiding oversimplifications:** "It's wrong to say 'everyone' when you only mean 'most', or 'no one' when you only mean 'just a few'. It's nice to make things simple, but not so simple that they're not true."

S-11 **comparing analogous situations: transferring insights to new contexts:** "Lots of things are like other things. Being lost in the city may be in some ways like being lost in your life. Maybe in both cases you need a map!"

S-12 **developing one's perspective: creating or exploring beliefs, arguments, or theories:** "It takes time to figure out what you really think, sometimes years! I should be ready to listen to what other people think and why. Then my own ideas can grow and grow."

S-13 **clarifying issues, conclusions, or beliefs:** "Often what people say is not as clear as they think. You should always be ready to say 'What do you mean?' or 'Could you explain that to me?'"

S-14 **clarifying and analyzing the meanings of words or phrases:** "Words are funny. Sometimes it sounds like you know them when you don't. Yesterday when my teacher asked me what 'democracy' meant, I thought I knew, but I found I couldn't explain it."

S-15 **developing criteria for evaluation: clarifying values and standards:** "If we are going to judge something as good or bad, we need a way to do it. But often we decide that something is good or bad and really don't know why we said so. People are funny!"

S-16 **evaluating the credibility of sources of information:** "We learn lots of things from other people, and from books and TV. But sometimes what we learn isn't so. We need to question what we hear people say and what we see on TV. Do they really know? Maybe and maybe not!"

S-17 **questioning deeply: raising and pursuing root or significant questions:** "My teacher often asks us questions that sound easy but aren't. The other day she asked us what a country is and it took us a lot of time to figure it out. I guess sometimes simple things aren't so simple."

S-18 **analyzing or evaluating arguments, interpretations, beliefs, or theories:** "The other day my brother and I argued about who should do the dishes. Finally we decided that we should do them together."

S-19 **generating or assessing solutions:** "It's interesting to try to solve problems. Sometimes there are even different ways to get the same job done."

S-20 **analyzing or evaluating actions or policies:** "I get mad when I am not allowed to do what my brother is allowed to do. My parents say it is because he is older than me, but sometimes I am not allowed to do what he did when he was my age. That's not fair!"

S-21 **reading critically: clarifying or critiquing texts:** "When I read I try to figure out exactly what is being said. Reading is like being a detective. You have to ask questions and look carefully for clues."

S-22 **listening critically: the art of silent dialogue:** "When I listen to someone, I ask myself whether I could repeat what they are saying and whether I could explain it to someone else. Sometimes I ask myself, 'Did anything like this ever happen to me?' This helps me see if I'm listening carefully."

S-23 making interdisciplinary connections: "I am finding out how I can use what I learn in one subject while I'm working on another. Lots of ideas work in different places."

S-24 practicing Socratic discussion: clarifying and questioning beliefs, theories, or perspectives: "I am finding out that you learn a lot more if you ask a lot of questions. I am also learning that there are different kinds of questions and that you can find out different things by asking them."

S-25 reasoning dialogically: comparing perspectives, interpretations, or theories: "It helps to talk to other kids when you are trying to learn. Sometimes they have good ideas, and sometimes it helps you to try to explain things to the other kids."

S-26 reasoning dialectically: evaluating perspectives, interpretations, or theories: "It even helps to talk to other kids who think differently from you. Sometimes they know things you don't and sometimes you find out that you need to think more before you make up your mind."

C. Cognitive Strategies — Micro-Skills

S-27 comparing and contrasting ideals with actual practice: "Lots of things we say we believe in, but then we don't do it. We say that everyone is equal but we don't give them an equal chance. We need to fix things so that we mean what we say and say what we mean."

S-28 thinking precisely about thinking: using critical vocabulary: "There are special words you can learn to help you talk about what goes on in your head. For example, inferences happen when you learn some things and decide other things because of that. Assumptions happen when you believe things without thinking about them. I try to watch my inferences and assumptions."

S-29 noting significant similarities and differences: "Sometimes it is important to see how alike things are that are different. Sometimes it is important to see how different things are that are alike. I always try now to see how things are both alike and different."

S-30 examining or evaluating assumptions: "To do a good job of thinking you have to pay attention to what you believe without thinking. Sometimes we go along with stuff without thinking about it. When you do, watch out! You probably missed something important!"

S-31 distinguishing relevant from irrelevant facts: "It may be true but is it related? We often forget to ask this. To figure things out you must stick to the point and not get other things mixed in."

S-32 making plausible inferences, predictions, or interpretations: "I sometimes decide things that aren't true. Then I have to stop and think about why I did that. I try to be more careful next time. Things often seem to be one way at the moment and then turn out to be different."

S-33 giving reasons and evaluating evidence and alleged facts: "Detectives and police look carefully for evidence so they can find out who really did it. We need to find evidence too, when we read and write and talk. We should try to find evidence before we decide who is right and wrong."

S-34 recognizing contradictions: "Sometimes kids say one thing today and another thing tomorrow. Sometimes parents and teachers do, too. That's confusing. You should decide what you really mean and then stick to it and not go back and forth and back and forth."

S-35 exploring implications and consequences: "When things happen, other things happen because of them. If you say something mean to someone, they may feel bad for a long, long time. It's important to see that, otherwise we won't notice all the things we are making happen."

How Would Naive Nancy and Selfish Sam Understand the Strategies ?

It should be clear that Naive Nancy and Selfish Sam would give different explanations of the 35 dimensions of critical thought. Nancy would deceive herself into thinking that she was thinking critically when she was not. Furthermore, most of her understandings would be so abstract that she would not be able to apply the principles to her experience. Selfish Sam would emphasize the usefulness of the various dimensions of critical thinking for getting what he wants, for protecting himself, and for using others to his advantage. However, he would show little interest in the principles that focus on fairmindedness, intellectual humility, and integrity.

The Interdependence of Traits of Mind

Just as the cognitive and affective dimensions are interdependent and intertwined, so also are the various individual strategies. For purposes of learning, we articulate separate principles and applications. In the beginning, the connections between them may be obscure. Nevertheless, eventually we begin to discover how progress with any one principle leads inevitably to other principles. To see this, let us look first at the individual strategies in the affective dimension.

Affective strategies are interdependent because the intellectual traits they imply develop best in concert with each other. Consider intellectual humility. To become aware of the limits of our knowledge, we need the courage to face our own prejudices and ignorance. To discover our own prejudices in turn, we often must empathize with and reason within points of view toward which we are hostile. To achieve this end, we must typically persevere over a period of time, for learning to empathically enter a point of view against which we are biased takes time and significant effort. That effort will not seem justified unless we have the confidence in reason to believe we will not be "tainted" or "taken in" by whatever is false or misleading in the opposing viewpoint. Furthermore, merely believing we can survive serious consideration of an "alien" point of view is not enough to motivate most of us to consider them seriously. We must also be motivated by an intellectual sense of justice. We must recognize an intellectual responsibility to be fair to views we oppose. We must feel obliged to hear them in their strongest form to ensure that we are not condemning them out of ignorance or bias on our part. At this point, we come full circle back to where we began: the need for intellectual humility.

To begin at another point, consider intellectual good faith or integrity. Intellectual integrity is clearly a difficult trait to develop. We are often motivated, generally without admitting to or being aware of this motivation, to set up inconsistent intellectual standards. Our egocentric or sociocentric tendencies make us ready to believe positive information about those we like, and negative information about those we dislike. We are likewise strongly inclined to believe what serves to justify our vested interest or validate our strongest desires. Hence, all humans have some innate mental tendencies to operate with double standards, which of course is paradigmatic of intellectual bad faith. Such modes of thinking often correlate quite well with getting ahead in the world, maximizing our power or advantage, and getting more of what we want.

Nevertheless, it is difficult to operate explicitly or overtly with a double standard. We therefore need to avoid looking at the evidence too closely. We need to avoid scrutinizing our own inferences and interpretations too carefully. At this point, a certain amount of intellectual arrogance is quite useful. I may assume, for example, that I know just what you're going to say (before you say it), precisely what you are really after (before the evidence demonstrates it), and what actually is going on (before I have studied the situation carefully). My intellectual arrogance may make it easier for me to avoid noticing the unjustifiable discrepancy between the standards I apply to you and the standards I apply to myself. Of course, if I don't have to empathize with you, that too makes it easier to avoid seeing my duplicity. I am also better positioned if I lack a keen need to be fair to your point of view. A little background fear of what I might discover if I seriously considered the consistency of my own judgments can be quite useful as well. In this case, my lack of intellectual integrity is supported by my lack of intellectual humility, empathy, and fairmindedness.

Going in the other direction, it will be difficult to use a double standard if I feel a responsibility to be fair to your point of view, see that this responsibility requires me to view things from your perspective empathically, and do so with some humility, recognizing I could be wrong, and you

67

right. The more I dislike you personally, or feel wronged in the past by you or by others who share your way of thinking, the more pronounced in my character the trait of intellectual integrity and good faith must be to compel me to be fair.

Distinguishing Macro-Abilities From Micro-Skills

Our reason for dividing cognitive strategies into macro-abilities and micro-skills is not to create a hard and fast line between the most elementary skills of critical thinking (the micro-skills) and the process of orchestrating those elementary skills, but rather to provide teachers with a way of thinking about two levels of learning. We use these two levels in most complex abilities. For intuitive examples, consider what is involved in learning to play the piano, learning to play good tennis, mastering ballet, or becoming a surgeon. In each of these areas, there is a level of skill learning which focuses on the most elementary of moves: for example, learning to practice the most elementary ballet positions at the bar, learning to play scales on the piano, or learning to hit various tennis strokes on the backboard. One must often return to this micro-level to ensure that one keeps the fundamentals well in hand. Nevertheless, dancing ballet is not practicing at the bar. Playing the piano is not simply playing scales. And hitting tennis balls against a backboard is not playing tennis. One must move to the macro level for the real thing. So, too, in critical thinking, students have to learn the fundamentals: what an assumption is, what an implication is, what an inference and conclusion are, what it is to isolate an issue, what it is to offer reasons or evidence in support of what one says, how to identify a contradiction or a vague sentence.

But thinking critically in any actual situation is typically doing something more complex and holistic than this. Rarely in thinking critically do we do just one elementary thing. Usually we have to integrate or make use of a variety of elementary critical thinking skills. For example, when we are reading (a macro-ability) we have to make use of a variety of critical thinking micro-skills, and we have to use them in concert with each other. We might begin by reflecting on the implications of a story or book title. We might then begin to read the preface or introduction and start to identify some of the basic issues or objectives the book or story is focused on. As we proceed, we might begin to identify particular sentences that seem vague to us. We might consider various interpretations of them. As we move along, we would doubtless dip into our own experience for possible examples of what the author is saying. Or we might begin to notice assumptions the author is making. We would be making all of these individual moves as part of one integrated activity: the attempt to make sense of, to follow, what we are reading. As always, the whole is greater than and more important than the parts. We do not read to practice our critical thinking micro-skills; we use our critical thinking micro-skills in order to read, or better, in order to read clearly, precisely, and accurately.

Standard instruction and many approaches to teaching critical thinking or thinking skills often fail here. They over-emphasize drill in micro-skills and neglect their *use*. Being able to find assumptions only when someone tells you to is of little value. Articulating and evaluating assumptions helps one only if one does it when appropriate. This requires thinkers to notice for themselves when a questionable assumption is made. Macro abilities cannot be taught through drill. They must be developed and practiced *in the context* of some reasoning. Keep this principle of interdependence in mind as you read through the various strategies.

Have We Left Out Any Important Strategies?

As you begin to use the principles of critical thinking we have formulated in your teaching, you may wonder whether our list is complete. You may wonder, in other words, whether we may have left out any important critical thinking principles. The answer to this is "Yes and no." "No" in the sense that all of the important critical thinking principles are at least implicit in the ones we have formulated. "Yes" in the sense that some of what is merely implicit might properly be made explicit.

To exemplify this point, consider these insightful suggestions which we recently received from Rex Dalzell from New Zealand.

> With respect to your list of strategies, I would like to suggest, with due intellectual humility, that the list could be usefully expanded by the addition of a further four strategies as follows:

Affective Strategies
Developing Intellectual Curiosity

In the affective area, I believe the development of an attitude of intellectual curiosity is of prime importance. Although there are elements of this dimension in other characteristics (e.g., independence of thought, intellectual perseverance, etc.), and while the whole notion of critical thinking implies the presence of this attribute, it seems to me sufficiently important to warrant an explicit category of its own.

Critical thinkers need to be curious about their environment, they need to seek explanations of apparent discrepancies and they need to speculate as to possible causes of these discrepancies. In short, they need to be predisposed to wonder about the world around them. This sense of wonder, this intellectual curiosity that seeks explanations and proffers solutions, is something that can be and needs to be encouraged and developed. For this reason I believe it would be helpful to include it as a separate stand-alone category in any over-all schema.

Developing Social Sensitivity

In addition to developing insight into egocentricity and sociocentricity so that desirable levels of self-awareness are achieved it is also necessary, I believe, for critical thinkers to develop a high level of social sensitivity. By this I mean that critical thinkers need to become sensitive to the social situation they find themselves in so that they can judge effectively when it is and when it is not appropriate to exercise, at least overtly, their critical thinking skills. It is my experience that with some critical thinkers, particularly the "born again, evangelical" variety, they are quite insensitive to the social milieu in which they find themselves. Without due regard for the sensitivity of the situation, they launch forth with their battery of critical thinking skills and often destroy any possibility of a productive outcome.

In addition to being able to recognize the limits of their knowledge and being able to suspend judgment, critical thinkers also need to know when to put their skills into operation and when and how to articulate the results. Listing social sensitivity as a separate category would, I believe, be useful in helping critical thinkers develop this skill.

Cognitive Strategies: Macro-Abilities
Observing Critically

In addition to reading critically and listening critically, I believe it is very important for critical thinkers to learn how to observe critically. Intellectual curiosity is a necessary but not sufficient condition for critical observation to occur. Critical thinkers need to "see" as well as "look at" what is in their environment. They need to be trained to see the details of their surroundings, physical as well as social, and to accurately recall just exactly what they have seen. Most, if not all, of the micro-cognitive skills depend on this critical observation as a basis for productive application. As with intellectual curiosity and social sensitivity it seems to me that critical observation is a skill that merits recognition in its own right.

Expressing Precisely

While precision is an integral feature of all critical thinking and is highlighted by such macro skills as clarifying issues, conclusions, or beliefs, clarifying and analyzing the meanings of words and phrases, the overall emphasis is on precision of analysis rather than on precision of expression. While precision of expression is implied in many of the listed skills — how else for example, could one engage successfully in Socratic discussion or reasoned dialogue or dialectic without such precision? — it seems to me that it would be helpful to list it as a separate skill. If critical thinkers are not able to express themselves with precision then their overall effectiveness is greatly reduced.

69

You may decide to add these four principles to your personal list, even though we received them too late to incorporate them formally in this volume. In any case, it would be quite instructive to try to fill out these descriptions and write an "application section" for each of them. Keep this awareness alive as you begin to work out your own unique application of critical thinking principles.

Important Note About Applications

The purpose of the following strategy list is to further clarify the basic principles of critical thinking, but not necessarily to provide applications of each strategy for each grade level. Teachers should experiment with the applications that seem appropriate and plausible for their students. Once you understand a range of applications (some at your grade level, some not), you will be able to begin to think up applications of your own. So do not assume that every application we provide is appropriate for your class. Experiment with an assortment of strategies and you will end up with a wide variety that works for your students. You can find many grade level examples of the applications in the remodeled lesson plan section of the book.

S-1 Thinking Independently

Principle: Critical thinking is independent thinking, thinking for oneself. Many of our beliefs are acquired at an early age, when we have a strong tendency to form beliefs for irrational reasons (because we want to believe, because we are praised or rewarded for believing). Critical thinkers use critical skills and insights to reveal and reject beliefs that are irrational. In forming new beliefs, critical thinkers do not passively accept the beliefs of others; rather, they try to figure things out for themselves, reject unjustified authorities, and recognize the contributions of genuine authorities. They thoughtfully form principles of thought and action; they do not mindlessly accept those presented to them. Nor are they unduly influenced by the language of another. If they find that a set of categories or distinctions is more appropriate than that used by another, they will use it. Recognizing that categories serve human purposes, they use those categories which best serve their purpose at the time. They are not limited by accepted ways of doing things. They evaluate both goals and how to achieve them. They do not accept as true, or reject as false, beliefs they do not understand. They are not easily manipulated.

Independent thinkers strive to incorporate all known relevant knowledge and insight into their thought and behavior. They strive to determine for themselves when information is relevant, when to apply a concept, or when to make use of a skill. They are self-monitoring: they catch their own mistakes; they don't need to be told what to do every step of the way.

Application: A critical education respects the autonomy of the student. It appeals to rationality. Children should be encouraged to discover information and use their knowledge, skills, and insights to think for themselves. Merely giving children "facts" or telling them "the right way" to solve a problem interferes with their questioning and replacing pre-existing beliefs with new knowledge.

Rather than asking children to place objects or pictures into pre-existing categories, the teacher can allow children to form their own categories. They can then discuss the reasons they had for forming each category. When different children have used different sets of categories to form groups, the teacher can ask such questions as these: *"When would it be best to group things this way? When would that way be best? Why would someone else make different groupings?"*

"Types of Literature" lessons could be remodelled so that children group and discuss writings they have read, entertaining different ways to classify them: *"Is this story like any other stories you've heard or read? Which? Why is it like this one?"* Children could collect and sort pictures of animals. The teacher can point out how their categories are like and unlike scientific categories. Older children could list and classify animals before reading zoological classification systems in their texts.

Text questions often presuppose what should be questioned: *"Why is this a good story title? Why did this story character do the wrong thing?"* Such questions can be remodelled: *"Is this a good title? Should this character have done that?"* The children can then be asked to support their answers with reasons which could then be probed and evaluated.

Rather than having children discuss only those ideas mentioned in their texts, the teacher can first have them brainstorm ideas and argue among themselves, for instance, about problems and solutions. Then when they read the text, they can compare it with their own ideas.

Before reading a section of text that refers to a map, chart, picture, or graph, students could first examine and discuss it: *"What does this show us? How can you tell?"*

In math, instead of following directions in their texts, children can be given a task to perform or problem to solve in small groups. *"How many paper clips would it take to go from here to the principal's office?"* The class can then discuss their solutions (and perhaps compare them to what is in their text). Younger children could figure out simple math problem through play-acting. *"Let's try to figure out the answer to 3 – 1. Let's have three of you stand here. Now, one of you walks away — that's 'minus one'. So what's left?"*

When a text tries to do too much of the children's thinking for them, the material can be examined in depth. *"Why does the text tell you about this? Why do the authors think this (concept, skill, procedure, step) is worth knowing? Why does the text tell you to do this step? What would happen if you didn't? If you did it differently?"*

Similar questions can be asked of pre-readers when they have been given directions for an activity or project: *"Why have I asked you to do this? Why did I suggest you do this first? What would happen if we didn't do it this way? Is there another good way we could do this?"*

Writing assignments should provide many opportunities for the student to begin to exercise independent judgment — by gathering and assembling information, by thinking about it, or by coming up with conclusions. The students can also discuss how to express and organize their thoughts in sentences and paragraphs.

In science, children could put their own headings on charts or graphs they make, or decide what kind of graph would be most helpful. They can design their own experiments rather than follow directions in their texts. *"How could we find out? What could we do? What would that tell us?"* Rather than reading their texts' account of what an experiment or study proved, the students can be asked what *they* think it means.

Children could review material themselves, rather than relying on their texts for summaries and review questions. The teacher could routinely ask students, *"What are the most important points covered in the passage (chapter, story, etc.)?"* as a discussion beginner. The class could brainstorm about what they learned when studying a lesson, unit, or story. Only after they have exhausted their memories should the teacher try to elicit any crucial points they neglected.

Lesson plans in which the strategy is used

S-2 Developing Insight Into Egocentricity or Sociocentricity

Principle: Egocentricity means confusing what we see and think with reality. When under the influence of egocentricity, we think that the way we see things is exactly the way things are. Egocentricity manifests itself as an inability or unwillingness to consider others' points of view, a refusal to accept ideas or facts which would prevent us from getting what we want (or think we want). In its extreme forms, it is characterized by a need to be right about everything, a lack of interest in consistency and clarity, an all or nothing attitude ("I am 100% right; you are 100% wrong."), and a lack of self-consciousness of one's own thought processes. The egocentric individual is more concerned with the *appearance* of truth, fairness, and fairmindedness, than with actually *being* correct, fair, or fairminded. Egocentricity is the opposite of critical thought. It is common in adults as well as in children.

As people are socialized, egocentricity partly evolves into sociocentricity. Egocentric tendencies extend to their groups. The individual goes from *"I am right!"* to *"We are right!"* To put this another way, people find that they can often best satisfy their egocentric desires through a group. "Group think" results when people egocentrically attach themselves to a group. One can see this in both children and adults: My daddy is better than your daddy! My school (religion, country, race, etc.) is better than yours. Uncritical thinkers often confuse loyalty with always supporting and agreeing, even when the other person or the group is wrong.

If egocentricity and sociocentricity are the disease, self-awareness is the cure. We need to become aware of our own tendency to confuse our view with "The Truth". People can often recognize when someone else is egocentric. Most of us can identify the sociocentricity of members of opposing groups. Yet when we ourselves are thinking egocentrically or sociocentrically, it seems right to us (at least at the time). Our belief in our own rightness is easier to maintain because we ignore the faults in our thinking. We automatically hide our egocentricity from ourselves. We fail to notice when our behavior contradicts our self-image. We base our reasoning on false assumptions we are unaware of making. We fail to make relevant distinctions (of which we are otherwise aware and able to make) when making them prevents us from getting what we want. We deny or conveniently "forget" facts that do not support our conclusions. We often misunderstand or distort what others say.

The solution, then, is to reflect on our reasoning and behavior; to make our beliefs explicit, critique them, and, when they are false, stop making them; to apply the same concepts in the same ways to ourselves and others; to consider every relevant fact, and to make our conclusions consistent with the evidence; and to listen carefully and openmindedly to others. We can change egocentric tendencies when we see them for what they are: irrational and unjust. The development of children's awareness of their egocentric and sociocentric patterns of thought is a crucial part of education in critical thinking. This development will be modest at first but can grow considerably over time.

Application: Although everyone has egocentric, sociocentric, and critical (or fairminded) tendencies to some extent, the purpose of education in critical thinking is to help students move away from egocentricity and sociocentricity, toward increasingly critical thought. Texts usually neglect obstacles to rationality, content to point out or have children point out irrationality and injustice. We recommend that children repeatedly discuss *why* people think irrationally and act unfairly. *"Why did he do that? What was he thinking? Why?"*

The teacher can facilitate discussions of egocentric or sociocentric thought and behavior whenever such discussions seem relevant. Such discussions can be used as a basis for having the children think about their own egocentric or sociocentric tendencies. The class can discuss situations in which people are most likely to be egocentric and how egocentricity interferes with our ability to think and listen. By discussing what people think (and how they think) when they are being egocentric and sociocentric, children can begin to recognize common patterns of egocentric thought. The class can discuss some of the common false assumptions we all make at times [e.g., "Anyone who disapproves of anything I do is wrong or unfair. I have a right to have everything I want. Truth is what I want it to be. Anyone who is different is bad. Our group (country, school, language, etc.) is better than any other."] Teachers can also have children point out the contradictions of egocentric attitudes: ["When I use something of yours without asking first, it is 'borrowing'; when you use something of mine, it is 'stealing'. Taking something without asking is O.K. (when I do it). Taking something without asking is wrong (when you do it)."] Sometimes story characters illustrate egocentricity.

The most real and immediate form of sociocentricity children experience is in the mini-society of their peers. Student attitudes present a small-scale version of the patterns which exist on a larger scale in societies. All of your students share some attitudes which are sociocentric. Furthermore, children divide themselves into "sub-cultures", each of which is narrower than the school-wide "culture". Honest and realistic exploration of these phenomena allows children to clarify and evaluate the ways in which "group think" limits them. *"What happens when I go along with my friends, even when I really don't want to? Should I always think the same as my friends?"*

Often texts try to discourage sociocentricity by encouraging tolerance — asking children to agree that people whose ways are different are not necessarily wrong. Yet, by keeping discussion general and not introducing specific advantages of different ways, children are left with a vague sense that they should be tolerant, rather than a clear sense that others have ways worth knowing about and learning from.

The standard approach to combatting sociocentricity and stereotyping usually fails to address children's real beliefs. As a result, "school knowledge" simply becomes a veneer over students real beliefs. Before beginning study of other peoples, the teacher could elicit children's ideas of that group, including stereotypes and misconceptions: *"What are these people like? (What is this animal like?) What do you think of when you think of them? How do they act in movies and on T.V.?"* After study, the children could evaluate these ideas in light of what they have learned. They could also discuss why they had them: *"Remember what you said about these people before we studied them? Which of our original beliefs were false or misleading? Why did we think that? Where did we get those ideas?"*

Lesson plans in which the strategy is used

S-3 Exercising Fairmindedness

Principle: To think critically, we must be able to consider the strengths and weaknesses of opposing points of view; to imaginatively put ourselves in the place of others in order to genuinely understand them; to overcome our egocentric tendency to identify truth with our immediate perceptions or long-standing thought or belief. This trait is linked to the ability to accurately reconstruct the viewpoints and reasoning of others and to reason from premises, assumptions, and ideas other than our own. This trait also requires the willingness to remember occasions when we were wrong in the past despite an intense conviction that we were right, as well as the ability to imagine our being similarly deceived in a case at hand. Critical thinkers realize the unfairness of judging unfamiliar ideas until they fully understand them.

The world consists of many societies and peoples with many different points of view and ways of thinking. To develop as reasonable persons, we need to enter into and think within the frameworks and ideas of different peoples and societies. We cannot truly understand the world if we think about it only from one viewpoint, as Americans, as Italians, or as Soviets.

Furthermore, critical thinkers recognize that their behavior affects others, and so consider their behavior from the perspective of those others.

Application: The teacher can encourage children to think fairmindedly when disputes arise or when the class is discussing issues, evaluating the reasoning of story characters, or discussing people from other cultures.

When disputes naturally arise in the course of the day, the teacher can ask the children to state one another's positions. They should be given an opportunity to correct any misunderstanding of their positions. The teacher can then ask them to explain why their classmate might see the issue differently than they do. *"What is Sue angry about? Why does that make her mad? Sue, is that right?"*

Children can be encouraged to consider evidence and reasons for beliefs they disagree with, as well as those with which they agree. For example, have them consider positions from their parents' or siblings' points of view. *"Why doesn't your mother want you to ...? Why does she think it's bad for you (wrong, etc.)? What does she think will happen? Why?"*

Rather than always having children argue their points of view, call on a student who doesn't have a position on the issue under discussion — who is still thinking things through. Help that student clarify the uncertainty. *"What makes sense about what each side said? What seems wrong? What aren't you sure about?"*

Although texts often have students consider a subject or issue from a second point of view, discussion is brief, rather than extended, and no attempt is made to have them integrate insights gained by considering multiple perspectives. If children write a dialogue about an issue from opposing points of view, or contrast a story character's reasoning with an opposing point of view, or role play, they can directly compare and evaluate different perspectives.

Children can be reminded of, and analyze, times that many members of a group or the class contributed something toward finding or figuring out an answer, solving a problem, or understanding a complex situation.

The class can discuss how hard it sometimes can be to be fairminded.

Lesson plans in which the strategy is used

S-4 Exploring Thoughts Underlying Feelings and Feelings Underlying Thoughts

Principle: Although it is common to separate thought and feeling as though they were independent, opposing forces in the human mind, the truth is that virtually all human feelings are based on some level of thought and virtually all thought generative of some level of feeling. To think with self-understanding and insight, we must come to terms with the intimate connections between thought and feeling, reason and emotion. Critical thinkers realize that their feelings are their response (but not the only possible, or even necessarily the most reasonable response) to a situation. They know that their feelings would be different if they had a different understanding or interpretation of the situation. They recognize that thoughts and feelings, far from being different kinds of "things", are two aspects of their responses. Uncritical thinkers see little or no relationship between their feelings and their thoughts, and so escape responsibility for their thoughts, feelings, and actions. Their own feelings often seem unintelligible to them.

When we feel sad or depressed, it is often because we are interpreting our situation in an overly negative or pessimistic light. We may be forgetting to consider positive aspects of our lives. We can better understand our feelings by asking ourselves, "How have I come to feel this way? How am I looking at the situation? To what conclusion have I come? What is my evidence? What assumptions am I making? What inferences am I making? Are they sound inferences? Do my conclusions make sense? Are there other ways to interpret this situation?" We can learn to seek patterns in our assumptions, and so begin to see the unity behind our separate emotions. Understanding ourselves is the first step toward self-control and self-improvement. This self-understanding requires that we understand our feelings and emotions in relation to our thoughts, ideas, and interpretations of the world.

Application: Whenever the class discusses someone's feelings (such as those of a character in a story), the teacher can ask children to consider what the person might be thinking to have that feeling in that situation. *"Why does he feel this way? How is he interpreting or looking at his situation? (How does he see things? What does he think she meant?) What led him to that conclusion? (Why does he think that?) What could he have thought instead? Then how might he have felt?"*

This strategy can be used to help students begin to develop an intellectual sense of justice and courage. Children can discuss the thoughts underlying passionate commitment to personal or social change: *"Why was she willing to do this? Was she scared? What else did she feel that helped her overcome her fears? Why? How did she look at things that helped her endure or stick with it?"*

Children can discuss reasons for greed, fear, apathy, and other negative or hampering feelings: *"Why are people greedy? What thoughts underlie greed? Why do people feel they need more money? What does less money mean to them? Why?"*

When discussing a case of mixed feelings, the teacher could ask, *"What was he feeling? What else? (Encourage multiple responses.) What led to this feeling? That one? Are these beliefs consistent, or contradictory? (Does it make sense to think all these things?) How could someone have opposite feelings about one situation? Is there a way he could reconcile these contradictions or make sense of these opposite feelings?"*

Children can also generalize about thoughts behind various emotions: behind fear, thoughts like — "This is dangerous. I may be hurt;" behind anger, thoughts like — "This is not right, not fair;" behind indifference, thoughts like — "This does not matter, no one can do anything about this;" behind relief, thoughts like — "Things are better now. This won't bother me anymore."

Lesson plans in which the strategy is used

S-5 Developing Intellectual Humility and Suspending Judgment

Principle: Critical thinkers recognize the limits of their knowledge. They are sensitive to circumstances in which their native egocentricity is likely to function self-deceptively; they are sensitive to bias, prejudice, and limitations of their views. Intellectual humility is based on the recognition that one should not claim more than one actually knows. It does not imply spinelessness or submissiveness. It implies the lack of intellectual pretentiousness, arrogance, or conceit. It implies insight into the foundations of one's beliefs: knowing what evidence one has, how one has come to believe, what further evidence one might look for or examine.

Thus, critical thinkers distinguish what they know from what they don't know. They are not afraid of saying "I don't know" when they are not in a position to be sure. They can make this distinction because they habitually ask themselves, "How could one know whether or not this is true?" To say "In this case I must suspend judgment until I find out x and y", does not make them anxious or uncomfortable. They are willing to rethink conclusions in the light of new knowledge. They qualify their claims appropriately.

In exposing children to concepts within a field of knowledge, we can help them see how all concepts depend on other, more basic concepts and how each field is based on fundamental assumptions which need to be examined, understood, and justified. The class should often explore the connections between specific details and basic concepts or principles. We can help children discover experiences in their own lives which help support or justify what a text says. We should always be willing to entertain student doubts about what a text says.

Application: Texts and testing methods inadvertently foster intellectual arrogance. Most text writing says, "Here's the way it is. Here's what we know. Remember this, and you'll know it, too." Behind student learning, there is often little more thought than, "It's true because my textbook said it's true." This often generalizes to, "It's true because I read it somewhere."

Teachers can take advantage of any situation in which the children are not in a position to know, to encourage the habit of exploring the basis for their beliefs. When materials call on the students to say or agree to what they are not in a position to know, we suggest the teacher encourage them to remember what is said in the materials but also to suspend judgment as to its truth. The teacher might first ask for the evidence or reasons for the claim and have the children probe its strength. They can be encouraged to explain what they would need to learn in order to be more certain.

We can model intellectual humility by demonstrating a willingness to admit limits in our own knowledge and in human knowledge generally. Routinely qualify statements: "I believe," "I'm pretty sure that," "I doubt," "I suspect," "Perhaps," "I'm told," "It seems," etc.

Children can discuss such experiences as getting a bad first impression, then learning they were wrong; feeling certain of something, then later changing their minds; thinking they knew something, then realizing they didn't understand it; thinking they had the best or only answer or solution, then hearing a better one. *"Did you feel sure? Why? What made you change your mind? What does this tell us about feeling sure of things?"*

The teacher can have the children brainstorm questions they have *after* study of a topic. Students could keep question logs during the course of thematic units or long projects, periodically recording their unanswered questions. Thus, they can come to see for themselves that even when they have learned what is expected of them, there is always more to learn.

Lesson plans in which the strategy is used

S-6 Developing Intellectual Courage

Principle: To think independently and fairly, one must feel the need to face and fairly deal with unpopular ideas, beliefs, or viewpoints. The courage to do so arises when we see that ideas considered dangerous or absurd are sometimes rationally justified (in whole or in part) and that conclusions or beliefs inculcated in us are sometimes false or misleading. To determine for ourselves which is which, we must not passively and uncritically accept what we have "learned". We need courage to admit the truth in some ideas considered dangerous and absurd, and the distortion or falsity in some ideas strongly held in our social group. It will take courage to be true to our own thinking, for honestly questioning our deeply held beliefs can be difficult and sometimes frightening, and the penalties for non-conformity are often severe.

Application: Intellectual courage is fostered through a consistently openminded atmosphere. Children should be encouraged to honestly consider or doubt any belief. Children who disagree with or doubt their peers, teacher, or text should be allowed to explain their reasons. Teachers should raise probing questions regarding unpopular ideas which their students have hitherto been discouraged from considering. The teacher should model intellectual courage by playing devil's advocate.

To help students begin to discover the importance of intellectual courage, the class could discuss such questions as these: *"Why is it hard to go against the crowd? If everyone around you is sure of something, why is it hard to question it or disagree? When is it good to do so? When might you hesitate? When should you hesitate? Is it hard to question your own beliefs? Why?"*

Children who have been habitually praised for uncritically accepting others' claims may feel the rug pulled out from under them for a while when expected to think for themselves. They should be emotionally supported in these circumstances and encouraged to express the natural hesitancy, discomfort, or anxiety they may experience so they may work their way through these feelings. A willingness to consider unpopular beliefs develops by degrees. Teachers should exercise discretion, beginning first with mildly unpopular rather than with extremely unpopular beliefs.

If, during the course of the year, an idea or suggestion which at first sounded "crazy" was proven valuable, the children can later be reminded of it, discuss it at length, and compare it to other events. *"How did this idea seem at first? Why? What made you change your mind about it? Have you had other similar experiences? Why did those ideas seem crazy or stupid at first?"*

Lesson plans in which the strategy is used

S-7 Developing Intellectual Good Faith or Integrity

Principle: Critical thinkers recognize the need to be true to their own thought, to be consistent in the intellectual standards they apply, to hold themselves to the same rigorous standards of evidence and proof to which they hold others, to practice what they advocate for others, and to honestly admit discrepancies and inconsistencies in their own thought and action. They believe most strongly what has been justified by their own thought and analyzed experience. They have a commitment to bringing the self they are and the self they want to be together.

People in general are often inconsistent in their application of standards once their ego is involved positively or negatively. For instance, when people like us, we tend to over-estimate their positive characteristics; when they dislike us, we tend to underrate them.

Application: Texts often inadvertently encourage the mental split between "school belief" and "real life belief" and between verbal or public belief and belief that guides action. There is an old saying to the effect that, "They are good prophets who follow their own teachings." And sometimes parents say, "Do as I say, not as I do." There is often a lack of integrity in human life. Hypocrisy and inconsistency are common. As educators, we need to highlight the difficulties of being consistent in an often inconsistent world.

As teachers, we need to be sensitive to our own inconsistencies in the application of rules and standards, and we need to help children to explore their own. Peer groups often pressure children to judge in-group members less critically than out-group members. Children need opportunities to honestly assess their own participation in such phenomena.

Texts often preach. They unrealistically present moral perfection as easy when it is often not. They ask general and loaded questions ("Do you listen to other views? Is it important to treat others fairly?") to which children are likely to simply respond with a "Yes!" Such questions should be remodelled and the "dark side" explored. For example, ask, *"When have you found it hard to listen to others?"* or *"Why are people often unfair?"*

Language Arts texts sometimes have children roundly criticize characters without taking into account the difficulties of living up to worthy ideals. Children should be encouraged to give more realistic assessments. *"Would you have done otherwise? Would it have been easy? Why or why not? Why do so few people do this?"*

When evaluating or developing criteria for evaluation, have children assess both themselves and others, noting their tendency to favor themselves.

Lesson plans in which the strategy is used

S-8 Developing Intellectual Perseverance

Principle: Becoming a more critical thinker is not easy. It takes time and effort. Critical thinking is reflective and recursive; that is, we often think back to previous problems to re-consider or re-analyze them. Critical thinkers are willing to pursue intellectual insights and truths in spite of difficulties, obstacles, and frustrations. They recognize the need to struggle with confusion and unsettled questions over time in order to achieve deeper understanding and insight. They recognize that significant change requires patience and hard work. Important issues often require extended thought, research, struggle. Considering a new view takes time. Yet people are often impatient to "get on with it" when they most need to slow down and think carefully. People rarely define issues or problems clearly; concepts are often left vague; related issues are not sorted out, etc. When people don't understand a problem or situation, their reactions and solutions often compound the original problem. Children need to gain insight into the need for intellectual perseverance.

Application:	Intellectual perseverance can be developed by reviewing and discussing the kinds of difficulties that were inherent in previous problems worked on, exploring why it is necessary to struggle with them over an extended period.

Studying the work of great inventors or thinkers through biography can also be of use, with children discussing why long-range commitment was necessary. In time, children will see the value in pursuing important ideas at length.

Texts discourage this trait by doing too much for children: breaking processes into algorithmic fragments and drilling the fragments. Texts try to remove all struggle from learning. Children should begin to see mental struggle as crucial to learning by discovering its reward in genuine understanding. Texts often present knowledge and knowledge acquisition (for example, scientific conclusions) as simple ("this experiment proved"), rather than the result of much thought, work, dead ends, etc.

Children should have some experiences slowly reading material they find difficult. Help them begin to see that if they are careful and stick to it, examining it one word, phrase, and sentence at a time, they can master it. Such in-depth reading can be done as a class or in small groups, sentence by sentence, with children interpreting and explaining as they go.

Children with hobbies, skills, or interests could discuss how they learned about them, their mistakes, failures, and frustrations along the way, and the tenacity their mastery required.

Raise difficult problems again and again over the course of the year. Design long-term projects that begin to develop perseverance. Of course, it is important to work with children on skills of breaking down complex problems into simpler components, so that they will see how to attack problems systematically.

Children can discuss experiences they have had wherein they came to understand something that at first baffled them or seemed hopelessly confusing and frustrating. *"What was it like to not understand or be able to do it? How did you come to understand it? What was that like? Did it seem worth it at the time? Was it worth it?"*

Texts will sometimes say of a problem that it is hard to solve, and leave it at that. This encourages an "Oh, that's very complicated. I'll never get it." attitude that prevents development of the critical spirit. Life's problems are not divided into the simple and the hopeless. To help children develop the sense that they can begin to attack even complex problems, you could divide the class into groups and have them discuss various ways in which the problem could be approached and see if they can break the problem down into simpler components. Children will not develop intellectual perseverance unless they develop confidence in their ability to analyze and approach problems with success. You should not overwhelm children with the task of *solving* problems so difficult that they have little hope of making progress, nevertheless, they can be expected to make some progress toward understanding and sorting things out.

Take a basic idea within a subject ("good story," "fairness," "communities," "living things," etc.). Have the children write their ideas on it and discuss them. Every month or so, have them add to, revise, or write more. (Or have discussions and record the key points.) At the end of the year, they can assess the changes in their understanding from repeated consideration over the course of the year, graphically illustrating their own progress through perseverance.

Illustrate how getting answers is not the only form of progress; show children how having better, clearer questions is also progress. Point out progress made. Sympathize with children's natural frustration and discouragement.

Have the children discuss the importance of giving sufficient thought to important decisions and beliefs, and the difficulty of becoming rational, well-educated, fairminded people.

When study and research fail to settle key questions, due to the inadequacy of available resources, the class could write letters to appropriate faculty of one or two colleges. Have children describe their work and results and pose their unanswered questions. The teacher may have to explain the replies. Children can then reopen the issues for further, better-informed discussion.

Lesson plans in which the strategy is used

S-9 Developing Confidence in Reason

Principle: The rational person recognizes the power of reason and the value of disciplining thinking in accordance with rational standards. Virtually all of the progress that has been made in science and human knowledge testifies to this power, and so to the reasonability of having *confidence* in reason. To develop this faith in reason is to come to see that ultimately one's own higher interests and those of humankind at large will best be served by giving the freest play to reason, by encouraging people to come to their own conclusions through a process of developing their own rational faculties. It is to reject force and trickery as standard ways of changing another's mind. It is to believe that, with proper encouragement and cultivation, people can develop the ability to think for themselves, to form reasonable points of view, draw reasonable conclusions, think clearly and logically, persuade each other by reason and, ultimately, become reasonable persons, despite the deep-seated obstacles in the native character of the human mind and in society as we know it. This confidence is essential to building a democracy in which people come to genuine rule, rather than being manipulated by the mass media, special interests, or by the inner prejudices, fears, and irrationalities that so easily and commonly dominate human minds.

You should note that the act of faith we are recommending is not blind faith, but should be tested in everyday experiences and academic work. In other words, we should have confidence in reason because reason works. Confidence in reason does not deny the reality of intuition; rather, it provides a way of distinguishing intuition from prejudice. When we know the source of our thinking and keep our minds open to new reason and evidence, we will be more likely to correct our prejudiced thought.

At the heart of this principle of faith in reason is the desire to make sense of the world and the expectation that sense can be made. Texts often don't make sense to children, sometimes because what they say doesn't make sense, more often because children aren't given time to make sense out of what they are told. Being continually called upon to "master" what seems nonsensical undermines the feeling that one can make sense of the world. Many children, rushed through mountains of material, give up on this early. ("If I try to make sense of this, I'll never finish. Trying to really understand just slows me down. Nobody expects me to make sense of this; they just want me to do it.")

Application: As a teacher, you can model confidence in reason in many ways. Every time you show your children that you can make rules, assignments, and classroom activities *intelligible* to them so that they can see that you are doing things for well-thought-out reasons, you help them understand why confidence in reason is justified. Every time you help them solve a problem with the use of their own thinking, or "think aloud" through a difficult problem in front of them, you help them develop confidence in reason. Every time you encourage them to *question* the reasons behind rules, activities, and procedures, you help them recognize that we should expect *reasonability* to be at the foundation of our lives. Every time you display a patient willingness to hear their reasons for their beliefs and actions you encourage confidence in reason. Every time you clarify a standard of good reasoning, helping them to grasp *why* this standard makes sense, you help them develop confidence in reason.

One reason children have little faith in reason is that they don't see reason being used in their everyday lives. Power, authority, prestige, strength, intimidation, and pressure are often used instead of reason. Many children develop a natural cynicism about reason which educators should help them overcome.

Critical education develops insight into the functions that various mechanical skills (such as use of grammar, sorting, counting, measuring, graphing) serve. Children need to learn, as early as possible, the relationship of human purposes to the function of such skills, and how they can be modified as human purposes change. Children will be more adept at using techniques and skills when they see them as *tools* whose appropriate use depends on human purposes. They will learn to see for themselves when to apply them, and when not.

Rather than asking children to perform mechanical skills merely for their own sake, the teacher can first give a reason for using the skill. State the function of the skill, for example, *"We will count the chairs in this room, to see if there are enough."* Next, the teacher can encourage children to consider whether the method being used is the only, or the best way to solve the problem: *"Can anyone think of another way to solve this problem? Which way do you think is best? Why?"* Teachers can also point out any arbitrary aspects of mechanical skills, such as using a particular length as a standard of measurement.

Texts often make knowledge acquisition seem mysterious, as though scholars have some sort of mystical mental powers. Making the reasoning behind what they study clear will help children begin to feel that knowledge and reason are within their grasp.

Give children multiple opportunities to try to persuade each other and you. Insist that children who disagree *reason* with each other, rather than using ridicule, intimidation, peer pressure, etc.

If you begin study of a new topic by discussing what they know about it, children can begin to realize that their initial knowledge is worthwhile. By allowing children to tackle problems and tasks on their own before explaining what to do, you help them experience the power of their own minds. By then showing them a better way that scholars have developed, children can see its superior power for themselves. Thus, as they learn, they can feel their minds grow.

Children could discuss examples from their own experience of persuasion through reason, and other techniques for changing someone's mind such as yelling, whining, forcing, tricking, or wearing someone down through repetition.

Lesson plans in which the strategy is used

S-10 Refining Generalizations and Avoiding Oversimplifications

Principle: It is natural to seek to simplify problems and experiences to make them easier to deal with. Everyone does this. However, the uncritical thinker often oversimplifies and as a result misrepresents problems and experiences. What should be recognized as complex, intricate, ambiguous, or subtle is viewed as simple, elementary, clear, and obvious. For example, it is typically an oversimplification to view people or groups as *all good* or *all bad*, actions as *always right* or *always wrong*, one contributing factor as *the cause*, etc., and yet such beliefs are common. Critical thinkers try to find simplifying patterns and solutions, but not by misrepresentation or distortion. Seeing the difference between useful simplifications and misleading oversimplifications is important to critical thinking.

Critical thinkers scrutinize generalizations, probe for possible exceptions, and then use appropriate qualifications. Critical thinkers are not only clear, but also *exact and precise*.

One of the strongest tendencies of the egocentric, uncritical mind is to see things in terms of black and white, "all right" and "all wrong". Hence, beliefs which should be held with varying degrees of certainty are held as certain. Critical thinkers are sensitive to this problem. They understand the important relationship of evidence to belief and so qualify their statements accordingly. The tentativeness of many of their beliefs is characterized by the appropriate use of such qualifiers as 'highly likely', 'probably', 'not very likely', 'highly unlikely', 'often', 'usually', 'seldom', 'I doubt', 'I suspect', 'most', 'many', and 'some'.

Application: Whenever children or texts oversimplify, the teacher can ask questions which raise the problem of complexity. For instance, if a child or text over-generalizes, the teacher can ask for or provide counter-examples. If a text overlooks factors by stating one cause for a problem, situation, or event, the teacher can raise questions about other possible contributing factors. (*"Was it all M's fault? Did N help create this problem? How? Why?"*) If different things are lumped together, the teacher can call attention to differences. (*"Is this situation 'just like' that one? What are some differences?"*) If only one point of view is expressed, though others are relevant, the teacher can play devil's advocate, bringing in other points of view.

Texts grossly oversimplify the concept of "characterization" by having children infer character traits from one action or speech (and thus leave children with a collection of un-integrated, fragmented, contradictory snap judgments, rather than a developed, consistent, complete understanding of characters). Children should analyze the whole character by considering the variety of attitudes, actions, and statements.

Texts often state such vague generalities as "People must work together to solve this problem." Such a statement glosses over complications which could be clarified in a discussion. *"Why don't people work together on this? How should they? Why? Why wouldn't this obvious solution work? So, what else must be done? How could these needs and interests be reconciled or addressed?"* The teacher may use analogies with children's' experiences to show the need for more careful explanations of a problem.

A common form of oversimplification in texts occurs when they describe *"the"* reason for or cause of a situation. Children have had a sufficient number of experiences with conflict to be able to see how sometimes both sides are partly to blame. By discussing these experiences, and drawing analogies, children can learn to avoid simple, pat, self-serving interpretations of events.

When discussing generalizations, the teacher could ask children for counter-examples. The class can then suggest and evaluate more accurate formulations of the claim. *"Is this always the case? Can you think of a time when an x wasn't a y? Given that example, how could we make the claim more accurate? (Sometimes .... When this is the case, that happens .... It seems that.... When this and that are both true, then ....)"*

The teacher can encourage children to qualify their statements when they have insufficient evidence to be certain. By asking for the evidence on which student claims are based and encouraging children to recognize the possibility that alternative claims may be true, the teacher can help children develop the habit of saying, "I'm not sure." and of using appropriate probability qualifiers.

Analogies and models (for example, in science) simplify the phenomena they represent. The class can examine ways such analogies and models break down. *"In what ways is this unlike that? How does this model break down? Why? What accounts for the differences? What does that tell us about our subject? Could the model be improved? How? Why is that better?"*

Lesson plans in which the strategy is used

S-11 Comparing Analogous Situations: Transferring Insights to New Contexts

Principle: An idea's power is limited by our ability to use it. Critical thinkers' ability to use ideas mindfully enhances their ability to transfer ideas critically. They practice using ideas and insights by appropriately applying them to new situations. This allows them to organize materials and experiences in different ways, to compare and contrast alternative labels, to integrate their understanding of different situations, and to find useful ways to think about new situations. Every time we use an insight or principle, we increase our understanding of both the insight and the situation to which we have applied it. True education provides for more than one way to organize material. For example, history can be organized in our minds by geography, chronology, or by such phenomena as repeated patterns, common situations, analogous "stories", and so on. The truly educated person is not trapped by one organizing principle, but can take knowledge apart and put it together many different ways. Each way of organizing knowledge has some benefit.

Application: Critical teaching, focusing more on basic concepts than on artificial organization of material, encourages children to apply what they have just learned to different but analogous contexts. Using similar information from different situations makes explanations clearer, less vague. Children could compare problems or conflicts from different stories: *"Do you remember the story we read called, '(_____)' What did we say about it? Is it like this story? Can we apply what we discovered to this situation? What does it tell us? What does this situation tell us about the other story?"*

When children master a new skill, or discover an insight, they can be encouraged to use it to analyze other situations. Combine the strategy with independent thought by asking children to name, recall, or find analogous situations.

When children have learned a scientific law, concept, or principle, they can enrich their grasp of it by applying it to situations not mentioned in the text. *"Is air like a liquid in this way?"* By exploring student understanding in this way, teachers can also discover children's misunderstandings of what they just learned.

After an idea has been covered, it can be brought up again, whenever useful.

Lesson plans in which the strategy is used

S-12 Developing One's Perspective: Creating or Exploring Beliefs, Arguments, or Theories

Principle: The world is not given to us sliced up into categories with pre-assigned labels on them. There are always many ways to "divide up" and so experience the world. How we do so is essential to our thinking and behavior. Uncritical thinkers assume that their perspective on things is the only correct one. Selfish critical thinkers manipulate the perspectives of others to gain advantage for themselves. Fairminded critical thinkers learn to recognize that their own ways of thinking and that of all other perspectives are some combination of insight and error. They learn to develop their points of view through a critical analysis of their experience. They learn to question commonly accepted ways of understanding things and avoid uncritically accepting the viewpoints of their peers or society. They know what their perspectives are and can talk insightfully about them. To do this, they must create and explore their own beliefs, their own reasoning, and their own theories.

Application: Perspective is developed through extended thought, discussion, and writing. Children who are unsure what to think can be given time to reflect and come to tentative conclusions. Children who have definite conclusions about the subject at hand can consider ideas from other perspectives, answer questions about what they think, or reflect on new situations or problems. Children can compare what they say they believe with how they act.

Texts rarely call upon children to thoughtfully react to what they read. Teachers can raise basic and important questions about what children learn, having them begin to discover and discuss underlying principles in their thought.

One-to-one Socratic questioning may facilitate development of perspective, especially for children who think they've exhausted their ideas. This strategy will also often coincide with evaluating actions and policies, arguments, or assumptions.

In general, we should look for opportunities to ask children what *they* believe, how *they* see things, what reasons seem most persuasive to *them*, what theory *they* think best explains what we are trying to explain, and so forth.

Explore big questions, helping children integrate details from different lessons and try to come to grips with the world. *"What things are most important in life? What's the difference between important and trivial? What are people like? What kinds of people are there? What's the difference between right and wrong? What is friendship?"* During such discussions, raise points made during study, and help children relate their general ideas to specifics they have studied.

Lesson plans in which the strategy is used

S-13 Clarifying Issues, Conclusions, or Beliefs

Principle: The more completely, clearly, and accurately an issue or statement is formulated, the easier and more helpful the discussion of its settlement or verification. Given a clear statement of an issue, and prior to evaluating conclusions or solutions, it is important to recognize what is required to settle it. And before we can agree or disagree with a claim, we must understand it clearly. It makes no sense to say "I don't know what you mean, but I deny it, whatever it is." Critical thinkers recognize problematic claims, concepts, and standards of evaluation, making sure that understanding precedes judgment. They routinely distinguish facts from interpretations, opinions, judgments, or theories. They can then raise those questions most appropriate to understanding and evaluating each.

Application: Teachers should encourage children to slow down and reflect before coming to conclusions. When discussing an issue, the teacher can ask children first, *"How would you describe the problem?"* The children should be helped to continually reformulate the issue in light of new information. They should be encouraged to see how the first statement of the issue or problem is rarely best (that is, most accurate, clear, and complete) and that they are in a better position to settle a question *after* they have developed as clear a formulation as possible.

When analyzing an issue, teachers can have children discuss such questions as these: *"Do we understand the issue? Do we know how to get an answer? Have we stated it fairly? Are the words clear? Are we evaluating anything? What standards should we use? Do we need any facts? How can we get the evidence we need?"*

When a statement is unclear, the class can discuss such questions as, *"How can we know whether or not this is true? What would it be like for this claim to be true? False? What evidence would count for it? Against it? Is there a clearer way to say this? Is there a more accurate way to say this? Can it be rephrased? Why would someone agree? Disagree?"*

This strategy provides a way of remodelling lessons that focus on "Fact/ Opinion" or which have vague passages of text.

To encourage children to distinguish fact from interpretation, the teacher could use questions like the following: *"Is this something that can be directly seen, or would you have to interpret or think about what you saw to arrive at this statement? Is this how anyone would describe the situation, or would someone else see it differently? What other ways of seeing this are there?"* Children might then talk about reasons for the interpretations.

Lesson plans in which the strategy is used

S-14 Clarifying and Analyzing the Meanings of Words or Phrases

Principle: Critical, independent thinking requires clarity of thought. A clear thinker understands concepts and knows what kind of evidence is required to justify applying a word or phrase to a situation. The ability to supply a definition is not proof of understanding. One must be able to supply clear, obvious examples and use the concept appropriately. In contrast, for an unclear thinker, words float through the mind unattached to clear, specific, concrete cases. Distinct concepts are confused. Often the only criterion for the application of a term is that the case in question "seems like" an example. Irrelevant associations are confused with what are necessary parts of the concept (e.g., "Love involves flowers and candlelight.") Unclear thinkers lack independence of thought because they lack the ability to analyze a concept, and so critique its use.

Application: There are a number of techniques the teacher can use to help children analyze concepts. Rather than simply asking them what a word or phrase means, or asking them for a definition, the teacher can use one of the techniques mentioned below.

When introducing concepts, paraphrasing is often helpful for relating the new term (word or phrase) to ideas children already understand. The teacher can also supply a range of examples, allowing children to add to the list. The class should discuss the purposes the concept serves. *"Why are you learning this? When would it be useful to use this word? What does it tell us?"*

When introducing or discussing a concept that is not within the children's experience, the teacher can use analogies which relate the idea to one with which children are familiar. Children could then compare the concepts.

When discussing words or phrases with which children are familiar, we suggest that teachers have children discuss clear examples of the concept, examples of its opposite (or examples which are clearly not instances of the concept), and examples for which neither the word or its opposite are completely accurate (borderline cases). Have children compare the facts relevant to deciding when the term and its opposite apply. Children could also discuss the implications of the concept and why people make a distinction between it and its opposite. *"Give me examples of X and the opposite of X. Why is this an X? What is it about this that makes you call it an X? What are you saying about it when you call it that? Why would someone say this? What are the practical consequences of calling it that? How do we feel about or treat X's? Why?"* (Do the same for the opposite.) When discussing examples, always start with the clearest, most obvious, indisputable cases and opposite cases. Only when those have been examined at length, should discussion move to the more problematic, controversial, difficult, or borderline examples. *"Why is this case different from the others? Why do you kind of want to call it X? Why do you not really want to call it X? What can we call this case?"*

When clarifying a concept expressed by a phrase rather than a single word, discuss cases in which the phrase applies, instead of merely discussing the individual words. For example, when clarifying the concept of a 'fair rule', though a general discussion of 'being fair' may be helpful, the more specific concept *'fair rule'* should be discussed and contrasted with its opposite.

For concepts that commonly have a lot of irrelevant associations, the teacher can have the children distinguish those associations which are logically related to the concept, from those which are not. Have the class brainstorm ideas associated with the term under discussion. *("What do you think of when you think of school?")* Then ask the children if they can imagine using the term for situations lacking this or that listed idea. *("If teachers and children gathered in a building to study, but there were no blackboards or desks, is it a school?")* Children may see that many of their associations are not part of the concept. They are left with a clearer understanding of what is relevant to the concept and will be less tempted to confuse mere association with it.

Assemble a variety of pictures — some which clearly illustrate the concept (say, 'tree'), some which illustrate the opposite, or are clearly not examples (such as grass), some which are borderline (large, tree-like bushes), and some you can't tell. Groups of children could sort the pictures into piles. The class can share the groupings, and children could be asked, *"What in the picture makes you put it with* these? Could you put it in a different pile? Why or why not? Why could you agree about these? Why couldn't your group agree about those?"

Whenever a text or discussion uses one term in more than one sense (such as a technical concept that is also an ordinary word), the teacher can ask the children to state how it is being used in each case or have them paraphrase sentences in which it occurs. Then the teacher can ask children to generate examples in which one, both, or neither meaning of the term applies. For example, children could distinguish ordinary from scientific concepts of work and energy. Children could also look at related words. 'Tired' and 'play' aren't related to the scientific concept 'work'.

When a text confuses two distinct concepts, children can clarify them. Children can distinguish concepts by discussing the different applications and implications of the concepts. *"Can you think of an example of A that isn't B? What's the difference?"* Older children could rewrite passages, making them clearer. For example, a social studies text explains how 'consensus' means that everyone in the group has to agree to decisions. The teachers' notes then offer an example wherein a group of children has to make a decision, so they vote, and the majority gets its way. The example, though intended to illustrate consensus, misses the point and confuses 'consensus' with 'majority rule'. The class could compare the two ideas, and so distinguish them. *"What did the text say 'consensus' means? What example does it give? Is this an example of everyone having to agree? What is the difference? How could the example be changed to illustrate the word?"*

Lesson plans in which the strategy is used

S-15 Developing Criteria for Evaluation: Clarifying Values and Standards

Principle: Critical thinkers realize that expressing mere preference does not substitute for evaluating something. Awareness of the process or components of evaluating facilitates thoughtful and fairminded evaluation. This process requires developing and using criteria or standards of evaluation, or making standards or criteria explicit. Critical thinkers are aware of the values on which they base their judgments. They have clarified them and understand *why* they are values. When developing criteria, critical thinkers should understand the object and purpose of the evaluation, and what function the thing being evaluated is supposed to serve. Critical thinkers take into consideration different points of view when attempting to evaluate something.

Application: Whenever the children are evaluating something — an object, action, policy, solution, belief — the teacher can ask them what they are evaluating, the purpose of the evaluation, and the criteria they used. With practice, children can begin to see the importance of developing clear criteria and applying them consistently. When discussing criteria as a class or in groups, rational discussion, clarity, and fairmindedness are usually more important than reaching consensus.

The class could discuss questions like the following: *"What are we evaluating? Why? Why do we need an X? What are X's for? Name or describe some good X's and some bad X's. Why are these good and those bad? What are the differences? Given these reasons or differences, can we generalize and list criteria? Can we describe what to look for when judging an X? What features does an X need to have? Why?"*

The teacher can take the children's reasons for beliefs, and make the standards explicit: "Oatmeal isn't good for breakfast 'cause it's yucky." The teacher can point out that the criterion used is taste, and could ask what other criteria are also important when evaluating foods.

Much of Language Arts instruction can be viewed as developing and clarifying criteria for evaluating writing. Children should continually evaluate written material and discuss their criteria. Specific points should be explained in terms of the values they support (such as clarity).

Lesson plans in which the strategy is used

S-16 Evaluating the Credibility of Sources of Information

Principle: Critical thinkers recognize the importance of using reliable sources of information. They give less weight to sources which either lack a track record of honesty, are not in a position to know, or have a vested interest in the issue. Critical thinkers recognize when there is more than one reasonable position to be taken on an issue; they compare alternative sources of information, noting areas of agreement; they analyze questions to determine whether or not the source is in a position to know; and they gather more information when sources disagree. They recognize obstacles to gathering accurate and pertinent information. They realize that preconception, for example, influences observation — that we often see only what we expect to see and fail to notice things we aren't looking for.

Application: When the class is discussing an issue about which people disagree, the teacher can encourage the children to check a variety of sources representing *different points of view.* (Texts miss a crucial point here. Having students examine twenty sources representing the same point of view does not teach this principle.)

The class can discuss the relevance of a source's past dependability, how to determine whether a source is in a position to know, and how motives should be taken into account when determining whether a source of information is credible: *"Is this person in a position to know? What would someone need, to be in a position to know? Was this person there? Could he have directly seen or heard, or would he have to have reasoned to what he is saying? What do we know about this person? What experience would you need to have to be an expert? What does he claim about this issue? Where did he get his information? Is there reason to doubt him? Has he been reliable in the past? Does he have anything to gain by convincing others? Why?"*

Finally, the teacher can use examples from the children's personal experience (for instance, trying to determine who started an argument) and encourage children to recognize the ways in which their own motivations can affect their interpretations and descriptions of events.

S-17 Questioning Deeply: Raising and Pursuing Root or Significant Questions

Principle: Critical thinkers can pursue an issue in depth, covering various aspects in an extended process of thought or discussion. When reading a passage, they look for issues and concepts underlying the claims expressed. They come to their own understanding of the details they learn, placing them in the larger framework of the subject and their overall perspectives. They contemplate the significant issues and questions underlying subjects or problems studied. They can move between basic underlying ideas and specific details. When pursuing a line of thought, they are not continually dragged off the subject. They use important issues to organize their thought and are not bound by the organization given by another.

Each of the various subject areas has been developed to clarify and settle questions peculiar to itself. (For example, history: How did the world come to be the way it is now?) The teacher can use such questions to organize and unify details covered in each subject. Perhaps more important are basic questions everyone faces about what people are like, the nature of right and wrong, how we know things, and so on. Both general and subject-specific basic questions should be repeatedly raised and used as a framework for organizing details children are learning.

Application: Texts fail to develop this trait of pursuing root questions by presenting pre-formulated conclusions, categories, solutions, and ideals, by avoiding crucial or thought-provoking issues or suggesting a too-limited discussion of them, by mixing questions relevant to different issues or by pursuing their objectives in a confusing way. To rectify these problems, teachers need to provide opportunities for children to come to their own conclusions, construct their own categories, devise their own solutions, and formulate their own ideals. They need to raise thought-provoking issues, allow extended discussion of them and keep the discussion focused, so that different issues are identified and appropriately addressed. The children, in turn, need to be clear about the objectives and to see themselves as accomplishing them in a fruitful way.

The class can begin exploration of an important topic, concept, or issue not discussed in any one place in their texts by looking it up in the table of contents, index, list of tables, etc. They can then divide up the task of reading and taking notes on the references. The class can then discuss their passages and pose questions to guide further research using other resources, and share their findings. Each student could then write an essay pulling the ideas together.

When a class discusses rules, institutions, activities, or ideals, the teacher can facilitate a discussion of their purposes, importance, or value. Children should be encouraged to see institutions, for example, as a creation of people, designed to fulfill certain functions, not as something that is "just there". Thus, they will be in a better position when they are adults, to see to it that it fulfills its goals. Or, for another example, ideals will be better understood as requiring specific kinds of actions, instead of being left as mere vague slogans, if the class examines their value.

When the text avoids important issues related to or underlying the object of study (such as moral implications), the teacher or children could raise them and discuss them at length.

Children can go through the assigned material, and possibly other resources, using an important issue(s) to organize the details, for example, making a chart or issue map. Socratic questioning, it should be noted, typically raises root issues.

When a lesson does raise important questions but has too few and scattered questions, the teacher can pull out, rearrange, and add to the relevant questions, integrating them into an extended and focused, rather than fragmented, discussion. Children can begin reading with one or more significant questions and list relevant details as they read.

Lesson plans in which the strategy is used

S-18 Analyzing or Evaluating Arguments, Interpretations, Beliefs, or Theories

Principle: Rather than carelessly agreeing or disagreeing with a conclusion based on their preconceptions of what is true, critical thinkers use analytic tools to understand the reasoning behind it and determine its relative strengths and weaknesses. When analyzing arguments, critical thinkers recognize the importance of asking for reasons and considering other views. They are especially sensitive to possible strengths of arguments that they disagree with, recognizing the tendency to ignore, oversimplify, distort, or otherwise unfairly dismiss them. Critical thinkers analyze questions and place conflicting arguments, interpretations, and theories in opposition to one another, as a means of highlighting key concepts, assumptions, implications, etc.

When giving or being given an interpretation, critical thinkers, recognizing the difference between evidence and interpretation, explore the assumptions on which interpretations are based and propose and evaluate alternative interpretations for their relative strength. Autonomous thinkers consider competing theories and develop their own theories.

Application: Often texts claim to have children analyze and evaluate arguments, when all they have them do is state preferences and locate factual claims, with very limited discussion. They fail to teach most techniques for analyzing and evaluating arguments. Texts that do address aspects of argument critique tend to teach such skills and insights in isolation, and fail to mention them when appropriate or useful. (See "Text Treatment of Critical Thinking and Argumentation" in the chapter, "Thinking Critically About Teaching: From Didactic to Critical Teaching".)

Instead of simply stating why they agree or disagree with a line of reasoning, children should be encouraged to place competing arguments, interpretations, or theories in opposition to one another. Ask, *"What reasons are given? What would someone who disagreed with this argument say?"* Children should then be encouraged to argue back and forth, and modify their positions in light of the strengths of others' positions.

Children can become better able to evaluate reasoning by familiarizing themselves with, and practicing, specific analytic techniques, such as making assumptions explicit and evaluating them; clarifying issues, conclusions, values, and words; developing criteria for evaluation; pinpointing contradictions; distinguishing relevant from irrelevant facts; evaluating evidence; and exploring implications. (See the strategies addressing these skills.)

When learning scientific theories, children should be encouraged to describe or develop their own theories and compare them with those presented in their texts. Children can compare the relative explanatory and predictive powers of various theories, whenever possible testing predictions with experiments or research.

Lesson plans in which the strategy is used

S-19 Generating or Assessing Solutions

Principle: Critical problem-solvers use everything available to them to find the best solution they can. They evaluate solutions, not independently of, but in relation to one another (since 'best' implies a comparison). They take the time to formulate problems clearly, accurately, and fairly, rather than offering a sloppy, half-baked, or self-serving description ("Susie's mean!" "This isn't going well, how can we do it better?") and then immediately leaping to solutions. They examine the causes of the problem at length. They reflect on such questions as, "What makes some solutions better than others? What does the solution to this problem require? What solutions have been tried for this and similar problems? With what results?"

But alternative solutions are often not given, they must be generated or thought up. Critical thinkers must be creative thinkers as well, generating possible solutions in order to find the best one. Very often a problem persists, not because we can't tell which available solution is best, but because the best solution has not yet been made available — no one has thought of it yet. Therefore, although critical thinkers use all available information relevant to their problems, including solutions others have tried in similar situations, they are flexible and imaginative, willing to try any good idea whether it has been done before or not.

Fairminded thinkers take into account the interests of everyone affected by the problem and proposed solutions. They are more committed to finding the best solution than to getting their way. They approach problems realistically.

Application: When presenting problem-solving lessons or activities, texts tend to provide lists of problem-solving steps which unnecessarily limit the process. For example, texts rarely encourage children to consider how others solved or tried to solve the same or a similar problem. They generally make "describing the problem" step one, without having the students reformulate their descriptions after further examination. They do not suggest analysis of causes. Texts often break problem-solving into steps and have children memorize the steps. They then drill the students on one or two steps. But children don't follow the process through. Thus, each step, practiced in isolation, has no meaning.

The best way to develop insight into problem-solving is to solve problems. When problems arise in the class, the children should be assisted in developing and implementing their own solutions. If the first attempt fails or causes other problems, they should consider why and try again. This way, they can learn the practical difficulties involved in discovering and implementing a workable solution and learn that some problems require perseverance.

When discussing a problem, we recommend that the teacher first have students state the problem, if that has not been done. They should explore the causes at length, exploring and evaluating multiple perspectives. Encourage them to integrate the strong points within each view. As the process of exploring causes and solutions proceeds, the children may find it useful to reformulate the description of the problem.

Rather than simply asking children if a given solution is good, the teacher could encourage an extended discussion of such questions as, *"Does this solve the problem? How? What other solutions can you think of? What are their advantages and disadvantages? What would happen if we tried this one? Would that help? Are we missing any relevant facts? (Is there anything we need to find out before we can decide which solution is best?) How will we know if a solution is a good one? Why do people/have people behaved in the ways that cause the problem? Can you think of other cases of this problem or similar problems? How did the people involved try to solve them? What results did that have? Did they solve the problems? Could we use the same solution, or is our case different in an important way? How do the solutions compare with each other? Why? Do any of these solutions ignore someone's needs? How could the various needs be taken into account?"*

Fiction often provides opportunities for analysis of problems and evaluation of solutions. Texts' treatments are often too brief, superficial, and unrealistic. They can be extended by having the class clarify the problem and analyze solutions as described above.

Social studies texts often provide opportunities for use of this strategy when they describe problems people or governments tried to solve. The children can evaluate the text's statement of the problem and its causes, evaluate the solution tried, and propose and evaluate alternatives. Children should be encouraged to explore the beliefs underlying various choices of solutions: *"Why do these people think this solution is best and those people want that one? What does each side claim causes the problem? What does each person assume? What sort of evidence or reasons would support each perspective or way of looking at things? What other ways of looking at the problem could there be? Would one solution be good for everyone? What is your perspective on this problem? (How do you see this problem?) Why?"*

Social studies texts provide innumerable opportunities for exploring crucial problems. *"What problems do we have in our [town, school]? Why? Who is involved in this? How do they cause the problem? How? Why? Who's affected? How? Why? What should be done? Why? Why not do it? What could go wrong? What do other people think should be done? Why? How can we find out more about the causes of this? How can we find out what different people want? Can we find a solution that would be good for everyone? Why or why not?"*

"What does this passage say was the problem? The cause? Explain the cause. Does it make sense? What other explanations make sense? What else was part of the cause? What was the solution tried? What were the effects? Who was affected? Did the solution work well? Why or why not? What should have been done differently?"

Lesson plans in which the strategy is used

S-20 Analyzing or Evaluating Actions and Policies

Principle: To develop one's perspective, one must analyze actions and policies and evaluate them. Good judgment is best developed through practice: judging behavior, explaining and justifying those judgments, hearing alternative judgments and their justifications, and assessing judgments. When evaluating the behavior of themselves and others, critical thinkers are aware of the standards they use, so that these, too, can become objects of evaluation. Critical thinkers examine the consequences of actions and recognize these as fundamental to the standards for assessing behavior and policy. Critical thinkers base their evaluations of behavior on assumptions which they have reasoned through. They can articulate and rationally apply principles.

Application: The teacher can encourage children to raise ethical questions about actions and policies of themselves and others. They can become more comfortable with the process of evaluating if they are given a number of opportunities to make and assess moral judgments: *"Why did X do this? What reasons were given? Were they the real reasons? Why do you think so? What might happen if someone acts this way? How would you feel if someone acted this way toward you? Why? Was this a good way to act? Why or why not?* (Help them make their standards explicit.) *Might someone else use a different standard (see this differently)?"*

Texts often falsely assume that people's stated reasons were their real reasons when the action doesn't fit the reason given. The children can be helped to see this. *"Why did M do that? What reason did M give? What did they do? What result did they say they wanted? What results did it actually have? Who was helped? Hurt? Why? Does that reason make sense as a reason for that action? Was the reason M gave the real reason? Why do you think so?"*

Children should also be called upon to generalize, to formulate principles of judgment: *"What makes some actions right, others wrong? What rights do people have? How can I know when someone's rights are being violated? Why respect people's rights? Why be good? Should I live according to rules? If so, what rules? If not, how should I decide what to do? What policies should be established and why? What are governments supposed to do? Why? What shouldn't they do? Why?"*

These generalizations can be further analyzed and tested by having children compare them to specific cases they have judged in previous lessons: *"Remember what you said last week about X? You said that it was wrong because .... Does it make sense to say that what Y did was right but X was wrong?"*

Lesson plans in which the strategy is used

S-21 Reading Critically: Clarifying or Critiquing Texts

Principle: Critical thinkers read with a healthy skepticism. But they do not doubt or deny until they understand. They clarify before they judge. Since they expect intelligibility from what they read, they check and double-check their understanding as they read. They do not mindlessly accept nonsense. Critical readers ask themselves questions as they read, wonder about the implications of, reasons for, examples of, and meaning and truth of the material. They do not approach written material as a collection of sentences, but as a whole, trying out various interpretations until one fits all of the work, rather than ignoring or distorting what doesn't fit their interpretation. They realize that everyone is capable of making mistakes and being wrong, including authors of textbooks. They also realize that, since everyone has a point of view, everyone sometimes leaves out some relevant information. No two authors would write the same book or write from exactly the same perspective. Therefore, critical readers recognize that reading a book is reading one limited perspective on a subject and that more can be learned by considering other perspectives.

Application: Children should feel free to raise questions about materials they read. When a text is ambiguous, vague, or misleading, teachers can raise such questions as, *"What does this passage say? What does it imply or mean? Assume? Is it clear? Explain it. Does it contradict anything you know or think is true? How do you know? How could you find out? Does this fit in with your experience? In what way? Why or why not? What might someone who disagreed with it say? Does the text leave out relevant or necessary information? Does it favor one perspective or way of looking at things? Which? Why do you suppose it was written this way? How could we rewrite this passage to make it clearer, fairer, or more accurate?"*

In Language Arts, rather than simply using recall questions at the end of fictional selections, have children describe the plot. Thus, children must pull out the main parts and understand cause and effect while being checked for basic comprehension and recall.

Children should continually evaluate what they read: *"How good is this selection? Why? Is it well written? Why or why not? Is it saying something important? What? How does it compare with other things we've read? Are some parts better than others? Which? Why?"*

They can evaluate unit, chapter, and section titles and headings in their texts. *"What is the main point in this passage? What details does it give? What ideas do those details support or explain? Is the heading accurate? Misleading? Could you suggest a better heading?"*

Often passages which attempt to instill belief in important U.S. ideals are too vague to give more than the vague impression that our ideals are important. Such passages typically say that the ideals are important or precious, that people from other countries wish they had them or come here to enjoy them, that we all have a responsibility to preserve them, and so on. Such passages could be reread slowly and deeply with much discussion.

The class could engage in deeper, critical reading by discussing questions like the following: *"Why is this right important? How is this supposed to help people? Does not having this right hurt people? How? Why?*

"Why would someone try to prevent people from voting or speaking out? How could they? Have you ever denied someone the right to speak or be heard? Why? Were you justified? Why or why not? What should you have done?

"Why are these rights emphasized? Do you have other rights? Why doesn't the text (or Constitution) say that you have the right to eat pickles? What are the differences between that right and those mentioned?

"Does everyone believe in this or want this? How do you know? Have you ever heard anyone say that tyranny is the best kind of government, or free speech is bad? Why?

"Why does the text say people have this responsibility? How, exactly, does this help our country? Why do some people not do this? What does it require of you? And how do you do that? Is it easy or hard? What else does it mean you should do?"

The teacher could make copies of passages from several sample texts which cover the same material and have the children compare and critique them.

Children can discuss their interpretations of what they read. Small groups of children can compare their paraphrases and interpretations, and check back in the book.

When students have misunderstood what they have read, rather than explaining what they missed, the teacher could have them reread more closely.

Lesson plans in which the strategy is used

S-22 Listening Critically: The Art of Silent Dialogue

Principle: Critical thinkers realize that listening can be done passively and uncritically or actively and critically. They know that it is easy to misunderstand what is said by another and hard to integrate another's thinking into one's own. Compare speaking and listening. When we speak, we need only keep track of our own ideas, arranging them in some order, expressing thoughts with which we are intimately familiar: our own. But listening is more complex. We must take the words of another and translate them into ideas that make sense to us. We have not had the experiences of the speaker. We are not on the inside of his or her point of view. When we listen to others, we can't anticipate, as they can themselves, where their thoughts are leading them. We must continually interpret what others say within the confines of our experiences. We must find a way to enter into their points of view, shift our minds to follow their train of thought.

Consequently, we need to learn how to listen actively and critically. We need to recognize that listening is an art involving skills that we can develop only with time and practice. We must realize, for example, that to listen and learn from what we are hearing, we need to learn to ask key questions that enable us to locate ourselves in the thought of another: "I'm not sure I understand you when you say ..., could you explain that further?" "Could you give me an example or illustration of this?" "Would you also say ...?" "Let me see if I understand you. What you are saying is .... Is that right?" "How do you respond to this objection?" Critical readers ask questions as they read and use those questions to orient themselves to what an author is saying. Critical listeners ask questions as they listen to orient themselves to what a speaker is saying: "Why does she say that? What examples could I give to illustrate that point? What is the main point? How does this detail relate to the main point? That one? Is he using this word as I would, or somewhat differently?" These highly skilled and activated processes are crucial to learning. We need to heighten student awareness of and practice in them as often as we can.

Application: The first and best way to teach critical listening is to model it. We should actively and constructively listen to what our students say, demonstrating the patience and skill necessary to understand them. We should not casually assume that we know what they mean. We should not pass by their expressions too quickly. Children rarely take seriously their own meanings. They rarely listen to themselves. They rarely realize the need to explain themselves or give examples. We are often in a position to help them do so by asking questions that show that we want to understand them.

Secondly, children rarely listen carefully to what other children have to say. They rarely take each other seriously. We can facilitate this process with questioning interventions. We can say things like: "Ron, did you follow what Trish said? Could you put what she said in your own words? Richard, could you give us an example from your own experience of what Jane has said? Has anything like that ever happened to you?"

Children can develop insight into listening skills, as well as improve their skills in distinguishing important from trivial details, noticing cause and effect relationships, and developing the concept 'plot' by discussing movies and TV shows they have recently seen. The children could draw pictures illustrating events and then groups of children can put the pictures in order as part of the discussion.

Older children can describe discussions, videotapes, or movies in writing, then compare their versions in small groups, trying to accurately reconstruct what they heard. Whenever possible, they should watch the piece a second time to verify their accounts or settle conflicting accounts of what they saw and heard. While watching a movie or video, they can be asked to take notes. Afterward, they can compare and discuss their notes. A teacher could periodically stop a movie or video and have the children outline the main point and raise critical questions.

The success of Socratic questioning and class discussion depends upon close and critical listening. Many assignments are understood or misunderstood through word of mouth. We need to take the occasion of making an assignment an occasion for testing and encouraging critical listening. In this way, we will get better work from our students, because in learning how to listen critically to what we are asking them to do, they will gain a clearer grasp of what that is, and hence do a better job in doing it. Children often do an assignment poorly because they never clearly understood it in the first place.

The class can also discuss listening, its importance and difficulty, and strategies for listening well. Such discussion should focus on students' own examples of listening well and of misunderstanding, stubbornness, and other problems, why they occurred, and ways of avoiding them in the future. *"What could you have done differently to listen better, check your understanding, help the other person listen better to you?"*

Lesson plans in which the strategy is used

S-23 Making Interdisciplinary Connections

Principle: Although in some ways it is convenient to divide knowledge up into disciplines, the divisions are not absolute. Critical thinkers do not allow the somewhat arbitrary distinctions between academic subjects to control their thinking. When considering issues which transcend subjects (and most real-life issues do), they bring relevant concepts, knowledge, and insights from many subjects to the analysis. They make use of insights from one subject to inform their understanding of other subjects. There are always connections between subjects. To understand, say, reasons for the American Revolution (historical question), insights from technology, geography, economics, and philosophy can be fruitfully applied.

Application: Young children can be encouraged to begin to explore the relationships between their different kinds of books. For example, they could compare pictures of animals in storybooks with pictures of real animals. *"How are these two rabbits alike? Different? Why are they different? Which one seems more like us? Why is this picture in this book? Why is that picture here? Which one shows how real rabbits look?"* Students could listen to stories about, or watch movies about animals and compare the "personalities" of real animals to storybook animals.

Students can evaluate stories they hear or read from the point of view of social studies (or science): *"Is this story realistic? Are the characters realistic, are people really like that? Would this character in that situation really act that way? Why or why not? Did the solution to the problem make sense?"*

Students should *use* math whenever it would be helpful.

Reading and writing can and should be taught in conjunction with every subject. One way to teach reading during other subjects would be to have children who cannot answer questions about what they read *skim* their texts to find the answer, rather than being supplied with answers. This approach more effectively teaches skill in skimming for specific information than the standard approach to teaching a lesson which drills children.

Teachers could also have children who misunderstood a sentence in their texts find it. Either the sentence was unclearly written, in which case, the children could revise it, or the student didn't read carefully, in which case the class could discuss why the sentence does not mean what the child thought.

Any time another subject is relevant to the object of discussion, those insights can be used and integrated. Some teachers allot time for coverage of topics in different subjects so that the topic is examined from the perspective of several subjects, that is, in thematic units.

Socratic questioning can be used to make subject connections clear. The teacher can use discussion of children's issues and problems to show the importance of bringing insights from many subjects to bear.

Lesson plans in which the strategy is used

S-24 Practicing Socratic Discussion: Clarifying and Questioning Beliefs, Theories, or Perspectives

Principle: Critical thinkers are nothing if not questioners. The ability to question and probe deeply, to get down to root ideas, to get beneath the mere appearance of things, is at the very heart of the activity. And, as questioners, they have many different kinds of questions and moves available and can follow up their questions appropriately. They can use questioning techniques, not to make others look stupid, but to learn what they think, help them develop their ideas, or as a prelude to evaluating them. When confronted with a new idea, they want to understand it, to relate it to their experience, and to determine its implications, consequences, and value. They can fruitfully uncover the structure of their own and others' perspectives. Probing questions are the tools by which these goals are reached.

Furthermore, critical thinkers are comfortable being questioned. They don't become offended, confused, or intimidated. They welcome good questions as an opportunity to develop a line of thought.

Application: Children, then, should develop the ability to go beyond the basic what and why questions that are found in their native questioning impulses. To do this, they need to discover a variety of ways to frame questions which probe the logic of what they are reading, hearing, writing, or saying. They can begin to learn how to probe for and question assumptions, judgments, inferences, apparent contradictions, or inconsistencies. They can begin to learn how to question the relevance of what is presented, the evidence for and against what is said, the way concepts or words are used, the consequences of beliefs. Not only do we need to question children, we also need to have them question each other and themselves.

Classroom instruction and activities, therefore, should stimulate the student to question and help make the children comfortable when questioned, so that the questioning process is increasingly valued and mastered. Questioning should be introduced in such a way that the students come to see it as an effective way to get at the heart of matters and to understand things from different points of view. It should not be used to embarrass or negate children. It should be part of an inquiry into issues of significance in an atmosphere of mutual support and cooperation. We therefore recommend that teachers cultivate a habit of wondering about the reasoning behind their students' beliefs and translating their musings into questions.

The teacher should model Socratic questioning techniques and use them often. Any thought-provoking questions can start a Socratic discussion. To follow up students' responses, use questions like the following: *"Why? If that is so, what follows? How do you know that? Is this what you mean ... or, ...? For example? Is this an example of what you mean ..., or this, ...? Can I summarize your point as ...? What is your reason for saying that? How does this relate to what we talked about last week (the story you heard yesterday)? What do you mean when using this word? Is it possible that ...? Are there other ways of looking at it? How else could we view this matter? Are you assuming that ...?"* (For more questions, see the section on Socratic discussion in the chapter, "Global Strategies: Beyond Subject Matter Teaching".)

Immediately after Socratic discussion, older children can write notes for five minutes, summarizing the key points, raising new questions, making new points, or adding examples. Later these notes could be shared and discussion continued.

To develop children's abilities to use Socratic questioning, the teacher could present an idea or passage to children and have them brainstorm possible questions. For instance, they could think of questions to ask story or historical characters or a famous person or personal hero on a particular subject.

Pairs of children can practice questioning each other about issues raised in study, trading the roles of questioner and questioned. The teacher may provide possible initial questions and perhaps some follow-up questions. Children could also be allowed to continue their discussions another day, after they've had time to think. As they practice Socratic questioning, see it modeled, and learn the language, skills, and insights of critical thinking, their mastery of questioning techniques will increase.

The direction and structure of a Socratic discussion can be made clearer by periodically summarizing and rephrasing the main points made. *"We began talking about this _____. Some of you said _____, others _____. These arguments were given .... Paige said that X couldn't be right but David disagreed. To find out, we decided we would need to find out _____. So how could we do that?"*

To practice exploring the idea of illuminating and probing Socratic questioning, children could evaluate different kinds of interviews, categorizing the questions asked. They could then think up probing follow-up questions that weren't asked. *"Why would you ask that? How could that be followed up? What would that tell you?"*

Lesson plans in which the strategy is used

S-25 Reasoning Dialogically: Comparing Perspectives, Interpretations, or Theories

Principle: Dialogical thinking refers to thinking that involves a dialogue or extended exchange between different points of view. Whenever we consider concepts or issues deeply, we naturally explore their connections to other ideas and issues within different points of view. Critical thinkers need to be able to engage in fruitful, exploratory dialogue, proposing ideas, probing their roots, considering subject matter insights and evidence, testing ideas, and moving between various points of view. When we think, we often engage in dialogue, either inwardly or aloud with others. We need to integrate critical thinking skills into that dialogue so that it is as useful as possible. Socratic questioning is one form of dialogical thinking.

Application: By routinely raising root questions and root ideas in a classroom setting, multiple points of view get expressed and the thinking proceeds, not in a predictable or straightforward direction, but in a criss-crossing, back-and-forth movement. We continually encourage the children to explore how what they think about x relates to what they think about y and z. This necessarily requires that their thinking moves back and forth between their own basic ideas and those being presented by the other children, between their own ideas and those expressed in a book or story, between their own thinking and their own experience, between ideas within one domain and those in another, in short, between any two perspectives. This dialogical process will sometimes become dialectical, that is, some ideas will clash or be inconsistent with others: *"What would someone who disagreed say? Why? How could the first respond? Why? Etc."*

When a lesson focuses on only one side of an issue or event, the teacher could have children discuss other views. *"What did the other (character, group of people) think? Why? (Use specific examples from a story or real life situation.) Would others see it this way? Would they use these words? How would they describe this? Why? What exactly do they disagree about? Why? What does X think is the cause? Y? Why do they differ?"*

Children could list points from multiple perspectives for reference, then write dialogues of people arguing about the issues. Small groups of children could role-play discussions in front of the class. The class as a whole (or groups of children) could then discuss the role-play: *What was each person's main point? Why did each believe that? What did they disagree about? Why? What did they agree about? Why?"*

Texts occasionally approach teaching dialogical thinking by having children discuss more than one perspective. Yet such discussion is simply tacked on; it is not integrated with the rest of the material. Thus, the ideas are merely juxtaposed, not synthesized. Rather than separate activities or discussions about different perspectives, the teacher can have children move back and forth between points of view. *"What did the fox want? Why? The bunny? Why? The fish? Why? Why did the fox think the bunny was wrong? How did the bunny answer? ... What beliefs do the sides have in common? How would the fish look at this dispute?"*

Lesson plans in which the strategy is used

S-26 Reasoning Dialectically: Evaluating Perspectives, Interpretations, or Theories

Principle: Dialectical thinking refers to dialogical thinking conducted in order to test the strengths and weaknesses of opposing points of view. Court trials and debates are dialectical in intention. They pit idea against idea, reasoning against counter-reasoning in order to get at the truth of a matter. As soon as we begin to explore ideas, we find that some clash or are inconsistent with others. If we are to integrate our thinking, we need to assess which of the conflicting ideas we will provisionally accept and which we shall provisionally reject, or which parts of the views are strong and which weak, or how the views can be reconciled. Children need to develop dialectical reasoning skills, so that their thinking not only moves comfortably between divergent points of view or lines of thought, but also makes some assessments in light of the relative strengths and weaknesses of the evidence or reasoning presented. Hence, when thinking dialectically, critical thinkers can use critical micro-skills appropriately.

Application: Dialectical thinking can be practiced whenever two conflicting points of view, arguments, or conclusions are under discussion. Stories provide many opportunities for this. Dialectical exchange between children in science classes helps them begin to discover and appropriately amend their preconceptions about the physical world.

The teacher could have proponents of conflicting views argue their positions and have others evaluate them. A dialogical discussion could be taped for later analysis and evaluation. Or the teacher could inject evaluative questions into dialogical discussion: *"Was that reason a good one? Why or why not? Does the other view have a good answer to that reason? What? And the answer to that objection? What evidence does each side use? Is the evidence from both sides relevant? Questionable, or acceptable? Compare the sources each side cites for its evidence. Which is more trustworthy? How can we know which of these assumptions is best? What is this side right about? The other side? Is one of these views strongest, does one side make more sense? Why or why not?"*

Lesson plans in which the strategy is used

S-27 Comparing and Contrasting Ideals with Actual Practice

Principle: Self-improvement and social improvement are presupposed values of critical thinking. Critical thinking, therefore, requires an effort to see ourselves and others accurately. This requires recognizing gaps between ideals and practice. The fairminded thinker values truth and consistency and so works to minimize these gaps. The confusion of facts with ideals prevents us from moving closer to achieving our ideals. A critical education strives to highlight discrepancies between facts and ideals, and proposes and evaluates methods for minimizing them. This strategy is intimately connected with "developing intellectual good faith".

Application: Since, when discussing our society, many texts consistently confuse ideals with facts, the teacher can use them as objects of analysis: *"Is this a fact or an ideal? Are things always this way, or is this what people are trying to achieve? Are these ideals yours? Why or why not? How have people tried to achieve this ideal? When did they not meet the ideal? Why? What problems did they have? Why? How* *can we better achieve these ideals?"* The children could discuss how to reword misleading portions of their text to make them more accurate.

Sometimes this strategy could take the form of *avoiding oversimplification.* For example, when considering the idea that we in this country are free to choose the work or jobs we want, the teacher could ask, *"Can people in this country choose any job they want? Always? What, besides choice, might affect what job someone has or gets? Would someone who looked like a bum be hired as a salesman? Does this mean they don't have this freedom? Why or why not? What if there aren't enough openings for some kind of work? How can this claim be made more accurate?"*

The teacher can facilitate a general discussion of the value of achieving consistency of thought and action: *"Have you ever thought something was true about yourself but acted in a way that didn't fit in with your ideal? Did you see yourself differently then?"*

Sometimes texts foster the confusion between ideals and actual practice by asking questions to which most people want to answer yes, for example: Do you like to help others? Do you listen to what other people have to say? Do you share things? Since none of us always adheres to our principles (though few like to admit it) you could rephrase such questions. For example, ask, *"When have you enjoyed helping someone? When not? Why? Did you have to help that person? When is it hard to listen to what someone else has to say? Why? Have you ever not wanted to share something? Should you have? Why or why not? If you didn't share, why didn't you?"*

Such discussion can also explore the rationalizations people use to cover intellectual dishonesty and inconsistency: *"What were you thinking? Why? Did you know you shouldn't, or did it seem OK at the time? Why?"*

Obviously, the more realistic our ideals, the closer we can come to achieving them. Therefore, any text's attempt to encourage unrealistic ideals can be re-modelled. For example, rather than assuming that everyone should always do everything they can for everyone anytime, allow children to express a range of views on such virtues as generosity.

Lesson plans in which the strategy is used

S-28 Thinking Precisely About Thinking: Using Critical Vocabulary

Principle: An essential requirement of critical thinking is the ability to think about thinking, to engage in what is sometimes called "metacognition". One possible definition of critical thinking is the art of thinking about your thinking while you're thinking in order to make your thinking better: more clear, more accurate, more fair. It is precisely at the level of "thinking about thinking" that most critical thinking stands in contrast to uncritical thinking. Critical thinkers can analyze thought — take it apart and put it together again. For the uncritical thinker, thoughts are "just there". "I think what I think, don't ask me why." The analytical vocabulary in the English language (such terms as 'assume', 'infer', 'conclude', 'criterion', 'point of view', 'relevance', 'issue', 'elaborate', 'ambiguous', 'objection', 'support', 'bias', 'justify', 'perspective', 'contradiction', 'consistent', 'credibility', 'evidence', 'interpret', 'distinguish') enables us to think more precisely about our thinking. We are in a better position to assess reasoning (our own, as well as that of others) when we can use analytic vocabulary with accuracy and ease.

Application: Since most language is learned by hearing words used in context, teachers should try to make critical terms part of their working vocabulary. When children are reasoning or discussing the reasoning of others, the teacher can encourage them to use critical vocabulary. New words are most easily learned and remembered when they are clearly useful.

When introducing a term, the teacher can speak in pairs of sentences: first, using the critical vocabulary, then, rephrasing the sentence without the new term: *"What facts are relevant to this issue? What facts must we consider in deciding this issue? What information do we need? How do you interpret that statement? What do you think it means?"* The teacher can also rephrase children's statements to incorporate the vocabulary: *"Do you mean that Jane is assuming that ...?"*

During discussions, participating children could be encouraged to explain the role of their remarks in the discussion: supporting a point, raising an objection, answering an objection, distinguishing concepts or issues, questioning relevance, etc. *"Why were you raising that point here? Are you supporting Fred's point or ...?"*

Lesson plans in which the strategy is used

S-29 Noting Significant Similarities and Differences

Principle: Critical thinkers strive to treat similar things similarly and different things differently. Uncritical thinkers, on the other hand, often don't see *significant* similarities and differences. Things superficially similar are often significantly different. Things superficially different are often essentially the same. Only through practice can we become sensitized to significant similarities and differences. As we develop this sensitivity, it influences how we experience, how we describe, how we categorize, and how we reason about things. We become more careful and discriminating in our use of words and phrases. We hesitate before we accept this or that analogy or comparison.

We recognize the purposes of the comparisons we make. We recognize that purposes govern the act of comparing and determine its scope and limits. The hierarchy of categories biologists, for instance, use to classify living things (with Kingdom as the most basic, all the way down to sub-species) reflects biological judgment regarding which kinds of similarities and differences between species are the most important *biologically*, that is, which distinctions shed the most light on how each organism is structured and lives. To the zoologist, the similarities between whales and horses is considered more important than their similarities to fish. The differences between whales and fish are considered more significant than differences between whales and horses. These distinctions suit the biologists' purposes.

Application: Texts often call on children to compare and contrast two or more things — objects, ideas, phenomena, etc. Yet these activities rarely have a serious purpose. Merely listing similarities and differences has little value in itself. Rather than encouraging children to make such lists, these activities should be proposed in a context which narrows the range of pertinent comparisons and requires some *use* be made of them in pursuit of some specific goal. For example, if comparing and contrasting two characters, children should use their understanding to illuminate the relationship between them, perhaps to explain factors contributing to conflict. Thus, only those points which shed light on the particular problem need be mentioned, and each point has implications to be drawn out and integrated into a broader picture.

"What does this remind you of? Why? How is it similar? Different? How important are the differences? Why? What does it tell us about our topic? How useful is that comparison? Can anyone think of an even more useful comparison?"

When comparing characters from literature, rather than simply listing differences, children should analyze and *use* their comparisons. *"Why are they different (personality, lives, problems, current situations)?"* Don't let them over-generalize from differences. Texts have children make sweeping statements from one difference in attitude or action. Such differences may not reflect difference in character as much as differences in situation. Relate differences in feelings and behavior to differences in how characters see things. Relate all significant differences between characters to the theme.

Children can compare models to what they represent, and so evaluate them: *"How much is the model like the real thing? Unlike it? What doesn't the model show? Why not? Could it? How or why not? What parts do they both have? Do they have similar parts? Why or why not? How important are the missing or extra parts? How like the original thing is this part? How is this model helpful? In what ways is it misleading? How good is this model? How could it be improved?"*

Lesson plans in which the strategy is used

S-30 Examining or Evaluating Assumptions

Principle: We are in a better position to evaluate any reasoning or behavior when all of the elements of that reasoning or behavior are made explicit. We base both our reasoning and our behavior on beliefs we take for granted. We are often unaware of these assumptions. Only by recognizing them can we evaluate them. Critical thinkers have a passion for truth and for accepting the strongest reasoning. Thus, they have the intellectual courage to seek out and reject false assumptions. They realize that everyone makes some questionable assumptions. They are willing to question, and have others question, even their own most cherished assumptions. They consider alternative assumptions. They base their acceptance or rejection of assumptions on their rational scrutiny of them. They hold questionable assumptions with an appropriate degree of tentativeness. Independent thinkers evaluate assumptions for themselves, and do not simply accept the assumptions of others, even those assumptions made by everyone they know.

Application: Teachers should encourage children to make assumptions explicit as often as possible — assumptions made in what they read or hear and assumptions they make. Teachers should ask questions that elicit the implicit elements of their claims. Although it is valuable practice to have children make good assumptions explicit, it is especially important when assumptions are questionable.

The teacher might ask, *"If this was the evidence, and this the conclusion, what was assumed?"* or *"If this is what he saw (heard, etc.), and this is what he concluded or thought, what did he assume?"* (*"He saw red fruit and said 'Apples!'*

and ate it." "He assumed that all red fruits are apples." or "He assumed that, because it looked like an apple, it was good to eat.")

The following are some of the probing questions teachers may use when a class discusses the worth of an assumption: *"Why do people (did this person) make this assumption? Have you ever assumed this? What could be assumed instead? Is this belief true? Sometimes true? Seldom true? Always false? (Ask for examples.) Can you think of reasons for this belief? Against it? What, if anything, can we say about this? What would we need to find out to be able to judge it? How would someone who makes this assumption act?"*

Lesson plans in which the strategy is used

S-31 Distinguishing Relevant From Irrelevant Facts

Principle: To think critically, we must be able to tell the difference between those facts which are relevant to an issue and those which are not. Critical thinkers focus their attention on relevant facts and do not let irrelevant considerations affect their conclusions. Whether or not something is relevant is often unclear; relevance must often be argued. Furthermore, a fact is only relevant or irrelevant in relation to an issue. Information relevant to one problem may not be relevant to another.

Application: When discussing an issue, solution to a problem, or when giving reasons for a conclusion, children can practice limiting their remarks to facts which are germane to that issue, problem, or conclusion. Often children assume that all information given has to be used to solve a problem. Life does not sort relevant from irrelevant information for us. Teachers can encourage children to make a case for the pertinence of their remarks, and help them see when their remarks are irrelevant: *"How would this fact affect our conclusion? If it were false, would we have to change our conclusion? Why or why not? What is the connection? Why does that matter? What issue are you addressing? Are you addressing this issue or raising a new one?"*

When sorting, evaluating, or grouping things or pictures, students can explain their reasons and why their reasons are relevant or important for what purpose. The teacher can use probing questions to have them fully explain themselves: *"Yes, seeing snow in this picture is one thing that tells us it's winter. Is there anything else relevant to figuring out what season it is, anything else that tells us the season? Why is that relevant or important for this?"*

Children could read a chapter of text or story with one or more issues in mind and note relevant details. Children could then share and discuss their lists. The children can then begin to discover that sometimes they must *argue* for the relevance of a particular fact to an issue.

Children who disagree about the relevance of a particular point to the issue discussed, should be encouraged to argue its potential relevance, and probe the beliefs underlying their disagreement: *"Why do you think it's relevant? Why do you think it isn't? What is each side assuming? Do these assumptions make sense?"*

Another technique for developing children's sensitivity to relevance is to change an issue slightly and have children compare what was relevant to the first issue to what is relevant to the second. ("What *really* happened?" versus "What does X

105

think happened?" Or *"Can* you do this?" versus *"Should* you do it?" Or "Which one *is* best?" versus "Which do people *think* is best?")

Lesson plans in which the strategy is used

S-32 Making Plausible Inferences, Predictions, or Interpretations

Principle: Thinking critically involves the ability to reach sound conclusions based on observation and information. Critical thinkers distinguish their observations from their conclusions. They look beyond the facts, to see what those facts imply. They know what the concepts they use imply. They also distinguish cases in which they can only guess from cases in which they can safely conclude. Critical thinkers recognize their tendency to make inferences that support their own egocentric or sociocentric world views and are therefore especially careful to evaluate inferences they make when their interests or desires are involved. Remember, every interpretation is based on inference, and we interpret every situation we are in.

Application: Teachers can ask children to make inferences based on a wide variety of statements, actions, story titles and pictures, story characters' statements and actions, text statements, and their classmates' statements and actions. They can then argue for their inferences or interpretations. Children should be encouraged to distinguish their observations from inferences, and sound inferences from unsound inferences, guesses, etc.

Sometimes texts will describe details yet fail to make or have children make plausible inferences from them. The class could discuss such passages. Or groups of children might suggest possible inferences which the class as a whole could then discuss and evaluate.

"What can we infer from or tell about this? How did you interpret that, what did you think it meant?"

Teachers can have children give personal examples of when they made bad inferences, and help them begin to recognize situations in which they are most susceptible to uncritical thought. The class can discuss ways in which they can successfully minimize the effects of irrationality in their thought. *"When do we tend to act irrationally? What could we do at those times to make more accurate interpretations, or understand the situation better?"*

Science instruction all too often provides "the correct" inferences to be made from experiments or observations, rather than having children propose their own. Sometimes science texts encourage poor inferences given the observation cited. Though the conclusion is correct, children should note that the experiment alone did not prove it and should discuss other evidence supporting it.

Children should interpret experiments, and argue for their interpretations. *"What happened? What does that mean? Are there other ways to interpret our results? What? How can we tell which is best?"*

Lesson plans in which the strategy is used

S-33 Giving Reasons and Evaluating Evidence and Alleged Facts

Principle: Critical thinkers can take their reasoning apart in order to examine and evaluate its components. They know on what evidence they base their conclusions. They realize that un-stated, unknown reasons can be neither communicated nor critiqued. They are comfortable being asked to give reasons; they don't find requests for reasons intimidating, confusing, or insulting. They can insightfully discuss evidence relevant to the issue or conclusions they consider. Not everything offered as evidence should be accepted. Evidence and factual claims should be scrutinized and evaluated. Evidence can be complete or incomplete, acceptable, questionable, or false.

Application: When asking children to come to conclusions, the teacher can ask for their reasons. *"How do you know? Why do you think so? What evidence do you have?"* When the reasons children supply are incomplete, the teacher may want to ask a series of probing questions to elicit a fuller explanation of student reasoning. *"What other evidence do you have? How do you know your information is correct? What assumptions are you making? Do you have reason to think your assumptions are true?"* etc.

When discussing their interpretations of written material, children should routinely be asked to show specifically where in the material they got that interpretation. The sentence or passage can then be clarified and discussed, and the student's interpretation better understood and evaluated.

"Why do think so? How do you know? What reasons do you have for thinking that? What facts or evidence do you have for that? Where did we get the evidence? (How do you know that?) Is the source reliable? How could we find out what other evidence exists? What evidence supports opposing views? Is the evidence enough or do we need more? Is there reason to question this evidence? What makes it questionable? Acceptable? Does another view account for this evidence?"

Lesson plans in which the strategy is used

S-34 Recognizing Contradictions

Principle: Consistency is a fundamental — some would say the *defining* — ideal of critical thinkers. They strive to remove contradictions from their beliefs, and are wary of contradictions in others. As would-be fairminded thinkers they strive to judge like cases in a like manner.

Perhaps the most difficult form of consistency to achieve is that between word and deed. Self-serving double standards are one of the most common problems in human life. Children are in some sense aware of the importance of consistency. ("Why don't I get to do what they get to do?") They are frustrated by double standards, yet are given little help in getting insight into them and dealing with them.

Critical thinkers can pinpoint specifically where opposing arguments or views contradict each other, distinguishing the contradictions from compatible beliefs, thus focusing their analyses of conflicting views.

Application: When discussing conflicting lines of reasoning, inconsistent versions of the same story, or egocentric reasoning or behavior, the teacher can encourage children to bring out both viewpoints and practice recognizing contradictions. *"What does X say? What does Y say? Could both views be true? Why or why not? If one is true,* must the other be false? Where, exactly, do these views contradict each other? On what do they agree? (What happened, causes, values, how a principle applies, etc.)"

Sometimes fiction illustrates contradictions between what people say and what they do. History texts often confuse stated reasons with reasons implied by behavior. They will often repeat the noble justification that, say, a particular group ruled another group for its own good, when they in fact exploited them and did irreparable harm. Children could discuss such examples. The teacher could use questions like the following: "What did they say? What did they do? Are the two consistent or contradictory? (Does what they said match how they acted, or are they opposite?) Why do you say so? What behavior would have been consistent with their words? What words would have been consistent with their behavior? If they meant what they said, what would they have done? If they said what they meant, what would they have said?"

When arguing opposing views, children should be encouraged to find points of agreement and specify points of dispute or contradiction. "What is it about that view that you think is false? Do you accept this claim? That one? On what question or statement does your disagreement turn? What, exactly, do you disagree with?"

The class can explore possible ways to reconcile apparent contradictions. "How could someone hold both of these views? How might someone argue that someone can believe both?"

Lesson plans in which the strategy is used

S-35 Exploring Implications and Consequences

Principle: Critical thinkers can take statements, recognize their implications — what follows from them — and develop a fuller, more complete understanding of their meaning. They realize that to accept a statement one must also accept its implications. They can explore both implications and consequences at length. When considering beliefs that relate to actions or policies, critical thinkers assess the consequences of acting on those beliefs.

Application: The teacher can ask the children to state the implications of material in their texts, especially when the text materials lack clarity. The process can help children better understand the meaning of a passage. "What does this imply, or mean? If this is true, what else must be true? What were, or would be, the consequences of this action, policy, solution? How do you know? Why wouldn't this happen instead? Are the consequences desirable? Why or why not?"

The teacher can suggest, or have children suggest, changes in stories, and then ask them to state the implications of these changes and comment on how they affect the meaning of the story.

Teachers can have children explore the implications and consequences of their own beliefs. During discussions, children can compare the implications of ideas from different perspectives and the consequences of accepting each perspective. "How would someone who believes this act? What result would that have?"

Lesson plans in which the strategy is used

Remodelling Language Arts Lessons

Introduction: Getting a Sense of the Whole

Language Arts are mainly concerned with skills of listening, speaking, reading, and writing. These basic skills are practiced through reading and discussing stories and pictures, and learning elements of grammar. Yet these basic skills are conceived superficially by textbook writers: I listen and read in order to be able to recall facts and follow directions; I speak and write in order to present facts, practice using proper formats (for example, question marks) and state my preferences. Texts do not seem to appreciate how all four activities are really practice in *thinking*. I may not have to think in order to remember what is said or written, but I must think in order to understand, evaluate, and incorporate what I hear and read. Similarly with speaking and writing, I don't have to think (much) in order to speak or write facts, compose summaries, and describe preferences, but I must think when I evaluate, try to communicate an important idea or belief, answer questions I have not considered before, or explain why I hold my beliefs. In other words, speaking and writing offer me a chance to develop and clarify my ideas and understanding. Numerous extended discussions are crucial to developing both listening and speaking skills.

Many stories presented in Language Arts curriculum provide material for fruitful, exploratory discussion about ethics, problem solving, emotions, and important issues and concepts. The suggested discussion questions, however, fail to take advantage of the stories to provide students practice engaging in thoughtful discussion. Rather than focusing on and pursuing crucial ideas in depth, many lessons merely contain a jumble of questions, having little relation to one another. Rather than asking students to evaluate a character's behavior (and explain and defend their evaluations), texts tend to simply ask students which characters they liked best.

We recommend, then, that discussions about stories become occasions for students to practice developing and explaining their ideas, and listening and responding to the ideas of others.

Students should be encouraged to probe beneath the surface of issues and ideas found in stories, to take their own ideas, and ideas of others, seriously. They should have a chance to think aloud when talking, consider what others say when listening, organize and expand on their ideas when writing, and analyze and evaluate when reading.

Generally, Language Arts materials fail to take advantage of opportunities to have students think fairmindedly (except, occasionally, when they have students take the "points of view" of animals or inanimate objects). Especially when discussing issues important to children, for instance, common disputes between parents and children, students should be encouraged to seriously consider points of view that oppose their own. Whenever possible, discussion should foster insight into egocentricity. Students should consider such questions as, "Is it ever hard to listen carefully to ideas with which you disagree? Why?"

Text questions frequently ask students what an important concept or idea means. Yet they do not have students analyze it in depth. They do not have them compare examples with examples of opposite ideas, discuss values implicit in using some concept (such as 'good sport'), or explore the implications of applying the concept.

When discussing feelings, texts rarely ask students to consider the relationship between what someone feels and what he or she thinks.

When text questions do not require students to state the issue or problem, the teacher should do so. Text questions fail to ask students to discuss at length the requirements for settling an issue or problem (that is, "Do we have to clarify ideas? Do we need facts? Are we evaluating anything? etc.") They typically don't have students discuss the criteria for judging solutions, compare possible solutions, or describe what is wrong with bad solutions.

Texts discourage independent thought by presenting techniques and concepts as self evident. Students are not required to consider alternative techniques or concepts. Nor do texts have students discuss the purpose of using a technique or concept.

Texts fail to teach critical vocabulary (such as 'infer,' 'relevant') even when such ideas are under discussion. Furthermore, the inferences students are asked to make are not distinguished from what they can observe or must guess. Students are asked to provide answers to questions even when the most appropriate response would be "I don't know" or "I can't tell." Furthermore, the texts lack valuable discussions concerning the potential problems caused by unjustified inferences.

The Language Arts In Perspective

Language arts, as a domain of learning, principally covers the study of literature and the arts of reading and writing. All three areas — literature, reading and writing — deal with the art of imagining, interpreting, and expressing *in language* how people *do live* and how they *might live* their lives. All three areas involve expression through command of language. Of course, there is no command of language separate from command of thought and no command of thought without command of language.

Very few children grow up to publish novels, poems, or short stories, but presumably all should begin to develop insight into the value of literature. Children should learn to enjoy the excitement of a good story. They should begin to see how stories can help us make sense of our lives. They should begin to learn how to express themselves clearly, precisely, and accurately. Through this process, they will begin to learn to *think* clearly, precisely, and accurately.

In words and ideas there is power — power to understand and describe, to take apart and put together, to create systems of beliefs and multiple conceptions of life. Literature displays this power, and skilled reading apprehends it. Unfortunately, most students leave school with little of this insight and skill. Few gain command of the language they use or even a sense of how to gain that command. To the extent that students have not achieved a command of the language in which they express themselves, they will struggle when called upon to interpret literature. They will find reading and writing frustrating and unrewarding. Because the foundations for such insights and skills are not typically laid in elementary education, it is difficult to develop them in students' minds later on. It is necessary to build for insights and skills over an extended period of time, over years, not just months. It is crucial that K–3 lay a solid foundation for intellectual and emotional development.

Present standard practice, K–12, does not sufficiently emphasize the sense-making function of language. Students, as a result, do not approach the written word with an attitude that what they read should make sense to them. So, very often when they make a mistake, they fail to catch it. Many students have the idea that reading means starting at the first word and plowing on to the last period. They don't realize that good reading means pausing, checking your understanding, skimming back and re-reading what was unclear, reading some sentences twice, etc. The way reading is taught causes students to put all writing into two categories: readable without problems or struggle, and impossible to read, so give up. They don't learn that if something they read doesn't make sense, there are things they can do to "crack the code". The place to establish the right attitudes and habits of reading is from the beginning, K–3.

The task of laying foundations for love of literature and language and for the command of language that that love presupposes needs to be clearly conceived and systematically addressed. It involves cultivating a new and different conception of literature, of reading, and of writing. It is a profound challenge. However, if we value students learning to think for themselves, we cannot ignore, we must meet, this challenge. If a basic goal of English classes is to instill a lifelong love of reading, we must seriously confront why most students end up with little or no interest in literature.

We need to think seriously about the world in which they live: the music they listen to, the TV programs and movies they watch, the desires they pursue, the frustrations they experience, and the values that are embedded in their lives differently. We must design our instruction so that students systematically and critically confront how they are actually living their lives and how, if they can gain some insights and skills, they might live their lives. For example, we should help our students see through the superficiality of most popular TV programs in comparison to great works of literature.

Most teachers can probably enumerate the most common features and recurring themes of, say, many students' entertainment: snugly animals, danger, excitement, fun, music, car chases, exploding planets, hideous creatures, mayhem, stereotypes, cardboard characters, all problems solvable in thirty minutes, and so on. The lyrics and values of most popular music are equally accessible, expressing as they do an exciting, fast-moving, sentimentalized, and superficial world of cool-looking "dudes".

Good English instruction must respect and challenge children's attitudes. Ignoring their preferences doesn't alter those preferences. Children must learn to assess for themselves the relative worth of popular entertainment and quality works. Children need opportunities to scrutinize and evaluate the forms of entertainment they prefer. They need to assess the messages they receive from them, the conceptions of life they presuppose, and the values they manifest.

As instruction is now designed, children typically ignore what they hear, read, and reiterate in school work. They may follow the teacher's request to explain why a particular story conveys an important truth, but for most this becomes a ritual performance for the teacher's benefit, having little influence on the child's actual beliefs and values.

Critical thinking can help children to begin the process of refining their tastes and establishing a foundation for insights into language. We should teach beginning with Kindergarten with this end in mind. In any case, under no conditions should we try to force or order children to say what they don't believe. A well-reasoned, if wrong-headed, rejection of a "good" story is better than mindless praise of it.

The problem is not that we don't expose students to important "content"; it is that we do not design instruction, on the whole, so that children must *think their way into and through* the content. To see this more clearly, we should make clear to ourselves the guiding ideals we want to underlie our instruction. We should then start to monitor our teaching to see whether these ideals are actually being cultivated by how we teach on a day to day basis.

Think about the Ideal Student

In addition to the need to enter sympathetically into the world of our students, appreciating how and why they think and act as they do, we must also have a clear conception of what changes we are hoping to cultivate. Consider language itself and the way in which an ideal student might approach it. We want children to become sensitive to language, striving to understand and use it thoughtfully, accurately, and clearly. We want them to begin to become autonomous thinkers and so begin to command rather than be commanded by language.

As Critical Reader

Critical readers approach stories as an opportunity to live imaginatively within another's world or experience, to consider someone else's view of things. They come to realize that the same story can legitimately be understood differently by different readers. They become interested in how others read a story. This experience is analogous to the recognition that the same situation can be understood differently by different people who bring a different point of view and different experiences, to the situation. Young children need many opportunities to read and interpret not only stories, but their own experiences as well. They need to begin to talk to others about what this or that story, what this or that character, what this or that situation *means*.

Young readers must learn that a story does not explain itself, but must be "figured out". They must learn to try out different possible meanings. They must begin to listen to and consider what other students think about what a story or element of a story means. They must begin to learn the difference between passive, impressionistic reading and active, reflective reading. They must begin to learn to question, organize, interpret, and synthesize. They must not only begin to interpret, they must also begin to recognize their interpretations *as interpretations*, and to grasp the value of considering alternative interpretations.

Only as they come to recognize their interpretations as such, will they begin to see the need to test, revise, and refine their interpretations. Only then will they begin to make ideas their own, accepting what makes most sense, rejecting what is ill-thought-out, distorted, and false, thus fitting their new understanding into their existing frameworks of thought. The best way to do this is by discussions and assignments — including many small groups engaged in cooperative learning — in which students express and consider alternative interpretations.

Consider, for example, the classic story, *The Deer-Slayer*, by James Fenimore Cooper. It begins with the lines: "In upper New York state, along the Hudson and Mohawk rivers, the warlike Iroquois

112

Indians were rampaging ... scalping, pillaging, massacring the white man who was trying to make a home in the wilderness that was part of America." As one reads on, one finds lines like: "mad to help any Indian .... Not one of them is a white man's friend", and "The Governor's raised the price on Indian scalps. Fifty pounds for each scalp you get." Throughout the story, one meets two kinds of Indians, good ones and bad ones. The "good" ones always work with and for the settlers. The bad ones are continually characterized as "savages" and "barbarians". They torture those they capture.

In this story, as well as others by Cooper *(The Last of the Mohicans* and *The Pathfinder)*, a foundation is laid for many self-serving myths about early American settlers and Native-Americans. The foundation is laid for hundreds of Hollywood movies about cowboys and Indians and, in line with this same "good guys-bad guys" view of the world, hundreds of movies about cops and robbers, "Americans" and their evil enemies, etc. Children are quite familiar with this simplistic picture of the world from the cartoons they watch on Saturday and Sunday mornings. James Fenimore Cooper's stories are not taught K–3, but the stories written for this level often reflect a similar simplistic way of thinking. We should design our reading instruction so that children are encouraged to question it.

As Critical Writer

Command of reading and command of writing go hand-in-hand. All of the understanding, attitudes, and skills we have just explored have parallels in writing. Critical writers recognize the challenge of putting their ideas and experiences into words. They recognize that inwardly many of our ideas are a jumble, some supporting and some contradicting other ideas, some vague, some clear, some true, some false, some expressing insights, and some reflecting prejudices and mindless conformity. Because critical writers realize that they only partially understand and only partially command their own ideas and experiences, they recognize a double difficulty in making those ideas and experiences accessible to others.

As young readers, children need to begin to recognize they must *actively* reconstruct an author's meaning; as writers, they need to begin to recognize the parallel need to *actively* construct their own as well as the probable meanings given by their readers. In short, while writing, critical writers engage in tasks that parallel the ones they engage in while reading. Both are challenging; both organize, engage, and develop the mind; and both require the full and heightened involvement of critical and creative thought. The sooner we begin to cultivate these insights and skills by the activities that take place in our classes, the better.

As Critical Listener

The most difficult condition in which to learn is in that of a listener. It is normal and natural for people to become passive when listening, to leave to the speaker the responsibility to express and clarify, to organize and exemplify, to develop and conclude. The art of becoming a critical listener is therefore the hardest and the last skill that students develop. Of course, most students never develop this art. Most students remain passive and impressionistic in their listening throughout their lives.

Yet this need not be the case. If we introduce young children to the arts of critical reading and writing, we can also introduce them to the art of critical listening. Once again, each of the understandings, attitudes, and skills of reading and writing have parallels in listening. Once again, we begin with basics. There is the same challenge to sort out, to analyze, and to consider possible interpretations, the same need to ask questions, to probe assumptions, and to trace implications. As listeners, we must follow the path of another person's thought. Listening is every bit as dialogical as reading and writing. Furthermore, we cannot go back over the words of the speaker as we can in reading, so there is all the more reason to emphasize the need for and the nature of active listening. There are many ways to encourage active listening K–3.

One of our most important responsibilities is to model active listening in front of our children. If a child says something, we must demonstrate by our response that we are "actively" engaged in a thoughtful process of figuring out, or at least trying to figure out, what the child is saying. We should draw the students into this process.

To sum up, the ideal English student, as you can see, is quite like the ideal student in other areas of learning; critical reading, writing, and listening are required in all subject areas. Yet the language arts are more central to education than perhaps any other area. Without command of one's native language, no significant learning can take place. Even other domains of learning must utilize this command. The ideal English student should therefore come close to being the ideal learner. While helping our children to gain command of reading, writing, and listening, we should see ourselves as laying the foundation for all thought and learning. The time to begin cultivating these ideals is as early as possible. The later we begin, the further away from the ideal will we end.

Ideal Instruction

Considering the ideal reader, writer, and listener paves the way for a brief overview of ideal instruction. In each case, we should use our understanding of the ideal as a model to move toward, as an organizer for our behavior, not as an empty or unrealistic dream. Reading, writing, and listening, as critical thinking activities, help to organize and develop learning. Each is based on a recognition that, if we actively probe and analyze, dialogue and digest, question and synthesize, we will begin to grasp and follow alternative schemes of meaning and belief.

Each of us lives in a somewhat different world. Each of us has somewhat different ideas, goals, values, and experiences. Each of us constructs somewhat different meanings to live by. And we do this from the early days of our lives, not only when we grow up. In ideal instruction, we want our children to discover and begin to understand different worlds so that they can better understand and develop their own. We want them to struggle to understand the meanings of others so they can better understand their own meanings. We want all children to begin this struggle, but each within the context of the stories and experiences that they are capable of understanding.

Unfortunately, most instructional guides in the language arts do not have a unified approach to this goal. They are often a patchwork, as if constructed by a checklist mentality, as if each act of learning were independent of the one that precedes or follows it. They typically lack a global concept of literature, language, reading, writing, and listening. Even grammar is treated as a separate, unconnected set of rules and regulations.

This is not what we want, and this is not how we should design our instruction. Rather, we should look for opportunities to tie dimensions of language arts instruction together. There is no reason for treating any dimension of language arts instruction as unconnected to the rest. Thus far, we have talked about reading, writing, listening, and literature as ways of constructing and organizing meanings. We can now use this central concept to show how one can tie grammar to the rest of language arts instruction, for clearly grammar itself can be understood as an organized system for expressing meanings.

Each "subject" of each sentence, after all, represents a focus for the expression of meaning, something that we are thinking or talking about. Each "predicate" represents what is said about the subject. All adjectives and adverbs are ways of qualifying or rendering more precise the meanings we express in subjects and predicates. By the same token, each sentence we write has some sort of meaningful relationship to the sentences that precede and follow it. The same principle holds for the paragraphs we write. In each paragraph, there must be some unifying thing that we are talking about and something that we are saying about it.

To put this another way, at each level of language arts instruction, we should aim at helping the student gain insight into the idea that there is a "logic" to the language arts. That is, that all the elements of the language arts make sense, and make sense not only in relation to each other, but also in relation to our everyday experience of the world.

This is a key insight that builds upon the idea of constructing and organizing meanings; it makes even more clear how we can tie all of the language arts together. Basic grammar has a logic to it, and that logic can be understood. Individual words and phrases also have a logic to them and, therefore, they too can be understood. When we look into language use with a sense that there is an intelligible structure to be understood, our efforts are rewarded. Unfortunately, we face a special obstacle in accomplishing this purpose.

Typically, young children treat the meanings of words as absolute and univocal. On this view, problems of meaning are settled by asking an authority for "the" meaning. Children have difficulty believing that the same word can have different meanings. We need to cultivate this recognition. But that is not all. We also need to foster their recognition that when we say something our words have implications that we should be responsible for. If we say "I promise", we have, for example, made a commitment that we should recognize.

To persuade children that it is possible to use words precisely, we must begin the process of demonstrating to them that all of the words in the language have established uses with established *implications* that they must learn to respect. For example, consider the words 'friend' and 'acquaintance'. If I call some people my friends, I imply that I know them well and am fond of them. If I call others acquaintances, I merely imply that I have met them, not that I know them well, not that I am necessarily fond of them. If I say that a country is democratic, I imply that the people rule that country. Each word in the language has established meanings which we must help students to learn to respect.

There is a parallel insight necessary for understanding how to arrange sentences in logical relationships to each other. Our language provides a wide variety of adverbial phrases that make connecting our sentences together easier. Here, as above, children need to begin to learn and respect this established logic. We need to look for opportunities to start this process.

Group I

Connectives	How they are used	Examples
besides what's more furthermore in addition	To add another thought.	Two postal cards are often more effective than one letter. *Besides*, they are cheaper.
for example for instance in other words	To add an illustration or explanation.	There is no such thing as an "unlucky number." *In other words*, this idea is pure superstition.

Group II

Connectives	How they are used	Examples
in fact as a matter of fact	To connect an idea with another one.	Last week I was ill. *In fact*, I had to stay in bed until Monday.
therefore consequently accordingly	To connect an idea with another one that follows from it.	The President vetoed the bill. *Consequently*, it never became a law.

Group III

of course to be sure though	To grant an exception or limitation.	He said he would study all day. I doubt it, *though.*
still however on the other hand nevertheless rather	To connect two contrasting ideas.	I like painting; *however*, I can't understand modern art.

Group IV

first next finally meanwhile later afterwards nearby eventually above beyond in front	To arrange ideas in order, time, or space.	*First*, drink some fruit juice. *Next*, have a bowl of soup. Then eat the meat. *Finally*, have some pie and coffee.
in short in brief to sum up in summary in conclusion	To sum up several ideas.	Scientists say that we should eat food that has all the proteins, fats, and vitamins we need. *In short*, they recommend a balanced diet.

Asking Key Questions

Language and grammar

Keeping in mind the idea that language and grammar are, on the whole, logical, we should ask questions that help children begin to discover this. What follows in the next paragraph is a variety of questions that ought to be raised in a variety of contexts. You would not, of course, raise them all at once. Some may be the basis of a series of cooperative learning activities in which student groups develop their own answers to one of these questions and report their answers, and how they came to these answers, to the class as a whole.

"What is a sentence? How is it different from a group of words? What is a paragraph? How is it different from a group of sentences? Why are some ways of using a word right and others wrong? What different kinds of sentences are there? When and how should each be used? Why follow the rules of grammar? How does punctuation help the reader? How does knowing about grammar help you to write? Read?"

Literature

Stories have their own logic. Events don't just happen. They make sense within the meanings and thinking of their authors. When we ask a question, there should be a method to it. The questions should lead students to discover how to come to terms with the logic of the story, at least to the meaning that they are giving to the story. In every case, we should have students support their answers by referring to passages in the story. It is not their particular answers that are of greatest importance, but rather how they support their answers with reasons and references to the story.

"What happened? Why? What is the author trying to convey? Why is this important? What is the main character like? How do you know? How do their experiences relate to my experience or to those of people around me? How realistic are the characters? How consistent? If they aren't (realistic, consistent), why not? What conflicts occur in the story? What is the nature of this conflict? What relationship does it have to my life? What meaning does that conflict have for the character? For me? What does this work tell me about the people and everyday life around me? Can I identify with them? Should I? How does the view presented in this work relate to my view? To what extent do I accept the way this story represents people? Are they like the people I know? To what extent or in what way would I change it to make it more 'lifelike'? How does it relate to ways of looking at things that I've found in other stories?"

These categories of questions would need, of course, to be formulated in different ways to be intelligible to students at different grade levels. In many cases you would have to build up to them with particular preparatory activities. None of these questions are intended as ready-made for this or that classroom. They are intended merely to stimulate your thinking about the general kind of questions that, sooner or later, in one form or another, must be raised.

Persuasive writing

All people spend a good deal of their time trying to persuade others to accept or believe something or other. Young children often develop considerable skill in persuading their parents to allow them to do this or that or to buy this or that. Persuasive writing, like all persuasion, has a straightforward logic. In it, a writer attempts to get the readers to take on the writer's perspective on something. We, as readers, need to grasp what is being said and judge whether or not to accept it, whether or not it makes sense to accept it. Young children need to be introduced into the art of rational persuasion. They need to learn how to express themselves clearly (If we don't know what they are saying how can we be persuaded?). They need to learn how to back up what they are saying with good reasons, with evidence, with relevant examples and illustrations from their experience, and with intelligible explanations.

They also need to learn to respond to the persuasive appeals of others with basic critical thinking tools. Television ads, television programs, peer groups, and adults — all attempt to persuade them. Children need to begin to learn how to develop their own persuasive appeals at the same time that they begin to learn how to rationally assess the persuasive appeals of others. As always, we need to learn to continually model these processes for them, finding ways to engage them in small groups carrying these processes out for themselves. In general, we need to help children begin to think analytically and reasonably.

"What, exactly, is the author trying to say? Why? How does the author support what he is saying with reasons, evidence, or experiences? What examples can I think of to further illuminate these ideas? What are the consequences of believing or doing as the author says? What kind of writing is this? How has the writer attempted to achieve her purpose? Have I good reason to accept what is being said? Doubt it? How could I check, or better evaluate, what is being said? What has been left out? Distorted? How do these ideas relate to mine?"

As always, these questions are meant to be merely suggestive, not necessarily to be the actual questions that you will ask this or that student. There are many possible reformulations of these questions which would render them more accessible, more understandable to young children. And, as always, children learn to be comfortable with analytic questions over time. We must be ever vigilant not to overwhelm them with more than they can take in at any given time.

Writing

Writing has a logic. Good substance poorly arranged loses most of its value. Whatever the principle of order chosen, thought must progress from somewhere to somewhere else. It must follow a definite direction, not ramble aimlessly. In the entire piece, as well as in each section and paragraph, ideally, each sentence should have a place of its own, and a place so plainly its own that it could not be shifted to another place without losing coherence. Children need to begin to discover that disorderly thinking produces disorderly writing and, conversely, orderly writing enhances orderly thinking. They need to change their misconceptions about the writing process: good writers begin with the first sentence and write each sentence perfectly until they get to the end. Children need practice pre-writing rough notes and increasingly refining their work until they are writing final copy.

We need to introduce children to the art of orderly, logical writing. We need to model this process for them. This can be done in a number of ways. If the students have a sufficient reading vocabulary, we can work with the class as a whole writing a short paragraph, asking for suggestions from the class as to how we might begin. Then, once a sentence is on the board we might ask if the sentence is clear, how we might express it more precisely. Then, we can ask for suggestions for a follow-up sentence, for one that elaborates further on what is said in the first sentence. Then, once satisfied with the formulation of that sentence, we might ask for an example to illustrate the point made in the first two sentences. And so we might proceed, working with the class to develop the paragraph. In this way, students can observe minds at work doing the labor of writing. A follow-up to this process might be to have the students work in groups, each group developing its own paragraph on a common main point. Then each group could choose a spokesperson to read its paragraph to the class as a whole and the class could then get both further experience in this process while gaining insight into how others think their way through a writing project. Over time we want students to become habituated to ask questions that help them develop their writing.

Conclusion

In order to foster basic learning in the language arts, it is essential that you develop for yourself a clear sense of the logic of language and of the unity of the language arts. If you model the insight that every dimension of language and literature makes sense, can be figured out, can be brought under our command, can be made useful to us, your children will be much more apt to make this same discovery for themselves. Remember, children are not used to unifying what they study. All too soon they become used to a steady diet of fragmented learning. They become used to forgetting, to studying the same thing over and over, and to everything being self-contained. On the whole, they do not learn organization skills.

Furthermore, most students do not learn the value of clear and precise language usage. Rather they learn to be satisfied with any words that occur to them to say or write. They do not become familiar with good writing. Disciplined thinking typically remains something foreign to them.

If you are to set in motion a new way to learn, a new set of attitudes and insights, a new unified, motivated basis upon which later teachers can build, you must develop patience with your own learning. You must be willing to have your own teaching strategies develop over time. Learning to teach in a critical manner takes a long time, but the implications are then significant — students who learn to use language clearly and precisely for the rest of their lives, students who listen and read critically for the rest of their lives, students who become critical and creative persons for the rest of their lives.

> *Everyone learning to deepen her critical thinking skills and dispositions comes to insights over time. We certainly can enrich and enhance this process, even help it to move at a faster pace, but only in a qualified way. Time to assimilate and grow is essential.*

Evaluative Thinking

(Kindergarten)

Objectives of the remodelled lesson

The students will:
- practice evaluating actions through role–play
- explore the relationship between a person's thoughts and feelings in particular situations
- develop criteria for evaluating people's behavior

Original Lesson Plan

Abstract

The students are put in groups of two or three and assigned a role-playing situation to act out while the rest of the class observes. A discussion follows which includes imagining what would have happened if any part of the situation had been changed, how the students felt about the situation, and whether they have had any similar experiences. The suggested role-play situations included these: a child who is nervous being in front of the class forgets the answer and another child laughs, two children agree to share a toy, and a student shouts a warning as another child starts to run into the street without looking.

from *About Me,* Bernard J. Weiss, et al., 1980. Holt Rinehart and Winston, Publishers. pp. 175–176.

Critique

This lesson is a confusing introduction to evaluative thinking because none of the questions asked call upon the students to evaluate anything. To evaluate accurately and fairly, students should understand what they are evaluating, and why. Critical thinkers are conscious of the standards they use when evaluating so that these, too, become objects of evaluation. Although reasonable people can disagree, making standards or principals themselves objects of evaluation makes rational discussion and agreement more likely.

Although the stories in the original lesson clearly suggest evaluative conclusions, neither the process of evaluation, standards of evaluation, or evaluative conclusions are elicited by the questions. Furthermore, this lesson encourages absolutistic (that is, "all or nothing") thinking, by using stories which describe cases of "all right" or "all wrong" whereas most real-life cases involve at least some degree of shared blame. The value of these exercises, as they stand, lies in showing how our behavior has consequences, and that changing our behavior can change the situation we are in.

Strategies used to remodel

S-20 analyzing or evaluating actions or policies
S-4 exploring thoughts underlying feelings and feelings underlying thoughts
S-15 developing criteria for evaluation: clarifying values and standards
S-35 exploring implications and consequences

Remodelled Lesson Plan S-20

The questions used in the original lesson can be used to elicit situations that the children are familiar with. However, since they don't require students to evaluate, we suggest that they be followed by questions which first call for an evaluation, then clarify what is being evaluated and why.

You might begin discussion of each situation by having students discuss what the characters felt and thought and why. "What happened? How did M feel about it? N? Why? What was each thinking? Why? What makes you think so?" **S-4**

To elicit and probe evaluations in the first situation, the teacher could ask, "Was it better for the second child to have laughed, or to have looked encouragingly? Why? What are we evaluating in this situation? Why is this important?"

The teacher could point out any standards of evaluation the students use. For example, if a student states "It was mean because it hurt his feelings," the teacher could say, "You used the *standard* of not hurting other people's feelings to *conclude* that this was wrong." **S-15**

If a variation is introduced, such as, "He wrote a funny answer on purpose when he forgot the right answer", the teacher can say, "Now we have a different story. How is this story different, and what do we want to say about it? Does this change make you think differently about this? Why or why not?" **S-35**

Listening Ears

(Kindergarten)

Objectives of the remodelled lesson

The students will:
* begin to develop insight into the importance and difficulty of listening to understand
* practice critical listening by restating other students' positions
* discuss how egocentricity can interfere with listening

Original Lesson Plan

Abstract

This lesson introduces the idea of listening by first asking students to sit quietly and listen to the sounds they hear, and then to discuss what they heard. Next, the children look at pictures of a mother rabbit with her babies (ears up and listening), a boy talking to his dog (ears up and listening), and students listening to a crossing guard. The teacher asks questions about who is listening and why, and why it's important to listen.

This is followed by a discussion in which students recall personal experiences of times it was important to listen. Finally, the teacher conducts a listening game of giving directions, and asking a student to follow them.

from *Let's Talk and Listen: Yellow Level Language for Daily Use,* Mildred A. Dawson, et al. Harcourt Brace Jovanovich. 1973. p. 4.

Critique

Although the objective of "Listening Ears" is to learn the importance of listening carefully, discussion is limited to the importance of listening to authorities for instruction and safety. A critical education requires that students be encouraged to listen to new ideas, and other points of view. Unless we understand a position well enough to present it ourselves, we cannot rationally agree or disagree with it. Since no one person can know everything, we should listen to others, distinguish what they know from what they don't know, and adjust our beliefs to accommodate what we have learned.

The original lesson doesn't distinguish *listening as hearing* from *listening as understanding,* and therefore ignores the difficulties of listening to understand. Children should begin to develop the insight that listening requires more than just hearing; it requires a sincere attempt to grasp what is said; listening is active. The biggest difficulties of listening arise from the complexity of the process of understanding, and our natural resistance to ideas different from our own. Listening is hardest when we don't *want* to listen.

Strategies used to remodel

S–22 listening critically: the art of silent dialogue
S–3 exercising fairmindedness
S–7 developing intellectual good faith or integrity
S–2 developing insight into egocentricity or sociocentricity

Remodelled Lesson Plan s–22

We believe that it is crucial to practice incorporating the aforementioned insights about listening into the solutions of genuine problems that arise at school. We encourage teachers to take advantage of as many problems, decisions, and disputes as possible. When students claim to disagree with each other, have them state each other's views fairly and accurately. Ask questions of clarification to elicit points overlooked. Later, you could facilitate a discussion in which students describe any problems they had in trying to listen, and why it was important to listen. **S–3**

Following is a list of questions the teacher can ask to further encourage students to think about the importance and difficulty of listening:

• Why should we listen to other people? Has anything bad happened to you because you didn't listen? When? Why should we listen to friends? Family? Classmates? Teachers? etc.

• When is it hard to listen? Why? Can you think of a time when you weren't listening to someone? Who was trying to talk to you? Why didn't you listen? What were you thinking? Why? **S–7**

• Do you ever act as though you are listening when you aren't? What's the difference between listening and *pretending* to listen?

• How do you feel when people don't listen carefully to you?

• Is it easy or hard to listen *a)* when you are angry, scared, or excited? *b)* to someone you like? *c)* to someone you don't like? *d)* when someone says something that sounds dumb or crazy to you? *e)* when someone says something that you think makes sense or is similar to what you think *f)* when you don't understand?

• How can you tell if someone is listening? What are the differences between being a good listener and not being a good listener? **S–2**

"Corduroy"

(K–1)

by Judy Calonico, Calaveras Unified
Schools, Pine Grove, CA

Objectives of the remodelled lesson

The students will:
- compare perspectives of a mother and daughter in a story
- explore the thoughts underlying the feelings regarding what makes things valuable
- generate and assess solutions
- clarify values and develop criteria to evaluate toys

Standard Approach

A Teddy bear named Corduroy sits on a shelf at a large department store. A little girl sees him and wants to buy him, but her mother says no because they are out of time and the teddy bear is missing a button. After the store closes, the bear searches for his button because he wants to be bought by the child. He looks all over the store and finally ends up in the bed department where he sees a button on a mattress and tries to pull it off. He falls off the mattress, knocks over a lamp and the night guard finds him and returns him to the toy department. The child returns, buys him, sews on the button and Corduroy happily joins her family.

Students are asked questions like the following: Who is Corduroy? Where is he? How did he get his name? Does anyone know what the material called corduroy looks and feels like? (Pass around a piece of corduroy.) Why did Corduroy go out into the store? Why was it important to find his button? Where was he when he tried to pull one up? Why couldn't he get it? How did the story end?

Critique

The original lesson focused on a lot of factual recall and a narrow line of questioning. No other point of view was suggested, nor was there any personal tie-in.

Strategies used to remodel

S–25 reasoning dialogically: comparing perspectives, interpretations, or theories
S–19 generating or assessing solutions
S–15 developing criteria for evaluation: clarifying values and standards
S–4 exploring thoughts underlying feelings and feelings underlying thoughts
S–26 reasoning dialectically: evaluating perspectives, interpretations, or theories

Remodelled Lesson Plan s-25

To lay the foundation for exploring thoughts underlying feelings and comparing perspectives in the story, the teacher could first set up a role play in which several children are wearing pictures of toys while a mother and child walk past shopping for the best toy. After a few minutes, stop and ask the toys how they felt, then ask the child how he or she was choosing, then ask the mother how she was choosing.

Read the story aloud and ask the following questions to encourage students to explore the story's meaning and assess Corduroy's solution:

What was Corduroy doing in the store after it closed? Why did he think it was important to find the button? Do you think it was important for him to find the button? How else could he have solved the problem of the missing button? Was it really necessary for him to have a button in order for him to be bought? **S-19** Do you think an adult would buy a teddy bear with a button missing? If not, why not? Why do you think the girl bought him anyway? **S-15** What would you have done? How did the girl feel after she bought Corduroy? Why? How do you know how she felt? What do you think Corduroy felt? Why? How do you know? **S-4**

"Can you think of a different way to end the story? If your favorite animal could think, what would he or she have thought while being bought?"

editors' note: The teacher could extend the discussion on the differences between the perspectives and standards of the girl and her mother (a common sort of difference between children and grown-ups). "Why do some people care about things like missing buttons and other people don't? How important was the missing button to the mother? Why? What reasons could she have? The girl? Why? Corduroy? Why? What was the most important thing about Corduroy for the mother? The girl? Why did the girl want Corduroy? Why didn't the missing button alter her feelings? Would the missing button have stopped any of the girl's plans for Corduroy? Why or why not? What does this difference between mother and daughter tell us about their values — what they think is important? Do you think the missing button is important? Why or why not? What's your best reason? What's the best reason on the other side? **S-15** Have you ever seen or experienced a similar disagreement? How was it similar? What do you think of it? What does that tell us about your values?" **S-26**

• With whom do you identify? Who do you understand? Who are you rooting for? Why?

"The Gingerbread Man"

(K–1)

by Pamela Lane-Stamm, Mattole Union
School District, Petrolia, CA

Objectives of the remodelled lesson

The students will:
- discuss the nature of what is real and not real
- practice suppositional thinking
- engage in dialectical thinking by evaluating the perspectives of the gingerbread man and the lady
- develop intellectual good faith by discussing the problem of selfishness

Standard Approach

> The teacher reads the classic story about the gingerbread man to the class. A lady makes up a gingerbread cookie batter, forms the gingerbread man and cooks him in the oven. But as she opens the oven door to take the gingerbread man out, he leaps off the cookie sheet and runs out the front door calling, "Run, run as fast as you can. You can't catch me, I'm the gingerbread man!" The lady, then a rabbit, and later a bear all try to catch the gingerbread man. But he outruns them all. The gingerbread man reaches a river that he must cross in order to stay ahead of his pursuers and a fox offers to take him across on his tail. As the river gets deeper, the fox coaxes him to climb onto his back and then his nose. Then the fox eats the gingerbread man.
>
> After listening to the story the children make pairs of gingerbread men out of construction paper and play a matching game. For an art project they can make rubbings of them. In addition, the children can take pictures of events in the story that are mixed up and sequence them into the same order in which they occurred in the story. They may also bake gingerbread.

Critique

Although the after-reading activities are a nice "hands–on" experience with gingerbread men and sequencing the pictures is a valuable way to recall the events that took place in the story, the story isn't discussed after the reading. Discussion should include the children's ideas concerning the realness of the story and the characters in the story. This topic alone would take up an hour or more and the children's thoughts on this matter suggest an evaluative as well as a descriptive judgment. It points to what the child considers to be serious and genuine, authentic and actual. From there, another discussion can take place from the position of assuming the events and characters are real, then what would have happened if ...? and present various situations and problems for the class to solve. The other activities could occur after these discussions.

Strategies used to remodel

S-14 clarifying and analyzing the meanings of words or phrases
S-18 analyzing or evaluating arguments, interpretations, beliefs, or theories
S-35 exploring implications and consequences
S-26 reasoning dialectically: evaluating perspectives, interpretations, or theories
S-7 developing intellectual good faith or integrity

Remodelled Lesson Plan

After the story has been read, the teacher can initiate a discussion about the concept of 'for real' with questions like these, "Was the gingerbread man 'for real'? Was the lady 'for real'? Were the rabbit, bear, and fox 'for real'? Is your desk, your head, a cartoon show, a hole in the ground, a hole in the air 'for real'?" Be ready for lots of unexpected answers and additional questions. After this, baking gingerbread men could be an additional activity, allowing the kids to smell, touch, and taste the ginger and molasses and perhaps discussing their realness as you go. **S-14**

On the following day, after rereading the story or using another text for retelling the story, initiate another discussion by asking about the differences and similarities of the two stories, if two texts are used. You might then talk about assumptions and ask, "Assuming these stories are 'for real', why did the gingerbread man think nobody could catch him? What was the gingerbread man assuming? (That he could trust the fox.) What were the fallacies in his thinking? **S-18** Could the gingerbread man have avoided being eaten? What would have happened if he hadn't been caught and eaten?" **S-35** After this, cutting out pairs of gingerbread men and playing a matching game would be a nice extension. Pairs of the other characters may also be made for the game.

editors' note: Students could also explore and assess the points of view of the gingerbread man and the lady. "Why did the lady feel that she was justified in wanting to eat the gingerbread man? What do you think her reasons were? Why did the gingerbread man feel that the woman shouldn't eat him? What do you think his reasons were? Do their reasons make sense to you? In what ways is the lady right? In what ways is the gingerbread man right? Why?" **S-26**

By discussing the selfishness of the lady, the students could recognize their tendency to judge others more strictly than they judge themselves. Ask the students, "How was the lady selfish? Would you have behaved differently towards the gingerbread man? Why or why not? Would it have been easy to behave unselfishly in this circumstance?" **S-7**

"Goldilocks and the Three Bears"

(K–2)

by Jim Georgevich, Billie Forman, Karen
Holub, and Betty Allen, Greensboro
Public Schools, Greensboro, NC

Objectives of the remodelled lesson

The students will:

- through Socratic discussion, clarify and explore the differing perspectives of storybook characters
- examine how people feel when their rights have been violated
- explore the feelings that underlie anger
- evaluate story characters' actions

Standard Approach

After reading the story, the teacher asks students about factual information to check for comprehension.

Critique

Students are rarely given a chance to think about how the different characters in this fairy tale would respond differently to the action of the story, and how those different responses are, in part, determined by different points of view. Students miss a valuable opportunity to think about, verbalize, and share ideas concerning different points of view and how different people will interpret the same sequence of events in different ways.

Strategies used to remodel

S–24 practicing Socratic discussion: clarifying and questioning beliefs, theories, or perspectives
S–4 exploring thoughts underlying feelings and feelings underlying thoughts
S–20 analyzing or evaluating actions or policies

Remodelled Lesson Plan s–24

The teacher will read the story to students and discuss with them how and why Goldilocks enters the Bears' house. They will discuss the events from Goldilocks' viewpoint: What reasons could she have for entering a stranger's house without permission? What do you think about these reasons? Discuss how Goldilocks might have felt when the bears came home and why.

Then, they will discuss events from the Bears' standpoint. Role play how the Bears felt finding an intruder in their house. "How did they feel? Why?

What do you suppose they were thinking? Why? **S–4** What actions did they take against Goldilocks? Were their actions justified? What are some other possible actions? What consequences resulted from the course of events? **S–20** How does this differ from real life?"

> *The reader should keep in mind the connection between the principles and applications, on the one hand, and the character traits of a fairminded critical thinker, on the other. Our aim, once again, is not a set of disjointed skills, but an integrated, committed, thinking person.*

"Goldilocks" II

(K–1)

by Judy Calonico, Calaveras Unified
Schools, Pine Grove, CA

Objectives of the remodelled lesson

The students will:
- practice fairmindedness by examining the bears' perspective through a similar experience and through discussion
- evaluate Goldilocks's behavior
- discuss significant differences between their experience and that of the bears

Standard Approach

> Read the story aloud to the class and ask simple recall questions (chronology), role-play the story, and discuss the specialized vocabulary and the origin of her name. Then ask questions about whether or not she should have done what she did.

Critique

The questioning was based on factual recall, vocabulary development, and a simple discussion of right and wrong.

Strategies used to remodel

S–3 exercising fairmindedness
S–20 analyzing or evaluating actions or policies
S–29 noting significant similarities and differences

Remodelled Lesson Plan s–3

> Read the story aloud just before a recess break, then have student helpers lay out snacks for all students. Explain to the students that the treat is not ready, but that it will be after recess. During the time they are out, remove some of the chairs and a portion of each child's snack. Leave evidence like crumbs or smears of peanut butter. Allow the children back into the room, let a minute or so pass, then ask them:
>
> What do you think happened here? How do you know this? How do you feel about this? Why? Is there a reason that this might have happened? We just finished reading the story "Goldilocks". What happened in that story? In what

ways are the bears like you? How do you think they felt? Were they right in feeling upset? What do you think Goldilocks was thinking as she explored the house of the bears? How did she feel? Was she right? What other choices might Goldilocks have made besides going into their home? What do you think this story is trying to teach us? **S–20**

editors' note: The teacher could also have students compare their experience with that of the bears. "How was this like what happened to the bears? How was it unlike it? How important are those differences? Why? Would the differences between the situations lead to different feelings and reactions? Why or why not?" **S–29**

Every trivial lesson you abandon leaves more time to stimulate critical thinking.

"A Toy for Mike"

(1ˢᵗ Grade)

Objectives of the remodelled lesson

The students will:
- practice suppositional thinking
- practice stating and clarifying the problem under discussion
- compare different solutions
- explain why some proposed solutions are not good

Original Lesson Plan

Abstract

Students read a story about Pat and Ann who have a problem. While they are trying to wrap a ball as a present for their friend Mike, the string breaks. They are in a hurry to go. Pat solves the problem by putting the ball in a bag they have decorated. Students are asked if they think Pat's plan was a good idea.

In the second section, entitled "Think About It", children read three problem statements ("Dad gets a flat when he is leaving for work"), and put a check next to two of the three solutions presented. ("Dad will ...Walk to work; Fix it; Wait for the rain to stop".) Then they discuss their choices and suggest other solutions.

from *Tag In And Out All Around,*
Theodore L. Harris et al. The Economy
Company, 1973. pp. T204–T205.

Critique

Although students are asked if they think Pat's solution is a good idea, they are not asked to state the problem, discuss the criteria for a good solution, or compare the solution to other solutions. The students should reflect on solutions and how to evaluate them, and begin to develop well thought-out, practical ideas about choosing good solutions. The "Think About It" activity is a classic work-book approach with two good answers and one absurd (or potentially dangerous) possibility. It is a "decode the words" lesson masquerading as a problem solving lesson. It could be improved with questioning and discussion.

Strategies used to remodel

S-19 generating or assessing solutions
S-13 clarifying issues, conclusions, or beliefs
S-31 distinguishing relevant from irrelevant facts

Remodelled Lesson Plan S-19

First, after the students read the story, we suggest asking, "What was Pat and Ann's problem? Why was it a problem? **S-13** How could they have solved it differently? How can we decide which solution is best? What facts are relevant? Why? What would a good solution involve?" **S-31**

Then, for each problem in the "Think About It" section, you might ask "What is the problem? What would you need to know to decide on a good solution? **S-13** What facts are relevant?" (Distance from work, availability of other transportation, availability of a spare tire.) **S-31** Encourage the use of "if, then" statements when describing the desirability of the solution ("If work is near home, then it's best to walk.").Discuss the solutions in the text that the children did not choose. Ask, "Why do you think this solution was a bad one? Does it make sense? What do you think would have happened had the person chosen this solution? Why?"

The critique should inform the remodel; the remodel should arise out of the critique.

"Moving Day"

(1ˢᵗ Grade)

Objectives of the remodelled lesson

The students will:
- explore the relationship between the thoughts and feelings about moving by examining a story character's assumptions and change of feelings
- practice Socratic discussion about moving and other major changes
- exercise fairmindedness by realizing that people often have very different feelings about major changes

Original Lesson Plan

Abstract

Students discuss their feelings about moving and read a story about Jud. Jud is unhappy about moving into an apartment,away from his friends and home. But when he moves, he discovers that he likes the elevator in his building, makes a new friend, and his feelings change.

Students are asked to describe Jud's feelings and explain his behavior, order story events, and find sentences in the story which answer a number of questions.

from *Sun and Shadow, Reading Skills 4*,
Margaret Early, et al., Harcourt Brace
Jovanovich. 1970. pp. 169–175.

Critique

Although students discuss how Jud first felt about moving to his new home and that he felt differently after he was there, they are not encouraged to recognize how the change in Jud's feelings arose from the change in his perception of his new situation. This lesson is a missed opportunity to have students practice seeing the relationship between thoughts and feelings and explore the character's assumptions. With practice they can begin to see how thoughts and feelings influence each other.

Strategies used to remodel

S–4 exploring thoughts underlying feelings and feelings underlying thoughts
S–30 examining or evaluating assumptions
S–3 exercising fairmindedness
S–24 practicing Socratic discussion: clarifying and questioning beliefs, theories, or perspectives

Remodelled Lesson Plan s-4

After reading the first half of the story, entitled "Moving Day", you might ask the following questions: How did Jud feel about moving? What did Jud think that made him feel sad? Angry? etc. (He would miss his friends, he would miss his house, it wasn't his decision.) What did he assume about his new home? (He wouldn't have any friends.) Could he have thought of something that would have made him feel less sad? What? (He will make new friends; it might be fun to live in a new place.) **S-30**

After completing the last half of the story, entitled "The Apartment", you could ask: What changed toward the end of the story? What did Jud learn that made him feel better? What makes you think so? Why would that make him feel better?

As an extension, the class could have a Socratic discussion: Does everyone feel the same about moving as Jud did? Why might someone else feel excited about moving? Afraid? etc. How do you feel about moving? Why might someone feel differently than you? **S-3** How can one person have so many different feelings about one event? Is moving an important event? Do people often have different, even opposite feelings about an important event? What are other important changes that people experience? Is that change like moving in some ways? How? Different? How? How might that affect our feelings about it? **S-24**

Susan, Tom, & Betty

(1ˢᵗ Grade)

Objectives of the remodelled lesson

The students will:
- practice Socratic discussion by learning how to distinguish and ask different types of questions
- practice making good inferences by evaluating the evidence in pictures
- distinguish cases in which they can make good inferences from those which they must guess or make up an answer, thereby developing intellectual humility
- make interdisciplinary connections by applying their categories of questions to questions in other subjects

Original Lesson Plan

Abstract

Students discuss three rows of pictures in which children are portrayed engaging in different activities: chasing a dog that took a jacket, coming home after a skating accident, getting the newspaper from the lawn, fixing a bike, meeting father at the airport, knocking over a can of paint while painting a wagon, receiving a dress, bringing flowers to the teacher, eating an ice cream cone. Students are asked to describe events preceding and following the scenes pictured, make judgments about the characters' personalities, and make up short stories about them.

from *Book I–1 Ginn Elementary English, Teachers' Edition*, 1968, by Silver Burdett & Ginn Inc. pp. 33–34.

Critique

This lesson lacks a firm purpose. It could be given an important objective such as teaching students that there are different kinds of questions. To take advantage of the hodge-podge of questions in this lesson, the remodel will focus on this task.

The section of the original lesson entitled "Interpreting the Pictures" provides four different kinds of questions without distinguishing them. Such lack of discrimination may lead students to believe that they can be equally certain in all cases. Some of the questions, such as, "Where is Tom in this picture?" and, "Is father just leaving or returning?" call upon students to make good inferences from pictures. Others, such as, "What do you think the dog will do with Susan's clothes?" and, "What do you think will happen after Susan gets in the house?" have more than one reasonable answer. (The dog might chew the clothes or bury them; Susan might clean her arm, or her mother or a babysitter might clean it.) Some questions, such as, "How can Tom get the paint off the floor?" (which assumes that he spilt the paint on the floor, as opposed to the ground or driveway) contain questionable assumptions — "How can Tom clean up the paint?" would be better. Still others can be answered only by guessing or making up a story "Where do you suppose Tom's father has been? Do you think someone suggested that Betty bring the flowers to her teacher or that she thought of it herself?"

The next section, entitled "Drawing Inferences", contains a number of leading questions such as, "Do you think Susan is thoughtful, careless, or careful?" and "In what ways might she have helped herself in these pictures?" Such questions discourage suspending judgment, and encourage questionable assumptions. (They could be reformulated or dropped.)

We suggest that discussion focus on distinguishing four kinds of questions: the answer is right there, the answer is implied (if we think, we can figure out the answer), there is more than one sensible answer (we have to make an answer up or make up a story), and questions with questionable assumptions (there is something wrong with the question).

Strategies used to remodel

S–24 practicing Socratic discussion: clarifying and questioning beliefs, theories, or perspectives
S–33 giving reasons and evaluating evidence and alleged facts
S–5 developing intellectual humility and suspending judgment
S–13 clarifying issues, conclusions, or beliefs
S–30 examining or evaluating assumptions
S–23 making interdisciplinary connections

Remodelled Lesson Plan S–24

You might begin the lesson by saying, "We're going to talk about these pictures. I'll ask you some questions about them and we'll talk about what kind of questions they are. You can ask more questions and we can talk about what kind of questions you asked." During the rest of the lesson, periodically ask students what questions they can think of. When they have been asked and answered, students can explain what kind of question it is.

Ask a question and have students answer (if they give different answers, let them argue a bit). "How did we answer this question? What did you do? Is this question asking what you know, or asking you to invent a possible answer? Can you see it right there, or did we have to figure out or infer the answer? Can we be sure? How? Is one answer more likely than others? Why? **S–33** Can we rule out any of these answers? Which? Why?" **S–5** As the questioning proceeds, you or the students could start to group the questions. "How did we answer this one? Were there any others like it?" **S–13**

"Is this a 'see it there' question, a 'figure it out' question, or a 'make up a story' question? Is there one obvious answer, or more than one answer that makes sense, or could we give any answer we want? Can we be sure of the answer? Why or why not? Does this question have a problem with it? Does it assume anything that we don't know for sure? What? Why don't we know that?" **S–30**

In subsequent lessons, you could have students use these categories to analyze the questions in their texts in other subjects as well as language arts.

"Do you remember when we talked about different kinds of questions? What different kinds of questions did we talk about? What kind of question is this? Why do you say so?" **S–23**

For a later, follow-up assignment, you could have the children hunt questions in their textbooks in small groups. They could copy each question and write what kind it is, and share and discuss their lists. Students could also compare questions within and between the categories and within and between subjects. **S–23**

The same can be done in discussions or in listening activities.

> *Macro-practice is almost always more important than micro-drill. We need to be continually vigilant against the misguided tendency to fragment, atomize, mechanize, and proceduralize thinking.*

"Help for the Hen"
(1ˢᵗ–2ⁿᵈ)

by Elizabeth Sanders, Diane Shope, and
Kim Dodgen, Greensboro Public
Schools, Greensboro, NC

Objectives of the remodelled lesson

The students will:
- clarify story characters' reasoning through Socratic discussion and critical vocabulary
- make interdisciplinary connections by researching an animal and figuring out what kind of story character it could be

Original Lesson Plan

Abstract

A hen asked different animals to help her, but none agreed, for various reasons. The bird finally told the hen to ask the fox for help. The hen asked the fox and the fox helped the hen eat the muffins. Questions were factual, in sequential order, and very detailed.

Critique

For this story, we would use Socratic questioning to help the children explore the characters' reasoning.

Strategies used to remodel

S-24 practicing Socratic discussion: clarifying and questioning beliefs, theories, or perspectives
S-28 thinking precisely about thinking: using critical vocabulary
S-23 making interdisciplinary connections

Remodelled Lesson Plan S-24

- Why didn't the hen tell from the very beginning what kind of help she needed?
- Why didn't the animals ask what the hen needed before refusing?
- Are the animals *assuming* that she is asking them to work?
- Did the way she made her request *imply* work? Is that what you thought? Why or why not?
- Does the illustration of the fox *imply stereotyping*? **S-28**

Follow-up: Think about another animal that you picture to be a villain. Pick a kind of animal that most people have bad feelings about (for example, snakes) and read about them. Then check to see if the assumption about the animal is accurate. If it wasn't accurate, what sort of character *would* the animal be? **S-23**

Messages Without Words

(2nd Grade)

Objectives of the remodelled lesson

The students will:
- practice reading critically by distinguishing main points from supporting details, providing more examples to support the text, and analyzing the implications of "Messages Without Words"
- explore the consequences that might result from making incorrect inferences about a person's non-verbal communications
- practice Socratic discussion of their text concerning non-verbal communications

Original Lesson Plan

Abstract

Students read and discuss a passage about how we receive "messages" from people through facial expressions and body movements. The discussion questions ask students to find main ideas of pages, make and justify inferences from pictures, discuss their own examples of non-verbal communication, and summarize the passage in one sentence.

from *Mustard Seed Magic,* Theodore L. Harris et al. Economy Company. 1972. pp. T62–T63.

Critique

The strength of this lesson lies in its subject matter, making inferences from body language. It encourages students to think about the many subtle clues that they take into account when drawing conclusions. The lesson does a poor job of teaching "finding the main idea". The first time students are asked to find the sentence that gives the main point, the "answer" is a question, not a statement. Students find a main point on each page, but don't look at how each is related to the passage as a whole. "Finding the main point" is done, according to this lesson, when students have located the sentence expressing it. Students aren't asked to consider what it means or why the passage was written. Deeper critical reading is possible with this selection.

Strategies used to remodel

S–21 reading critically: clarifying or critiquing texts
S–35 exploring implications and consequences
S–24 practicing Socratic discussion: clarifying and questioning beliefs, theories, or perspectives

Remodelled Lesson Plan s-21

The original asks, "Read the sentence that tells the main idea of these paragraphs". Since there is no sentence on page one that states the main point, students can be helped to *formulate* the main idea. "What is this page about?" If students answer with the phrase, "messages without words", you could ask, "What does that mean? What about messages without words?" If they give the first sentence, they could reformulate it as a statement. If they give a detail or example, you could ask, "What is that example for? What is its point? How could we tell someone the most important point or main idea of this page?" Encourage students to think up questions concerning the meaning of the text as they read. The class can then discuss the students' questions.

Discuss the different ways of sending nonverbal messages mentioned in the text as well as other examples. You could have students brainstorm examples or raise your own examples. "How do you say, 'I don't know.' without words?"

Ask the students if all of the people in the examples intended to send a message, or were some of them just reacting without especially intending to communicate. (For example, the boy who runs probably isn't trying to communicate even though we can get the message.) "Does 'messages without words' imply that the 'sender' means to send messages? If so, what would be a less misleading phrase? Why would that be better? Does it reflect the passage?" **S-35**

Students can also discuss the problems that can be caused when non-verbal communications are mis-interpreted. For example, "What might happen if you thought that your friend's expression meant that she was angry with you when she wasn't?" Solicit possible consequences from the class. Students could then think of other, similar situations. Then discuss with the class how one might prevent the negative consequences of mis-reading non-verbal messages. Students could play act these situations. **S-35**

After the selection has been read and discussed, the class could pursue its deeper meaning and purposes: What is the main point of this selection? Why was it written? Why is this idea important? How can it help you think about things differently? In what ways are messages without words similar to messages through words? Different? What accounts for the similarities and differences? **S-24**

Also, the students could perform field research: noticing and writing down examples of non-verbal communication. These lists can be shared and categorized or analyzed by small groups of students.

Sentences That Ask

(2ⁿᵈ Grade)

Objectives of the remodelled lesson

The students will:
- learn the mechanics of writing questions correctly, by formulating and writing appropriate questions
- practice inferring facts about other students from their choice of questions
- practice fairmindedness by writing questions their parents might ask
- discuss how changing an issue can change which questions are appropriate and which facts are relevant

Original Lesson Plan

Abstract

First, students read two sentences in their textbooks: "Think of your pet or a pet that you would like to have. Talk about your pets." The teacher then encourages the students to discuss their pets by asking each other questions.

Next, the students read, "This sentence asks a question: What is your pet?" Students each think of three questions about pets. The teacher writes some of them on the board, calling attention to the question mark and to the fact that all sentences begin with a capital letter. Finally, the children copy three or four of the board questions. The teacher stresses the punctuation rule before work begins.

from *Language for Daily Use, Level 2 Red,* Dorothy S. Strickland et al. 1973 Harcourt Brace Jovanovich, Inc. p. 19.

Critique

This lesson over-emphasizes drilling the mechanics of writing questions (begin with a capital letter; end with a question mark) at the expense of exploring the necessary *function* of questioning. Children need to learn to formulate appropriate questions, and to see the ways in which these questions can elicit useful responses. The lesson can be expanded so that asking good questions becomes the topic, and learning the correct form is a by-product.

In the lesson, students are asked to think of any three questions they could ask about a pet, but they are given no guiding purpose for formulating them. This approach misses the opportunity to show students the ways in which their needs and purposes determine their questions, and is therefore an incomplete introduction to questions.

We have added extensions which give students practice distinguishing relevant from irrelevant information and practicing fairmindedness.

Strategies used to remodel

S–31 distinguishing relevant from irrelevant facts
S–32 making plausible inferences, predictions, or interpretations
S–3 exercising fairmindedness

Remodelled Lesson Plan

First, instead of having students ask any three questions about pets, the teacher can ask them to think of at least three questions they might ask a pet seller to determine if a particular animal would be a good pet for them. This will give students a guiding purpose, though any reasonable purpose will do for formulating appropriate questions. "What would you want to know? What facts about the animal seem relevant or important to you? Why would you want to know that?" **S–31**

After the students have listed their questions, and have corrected any mechanical errors such as forgetting a question mark, the teacher can write one student's questions on the board so that the class can discuss what that student wants in a pet. "What can we infer about what Sue wants in a pet? Can we tell what animal she's referring to? Why or why not?" **S–32**

Then, when a number of students' responses have been covered, have the students imagine that they are going home to ask their parents if they can have the pet they want. "What questions do you think your parents would ask? What facts would *they* think are relevant or important to know?" **S–31** (Students could trade papers to double-check the mechanics. "Does each question begin with a capital and end with a question mark?") The class could then discuss the things that most concern the parents and why. This activity gives the students practice in fairmindedness as well as more practice formulating and writing questions properly. **S–3**

Next, to give students practice seeing how changing a problem slightly can change the nature of the pertinent questions, students could imagine that they have moved (from a house with a yard to an apartment, for instance) and list questions that they would now ask when choosing a pet. "How did your questions change when the situation changed? Why are different facts relevant? Did you have to change your mind about the pet that was best for you? Why or why not?" **S–31**

"Two Ways to Win"

(2nd Grade)

Objectives of the remodelled lesson

The students will:
- use analytic terms such as assume, infer, and imply to analyze and assess story characters' beliefs
- clarify 'good sport' by contrasting it with its opposite, 'bad sport' and exploring its implications

Original Lesson Plan

Abstract

Students read a story about a brother and sister named Toby and Cleo . They are new in town and worried about making new friends. They ice skate at the park every day after school, believing that winning an upcoming race can help them make new friends (and that they won't make friends if they don't win). Neither wins; Cleo, because she falls, Toby, because he forfeits his chance to win by stopping to help a boy who falls. Some children come over after the race to compliment Toby on his good sportsmanship and Cleo on her skating.

Most of the questions about the story probe the factual components. Some require students to infer. Questions ask what 'good sport' means and if Cleo's belief about meeting people is correct.

from *Mustard Seed Magic,* Theodore L. Harris et al. Economy Company. 1972. pp. 42–46.

Critique

The original lesson has several good questions which require students to make inferences. Since the text does not explicitly state that the children had just moved, the question,"Have Toby and Cleo lived on the block all their lives?" is a good one. The text also asks students if they know who won the race. Since they do not, this question encourages students to suspend judgment. Although 'good sportsmanship' is a good concept or phrase for students to discuss, the text fails to have students practice techniques for clarifying it in sufficient depth. Instead, students merely list the characteristics of a good sport (a central idea in the story) with no discussion of what it means to be a bad sport or sufficient assessment of specific examples. The use of opposite cases to clarify concepts helps students develop fuller and more accurate understandings. With such practice a student can begin to recognize borderline cases as well — where someone was a good sport in some respects, bad in others, or not clearly either. This puts students in a better position to develop criteria for judging behavior.

144

Strategies used to remodel

S–18 analyzing or evaluating arguments, interpretations, beliefs, or theories
S–33 giving reasons and evaluating evidence and alleged facts
S–14 clarifying and analyzing the meanings of words or phrases
S–7 developing intellectual good faith or integrity
S–30 examining or evaluating assumptions
S–28 thinking precisely about thinking: using critical vocabulary

Remodelled Lesson Plan *S–18*

Where the original lesson asks, "What does 'a good sport' mean?", we suggest an extension which has students analyze the concept at length. The teacher can make two lists on the board of the students' responses to the question, "How do good sports and bad sports behave?" Students could go back to the story and apply the ideas on the list to the characters in the story, giving reasons to support any claims they make regarding the characters' sportsmanship. **S–33** In some cases there might not be enough information to determine whether a particular character is a good or bad sport. Or they might find a character who isn't clearly one or the other, or has some characteristics of both good and bad sports. Again, students should cite evidence from the story to support their claims. The students could also change details of the story to make further points about the nature of good and bad sportsmanship. (If the girl had pushed Cleo down in order to win the race, that would have been very bad sportsmanship.)

To further probe the concept of good sportsmanship, ask questions like the following: How did Toby impress the other children? Why did they think he did a good thing? If you had seen the race, what would you have thought of Toby? Why do we value the kind of behavior we call 'good sportsmanship'? Why don't we like bad sportsmanship? **S–14** Why are people ever bad sports? Is it easy to be a good sport? Why or why not? **S–7**

There are a number of places in the lesson where the teacher could introduce, or give students further practice using critical thinking vocabulary. Here are a few examples: What can you *infer* from the story title and picture? What parts of the story *imply* that Toby and Cleo will have some competition in the race? What do Toby and Cleo *assume* about meeting new people and making new friends? Is this a good or a bad *assumption*? Why? Why do you think they made this assumption? Have you ever made similar assumptions? Why? **S–30** What can you *infer* that Cleo felt at the end of the story? What *evidence* do you have? **S–28**

"Marvin's Manhole"

(2nd Grade)

Objectives of the remodelled lesson

The students will:
- develop, consider, analyze, and evaluate interpretations of a story
- evaluate the evidence for and against each interpretation
- practice reasoning dialectically in an essay

Original Lesson Plan

Abstract

The students read "Marvin's Manhole", a story about a boy who rejects his mother's explanation of the purpose of a manhole and decides that there is a "scary thing" living under his street. Marvin tries to make contact with the thing, but fails. One day he finds the manhole open. After looking for the thing, Marvin climbs into the manhole, has a scare, and meets a workman who confirms his mother's explanation.

Students are asked to recall details, discuss Marvin's personality, discuss parts of Marvin's reasoning, read an emphasized word as Marvin would have said it, discuss some of the pictures, discuss Marvin's feelings, and describe what may have happened after the end of the story.

from *People Need People,* Eldonna L.
Evertts. Holt Publishing. 1977.
pp. T222–T231.

Critique

This lesson fails to take advantage of the ambiguous nature of Marvin's story. It is unclear whether Marvin really believes in the existence of the "scary thing," or is merely pretending to believe in it. Much of Marvin's behavior can be interpreted either way. This lesson misses the opportunity to have students argue for one interpretation over another, or see how each interpretation affects the readers' understanding of the details in the story.

Early in the story, when Marvin hits the manhole cover with his baseball bat and runs away, the reader could interpret his actions as bravely trying to get the scary thing to come out, or as part of a game. The faultiness of Marvin's reasoning (for example, when he concludes that the scary thing eats the bread he leaves on the street overnight) suggests that he's pretending or playing. Yet, when he discovers that the manhole cover is open, he behaves as though he believes in the thing.

The suggested questions do nothing to explore the possible different points of view. Only one question raises the issue of Marvin's belief, "How strongly do you think Marvin believed in the scary thing by this point in the story?" Another assumes his belief in the thing, "Do you think Marvin finally believed what his mother had told him about the manhole?" The different interpretations, then, could become the main focus of the lesson.

Strategies used to remodel

S-18 analyzing or evaluating arguments, interpretations, beliefs, or theories

S-28 thinking precisely about thinking: using critical vocabulary

S-33 giving reasons and evaluating evidence and alleged facts

S-26 reasoning dialectically: evaluating perspectives, interpretations, or theories

Remodelled Lesson Plan *s-18*

The process of sorting out the different interpretations of the story can begin with Marvin's claim that he thinks there is a scary thing in the manhole. The teacher might ask the students, "Why do you think Marvin said that there was a thing in the manhole?" Encourage a discussion of the question. Then focus on the issue, "Does Marvin really believe in the scary thing?"

Keep raising this issue as the students discuss various parts of the story and allow discussion. "Does this part of the story *support*, or *weaken* your *interpretation*? **S-28** How? If you think he does believe in the thing, why do you think he did this? If you think he doesn't believe in the thing, why do you think he did this?" **S-33**

Accept any position a student may maintain. The possibilities include: Marvin believed in the thing the whole time; Marvin believed part of the time; Marvin was pretending to believe in the thing; Marvin believed in the thing, but didn't really think it was scary.

Encourage the students to use "if, then" statements when discussing the implications of their ideas — "If Marvin *really* believed in the thing, he made a *questionable inference* when he *concluded* that the thing ate the bread." Finally, after the story has been read and discussed, review the different positions taken, and assign a writing exercise. Have the students evaluate the interpretations. "Which interpretation is strongest? Support your position with details from the story. Explain the weaknesses of another interpretation." **S-26**

"The Camel and the Jackal"

(3ʳᵈ Grade)

Objectives of the remodelled lesson

The students will:
- discuss the moral of the story by evaluating the actions of the characters
- develop intellectual good faith by discussing the concept of revenge
- practice intellectual perseverance by discussing the difference between justice and revenge in depth
- practice giving reasons for moral judgments

Original Lesson Plan

Abstract

Students read a story about two animals. The jackal wants to cross the river to get crab to eat, but he can't swim. So he tells the camel that there is sugar cane (which the camel loves) across the river. After they cross the river and the jackal has eaten his fill, he runs to the sugar cane field and laughs and sings, catching the attention of people nearby. He hides while the people attack the camel and chase him away. The jackal explains to the camel, "I always laugh and sing after dinner." The camel takes him back across the river. Halfway across, the camel says, "I always roll over after dinner." He does so, and the jackal falls into the water.

The students are asked to recall story details, decide which animal is smarter, and which they like the most.

from *Fun All Around,* Nila Banton Smith et al. The Bobbs-Merrill Company, Inc. International Reading Association. 1964. pp. 200–3, T35.

Critique

The questions in the text fail to probe into the moral nature of the story, and fail to lay a foundation from which the students can apply the moral to their own lives. This lesson is a missed opportunity for discussing the concepts of revenge and justice.

Strategy used to remodel

S–20 analyzing or evaluating actions or policies
S–7 developing intellectual good faith or integrity
S–8 developing intellectual perseverance

Remodelled Lesson Plan s-20

In order to take advantage of the moral nature of the story, the class can discuss and evaluate the actions of the animals. The teacher could interrupt the story after each deception or trick and ask, "Was this fair? Why or why not? Could he have done something better? What? What makes you think that would be better?"

At the end of the story, ask, "Is this the best way for the camel to have taught the jackal a lesson? Why or why not? Did the jackal purposefully attract the people's attention? How can you tell? If not, does it make you feel differently about the camel's reaction? Why or why not?"

To have students begin to develop intellectual good faith, the class can discuss what they would have done if they were the camel: If you had been in the camel's place, would it be easy for you not to pay him back? What would you have thought of the camel if he hadn't tricked the jackal? Why? **S-7**

The teacher could also lead an extended discussion about the relationship between justice and revenge, which will be a good experience for developing intellectual perseverance. Encourage them to give examples. "Do you think the camel was being fair (seeking justice) or getting revenge (paying the jackal back)? Why? What is the difference between these two things? Is revenge ever OK, or is it always bad? Why or why not? Was the camel justified? Why or why not? What is the difference between teaching someone a lesson and two wrongs? In your own life, how can you decide if paying someone back would be right or wrong, smart or foolish?" **S-8**

"Friends"
(3rd Grade)

by Marilyn Barnes, Claremont U.S.D.,
Claremont, CA

Objectives of the remodelled lesson

The students will:
- explore a problem story characters have and discuss solutions
- think independently by creating a different ending to the story or predicting a new problem
- develop criteria for friendship by clarifying their values
- make interdisciplinary connections by using their knowledge about animals to imagine new stories

Standard Approach

Students read Helme Heine's story "Friends" which is about three friends: a rooster, a pig, and a mouse. The three begin each day with one another, play together, and eventually try to spend the night together. After swearing to be friends forever, they run into the problem of where to sleep: a small hole in the wall, a pigsty, or a chicken coup. None suit all of the friends, so they each vow to dream about each other since they can't sleep in the same place.

Critique

The teacher asks students to list qualities of a good friend (the main idea of the story) without discussing the qualities of people we don't want as friends. Thus, the lesson fails to assist students in understanding how people develop criteria for evaluation. The teacher neglects to ask students what happens to friends when they can't agree on something. By having students write a different ending for the story, students will begin to practice independent thinking.

Strategies used to remodel

S–19 generating or assessing solutions
S–1 thinking independently
S–15 developing criteria for evaluation: clarifying values and standards
S–23 making interdisciplinary connections

Remodelled Lesson Plan S–19

One of the most interesting things a teacher can do with this story is to have the students identify with the characters in the story and analyze the qualities of their friendship.

150

While discussing qualities of a good friend, students could also explore qualities of those they would not like to be friends with.

The problem arises when the friends cannot find a suitable place to sleep together. Question the students as to why the sleeping arrangement was a problem. Then have the students work together to come up with another agreeable solution.

Asking students to create a new ending, or better yet, another conflict, and then solving this new conflict encourages students to think for themselves. **S-1**

editors' note: When discussing friends, the teacher could ask the students to explain why they chose the particular qualities that they wanted and did not want in a friend. "Why is this a 'good friend' quality? Why is this one undesirable? Do people, like the animals in the story, need to spend all their time together to be good or best friends? Why or why not?" **S-15**

This lesson also offers a good opportunity to make interdisciplinary connections. The students can relate what they've learned about animals in science (the study of animals) to this story idea. The class could pick other animals and students could predict what problems their differing needs might cause in a friendship. For example, fish and rabbits might have problems being friends because fish need to live in water and rabbits need to live on the ground. **S-23**

"The Horse Was in the Parlor"

(3rd Grade)

Objectives of the remodelled lesson

The students will:
- practice examining perspectives and assumptions
- discuss story characters' evaluative assumptions about root questions concerning snobbery and superiority
- develop their perspectives on judging people and being judged by them

Original Lesson Plan

Abstract

The students read a story about Pat and Nora, who move into a new, nicer house. They decide to use their old house as a barn for their animals. Nora's aunt, a snobbish woman who had angered the couple by "looking down her nose" at them, writes to say that she will visit again. Nora works hard to make everything ready. When the aunt arrives, not knowing they have moved, she enters the old house. She thinks that Pat and Nora are living with their animals and says that she will never visit again. After she learns of her mistake and sees the new house, she becomes friendlier toward the young couple.

After reading the story, the students are asked to recall details, describe the characters' personalities, say who they liked the most, and reread the funniest parts of the story.

from *Fun All Around,* Nila Banton Smith
et al. The Bobbs-Merrill Company, Inc.
International Reading Association. 1964.
pp. T25, 114–120.

Critique

This lesson misses the opportunity, that the story offers, to have students evaluate the main characters, and explore perspectives. It also fails to explore the problem of snobbery and questions about "the right sort of person". By filling in the missing pieces in people's reasoning, we can better understand what they think and why.

Strategies used to remodel

S–17 questioning deeply: raising and pursuing root or significant questions
S–30 examining or evaluating assumptions
S–34 recognizing contradictions
S–33 giving reasons and evaluating evidence and alleged facts
S–12 developing one's perspective: creating or exploring beliefs, arguments, or theories

Remodelled Lesson Plan s–17

The teacher can take advantage of the ethical nature of the story by having students evaluate the characters and explore their beliefs and underlying assumptions. The class could be split into groups, each of which could brainstorm two lists: What Aunt Bridget thinks; What Nora thinks. The groups would then organize the lists into two columns, putting opposing beliefs next to each other. They can then fill in the missing pieces and check for internal consistency.

The class can use the following questions: What does it mean to "look down your nose" at someone? What did Aunt Bridget think of Nora and Pat? (She is more important than they are.) What was she assuming? (You're a more important person if you have a nicer house.) **S–30**

• What did Nora think of Aunt Bridget's attitude? Did she agree with her Aunt's reasoning, or the assumption that your house shows how important you are? How do you know? How did Nora try to change her Aunt's opinion of her? What does that assume? (Although Nora criticizes her Aunt for her pride, she seems to accept the assumption that your house shows how important you are.) **S–34**

• What did Aunt Bridget assume when she went into the old house? How did she feel when she learned of her mistake? Why? How do you know? **S–33**

The class could also discuss Aunt Bridget's assumption of superiority, whether they agree with it, why or why not, why they think Aunt Bridget has that belief, and what reasons she might use to justify it. **S–30**

The class could relate the ideas in the story to their own experiences. "Have you ever worried about what other people thought of you? What assumptions were the people making? Do you agree with those assumptions? Do you use those assumptions when you form opinions of others? When is it important to worry about what other people think of you? When is it not important? What makes some people better than others? In what ways are some people better? Why?" Discuss at length. **S–12**

153

"Aha! A Sleuth!"

(3rd Grade)

by Dr. Judie Davie, Mary E. Weinberg,
and Dorothy H. Williams, Greensboro
Public Schools, Greensboro, NC

Objectives of the remodelled lesson

The students will:
- clarify and analyze the meaning of 'sleuth' by synthesizing what they know about popular sleuths
- clarify and analyze the concept of a mystery through deep questioning
- gain insight into how they engage in sleuth-like behavior themselves by transferring the concept to everyday contexts
- make interdisciplinary connections by applying the concept 'sleuth' to academic disciplines that require sleuth-like behavior

Original Lesson Plan

Abstract

The reading unit was an introduction to a unit on mysteries. At the end of this lesson, students will be able to describe what a sleuth is and identify who he is. They were to identify other detectives that they knew, identify synonyms for 'sleuth', and describe traits that sleuths have. Based upon the title "Aha! A Sleuth", they next predict what the story is about. After reading the story, they name persons, places, and things that might help detectives find clues to solve mysteries.

Critique

The original lesson was a literal assignment. The plan did not provide an opportunity to discuss sleuths or mysteries. The questions were not probing and did not stimulate critical thinking. The lesson fails to encourage students to relate these ideas to their own lives or to other disciplines.

Strategies used to remodel

S–14 clarifying and analyzing the meanings of words or phrases
S–17 questioning deeply: raising and pursuing root or significant questions
S–11 comparing analogous situations: transferring insights to new contexts
S–23 making interdisciplinary connections

Remodelled Lesson Plan *S-14*

The teacher could introduce the lesson by having photos of sleuths hanging in the room and the lesson title written on the board. Here are some trigger questions:

• Can you identify these people? How do you know who they are? What do they do?

Introduce the term 'sleuth' and ask, "What is a sleuth? What are other terms for sleuth? What makes a sleuth a sleuth? What is the job of a detective? How do we know this?"

• If a sleuth solves mysteries, what is a mystery? How do you know a story is a mystery? (Explain related topics on how this title suggests that it may be a mystery.)

Read the text. Then discuss the following questions: What is the mystery in "Aha! — A Sleuth"? Is a crime always a mystery? Is a mystery always a crime? Who commits crimes? What would you do to stop a crime? What would you have done differently than the sleuth? How would you have solved the crime? *S-17*

editors' note: To help students relate the lesson to their own lives, have them discuss how we all engage in some sleuth-like behavior in everyday life. ("Oh, Mom must have gone to the store, because she and the grocery list are gone." "My sister must be home, because her purse is on the table." etc.) "Can you think of times you reasoned from 'clues' to figure something out? (You might supply your own example first.) Was there a 'mystery' or question? What clue or clues did you notice? What did you conclude? Were you right? Was your reasoning strong? Why or why not? What should you have concluded? How is this like or unlike the principles of good sleuthing?" *S-11*

This lesson offers a great opportunity to assist students in making interdisciplinary connections. Ask students what other jobs, besides a detective, require sleuth-like behavior or skills (automobile mechanic, doctor, or scientist). Ask the students to name ways that a scientist is a sleuth. Call attention to the fact that because they have studied science in school, they have, in some ways, been scientists. Finally, ask them to recall some of the experiments they have performed and to determine how they acted sleuth-like while designing, doing, and interpreting those experiments.

If the students have studied any history, they could compare sleuthing to figuring out what happened in the past. *S-23*

"Poor Little Puppy"

(3rd Grade)

Objectives of the remodelled lesson

The students will:
- explore the nature of pride and shame by exploring thoughts underlying feelings and clarifying values
- examine story characters' assumptions

Original Lesson Plan

Abstract

Students read a story about Sam and Sally who have a new puppy, Lady (a dachshund), of which they are very proud. One day a big boy comes by and makes fun of Lady — "She's two dogs long and half a dog tall. She's good for play, but that's about all." Sam and Sally begin to compare Lady to other people's dogs and realize that there are many things she cannot do. They try to teach her several new tricks, to no avail. The children feel ashamed of their puppy. This makes Lady sad. Sam and Sally have given up in dismay when a little boy comes by and loses his ball down a deep hole. Lady saves the day by digging the ball out. Sam and Sally are again proud of Lady.

Students are asked to answer factual questions about the story and discuss the following questions: What kind of boy was the big boy who made fun of Lady? What would you have said if someone had made fun of your dog? Why did Lady not learn to do the tricks that Sam and Sally tried to teach her? Why was digging for a ball a trick she did not have to learn?

from *Fun All Around,* Nila Banton Smith, et al. The Bobbs-Merrill Company, Inc. International Reading Association. 1964. pp. T12–T13, 24–33.

Critique

This lesson fails to have students evaluate the characters' assumption that you can only be proud of your dog if it can do tricks. The characters hold this assumption through most of the story including the end, but its justification is never questioned. This is an important point because it is this assumption that leads to the shame the children feel towards Lady, and their dissatisfaction in turn hurts Lady's feelings. The discussion, then, should be focused on the feelings of the characters, how their assumptions affected their feelings, and when we should feel pride in or shame toward our loved ones.

Strategies used to remodel

S-4 exploring thoughts underlying feelings and feelings underlying thoughts
S-30 examining or evaluating assumptions
S-15 developing criteria for evaluation: clarifying values and standards

Remodelled Lesson Plan s-4

In order to probe the central ideas of pride and shame, when the story has been read, the teacher can supplement the original questions with the following: How did Sam and Sally feel about Lady at first? Why? What happened to make them ashamed of Lady? What did they assume? (Dogs aren't good unless they can do tricks.) Is it a good assumption? Why or why not? Why do you think they made that assumption? (Discuss at length.) **S-30** How did they act toward Lady when they felt ashamed? How did that make Lady feel? Why? How else could they have reacted to the boy's teasing? Why did they become proud again? What changed? Why? (They learned about something Lady could do well. Their assumption didn't change.)

The students can then clarify their values and explore reasons for pride and shame. "What reasons should people have for being proud of their puppies? Ashamed? (Compile lists and compare.) Would everything on the 'proud' list have to be true of your pet for you to be proud of it? Why or why not? If (item on pride list) would make you proud of your dog, what does that tell us about your values? If (item on shame list) would make you ashamed of your dog, what does that tell us about your values? Why are these things important to you?" **S-15**

"Kate and the Big Cat"

(3ʳᵈ Grade)

Objectives of the remodelled lesson

The students will:
- practice reading critically by making inferences and analyzing the concept of being treated like a baby
- practice thinking fairmindedly by considering parents' views on "being treated like a baby"
- compare relevant and irrelevant facts for two distinct questions

Original Lesson Plan

Abstract

Students read a story about Kate, who has just moved to a new apartment. Kate has two problems. First, she feels that her parents treat her like a baby. She is discouraged when they hesitate to leave her alone in the new apartment. Her second problem arises while she is alone. As a circus caravan passes by her apartment, a cage door swings open and a tiger jumps out. Kate, after being frustrated by a disbelieving police officer on the phone, devises an ingenious plan for trapping the tiger.

Before reading the story, students are asked to imagine a story that they might write to go with the unit and story titles. Then students read part of the story and state Kate's problem and how they would solve it. Later students are asked to distinguish important from unimportant details concerning what the police would need to know to capture the tiger; predict what Kate will do after the policeman doesn't believe her; and distinguish true from false statements.

from *Air Pudding and Wind Sauce,*
Theodore L. Harris et al. The Economy
Company. 1972. pp. T26–T34.

Critique

Two exercises in this lesson give students valuable critical thinking practice: one has students distinguish relevant from irrelevant facts; another (Rereading Section), requires students to make inferences, rather than simply finding facts in the story.

This lesson, however, fails to have students probe the all-important concept of 'being treated like a baby', or practice fairmindedness by taking Kate's parents' point of view on the subject. Furthermore, in some cases, this lesson leads students to confuse their pure imaginings with good inferences.

Strategies used to remodel

S–21 reading critically: clarifying or critiquing texts
S–32 making plausible inferences, predictions, or interpretations

158

S-14 clarifying and analyzing the meanings of words or phrases
S-3 exercising fairmindedness
S-31 distinguishing relevant from irrelevant facts
S-5 developing intellectual humility and suspending judgment
S-33 giving reasons and evaluating evidence and alleged facts

Remodelled Lesson Plan *S-21*

In the "Story Motivation" section, rather than asking students to pretend that they are the author who will write the story to go along with the titles, we suggest asking them "What can we infer that this story is about? Why?" Have them distinguish what they are sure of, from what is merely possible. (They can infer that there is a big cat; a tiger; someone named Kate; and that the tiger and Kate will have an interaction involving a trick, a trap or a deal. It is fairly safe to assume that the cat is on the loose.) *S-32*

In the "Guided Reading and Comprehension" section we suggest that after the children have described Kate's problem, they discuss what being treated like a baby means. "What does it mean? Why doesn't she like it? How would Kate rather be treated? Give examples. Why would she want to be treated like this?" *S-14*

The teacher could also have students consider Kate's parents' point of view: How would her parents describe their treatment of Kate? Why were they reluctant to let Kate stay at home? Did they think they were treating her like a baby? Why or why not? Discuss at length. *S-3*

Instead of having students mark the important things Kate should have said to the police when calling for help, we suggest asking of each detail cited, "Is this most relevant for informing the police about the tiger? Why or why not?" Then change the problem, and repeat the process for the new problem so that students can see how different problems require different facts. For instance, the teacher may point out that the policeman probably didn't believe Kate because it seemed unlikely that a tiger would be wandering near an apartment. "If this is true, which of these facts would have helped Kate convince the policeman that she was serious? Why? Why is that more relevant than this? Why did changing the focus of our discussion change which facts are most pertinent?" *S-31*

In the "Story Motivation" section preceding part two, students are asked to say what they think Kate will do about the tiger. In order to discourage students from confusing guesses about the story with inferences, we suggest adding a question such as this, "Do we have any way of *knowing* what Kate might do?" (The students have good reason to conclude that Kate will trap the tiger, but no reason to conclude that she will use any particular method.) *S-5*

The "Rereading" section asks students which statements in a list are true. We suggest asking, "Did the story say this or did you have to *infer* it?" Have students either tell where they found the answer or explain how they figured it out. *S-33*

159

Adjectives

(3rd Grade)

by Dale Russell & Hazel Farmer, Greensboro Public Schools, Greensboro, NC

Objectives of the remodelled lesson

The students will
• begin to more deeply understand parts of speech
• think independently when writing sentences using adjectives to describe a food
• guess what food another student was describing
• consider adjectives in relation to the other parts of speech, noting significant similarities and differences
• discuss the importance of being able to identify parts of speech, thereby pursuing root questions

Standard Approach

> Students use adjectives to complete sentences on a worksheet. "I saw a _____ bird yesterday."

Critique

Students may not truly understand what an adjective is from this drill. Students' independent thinking is limited.

editors' note: Because the standard approach teaches each part of speech in isolation from the rest, most students fail to understand the relationships of different kinds of words in sentences. Thus, they can't *use* their conceptions of the parts of speech to read or write more clearly, precisely, or grammatically.

Strategies used to remodel

S–17 questioning deeply: raising and pursuing root or significant questions
S–1 thinking independently
S–29 noting significant similarities and differences

Remodelled Lesson Plan s–17

> Make three lists of adjectives on the board. Use the following headings: describe a bird, describe a race car, describe an apple. The teacher will add irrelevant words or non-adjectives to the lists, and later ask students if any words don't belong.

The teacher will do a balloon mapping activity on the board with the class using a food as the subject. Students will suggest adjectives that describe four characteristics of the chosen food.

Looks   **Feels**
                                                 (in your mouth)

Food

Smells   **Tastes**

Independent assignment: In a bag, have names of foods written on slips of paper. Each student chooses one. Give each student a sheet with a balloon map on it. Students fill in the name of the food they chose, then write adjectives and attach them to the appropriate characteristic (looks, feels, smells, or tastes).

Students then use their maps to write sentences describing the food they chose without saying what it is or whether they like it. **S–1**

One student will read his or her sentences, and classmates will guess the name of the food and whether it was liked or disliked. Those who correctly guess will explain how they came to their conclusions. "How did you figure that out? Did one adjective tip you off, or was it the combination?"

The teacher then asks, "What is an adjective? What do adjectives do for us? How do adjectives make sentences better? More interesting, precise, vivid?" **S–1**

editors' note: These questions could also be asked: Could all of those adjectives have applied to another food? If so, what adjectives could we add to this to make it describe only the food meant? Which adjectives were most helpful for figuring out which food was meant? Why?

"Why can it be helpful to know what kind of word each is? Why do we need to know if a word is an adjective?" The teacher could discuss how modifiers should be next to the words they modify. Students could find sentences with adjectives in their texts, rewrite them so that the modifier is in a wrong place, and compare them with the original sentences. "What does it sound like this sentence means? Why? Why did the author place the adjective in the place that he did?"

Students could examine a few sentences with adjectives and discuss the purpose of each adjective (to tell us which one, because without it, it could mean the other one; to tell us more about it so we can picture it clearly — imagine it better).

Students could compare noun, verb, and adjective forms of the same root: Salty, the salt, to salt your food. "How are these words alike? Different? What does your dictionary say about each? Give me a sentence for each. How does each word fit in with the rest of its sentence?" **S–29**

It would be a good idea to refer to adverbs and explain that another reason for knowing if a word is an adjective is to know how it should end: 'graceful' modifies 'girl', but she "walks gracefully".

Critical Thinking Handbook: K–3

Listening Game

(3rd Grade)

Objectives of the remodelled lesson

The students will:
- practice critical listening skills and develop insight into critical listening by discussing listening, comparing listening to reading, comparing active to passive listening, and discussing ways to listen actively and accurately
- explore the implications of changes to a story retold five times
- discuss how to judge the accuracy of conflicting versions of a story
- recognize when to suspend judgment
- explore how one's point of view can shape one's interpretation of events

Original Lesson Plan

Abstract

In this lesson, five students are asked to leave the room. Next, the teacher reads the story "The Dizzy King" asking that the remaining students listen very carefully. When the story is finished, one student from class brings in student #1 and retells the story. Then student #1 tells the story to student #2, etc. After all the students have been told the story, the class discusses how the details of the story changed. "Were details left out? Added?"

from *Using Our Language,* Dr. Anne D. Ross. Bowmar Noble Publishing Inc. Economy Co. 1977. p. 55.

Critique

Although this lesson is about listening clearly and carefully, it doesn't discuss or teach strategies for skilled listening, such as self-regulation and correction, or the need to test oneself by reiterating a sensible version of what one has heard. This lesson oversimplifies the difficulties of listening carefully and fairmindedly. The only kinds of mistakes it refers to are altering details, leaving details out, or adding new ones. It fails to address the effect these changes have on the *meaning* of what was heard.

This lesson addresses only the problem of remembering a number of details from a story. Since the story doesn't involve, or appeal to, anyone's self interest, the lesson overlooks the motives people have for changing stories. Although listening to remember details is an important skill, children face more profound problems when listening carefully to understand the story as a whole: distinguishing credible from un-credible sources of information, recognizing contradictions, determining the effect of point of view, and suspending judgment when they don't have enough information to know.

The lesson could also increase students' insight by relating listening to reading, writing, and speaking.

162

Strategies used to remodel

S-22 listening critically: the art of silent dialogue
S-35 exploring implications and consequences
S-9 developing confidence in reason
S-11 comparing analogous situations: transferring insights to new contexts
S-8 developing intellectual perseverance
S-16 evaluating the credibility of sources of information
S-2 developing insight into egocentricity or sociocentricity
S-34 recognizing contradictions
S-5 developing intellectual humility and suspending judgment

Remodelled Lesson Plan S-22

The class could first have a discussion about the differences between active listening and passive listening. Students could also compare listening to reading. "If someone is talking and you're interested in what he or she is saying, do you listen differently than usual? In what ways? Why? How does that compare to times you weren't really listening? Why do people sometimes not listen carefully? How is listening easier than reading? Harder? Why? What do these two have in common? Why? What can you do to listen better?"

Then, after playing the original game and discussing how the story changed, the teacher could add the following questions: Was anything in a rearranged order? Was something *important* left out of some versions? What? Why was it important? Did each version of the story make sense? Did any of the changes affect the meaning of the story? Which changes? How did they change the meaning? Why did some changes not affect the meaning of the story? **S-35**

• How was student #2's version affected by the changes made by student #1? Did any of the distortions from the first re-teller show up in the last version?

Then, to develop insight into careful listening, students could explicitly discuss listening: What were you doing as you listened? While you were listening, did something not make sense? Did you ask for clarification? Why or why not? What question or questions could you have asked? **S-9**

• Do you listen differently when you know you will have to remember and repeat what you are hearing? How? Why? Do you read differently when you know you're expected to remember what you read? Do you speak or explain things differently when your audience has to understand and remember what you say, than you do when you're just talking for normal purposes? How? Are there ways speakers can make it easier for listeners to understand and remember what they say? What? Why would that help? How do writers help their readers follow, understand, and remember the key points? Could speakers use any of these techniques? Which? Why? How would that help? **S-11**

The experiment could be repeated after this discussion. Encourage students to stop the teller to ask questions or to get clearer explanations as they listen. "What was different this time? Did thinking about listening help you listen better?" **S-8**

Students could retell TV shows and correct each other.

Extension S–16

The teacher could extend this lesson to stress the importance of determining credibility.

We suggest adding a detailed discussion of the motivations people have for changing or distorting stories. "Did you ever hear two or more different versions of the same story?" If you need examples to get the students on track, mention how siblings might explain a quarrel differently to their parents.

After getting a number of examples, have students discuss them. You could use questions such as these: Why do you think the people told different stories? (To avoid blame; to make one's self or friend look good; to make someone else look bad; because they saw different parts; because they made different inferences.) **S–2** Could all of the versions of the story be true? Why or why not? Which part of that version contradicted the other version? **S–34** Could you tell if any particular version of the event was true? Were parts of the story true but not other parts? Can you always find out the truth? Tell us about a time you had to suspend judgment, and why. What could you do to find out what really happened? **S–5**

> *Though everyone is both egocentric and critical (or fairminded) to some extent, the purpose of education in critical thinking is to help students move away from egocentricity, toward increasingly critical thought.*

"Any Old Junk Today?"
(3rd Grade)

Objectives of the remodelled lesson

The students will:
* engage in dialogical reasoning by comparing two perspectives on what gives things value
* pursue root questions by distinguishing relevant from irrelevant story details and clarifying values
* pinpoint contradictions between opposing perspectives

Original Lesson Plan

Abstract

Students read a story about Eddie Wilson and his father. Eddie collects things that he calls "valuable property", but his father calls "junk". One day, when the family goes to an antique store, Eddie buys two things. At first his father is angry and wants to throw them away. But then he decides he wants one of the objects, and buys it from Eddie. Eddie's mother buys the other. Eddie's father is proud of the profit Eddie has made, and suggests that they go into business together "selling junk".

In the discussion questions, students are asked to do the following things: recall story details; guess Eddie's mother's attitude; list objects found in antique stores; make and justify inferences; describe the difference between junk and antiques; calculate Eddie's profit; and select a sentence which expresses the main idea of the story. ("What is the Main Idea? Write X before the group of words that best tells the main idea of 'Any Old Junk Today?' 1. Eddie's father did not like Eddie's junk. 2. Eddie took a collection to school. 3. Eddie bought a coffee grinder. 4. Eddie found something that was valuable both to him and to his father. 5. Eddie had an enjoyable day.")

from *Air Pudding and Wind Sauce,*
Theodore L. Harris, et. al. The Economy
Co. 1972 pp. T37–T41.

Critique

This story describes a clash of two perspectives. The disagreement between Eddie and his father provides an excellent model for many conflicts. It includes a specific issue ("Does Eddie collect *junk* or *valuable property?*"); two sets of incompatible concepts applied to the same things; and two lines of reasoning based on contradictory evaluative assumptions (objects which look interesting or appealing are valuable; only those objects which can be used or sold for profit are valuable). Yet the suggested questions fail to take advantage of the story.

Students are not required to engage in careful critical reading of the story, analysis of the reasoning, or evaluation of the assumptions or arguments implied by numerous details. Although students are asked "What is the difference between junk and antiques?", they do no detailed clarification of concepts, nor apply their insights to the issue. In short, the text misses an ideal opportunity for students to engage in dialogical thought on a topic on which adults and children often disagree: grown-ups' inexplicable value system.

Most of the inferences required by the lesson only ask students to make calculations about the financial exchanges. The text identifies the key concepts for the students, thereby discouraging independent thought; students should practice identifying key concepts. The authors assume Mr. Wilson's point of view by referring to Eddie's collection as junk, thereby discouraging openmindedness.

Strategies used to remodel

S–25 reasoning dialogically: comparing perspectives, interpretations, or theories
S–3 exercising fairmindedness
S–1 thinking independently
S–35 exploring implications and consequences
S–31 distinguishing relevant from irrelevant facts
S–17 questioning deeply: raising and pursuing root or significant questions
S–34 recognizing contradictions
S–13 clarifying issues, conclusions, or beliefs
S–15 developing criteria for evaluation: clarifying values and standards
S–12 developing one's perspective: creating or exploring beliefs, arguments, or theories
S–8 developing intellectual perseverance

Remodelled Lesson Plan S–25

Rather than using the questions in the original lesson, we suggest that the teacher make the disagreement between Eddie and his father the focus of discussion. After students have read the story once, ask, "How would you describe the dispute between Eddie and Mr. Wilson through most of the story? What is the issue? (Is Eddie's collection junk or valuable property? Should Eddie keep collecting things? What makes some things more valuable than other things? etc.)" If students give a one-sided formulation ("Why doesn't Eddie's father like that 'swell' stuff?" "Why does Eddie collect all that junk?") ask how the other side sees the issue. Insist on a fair formulation; one that doesn't favor either side. **S–3**

"What are the key terms? How does Eddie describe his collection? What is it from his father's point of view?" **S–1** Students could then clarify the terms ('junk', 'valuable property', 'rubbish', 'antique', etc.) — at least one term from each point of view. Ask them for clear examples of each concept. Have them discuss disputed and unclear cases. (Keep lists.) Ask them what calling an object "x" implies about it. (For example, junk or rubbish should be thrown away.) **S–35**

While rereading the story, students could note every detail relevant to the issue; anything that sheds light on the points of view of the main characters. **S–31**

Relevant details:
• Eddie collects what he calls "valuable property".
• Mr. Wilson calls Eddie's collection 'junk'.
• Eddie says, "I had a very enjoyable day today" whenever he collects something.

- Mr. Wilson says, "This junk collecting has to stop. Every week the neighbors put out all their rubbish, and every Saturday you bring most of that rubbish to our house."
- Mr. Wilson says that the telephone pole was "different. I could use that pole." He says that the pole was the "only thing we were ever able to use."
- Eddie disagrees with his father's characterization of his collection of "junk".
- Mr. Wilson explains to Eddie that "antiques are old things."
- When his father tries to explain 'antique', Eddie asks, "You mean junk?"
- Mr. Wilson says, "Certainly not! Antique things are very valuable. They sell for a lot of money."
- Regarding antiques, Eddie says, "Looks like junk to me."
- Eddie thinks he can find valuable property in the antique store.
- Eddie thinks the carriage lamp looks like valuable property
- Eddie buys a grinder with "swell wheels".
- Eddie looks at a "swell old" rusty lock.
- Mr. Wilson calls the rusty lock "junk".
- When he hears Eddie say he had an enjoyable day, Mr. Wilson inferred Eddie had bought "junk", got mad, and stopped the car.
- Eddie defends his purchases by saying, "Please, Dad. That isn't junk. It's valuable antique property."
- Mr. Wilson starts to dump Eddie's purchases in the rubbish can.
- Mr. Wilson says, "Say! This could be a good carriage lamp!" and pays Eddie for it.
- Eddie says, "When I grow up, I'm going to sell junk. I can make a lot of money selling junk."
- Mr. Wilson says, "How about us selling junk together?"

When they have finished, let them share the details and discuss their significance. **S–17** Students can clarify the issue, point out contradictions between Eddie's beliefs and his father's and any inconsistencies or changes of mind within each perspective. "What does Eddie assume? His father? Where, exactly do they disagree? What beliefs of Eddie contradict his father's beliefs? **S–34** What, exactly, changed at the end of the story? Assumptions? Use of terms? Values? etc." **S–13**

The students can then explore their own perspectives. They might review the lists of objects made when clarifying terms and discuss and compare the criteria they used with those of the characters. Ask, "What is your point of view on the assumptions we found? What do you think gives objects value?" Discuss at length. **S–15** The teacher may want to split the class into pairs or small groups for discussion. **S–12**

Finally, students could write an essay or dialogue in which they present arguments about the issues and ideas covered in the discussion. **S–8**

When texts teach skills and concepts, they describe how to use it (and when and why), but the practice is drill: Perform this operation on, or apply this distinction to, the items below. (Of the sentences below, rewrite those that are run-ons. What is X percent of Y? Put your results in the form of a bar graph using the following headings .... Locate N on the map on page 63.) Even when students can produce the correct results and repeat the explanations, they don't necessarily understand the functions and purposes of the skills and concepts, and so fail to use or apply them spontaneously when appropriate.

Remodelling Social Studies Lessons

Introduction: Social Studies in Perspective

Social studies is nothing more or less than the study of how humans live together as a group in such a way that their dealings with one another affect their common welfare. All of us, like it or not, engage in social study. In our everyday lives, we all attend to, generalize, and reason about how we are living together in our respective groups. We pay special attention to the groups that are of immediate interest to us. But we develop concepts of other groups as well. We make judgments about how our welfare is affected by other groups behaving as they do. We make judgments about the effect of our group's behavior upon other groups. We gather evidence from experience, from books, and from the media that we use to justify conclusions we come to about our own groups, our own society, and about other groups, including that of other societies.

All children, as a result of thousands of hours of TV watching and thousands of interactions with others, internalize hundreds of judgments about people and groups, and about what is and is not appropriate social behavior, before they enter any school room. Piaget's studies of children, particularly his study for UNESCO, illustrate this point well. Consider the following excepts from his interviews of children of different ages from different nations. In them we have evidence that the everyday realities of children's lives typically have a more profound effect on what they learn about the nature of social behavior than what we think we are teaching them in the classroom:

Michael M. (9 years, 6 months old): Have you heard of such people as foreigners? *Yes, the French, the Americans, the Russians, the English ….* Quite right. Are there differences between all these people? *Oh yes, they don't speak the same language.* And what else? *I don't know.* What do you think of the French, for instance? Do you like them or not? Try and tell me as much as possible. *The French are very serious, they don't worry about anything, an' it's dirty there.* And what do you think of the Russians? *They're bad, they're always wanting to make war.* And what's your opinion of the English? *I don't know … they're nice ….* Now look, how did you come to know all you've told me? *I don't know … I've heard it … that's what people say.*

Maurice D. (8 years, 3 months old): If you didn't have any nationality and you were given a free choice of nationality, which would you choose? *Swiss nationality.* Why? *Because I was born in Switzerland.* Now look, do you think the French and the Swiss are equally nice, or the one nicer or less nice than the other? *The Swiss are nicer.* Why? *The French are always nasty.* Who is more intelligent, the Swiss or the French, or do you think they're just the same? *The Swiss are more intelligent.* Why? *Because they learn French quickly.* If I asked a French boy to choose any nationality he liked, what country do you think he'd choose? *He'd choose France.* Why? *Because he was born in France.* And what would he say about who's the nicer? Would he think the Swiss and the French equally nice or one better than the other? *He'd say the French are nicer.* Why? *Because he was born in France.* And who would he think more intelligent? *The French.* Why? *He'd say that the French want to learn quicker than the Swiss.* Now you and the French boy don't really give the same answer. Who do you think answered best? *I did.* Why? *Because Switzerland is always better.*

Marina T. (7 years, 9 months old): If you were born without any nationality and you were given a free choice, what nationality would you choose? *Italian.* Why? *Because it's my country. I like it better than Argentina where my father works, because Argentina isn't my country.* Are Italians just the same, or more, or less intelligent than the Argentinians? What do you think? *The Italians are more intelligent.* Why? *I can see the people I live with, they're Italians.* If I were to give a child from Argentina a free choice of nationality, what do you think he would choose? *He'd want to stay an Argentinian.* Why? *Because that's his country.* And if I were to ask him who is more intelligent, the Argentinians, or the Italians, what do you think he would answer? *He'd say Argentinians.* Why? *Because there wasn't any war.* Now who was really right in the choice he made and what he said, the Argentinian child, you, or both? *I was right.* Why? *Because I chose Italy.*

The fact, then, that children form much of their thinking about how humans live together in groups as a result of their own native egocentrism, buttressed by the sociocentrism of those around them in everyday life, is one major problem for instruction. But it is not the only problem. The other major problem lies in the fact that when highly intelligent and well educated scholars from different societies study how humans live together in groups they sometimes differ significantly in the conclusions they come to. To put this another way, human social behavior can be studied from different points of view. And the conclusions one comes to about human behavior in part depend on the point of view from the perspective of which one studies behavior. That is why there are different schools of thought in social studies.

We believe that these two major problems for social studies instruction entail an important general strategy for teaching. To combat the first problem, it is essential that the bulk of activities focus on engaging the student's own thinking, so that the thinking that students actually use on social problems in their everyday lives are explicitly discovered by the students and, where appropriate, challenged. To combat the second major problem, it is essential that students discover and enter into dialogue with more than one point of view, indeed with multiple points of view. These two needs come together if we turn progressively away from a didactic approach to teaching and focus progressively on a critical approach (See Chapter 8, "Thinking Critically About Teaching", for a fuller account).

The major problem to overcome in remodelling social studies units and lessons, then, is that of transforming *didactic* instruction within *one* point of view into *dialogical* instruction within *multiple* points of view. As teachers, we should see ourselves not as dispensers of absolute truth nor as proponents of uncritical "relativity", but as careful, reflective seekers after truth, as involved in a search in which we invite our students to participate. We continually need to remind ourselves that each person has a somewhat different point of view, that each point of view rests on assumptions about human nature, that thinking of one point of view as *the truth* limits our understanding of the very thing we want to grasp. Practice entering into and coming to understand divergent points of view, on the other hand, heightens our insight into the real problems of our lives.

Children, as we have already underscored, already face the kinds of issues studied in social studies and are engaged in developing views on questions like the following:

> What does it mean to belong to a group? Does it matter if others do not approve of me? Is it worthwhile to be good? What is most important to me? How am I like and unlike others? Whom should I trust? Who are my friends and enemies? What are people like? What am I like? How do I fit in with others? What are my rights and responsibilities? What are others' rights and responsibilities?

We humans live in a world of human meanings. There is always more than one way to give meaning to our behavior. We create points of view, ideologies, religions, and philosophies that often conflict with each other. Children need to begin to understand the implications of these crucial insights: that all accounts of human behavior are expressed within a point of view; that no one account of what happened can possibly cover all the facts; that each account stresses some facts over others; that when an account is given (by a teacher, student, or textbook author), the point of view in which it is given should be identified and, where possible, alternative points of view considered; and finally, that points of view need to be critically analyzed and assessed. Of course, the introduction of children to these truths must take place slowly, concretely, and dialogically. We must be on the alert for occasions that facilitate student discoveries in this area. We must be patient and think in terms of their development of insights over a period of years.

Adults, as well as children, tend to assume the truth of their own unexamined points of view. People often unfairly discredit or misinterpret ideas based on assumptions differing from their own. To address social issues critically, students must continually evaluate their beliefs by contrasting them with opposing beliefs. From the beginning, social studies instruction should encourage dialogical thinking, that is, the fairminded discussion of a variety of points of view and their underlying beliefs. Of course, this emphasis on the diversity of human perspectives should not be covered in a way that implies that all points of view are equally valid. Rather, children should learn to value critical thinking skills as tools to help them distinguish truth from falsity, insight from prejudice, accurate conception from misconception.

Dialogical experience in which children begin to use critical vocabulary to sharpen their thinking and their sense of logic, is crucial. Words and phrases such as 'claims', 'assumes', 'implies', 'supports', 'is evidence for', 'is inconsistent with', 'is relevant to' should be carefully and progressively integrated into such discussions. We should begin to introduce children to the vocabulary of educated thinking as soon as possible, but we should start from simple, intuitive examples that come from their own experience.

Formulating their own views of historical events and social issues enables children to begin to synthesize data from divergent sources and to grasp important ideas. Too often, children are asked to recall details with no synthesis, no organizing ideas, and no distinction between details and basic ideas or between facts and common U.S. interpretations of them. Children certainly need opportunities to explicitly learn basic principles of social analysis, but more importantly they need opportunities to *apply* them to real and imagined cases and to develop insight into social analysis.

Children should, in other words, begin to become as adept in using critical thinking principles in the social domain as we expect them to become in scientific domains of learning. We, on our part, should begin as soon as possible to foster an attitude of applying sound standards of judgment to every area of learning and we should do so in concrete, engaging ways, so that children begin to discipline their thinking with the skills of critical thinking.

171

Traditional lessons cover several important subjects within social studies: politics, economics, history, anthropology, and geography. Critical education in social studies focuses on basic questions in each subject, and begins to prepare children for their future economic, political, and social roles. At the K-3 level, we can but touch the surface of these important domains, but we should not under-emphasize the significance of this introduction.

Some Common Problems with Social Studies Curriculum Materials

- Questions suggested often ask for recall of a random selection of details and key facts or ideas. Minor details are often given the same emphasis as important events and principles. Children come away with collections of sentences but little sense of how to distinguish major from minor points. The time and space given to specifics should reflect their importance.

- Often the answers to review questions are found in bold or otherwise emphasized type. Thus, children need not even understand the question, let alone the answer, to complete their assignments.

- Materials rarely have students extend insights to analogous situations in other times and places. Students do not learn to *use* insights or principles to understand specifics. They do not learn to recognize recurring patterns.

- Students are not encouraged to recognize and combat their own natural ethnocentricity. Materials often encourage ethnocentricity in many ways. They often present U.S. ideals as uniquely ours when, in fact, every nation shares at least some of them.

- Ethnocentricity is introduced in word choices that assume a U.S. or Western European perspective. For example, cultures are described as "isolated" rather than as "isolated from Europe". Christian missionaries are described as spreading or teaching "religion" rather than "Christianity". Cultures are evaluated as "modern" according to their similarity to ours.

- Materials often encourage student passivity by providing all the answers. Children are not held accountable for suggesting answers on their own. Materials usually err by asking questions students should be able to answer on their own, and then immediately providing the answer. Once students understand the system, they know that they don't have to stop and think for themselves because the text will do it for them in the next sentence.

- Materials often emphasize the ideal or theoretical models of government, economic systems, and institutions without helping children to begin to recognize real (hidden) sources of power and change. Materials rarely prepare children to distinguish ideals from the way a system might really operate in a given situation.

- Explanations are often abstract and lack detail or connection to that which they explain, leaving children with a vague understanding.

Some Recommendations for Action

Students in social studies, regardless of level, should be expected to begin to take responsibility for their own learning. This means that they should begin to develop the art of independent thinking and study and begin to cultivate intellectual and study skills.

Discussions and activities should be designed or remodelled by the teacher to begin to develop the students' use of critical reading, writing, speaking, and listening. Furthermore, students should begin to get a sense of the interconnecting fields of knowledge within social studies, and the wealth of connections between these fields and others, such as math, science, and language arts.

The students should not be expected to memorize a large quantity of unrelated facts, but rather to begin to think in terms of interconnected domains of human life and experience. This includes elementary forms of identifying and evaluating various viewpoints; gathering and organizing information for interpretation; distinguishing facts from ideals, interpretations, and judgments; recognizing relationships and patterns; and applying insights to current events and problems.

Unifying Social Studies Instruction

- What are people like? How do people come to be the way they are? How does society shape the individual? How does the individual shape society?

- Why do people disagree? Where do people get their points of view? Where do I get my point of view?

- Are some people more important than others? From what point of view?

- How do people and groups of people solve problems? How can we evaluate solutions?

- What are our biggest problems? What has caused them? How should we approach them?

Keep in mind that it takes a long time to develop a child's *thinking*. Our thinking is connected with every other dimension of us. Our children enter our classes with many "mindless" beliefs, ideas which they have unconsciously picked up from TV, movies, small talk, family background, and peer groups. Rarely have they been encouraged to think for themselves. Thinking their way through these beliefs takes time. We therefore need to proceed very patiently. We must accept small payoffs at first. We should expect many confusions to arise. We must not despair in our role as cultivators of independent critical thought.

In time, children will develop new modes of thinking. In time they will become more clear, more accurate, more logical, more openminded — if only we stick to our commitment to nurture these abilities. Social studies provide us with an exciting opportunity, since they address issues central to our lives and well-being.

Of course, it is not easy to shift the classroom from a didactic-memorization model to a critical one, but, if we are willing to pay the price of definite commitment, it can be done. Over time, students can learn to live an "examined" life, one in which they come to terms with the social nature of their lives, if only we will carefully, systematically, and encouragingly cultivate it.

Do Communities Change?

(Kindergarten)

Objectives of the remodelled lesson

The students will:
- practice evaluating community changes
- clarify their values by developing criteria for evaluating changes in a community
- practice fairmindedness

Original Lesson Plan

Abstract

First, students review changes that have occurred in their personal lives such as height and weight. Then they discuss a number of common community changes and express their feelings about them.

from *Me*, Harlan S. Hansen, et al.
Houghton Mifflin Company. 1976,
pp. 126–7.

Critique

This lesson simply asks children to recognize changes and to indicate whether or not they like the changes. The opportunity to *evaluate* the merits of changes based on reasons other than personal preference is ignored. The original lesson also overlooks the importance of children learning that different people judge changes differently, according to their points of view.

We recommend that the teacher write key words from the children's responses. This helps make the connection between words and writing. Then, when discussing particular reasons, the teacher could point and read the words out loud reinforcing that connection as well as graphically illustrating the use of writing for keeping track of many ideas.

Strategies used to remodel

S–20 analyzing or evaluating actions or policies
S–15 developing criteria for evaluation: clarifying values and standards
S–13 clarifying issues, conclusions, or beliefs
S–3 exercising fairmindedness

Remodelled Lesson Plan S–20

In order to allow students to evaluate changes, the question from the original lesson, "How do you feel about this kind of change in your community?" could be followed by, "Is this a good change or a bad change? Why?"

To help the children clarify their conclusions, you could also take note of their responses and discuss each one for its implications. ("One of you said a change was bad because it left less room to play. Is less room for children to play always a bad change, or just in that one case?") When referring to their responses, you can point out the features that good changes have in common, and then do the same for bad changes."How was reason X like reason Y? What did the good changes have in common? Is that part of why they were good?" Etc. **S-15**

The class could then discuss why it is important to be clear about these reasons. The children can thus begin to see that knowing what makes a good change good helps when you have to make changes. **S-13**

In addition, the students could use this lesson to practice fairmindedness. "Do you think someone else might like a change that you didn't? Imagine that someone disagreed with you about *this* change? Why might someone think otherwise?" If students cannot think of any reason someone would disagree with them, the teacher could provide examples. Discuss at length. **S-3**

> *Getting experience in lesson plan remodelling: How can I take full advantage of the strengths of this lesson? How can this material best be used to foster critical insights? Which questions or activities should I drop, use, alter or expand upon? What should I add to it?*

How Is My School Like My Home?

(Kindergarten)

Objectives of the remodelled lesson

The students will:
- begin to develop intellectual humility by distinguishing what they can reasonably conclude from what they cannot
- give reasons and examine evidence for concluding whether or not pictures depict home scenes or school scenes
- develop confidence in their abilities to figure things out

Original Lesson Plan

Abstract

Students discuss some of their basic needs, such as love, food, shelter, and clothing and how they meet those needs. Then they are given twelve pictures of children at home or school having these needs met. Students are asked what need is being met in each. Finally, they sort the pictures into two groups: needs met at home; needs met at school.

from *Me,* Harlan S. Hansen, et al.
Houghton Mifflin Company. 1976,
pp. 106–7.

Critique

This lesson mixes two concepts together: where needs are met and how to identify school versus home in photographs. This lesson should be introduced by telling the children that they get their needs met both at home and at school. Then the lesson should be divided into two lessons, one, focusing on needs and the other on home versus school. The rest of the critique and the remodel addresses the later.

Young children have an especially hard time saying they don't know. They need practice distinguishing cases in which they do have enough information to know, from cases in which they don't. This lesson misses the opportunity to have them do so.

Strategies used to remodel

S–5 developing intellectual humility and suspending judgment
S–33 giving reasons and evaluating evidence and alleged facts
S–9 developing confidence in reason

Remodelled Lesson Plan s-5

We suggest that the teacher encourage suspension of judgment by adding pictures that aren't clearly home or school, such as two children playing on a swing-set. The teacher could ask of each picture "Can you *infer* or tell if this is at school or at home? Why do you say so?" If the cases aren't clear cases, but there are some clues that point to the likelihood of it being a school or a home, have students give the reasons that they inferred that it was at home or school and help them evaluate their reasons to see if they are solid. For example, suppose a student responds, "The reason I think it is a school, is because there are five children working on a project, and that happens more often at school than at home." The teacher could ask the rest of the class if they agree. If necessary, the teacher could say that the reason given was a good one because it makes sense — one would normally see five children working together at school rather than at home. On the other hand, if a student were to say, "I think this is a school because it has a swing-set in it.", and the other children don't question the conclusion, the teacher could point out that some children have swing-sets at their houses. Then the teacher might ask the student if there is anything else in the picture that might give a clue or evidence that shows whether it is at home or at school. **S-33**

Even if the picture is clear, the children could be asked to point out other clues in it that support the conclusion. "What else makes you think it's ...? Why?"

After doing this, the teacher can point out to the students that they can often figure things out by thinking carefully. The students could look at family photographs and try to figure out whether they were taken at home or away from home, and explain why. **S-9**

Tools (Two Remodelled Lessons)

(Kindergarten)

The first remodel below appeared in the first edition of this book. The remodelled lesson was then further remodelled by Susan Lara Fulton during a workshop. Her work follows the first remodel, illustrating how the remodelling process is an on-going critical, not a one-step, process.

First Remodel

Objectives of the remodelled lesson

The students will:
* think independently and analyze the concept 'tool' by categorizing examples
* deepen their understanding of the concept by discussing things which are not tools but which are *used as* tools

Original Lesson Plan

Abstract

Students are asked to comment on what tools can be used to make specific tasks easier; to review pictures of tools and tell what jobs they help people do; to state which of the pictured tools are in their classroom; to draw pictures of tools which are in the classroom but not already pictured on their activity sheets; to divide pictures into two categories: "tools in the classroom" and "tools not in the classroom"; to discuss what kinds of jobs tools help people do and whether more than one job can be done by certain tools; and to classify tools as cleaning, cutting, or lifting tools. All of the tools are ones that students are probably familiar with.

from *Me,* Harlan S. Hansen, et al.
Houghton Mifflin Company. 1976,
pp. 140–143.

Critique

This lesson is doing too much of the thinking for students by providing the list of tools and the categories for them. Furthermore, the division of tools into those found in the classroom versus those found outside the classroom doesn't seem particularly useful. The concept 'tool' can be further extended by having students discuss objects not usually thought of as tools which can be used as tools.

Strategies used to remodel

S–1 thinking independently
S–14 clarifying and analyzing the meanings of words or phrases

Remodelled Lesson Plan s-1

> To foster independent learning, rather than giving students a set of categories, students can list tools they've seen used and develop their own ways to categorize them. Encourage students to accept multiple sets of categories as appropriate.
>
> Then, in order for children to develop a clear concept of tools and the value of tools, the teacher could add examples of objects not ordinarily thought of as tools. For example, some Latin women use scarves, that we think of as decorative clothing, for carrying groceries and babies. People who lived a long, long time ago used rocks as tools. People pass the hat to collect and carry money. We can use sticks to draw or write in the dirt. We can use a piece of paper as a megaphone.
>
> The students can then think of examples of things they use as tools. They could then be asked whether that use is typical (what the thing was designed to do) or unusual (used in a way not intended in the original design). **S-14**

Second Remodel

by Susan Lara Fulton, St. Basil's
School, Vallejo, CA

Objectives of the remodelled lesson

The students will:
- clarify and analyze the word 'tool'
- understand the defining characteristics of tools through exploring examples, categorizing, and problem solving

Original Lesson Plan

> The remodel of "Tools" (see above).

Critique of the Remodelled Lesson

The remodelled lesson above fails to have the students attempt to formulate a definition of 'tool'. This requires in-depth critical thought. Classifying is a great way to use critical thinking, provided the students do their own classifying. It fosters their own independent thinking and encourages them to clarify various ideas about and purposes for tools.

Strategies used to remodel

S–1 thinking independently
S–14 clarifying and analyzing the meanings of words or phrases
S–9 developing confidence in reason

Remodelled Lesson Plan *s–1*

Rather than beginning the lesson by asking for examples, students are asked first for a definition of the word 'tool'. It is much more difficult to define by word than to define by example. Whether or not the students are able to define by word, the next step is to define by example. Continue with examples and try to have the students draw out the worded definition by examination of the examples and counter-examples (examples that fit the proposed definition but are clearly not tools). **S–14**

Classify tools as per the remodelled lesson plan. Then, follow through with the suggestion of adding examples of objects not ordinarily thought of as tools. However, present the examples by asking questions: "Why do you think a stick can be a tool?" or "How do you think a stick can be used as a tool?" Then have the students come up with other examples.

An added extension of this lesson could include a little play acting or problem solving. Present the students with a problem or situation which needs a little creative tool-making and see how they solve the problem. Example: The handle on the cupboard door is wobbly. The screw is loose and needs to be tightened, but we have no tools. How do we fix the door? The objective, of course, would be to find something in the classroom which would substitute for a screwdriver. **S–9**

Why Did the Girl Say "No"?

(1ˢᵗ Grade)

Objectives of the remodelled lesson

The students will:
• practice critical vocabulary
• make plausible inferences regarding people's values based on choices they made

Original Lesson Plan

Abstract

Students are asked to examine decisions and figure out what was important to the person who made it. Among the decisions they examine is the following: A teacher chooses between a pair of worn, comfortable-looking shoes and a pair of fashionable, less comfortable-looking shoes. Students are expected to say whether the teacher most values comfort or fashion. Students then look at a picture story (while the teacher reads), of a girl pulling her nice clean wagon while her little brother runs along beside her. He falls in a muddy puddle. The girl imagines two scenarios: she gives him a ride and her mother is happy with her but her wagon is muddy; she doesn't give him a ride and her wagon stays clean but her mother is mad. The girl tells her brother "No!".

from *Things We Do,* Frank L. Ryan, et al.
Houghton Mifflin Co. 1976.
pp. T116–T117.

Critique

This lesson fails to seize the opportunity to introduce critical vocabulary. It also overlooks the chance to have children make plausible inferences beyond the most obvious, surface ones.

Strategy used to remodel

S–28 thinking precisely about thinking: using critical vocabulary
S–32 making plausible inferences, predictions, or interpretations

Remodelled Lesson Plan S–28

The teacher could rephrase questions and comments to include critical thinking vocabulary. For concepts that you are introducing, first use the new term, and then words the students are familiar with. For example, ask, "What did the girl's response *imply* or *tell us* about what she thinks is most important?" The teacher could also rephrase student responses to include the vocabulary. For example, if a student says "I think comfort is most important to you.", say, "You *inferred* from my choice that I value comfort more than looks." Continue this process with the story of the girl.

The teacher can use this exercise to help students notice what things imply beyond what is said. In the first example, one can predict some other kinds of choices the teacher choosing comfortable shoes would make: Can you predict what choice I would probably make between wearing blue jeans and a dress? How were you able to infer or predict this? What other choices does my choice *imply?* What other choices do you think I'd make? **S–32**

> *In teaching for critical thinking in the strong sense, we are committed to teaching in such a way that children learn as soon and as completely as possible how to become responsible for their own thinking.*

Martin Luther King, Jr.'s Birthday

(1ˢᵗ Grade)

Objectives of the remodelled lesson

The students will:
- practice making the distinction between facts and ideals
- practice reading critically by clarifying terms and recognizing assumptions in their text

Original Lesson Plan

Abstract

Students are told that January 15 is Martin Luther King's birthday; he was an important leader of African–Americans; he believed in peace; he was given the Nobel Peace Prize. The teachers' text mentions some discriminatory social policies that King opposed.

from *At School,* Virginia Finley, et al. Tiegs-Adams: People And Their Heritage, 1983. by Silver Burdett & Ginn, Inc. p. 91.

Critique

The lesson is vague because it does not explain the variety of problems that African–Americans faced and therefore why King was an important leader. It also confuses ideals with actual practice by neglecting to discuss the oppression of many African–Americans today, and therefore may suggest that the race problems have been solved. Furthermore, King was a leader in the Civil Rights Movement; not only African–Americans followed him. The text, however, refers to him merely as a leader of African–Americans.

Strategies used to remodel

S–30 examining or evaluating assumptions
S–21 reading critically: clarifying or critiquing texts
S–27 comparing and contrasting ideals with actual practice
S–7 developing intellectual good faith or integrity
S–10 refining generalizations and avoiding oversimplifications

Remodelled Lesson Plan

To help students clarify their texts, you might have them read the lesson and ask, "What does the text mean by 'his people'? What does 'his dream was about a better life for his people' assume about their lives? (That their lives were not good enough). **S–30** Do you know about any of the problems that African–Americans faced that King was struggling against?" **S–21**

You might point out that among the problems African–Americans faced was the lack of some of our country's freedoms — freedoms all citizens are supposed to have. Discuss a few: many African–Americans weren't allowed to vote, they couldn't get jobs they wanted because of prejudice and inferior education, they often couldn't live where they wanted because Caucasians wouldn't sell or rent houses to them, etc. Stress that these examples show the difference between ideals and actual practices. **S–27** Point out that good citizens work to change the practices that contradict our ideals. You may also want to point out some of the other examples of discriminatory treatment of African–Americans if the students are unfamiliar with them (separate bathrooms, water fountains, restaurants, schools, "back of the bus", etc.) **S–7**

Next, you could ask questions like these: "Why was King an important leader? (He worked, sacrificed, even spent time in jail, in order to bring the country closer to its ideals.) For whom was King a leader?" (He was a leader for most people who supported the Civil Rights movement, whatever their race.) **S–10**

Telling me that this is an important concept doesn't mean much if you never mention it again.

Our Country's Birthday

(1ˢᵗ Grade)

Objectives of the remodelled lesson

The students will:
- practice critical reading by clarifying statements in their text
- distinguish the phrases 'freedom from England' and 'freedoms of individuals'
- begin to develop a concept of personal freedoms in the U.S.
- practice making the distinction between facts and ideals in their lives and in their country

Original Lesson Plan

Abstract

Students read and discuss a passage about the 4ᵗʰ of July. Students are informed that, on July 4, 1776, Americans said they wanted to be free from England and we celebrate the day because we are proud to be free. In the discussion they are told that with freedom comes responsibility, and that freedom can be lost if tyrants take over.

from *At School*, Virginia Finley, et al. Tiegs-Adams: People And Their Heritage, 1983. by Silver Burdett & Ginn, Inc. p. 81.

Critique

This lesson confuses two different senses of 'freedom': 'freedom (of the country) from England' and 'freedom of individual Americans'. The first, we achieved after the Revolutionary War. The second, we must continually strive to achieve and perfect. The text, by skipping back and forth between the two, implies that the struggle to achieve individual freedom ended with our separation from England. Therefore, it confuses actual practice with ideals. Furthermore, by suggesting that the primary danger to freedom is the possibility of a tyrant taking over, the text neglects the more constant problem of some people not having freedoms. Some groups, such as African–Americans, women, and Native–Americans have only recently acquired freedoms equal to or approaching those of other Americans. During the McCarthy era, many Americans lost freedoms. Students need to see how the ideal of individual freedom has been violated in the past, to begin to understand what safeguarding these freedoms really involves.

Strategies used to remodel

S-21 reading critically: clarifying or critiquing texts
S-14 clarifying and analyzing the meanings of words or phrases
S-7 developing intellectual good faith or integrity
S-27 comparing and contrasting ideals with actual practice

Remodelled Lesson Plan S-21

After the students have read the text, the teacher could draw the students' attention to the two uses of 'freedom' in the passage. "What does 'free from England' mean?" If they cannot answer, you might point out that when colonists were under English rule they weren't allowed to make many important decisions for themselves because they weren't fully represented in the English government.

Students could then reread the last sentence on the page. "What does the text mean by 'we are proud to be free'? Does the text mean merely that we are proud to be free from England?" Allow time for students to respond. If the students haven't recognized the different meaning of 'freedom', you might mention our individual freedoms. Tell the students about one of our freedoms (such as freedom of religion) and explain what it means (no one can force us to believe in or practice a particular religion). "Do you know of any other freedoms that we have? What? What does that mean? Why is it important or valuable?" You may also supply important freedoms the students miss. **S-14**

You could then say that having these freedoms is an important American ideal and ask the students if they know what an *ideal* is — something that we value highly, and try to achieve. Point out that success is a matter of degree (like cold, warm, and hot), rather than simply a matter of all or nothing (like a light switch). "Do you have any ideals that you have trouble practicing?" The teacher may use a personal example here, such as "Being kind and pleasant to my friends is an ideal, but sometimes I lose my temper and snap at them. This makes me feel bad because I haven't lived up to my ideals. I know I have to try harder. What are some ideals you want to live up to? Why? Are they hard to live up to? Why? Why try?" **S-7**

Return the discussion to American ideals. "Since we achieved freedom from England we have had these ideals, though in some ways we have not practiced them since then." Use examples here such as treatment of Native–Americans, that women couldn't vote until 1920, and that in the 1950's many people got into trouble because of friends they had, or political groups they joined. "Why have we had these problems living up to our ideals as a nation?" **S-27**

Rules

(1ˢᵗ Grade)

Objectives of the remodelled lesson

The students will:
*   probe deeply into the nature of rules by comparing different kinds of rules and exploring their purposes
*   refine generalizations by analyzing legitimate exceptions to rules and their justifications
*   develop insight into egocentricity by exploring people's reasons for breaking rules

Original Lesson Plan

Abstract

Half of the lessons in this unit focus on a class planning a field trip and discussing rules they need to make. The rest discuss laws, police, and rules in the home. The unit covers the following points: We need rules to keep us safe, and to give everyone a fair chance. Bad consequences would arise if we had no rules. Laws are necessary. Police help us. Families have rules. Rules help families. Everyone is responsible for following rules.

from *At School*, Virginia Finley, et al.
Tiegs-Adams: People and Their Heritage, 1983. by Silver Burdett & Ginn, Inc. pp. 34–39.

Critique

To understand rules deeply, students need to recognize how rules are based on human purposes and therefore can and should be applied or changed to fit those purposes. Students should practice evaluating rules and explaining how to change them and why. They should also discuss how human needs, and a sense of right and wrong, often require suspending or making exceptions to rules. Students should learn to recognize that rules should be changed if they do not meet the alleged purpose, or when the purpose itself should be rejected. In addition, students should think about their impulses to apply rules inconsistently and to break them.

Strategies used to remodel

S–17 questioning deeply: raising and pursuing root or significant questions
S–29 noting significant similarities and differences
S–20 analyzing or evaluating actions or policies
S–15 developing criteria for evaluation: clarifying values and standards
S–10 refining generalizations and avoiding oversimplifications
S–2 developing insight into egocentricity or sociocentricity

Remodelled Lesson Plan s–17

The class or small groups of students could discuss rules in-depth.

• What is a rule? What different kinds of rules are there? How and why are they different? Does breaking them have different consequences? Does it follow that it is worse to break one kind of rule than another? (Compare games to safety rules, for example.) Small groups of students could list categories of rules and write short answers to these questions. **S–29**

• Do you ever make rules? Why do you make them? (Have students discuss a variety of rules and their purposes.) How well does each work? Why? Can they be improved? How? **S–20**

• Are there good rules and bad rules? What's the difference between good rules and bad ones? (Have students give examples of each and explain why the bad rules are bad and the good rules good.) What is this rule's purpose? Is the purpose worthwhile? Does the rule achieve its purpose? Should the rule be dropped, or changed, or should there be exceptions to it? **S–15**

• Why is it sometimes OK to ignore or suspend rules? (If the teacher has recently made an exception to a rule in class, students may discuss its justification. Encourage students to give their own examples of legitimate exceptions to rules.) **S–10**

• Why do we sometimes break rules when we shouldn't? (Students can discuss when they wanted to break or did break a rule.) Why did you feel that way? What were you thinking at the time? What were the consequences? Did you think the rule was a good rule? Do you feel differently when you break a rule than when someone else does, for example, borrowing without permission? **S–2**

To sum up, students could give examples of rules they would like to change, and have them discuss why they think they should be changed. The teacher could point out to the students when their reasons fall into the aforementioned categories, that is, when the rule doesn't meet the purpose or the purpose should be rejected. Encourage further class discussion of examples given.

When discussing rules, keep in mind the points below.

A. All rules have a purpose.

B. Analyzing the purpose helps us evaluate rules.

C. All rules have advantages and disadvantages.

D. To justify changing a rule you must show that either: *1)* the rule doesn't meet the purpose or *2)* the purpose should be rejected.

E. All rules have exceptions.

About Families &
Needs and Wants

(1ˢᵗ Grade)

by Mary J. B. Hesser, Gloria Dei
Lutheran School, Sacramento, CA

Objectives of the remodelled lesson

The students will:
- engage in Socratic discussion about families and about needs and wants
- develop their perspectives on the concept 'family'
- clarify and analyze the difference between 'needs' and 'wants'
- probe into the nature of needs and wants, and consider the implications of different individuals having conflicting needs and wants

Original Lesson Plan

Abstract

The unit includes eight lessons discussing the make-up of families, recognizing family structures, differences and similarities in families, how families change, jobs family members may have, wants and needs of a family, and holidays families may celebrate. I have chosen two lessons from this unit, "Recognizing Family Structures" and "Wants and Needs of a Family" to remodel. In the first lesson, students are asked to interpret pictures of families, identify "big" and "small" families, and relate the pictures to their own circumstances (at least regarding size). The second lesson asks students to view various pictures and classify examples of wants and needs. The teacher is directed to introduce vocabulary including money, income, and buying.

Critique

The entire unit can be beneficial to first graders by helping them explore their environment, define and clarify their sense of self in relation to family and society, and compare and contrast others' experiences of family to their own. However, both lessons I have chosen impose definitions on the students and presuppose their appropriateness. To help students broaden their thinking and interpretation in reference to their experiences of family, I would drop the text's statements and substitute Socratic questioning strategies to encourage the students to think out their own definitions of family and family structures, how they arrived at those definitions, how they are affected when someone else's definition opposes their own, and what stereotyping is and how it is practiced.

Lesson 2 would also involve dropping the text and substituting questioning techniques to develop student thinking regarding what wants and needs are, how they change, etc. Ideally, this could lead to a Socratic discussion of the world's resources and individual student's egocentricity in relation to our use of these limited resources.

Strategies used to remodel

S–24 practicing Socratic discussion: clarifying and questioning beliefs, theories, or perspectives
S–12 developing one's perspective: creating or exploring beliefs, arguments, or theories
S–14 clarifying and analyzing the meanings of words or phrases
S–17 questioning deeply: raising and pursuing root or significant questions
S–35 exploring implications and consequences
S–4 exploring thoughts underlying feelings and feelings underlying thoughts

Remodelled Lesson Plan s–24

Lesson 1

Lesson 1 would include questions to facilitate discussion such as: What is a family? Is _____ a family? Why? Are you part of a family? Are some kinds of family good and some bad? Can one person be a family? Why or why not? How does it feel to be in your family? What if you could choose your family, tell us what you'd imagine about it. **S–12**

editors' note: "Who do you think of as members of your family? When you think of family, do you think of your grandparents, uncles, aunts, and cousins? Why or why not?"

Lesson 2

"The book says people have many needs and wants. What is a need? What is a want? Do people have many needs and wants? Give me some examples of need and wants. Why do you say X is a need? Why do you think Y is a want? **S–14** Do different people think differently about wants and needs? How? Can a want change to a need or a need to a want? How? Why? Are other people's needs and wants important to you? Why or why not?" **S–17**

"Can groups of people have wants and needs? Can nations have needs? Does the Earth have needs? What if your wants and needs affect what others want and need?" **S–35**

editors' note: "Do wants and needs feel the same? How can we tell which are wants and which are needs? Why might the difference between needs and wants be important?" **S–14**

"How might the way we are thinking affect what we want? Can you think of any examples of how changing the way you were thinking changed what you wanted?" **S–4**

Emotions: Anger

(1ˢᵗ — 3ʳᵈ Grades)

Objectives of the remodelled lesson

The students will:
- discuss the relationship between thoughts and feelings and analyze feelings using critical vocabulary
- examine assumptions that lead people to feel certain ways

Original Lesson Plan

Abstract

We have selected two lessons on anger from a series of lessons on children and emotions. In the first lesson, students are asked to interpret what a boy in a picture is feeling and cite specific context clues to support their interpretations. They then discuss what makes them feel angry. Following this, students review two sets of pictures in which someone is allegedly portrayed as being angry. Students are asked "Why are they angry? When do you feel this way?" In summary, students are asked to mention things that make people angry, and to discuss whether they think everyone is angry sometimes.

In the second lesson, students are asked to describe a picture (of three children working together, shooing away a girl who wants to join them) and infer that the girl is angry. They discuss two ways she could keep from being angry (by playing by herself, by bringing materials to the group to gain admittance).

from *Things We Do,* Frank L. Ryan,
et al. Houghton Mifflin Co. 1976.
pp. T66–T69.

Critique

Critical thinking requires understanding oneself. When feelings are discussed in terms of the thoughts associated with them, they can be more fully explored. We can probe the bases of our feelings by understanding the thoughts behind them. Thinking about our thoughts helps us better understand our feelings. The reverse is also true. Using the insight that our thoughts and feelings are connected, we can use our feelings to better understand our thinking. This lesson misses the opportunity to develop this crucial insight. Students should practice discussing their feelings and thoughts in relation to one another, and finding the assumptions underlying their feelings.

Strategies used to remodel

S–4 exploring thoughts underlying feelings and feelings underlying thoughts
S–28 thinking precisely about thinking: using critical vocabulary
S–5 developing intellectual humility and suspending judgment
S–30 examining or evaluating assumptions

Remodelled Lesson Plan s–4

This remodel will stress the relationship between thoughts and feelings, and how changing the way one thinks about a situation can change the way one feels.

In the first lesson, follow the question "Why do you think the people in these pictures are angry?" with "What kinds of things are they probably thinking?" Use critical thinking vocabulary whenever possible. The class could use the following format:

What happened?
How did the person feel?
What was assumed?
What was concluded? **S–28**

In the second lesson, after asking "How do you think the girl who is being told to stay away feels?" and "Why?", encourage different responses, rather than forcing the conclusion that the girl is angry. Some students, for example, may recognize that the girl may feel hurt. For each response ask, "If she feels..., then what is she probably thinking?" **S–5** The original lesson asks, "What could the girl do to keep from being angry?" If the students don't mention them, point out that there are two ways to change how you feel: you can change the situation, or change how you think about the situation.

When doing a unit on emotions, the class should discuss as great a variety of emotions as the student can name. For each emotion, have students give examples of when people may feel that way. These examples could also be put into the above format. Then the students can discuss the kinds of assumptions operating behind different emotions. **S–30**

Examples (using format)
A. Student states, "I got mad at Sally because she pushed me down." Use questions to elicit explanations.
  1. You felt mad.
  2. You *felt* Sally push you down and it hurt.
  3. You *assume* that people should not hurt each other.
  4. You *concluded* that Sally was wrong to push you down.
B. Student states, "I was excited because my birthday was the next day."
  1. You felt excited.
  2 You *knew* your birthday was the next day.
  3. You *assumed* that birthdays are fun.
  4. You *concluded* that you would have fun.

Students could also discuss whether everyone would always think and feel the same way in a given situation.

The Pledge of Allegiance

(1st–3rd Grades)

Objectives of the remodelled lesson

The students will:
- discuss the meaning of the Pledge of Allegiance
- begin to develop a concept of 'good citizenship'
- develop an appreciation for 'our republic', 'liberty', and 'justice'
- begin to develop insight into sociocentricity and the need for integrity by comparing ideals to actual practice and comparing U.S. and French ideals
- explore the relationships between symbols and what they represent

Standard Approach

The teacher explains the difficult words in the pledge, and the class discusses the flag and the importance of patriotism.

Critique

The lessons we reviewed on the subject over-emphasized the flag, while de-emphasizing allegiance to the country. They tended to confuse our ideals with our practice, thereby failing to suggest that it takes work to better live up to ideals. The common belief that loving your country means finding no fault with it is a major obstacle to critical thought. Fairminded thinking requires us to consider criticisms.

The lessons we reviewed do not fully explain the ideas in the pledge; therefore, students are making a promise they don't understand. Ideas as important and complex as 'good citizenship' aren't covered in sufficient depth.

Furthermore, many lessons lead students to believe that our ideals are uniquely American, ignoring how many other countries have similar ideals. This practice encourages sociocentric stereotyping of non-Americans. Therefore, we suggest that students discuss ideals that others share with us.

The remodel can be substituted for any lesson on the pledge. Some teachers may also want to have students critique the pledge lesson in their text.

Strategies used to remodel

S–14 clarifying and analyzing the meanings of words or phrases
S–32 making plausible inferences, predictions, or interpretations
S–27 comparing and contrasting ideals with actual practice
S–7 developing intellectual good faith or integrity
S–29 noting significant similarities and differences
S–2 developing insight into egocentricity or sociocentricity

193

Remodelled Lesson Plan

We have designed this lesson as a complete third grade level discussion. We believe, however, that the pledge should be discussed as early as the children recite it. For first and second grades, use as much of this lesson as your students can understand.

Teachers of second and third grades may have a pre-activity. Groups of students could use the dictionary to look up the words in the pledge and rewrite the pledge in their own words. We then recommend a thorough discussion of the pledge, such as that described below.

• A pledge is a promise. What is a promise? Why keep promises? How do you feel when someone breaks a promise to you? Is something a promise if you have no choice about whether or not to make it? **S–14**

• Allegiance is loyalty. (Use 'allegiance to a friend' as an analogy to enhance discussion.) So we are making a promise to be loyal. Loyal to what? (Flag and country.) The flag is a symbol of our country. (If necessary, discuss the meaning of 'symbol'.) To be loyal to the flag is to show respect for it. We do this as a way of showing respect for our nation. (Discuss our country's name.)

• "And to the republic for which it (the flag) stands." Our country is a republic. That means that we have the right to pick our leaders. (Compare this to other forms of government.) Do people in every country get to pick their leaders? If we select our leaders, then who is responsible for our government? **S–32** Why? (Discuss how the country is made up of land, people, and government, and so we have to care for all three.)

• Our country has ideals, some of which are in the pledge. (Discuss 'ideals'.) 'Indivisible' means something that stays whole, and is not split into parts. (Use households as an analogy to generate a discussion of why unity is important.) (Define 'liberty' and 'justice'.) We say "with liberty and justice for all." Why are these things important? How do you feel when you are treated unfairly? How would you feel if you couldn't decide anything for yourself? (Then discuss that last phrase, and ask who is meant by 'all'?) Is the idea that everyone is free and is always treated fairly a fact or an ideal? **S–27** What is the difference between a fact and an ideal? (Discuss) Are freedom and fairness easy or hard for a country to achieve? (Discuss) **S–7**

• Therefore, when we say the pledge, we promise to respect the flag and be good citizens. Since we live in a republic, the citizens are responsible for the government. So we promise to take care of the land, keep our country whole, and strive to make our government treat everyone fairly and let people be free.

The teacher should point out that the students are not required to say the pledge, that they have a choice to decide whether they want to make this promise this way.

You might want to tell the students that the French people hold the ideals of liberty, brotherhood, and equality. Have the students compare these to our ideals, then ask, "What do French and American points of view have in common?" (This could be a good place to have students critique the implications of their texts and why it was written that way: the tendency to want to think of ourselves as the only good people.) **S–2**

The next section is an introduction to the idea of a symbol. It helps the students distinguish between symbols and that which they represent.

Symbols S–29

You might begin with our flag, the skull-and-crossbones sign, and traffic lights as examples of symbols. Ask the students for more examples. Then ask, "Is there a symbol for you?" Use the analogy of the students' names as symbols of them in the following discussion: Is a symbol the same as the thing it symbolizes or stands for? Is the symbol as important as what it symbolizes? Why might people get upset when a symbol is mistreated? Is it right to treat or react to the symbol the way you treat or react to the thing it symbolizes? Why or why not?

The purpose of this handbook is to explain critical thinking by translating general theory into specific teaching strategies.

Sue's Mistake

(2nd Grade)

Objectives of the remodelled lesson

The students will:
- probe deeper into the concept of 'learning from a careless mistake'
- develop intellectual humility by avoiding the questionable conclusion suggested by the text

Original Lesson Plan

Abstract

The students' text tells about a student, Sue, who forgot her field-trip permission slip. Her father brings it to her, and she apologizes. The discussion includes the following ideas: Sue's mistake inconvenienced her father. Everyone makes mistakes. When we make mistakes we should apologize and thank anyone who helps us. We should learn from our mistakes. The reinforcement activities suggest the following situations for role play: a child breaks a window; a child scatters raked leaves; a child leaves his jacket outside; a child forgets to give water to his pet dog.

from *At School*, Virginia Finley, et al.,
Tiegs-Adams: People and their Heritage,
1983. by Silver Burdett & Ginn, Inc.
pp. 42–3.

Critique

This lesson reinforces a common and damaging confusion between feeling sorry only because someone's angry, and genuinely regretting an action and so avoiding repeating it. Although Sue apologized, students are not in a position to know if she really did learn from her mistake.

Strategies used to remodel

S–5 developing intellectual humility and suspending judgment
S–14 clarifying and analyzing the meanings of words or phrases

Remodelled Lesson Plan

First, since the question "Did Sue learn from her mistake?" encourages students to come to a conclusion when the evidence provided is inadequate, you could replace it with "How could we tell if Sue learned from her mistake? If Sue did learn, how would she behave in the future? What exactly did she do wrong? How could she avoid doing things like that?" **S–5** These questions will

196

give students practice distinguishing learning from a mistake in a practical sense, from substituting verbal rituals for a change in behavior.

Then, after the role–playing exercises in the original lesson (which encourage students to accept responsibility and say "I'm sorry"), have a general discussion of how learning from a mistake involves more than simply apologizing. Such a discussion enables students to analyze the concept of 'learning from a mistake.'

• How can you tell if someone has learned from a mistake? Do you ever say you're sorry, but then do it again? Why? Does saying that you're sorry mean that you've learned from your mistake? What if you repeat the mistake and the apology again and again? When can someone tell that you have learned from a mistake? (When you make things right — as in the text, by raking up the scattered leaves — and when you make an effort to not repeat it.) Have students give other examples from their experience, and ask if the case is one of *learning* from a mistake. **S–14**

Getting experience in lesson plan critique: What are the strengths and weaknesses of this lesson? What critical principles, concepts, or strategies apply to it?

Schools in India

(2nd Grade)

Objectives of the remodelled lesson

The students will:
- practice clarifying the concept 'school' by comparing their initial ideas to village schools in India, thereby improving their ability to distinguish relevant from irrelevant facts and sociocentric associations from the concept

Original Lesson Plan

Abstract

The students read and discuss their text, which covers the following points: since India is poor, not all children can go to school; not all schools have school buildings; sometimes villagers build school buildings; many adults go to school at night; children in India learn reading, writing, health, and practical skills.

from *Families and Social Needs,* Frederick M. King et al. Laidlaw Brothers, Doubleday & Company, Inc. 1968. pp. 119–121, T107–T109.

Critique

In order to think clearly and accurately about ideas, it is necessary to distinguish features which are necessarily related to an idea from those which we simply associate with the idea. The original lesson does not emphasize what is fundamental to all schools. We have used this lesson to show how to give students practice in struggling to clarify a concept and distinguishing their sociocentric associations with it from its essential characteristics. This material could encourage stereotyping by giving the impression that all Indian schools are small village schools with no electricity or other modern conveniences.

Strategies used to remodel

S–14 clarifying and analyzing the meanings of words or phrases
S–31 distinguishing relevant from irrelevant facts
S–2 developing insight into egocentricity or sociocentricity
S–10 refining generalizations and avoiding oversimplifications

Remodelled Lesson Plan S–14

To explore students' initial associations with the concept 'school', you might begin by asking them, "What do you think of when you think of school? Which of these are necessary for calling something a school? Are any of these things *not* necessarily related to a place being a school? Which? Why?" (Mark those items students have identified as irrelevant.) You might have a student or a few students (who need writing practice) make a permanent list of the items for later comparison to material discussed in the lesson. **S–31**

When the lesson has been read and recapped, the class could again examine their lists. Students could go through their texts again, noting pertinent points. The children are now in a position to analyze and evaluate their original conception in light of what they have read. "Remember the things that you said are necessary for a place to be a school? Which of those things do Indian schools share? Which do they not share? Should we call the schools in India 'schools'? Why or why not? Were any of your initial ideas about what makes a school a school too limiting? Which? Why? Why isn't that related to school-ness? What are the most important characteristics of schools? Why are they the most important?"

"Why did you have the ideas about schools that you did before you read? Where did you get those ideas? Do all of the schools you know about have those characteristics? Then why aren't all of these features relevant?" You might then explain that people have a tendency to confuse their associations and experiences with the real, essential meanings of words. Have students briefly discuss the problems this can cause when people read, hear, or see peoples whose experiences are very different. **S–2**

To address the possible stereotyping and generalization problem, the class could also consider other kinds of schools in India. "Are all Indian schools like these? Since there are cities in India and schools in the cities, do you think those schools are like the schools in the text? Like ours?" **S–10**

At the Television Studio

(2nd Grade)

Objectives of the remodelled lesson

The students will:
- discuss the credibility of ads by exploring their purpose
- learn to recognize common "tricks of the trade" in children's commercials
- discuss ways of being a smart consumer
- develop critical listening skills by analyzing ads and distinguishing relevant from irrelevant facts

Original Lesson Plan

Abstract

This lesson shows a woman who works for a television studio, taking pictures of a dog for a dog-food commercial. The text explains that commercial television is funded through the sale of commercials and that a dog food company buys commercial time which pays for a show about pets.

The teacher tells the students that the purpose of advertising is to convince the consumer to buy the product. This is why thousands of dollars are spent on one television commercial. The students are asked why they think people buy things that they see advertised on television and to name some of the things that they have wanted to buy after viewing a commercial.

from *In Neighborhoods,* Virginia Finley, et al. Tiegs-Adams: People and Their Heritage, 1982. by Silver Burdett & Ginn, Inc. p. 9.

Critique

This was one of a very few lessons that discussed advertising, so we decided to focus our critique and remodel on that aspect of the lesson. Since most school-age children have been exposed to and influenced by commercials, a lesson on evaluating advertising could be an opportunity to help students recognize manipulative techniques, and so be in a better position to decide how to spend their money.

The most serious problem with this lesson is that it doesn't explicitly have students follow out the implications of the statement "the purpose of advertising is to convince the consumer to buy". Therefore it does not cover the ways in which ads are often designed to mislead the audience. When the lesson asks students why people buy products they've seen advertised, it should also have students reflect on the *adequacy* of those reasons. Although it asks the students to name things they have wanted after seeing commercials, it fails to have students examine the ways ads influence them. The students should be asked why they wanted those products and discuss whether those products met their expectations. Furthermore, rather than using a dog food commercial as its example, it should have used a commercial aimed at children. And finally, by not discussing how a smart consumer would decide which product to buy, the lesson doesn't help the student overcome the influence of commercials or develop insight into critical listening.

Strategies used to remodel

S–16 evaluating the credibility of sources of information
S–35 exploring implications and consequences
S–22 listening critically: the art of silent dialogue
S–31 distinguishing relevant from irrelevant facts

Remodelled Lesson Plan S–16

Before doing this lesson, the teacher may want to spend some time watching children's commercials. The class can discuss the following questions: What are commercials and other advertisements? Why are they made? What does this purpose imply about ads? If I want you to buy something, what kinds of things might I say? Would I say anything bad about it? Why not? Have any of you ever wanted something after seeing a commercial for it? Why did you want it? Have you ever gotten something you wanted after seeing an ad? Was it what you expected it to be like? Have you ever been disappointed in a product when an ad had convinced you that you would love it? **S–35**

Point out that although advertisers cannot lie, they can use any misleading or manipulative technique short of an outright, provable lie. If students have trouble understanding this, you might use an example of a child defending herself as an analogy. For example, a child may truthfully say, "I didn't touch the lamp" when she knocked the table the lamp was on, causing it to fall and break. In a case like this, we would not praise the child for telling the truth.

Students could also brainstorm details in commercials they've seen and discuss the techniques used in them. The teacher could summarize these descriptions and comments on the board. "Tell me about some commercials you've seen. How do they try to get you or your parents to buy the product or use the service?" (Commercials show children playing with toys and acting as though they are having a great time. They claim that everyone wants their product and suggest that you will be the only one left out if you don't get it. Announcers and actors use an excited tone of voice. Cereal companies advertise toys and contests that they put in or on boxes. Showing food and showing people eating food makes you hungry for it.) The class or small groups of students could then discuss the items they listed. For each, ask, "Is this misleading? What kinds of things should we look out for when we watch ads?" If the students miss the following points, you could mention them: children in commercials are actors paid to look like they are having fun; there may be no difference between an advertised, more expensive product and an un-advertised, cheaper product; some aspects of commercials have nothing to do with the product (such as cartoon characters designed as advertising gimmicks). "How can we prevent ads from tricking us?" **S–22**

Then discuss what being a smart consumer entails. Ask students how they should decide which product is the best to buy. "How can we find out or figure out what would be worth the money? What kinds of things are good to know about toys or food if we want to be smart shoppers? How can we find these things out?" **S–31**

Finally, teachers with access to VCR's could videotape commercials for children's products and show them in class for students to analyze. **S–22** If you don't have access to a VCR, you could bring in other forms of advertising for children's products.

Getting experience in lesson plan critique: What are the strengths and weaknesses of this lesson? What critical principles, concepts, or strategies apply to it?

We Need Rules

(3rd Grade)

by Sharon Hochstettler, Prescott
U. S. D. #1, Prescott, AZ

Objectives of the remodelled lesson

The students will:
- discuss what it is to be a good school citizen and a bad school citizen
- clarify concepts of good rules and bad rules through an experiment of creating and following their own rules in the classroom
- discuss their experiment and weigh the advantages and disadvantages of being a rule maker
- transfer the concepts of good citizenship and personal freedoms to the city government level by visiting a judge and discussing a local gun control proposition

Original Lesson Plan

Abstract

The students read about rules at home and in the community. The entire lesson explores literal recall of laws, rules, and elections. Students bring in articles, read books, and invite public officials to class to learn who writes the laws. Students are encouraged to read about famous leaders.

from *The World and Its People,* Richard H. Loftin. Silver Burdett Publishing Co., 1984. pp. 163–167.

Critique

Citizenship vocabulary is introduced. However, most terms are those the student would already know. The manual provides teachers with "right" answers. There is no attempt to involve the student in assessing good and bad laws, nor to apply this information to significant issues in the students' lives. The text does not discuss the difficulty of making good laws or rules nor the difficulty in following them.

Strategies used to remodel

S–20 analyzing or evaluating actions or policies
S–11 comparing analogous situations: transferring insights to new contexts
S–6 developing intellectual courage
S–12 developing one's perspective: creating or exploring beliefs, arguments, or theories

Remodelled Lesson Plan

To clarify the concept of good citizenship, students will contrast a good school citizen and a bad school citizen. Then students will discuss how the school rules are made and the advantages and disadvantages of making such rules. A small group within the class will make up a set of rules to be followed for a week.

After a week, the class will critique the rules, discuss the advantages and disadvantages of being a rule maker, and apply the concept of good citizenship to rule makers. "Which of your rules were good rules? Which were bad rules? Why were these good and those bad? What does this tell us about the differences between good and bad rules? What is good about being a rule maker? What is bad about it? What is good and bad citizenship in a rule maker?" **S–20**

Our school is a block and a half from the county courthouse and across the street from the county jail. Students will next transfer what they have learned in the classroom to their county government. While interviewing a district judge, they will question the judge about advantages and disadvantages of being someone who carries out the laws.

Good and bad laws will be discussed. It is not against the law in Prescott to wear six-shooters. The National Rifle Association is strong in this area and our local state assemblyman has introduced a bill allowing citizens to carry concealed weapons. Discuss the advantages and disadvantages of such laws. **S–11**

Finally, students will visit the county jail and explore the consequences of not following laws, whether good or bad. "What are the consequences of not following rules? Is it ever worth the punishment not to follow a rule? Why or why not?" **S–6**

Following the above projects, students discuss the lives of Americans who have made laws, broken laws, and followed laws. Some famous leaders might include Woodrow Wilson, Franklin Delano Roosevelt, Martin Luther King, Oliver North, or George Washington. **S–12**

Looking to the Future

(3rd Grade)

Objectives of the remodelled lesson

The students will:
- discuss the implications of a passage to determine whether or not the text is misleading, thereby reading critically and developing the intellectual courage to question their texts
- discuss how to evaluate sources of information

Original Lesson Plan

Abstract

On two pages, students read about a slum in Washington, D.C. with unsafe housing conditions. Bulldozers came to Lafayette Square and knocked down thousands of houses, replacing them with new houses and apartments for the people to live in.

from *At School,* Eleanor Thomas, et al. Tiegs-Adams: People and their Heritage, 1983. by Silver Burdett & Ginn, Inc. pp. 180–1.

Critique

This student text may lead students to believe that slums no longer exist in Washington, D.C. By mentioning only one case, a case in which improvements were made, it overlooks the majority of cases in which improvements were not made. It does not mention or allude to the work that remains to be done. Since the student text is misleading, the student should be given a chance to critique it. Students need practice critiquing written material. They need to practice discussing the implications of claims.

Strategies used to remodel

S–21 reading critically: clarifying or critiquing texts
S–14 clarifying and analyzing the meanings of words or phrases
S–35 exploring implications and consequences
S–16 evaluating the credibility of sources of information
S–6 developing intellectual courage

Remodelled Lesson Plan s–21

First, students could read the original passage. The teacher can use the following questions as a pre-activity: What is a slum? Why are there slums? Why do people live in slums? What would it be like to live in a slum? Must there be slums? How can people get rid of slums? **S–14**

Then, the students could read the passage again, and discuss the following questions. "What does the text say about Washington, D.C.? When the text says 'In one part of Washington, houses were very old ... ' does that imply that the city had only one slum? Does the passage imply that there are no more slums in Washington?" Discuss at length. (The teacher may use a similar example, such as, "One girl in this room has a red dress." "Does that mean that no other girl in the room has a red dress? Would people usually think that that's what it means?" [Though a logician would say "no" most people would say "yes".]) **S–35**

Next, the teacher could ask, "How could we find out about the slums? Why do you think the text was written this way?" The teacher may mention that there are a variety of points of view on the causes of, and solutions to, the slum problem.

For further discussion of slums, or for reinforcement, students could discuss the following questions: Is getting rid of slums a difficult or easy problem? Why? Do we understand the causes of slums? What do we agree about? Disagree? How is this problem different from one like who should get to pick which TV show to watch? How can we find out what a city is like if we can't go there? What different sources of information might we find? Which of these would most likely leave out problems like slums? Which of these would be most likely to include such problems? Why do you think so?" **S–16**

"When can you assume that what you read is true? Under what conditions should you be skeptical and check other sources? (When someone is 'selling' products or ideas or wants to make things look good.) What kinds of materials can you trust? Why? Have you ever not believed what you heard or read? Have you ever tried to mislead someone? Why?" **S–6**

> *Critical thinkers realize that everyone is capable of making mistakes and being wrong, including authors of textbooks.*

Does Earth Move?

(3rd Grade)

Objectives of the remodelled lesson

The students will:
- discuss the importance and difficulty of openmindedness and intellectual courage by discussing Galileo's trial
- evaluate behavior and discuss thoughts underlying feelings of various parties involved
- relate the issues raised to their own lives

Original Lesson Plan

Abstract

This lesson covers the following points: Copernicus disagreed with others and said that the Sun, not the Earth, is the center of the solar system; later Galileo began to agree with Copernicus; some people got mad and had Galileo arrested. Students discuss the differences between the old and new ideas about the solar system and perform an experiment which shows why it is hard to say which theory is correct. Students play-act "Galileo's Trial" and discuss whether or not people forgot about Galileo's ideas after he had been put under house arrest.

from *Who Are We?*, Sara S. Beattie, et al.
The Houghton Mifflin Co. 1976.
pp. T68–T71.

Critique

This lesson misses the opportunity to discuss the importance of openmindedness and intellectual courage. Galileo's life presents an excellent example of someone who was punished for having a good idea, because the people around him were closedminded and refused to listen. Yet the lesson, because it doesn't relate the material to the students' lives, fails to foster insight into the importance of putting aside prejudices and fears, listening openmindedly, and speaking out for one's beliefs. Nor does it foster insight into the students' egocentricity by having students reflect on times when they have closedmindedly rejected a new idea.

Strategies used to remodel

S–6 developing intellectual courage
S–4 exploring thoughts underlying feelings and feelings underlying thoughts
S–7 developing intellectual good faith or integrity
S–20 analyzing or evaluating actions or policies
S–2 developing insight into egocentricity or sociocentricity
S–34 recognizing contradictions

Remodelled Lesson Plan s-6

When discussing Galileo's trial, encourage students to reflect on the importance of intellectual courage and openmindedness, by having the class discuss what their text describes.

• Why did people get mad at Galileo? What were they assuming? (That is, what might they have been thinking that made them angry?) **S–4** Who was in a better position to know if he was right, Galileo or his critics? Why? What should have happened?

• If Galileo was punished for speaking out, do you suppose other people felt free to say they agreed with him? If you had lived then and knew about this, would you have spoken out for his ideas, or kept quiet to keep out of trouble? How might you have felt about that? Which do you think is wiser, saying what you think or staying out of trouble? **S–7**

• Should Galileo have changed his mind or kept quiet because everyone disagreed with him? **S–20**

• Have you ever gotten mad when someone questioned a belief of yours? Is that a good thing to do? Why or why not? **S–20** Did you ever miss out on learning a new idea because you were angry and wouldn't listen? What can you do about this problem? **S–2**

• Have you ever been in Galileo's position where you said something that everyone disagreed with? How did the other people react? How did you feel? Why? Did you change your mind? Why or why not? Was it hard to speak out? Why or why not? **S–4**

• Is there something wrong with believing that other people should listen carefully to you, and take your ideas seriously, but you don't have to listen to them? **S–34**

An Oil-Drilling Community

(3rd Grade)

by Sharon Hochstettler, Prescott
U. S. D. #1, Prescott, AZ

Objectives of the remodelled lesson

The students will:
- exercise fairmindedness by considering negative aspects of petroleum use left out of the text
- critique the presentation in the text
- transfer what they learn about oil to the local question of a copper mine

Original Lesson Plan

Abstract

The student text describes vocabulary related to oil drilling, such as: petroleum, derrick, Alaskan pipeline, non-renewable resources and renewable resources. Where oil is found and how it is used are described. Students use maps and graphs to see where oil is found and what places (states and countries) have the most oil. Students are asked to explain why the Alaskan pipeline is raised above ground level.

> from, *The World and Its People,* Richard H. Loftin, Silver Burdett Publishing Co., 1984, pp. 147–150.

Critique

This lesson focuses on literal recall of minor details and ignores one of the most profound problems facing our environment today. It presents a biased view of the Alaskan pipeline. The student can easily see what conclusions are expected.

Strategies used to remodel

S–3 exercising fairmindedness
S–21 reading critically: clarifying or critiquing texts
S–11 comparing analogous situations: transferring insights to new contexts
S–12 developing one's perspective: creating or exploring beliefs, arguments, or theories

Remodelled Lesson Plan s-3

Since the two biggest problems in the original lesson are one-sidedness and lack of application to the students, my suggestions focus on addressing them.

Before beginning the unit, students will bring in current articles and pictures pertaining to the uses of oil and the damage oil drilling and transportation have caused. Since our community is presently involved in a heated debate over the development of a copper mine in the area, articles pertaining to the mine including reference to the environmental impact study should also be included.

Students will read the text, and identify the various uses of petroleum that it mentions. "How is the oil obtained? What is life like on the offshore oil platform? What is life like on the land near the offshore oil platform? How is life changed for people living far from the drilling site? For animals? What assumptions did the text make about these questions? In what ways did the articles agree and differ from the text?" **S–21**

Students in small groups will then write charts showing the benefits of oil. A subsequent activity will be a chart outlining problems caused by our dependence on oil. These charts will then be compiled by the entire class. Next, the class will do the same activity for copper mining in Prescott, Arizona.

"What might life be like in a copper mine? What might life be like for people living near the mine? How is life changed for people and others living far from the mining site?" **S–11** Local speakers, for and against the mine, would be invited to present their ideas to the class. Students would then choose a concluding writing activity, such as letters to companies, editors, poems, creative writing stories. **S–12**

editors' note: Students can sum up with a general evaluation of our petroleum use by examining charts of positive and negative points. "Given the pluses and minuses of our heavy use of petroleum, do you think continuing to use so much of it is a good thing? Why or why not? If you think its a bad idea, what could we do instead?"

Small groups of students could take items from the list of uses of petroleum and try to think of ways to cut down on petroleum products.

"What bad things about petroleum use were mentioned in your text? What other bad things did we discuss? Why weren't these mentioned in the text?" **S–21**

Farms Yesterday and Today

(3rd Grade)

by Joanne Alford, Edwina Monroe, and
Alice Newell, Greensboro
Public Schools, Greensboro, NC

Objectives of the remodelled lesson

The students will:
- name ways in which farms have changed
- state reasons why farms have become more productive
- pursue root questions by exploring the effects of technology on life on farms through research, writing, and discussion, thereby developing intellectual perseverance and confidence in reason
- transfer insights from this lesson to future discussions regarding technology

Original Lesson Plan

Abstract

Students compare how farms started, grew, and changed to meet the needs of the community. They study a variety of farms and products, learn how machines produce more products on fewer farms, and make a survey to determine what products are grown in which states. Nine vocabulary words are highlighted. Visuals are provided to compare and contrast. There are check-up questions for recall and critical thinking. Research idea: locate present-day farm machines (plows, tractors, harrows, and planters) and compare them with those used long ago.

Critique

The basic idea of helping students to be more aware of practices concerning a real social issue involving an old and new point of view, is good. Empathy building exercises help students appreciate the progress of modern technology by looking at how it affects the industry today. Students could also develop other ideas about technological advances on the basis of what they know. They should also examine the conclusion that things have improved over time through the education of the farmers and scientific breakthroughs.

Strategies used to remodel

S–17 questioning deeply: raising and pursuing root or significant questions
S–33 giving reasons and evaluating evidence and alleged facts
S–13 clarifying issues, conclusions, or beliefs
S–9 developing confidence in reason
S–8 developing intellectual perseverance
S–23 making interdisciplinary connections
S–11 comparing analogous situations: transferring insights to new contexts

Remodelled Lesson Plan *S–17*

The remodel will focus on the question: Are modern farms more productive than farms in the past?

Students will brainstorm about farm life in the past and present. After a discussion which would include vocabulary, visuals, and reports, the teacher will introduce questions. "Are farms more productive? Why or why not? (Put their reasons on the board.) Are these good conclusions? Explain."

Finally, ask, "If we agree that farms are more productive, then what evidence can we give that supports our conclusion?" *S–33*

editors' note: To address the criticism that the standard approach doesn't have students examine the conclusion that things have improved, the question could be broadened to, "Are modern farms *better* than farms in the past?" The class could brainstorm about the question's meaning and break it down into sub-questions: Are farms more productive or efficient? Are farms more fun to live on? Do farms produce better food? etc. *S–13*

Students could form themselves into groups each of which will explore one sub-question in an extended activity that has them read, write a rough draft response, discuss these drafts, and rewrite them into a group paper. The teacher could duplicate these papers for the whole class to read. *S–9*

Class discussion of these papers could then explore the question, "In what ways have farms changed, and which are changes for the better?" *S–8*

Each student could write two drafts of an individual essay (you could also tell students that they can use the group papers as references). *S–9* Make all essays available for student perusal. This project (longer than the original) includes reading, research, writing, science, technology, economics, environment, and critical thinking and is a more neutral exploration than the original. *S–23*

This topic could be even further expanded to, "How has technology changed things — in what ways for the better and in what ways for the worse?"

Later in the year, when the class discusses technology in general or some specific technological advance, the teacher could remind students of this lesson. "How does what we said about farms and technology apply here? What does our work then tell us about this case? How is this different?" *S–11*

City Park

(3ʳᵈ Grade)

Anonymous

Objectives of the remodelled lesson

The students will:
- practice independent thinking by making their own list of things that they like in parks
- exercise fairmindedness by considering features other groups of people might want in a park
- give reasons for their park design
- analyze and evaluate the park design policies
- develop intellectual perseverance by revising their park designs after getting feedback from the class
- discuss and analyze their methods and processes, thereby deeply exploring social studies

Original Lesson Plan

Abstract

Students are given the task of designing a park (within budget). They have its dimensions and a price list. They are told that it has a hill, a stream, a small tree, and a large tree (which they can place wherever they want). They are told to list the features they want, star their favorites, and make sure they are within budget. Students draw the natural features on butcher paper, draw and cut out pictures of materials and equipment, and glue them to the design of the park.

Critique

editors' note: To fairmindedly consider the needs of the other age groups that might use the park, students should engage in extended discussion. Students could assess the various parks designed by their classmates and revise their work. By changing the lesson from an individual to a collaborative effort, students will have more ideas to work with, can produce a better product, and can analyze the methods they used — the design process and the group management process. Thus, the lesson becomes a more realistic version of what adult group planners do, including the social aspects.

Strategies used to remodel

S–1   thinking independently
S–3   exercising fairmindedness
S–33 giving reasons and evaluating evidence and alleged facts
S–20 analyzing or evaluating actions or policies
S–8   developing intellectual perseverance
S–17 questioning deeply: raising and pursuing root or significant questions

Remodelled Lesson Plan

Present the problem. The size of the proposed park is 300 feet by 200 feet. Compare this to some known landmark such as the school yard or a football field.

With the whole class, brainstorm a list of features they like in parks. **S–1** You may want to talk about features other groups of people like. "Who will use this park? For what — what would they like to do there? What would these people need to be able to use the park that way? What would little kids like to have in the park? Teen-agers? Grown-ups? What would be a fair way to decide how to give everyone some things they want?" **S–3**

Put students into groups of 3 or 4. Tables are helpful, but students may also work on the floor. Give students butcher paper, rulers, paper, felt pens, scissors, tape or glue, and the worksheets.

Allow ample time when the plans have been completed for each group to make a presentation to the class explaining the merits of its project. "Why did you include those things? Why did you put this there?" **S–33** Encourage questions from the rest of the class to analyze and evaluate each project, and compare the parks. "What do you like about this design? Why is that good? How would this be used? Can you see any problems arising from this design? Is one of the designs better than the rest?" The teacher could help students see the values presupposed in the various designs and evaluations of the parks. **S–20**

The class could do one of the following extensions:

Take a field trip to a nearby park and sketch its layout.

Redesign the school playground.

Draw a park exactly to scale.

Make a three-dimensional model of your park.

Research the actual cost of materials and equipment to build your park.

Write an essay explaining the merits of your park design.

After discussion of the plans, allow interested students to make revisions that will improve their parks and re-submit them to the class. "What changes did you make? Why? Why is that better? Is anything lost by making that change? Why didn't you do it that way before?" **S–8**

editors' note: This lesson has rich potential for deeply exploring social studies at the "micro-level". To take advantage of this, the teacher could have the class discuss the processes used by each group — how they divided the task into subtasks, how they addressed disagreement, etc. "What did your group do first? Why? Then what? Did you have any problems? (disagreement within the group, forgetting a crucial element and so having to completely redo the design, not keeping track of the budget, etc.) What? Why? How did you solve it? How would you avoid that problem in the future? Did any other groups have the same problem or a similar problem? How did you deal with it? How did that work? Did any other group approach the task differently than this group? How? What did you do first? Why? Now that you've finished this project, what would you do differently if you did it again? Why? What would you do the same way? Why?" **S–17**

The Health Department

(3rd Grade)

Objectives of the remodelled lesson

The students will:
- pursue basic questions regarding the functions of government and the need for regulatory agencies
- develop insight into egocentricity by exploring why people who work with food might be careless by comparing their perspective to that of Health Department workers
- practice reference skills by using their texts as a reference

Original Lesson Plan

Abstract

The student text describes a number of functions of the Health Department, including these: testing for germs; checking the quality of food and the cleanliness of workers and machines; working in clinics. The "Providing background" section in the teacher's notes explains the progress in disease control and medicine, offers the word 'epidemic', and mentions our longer life span.

from *At School,* Virginia Finley, et al. Tiegs-Adams: People and their Heritage, 1979. by Silver Burdett & Ginn, Inc. pp. 66–67.

Critique

This lesson is a missed opportunity to have students discuss one of the most profound problems in human nature. The need for regulatory agencies is a symptom of a greater problem than poor food quality and lack of cleanliness; it is a symptom of our tendency to ignore the rights and needs of others when our own interest is involved. Using a specific example like the need for the Health Department, can highlight for students the ideal of government as a protector of peoples' rights from people with more narrow interests. This helps lay the foundation for students' views on the purposes and functions of government. Since this is a key area, we have included several of the innumerable possible extensions. Teachers using this text may want to rob time for some of these by dropping trivial lessons and activities.

Strategies used to remodel

S–17 questioning deeply: raising and pursuing root or significant questions
S–2 developing insight into egocentricity or sociocentricity
S–25 reasoning dialogically: comparing perspectives, interpretations, or theories
S–19 generating or assessing solutions
S–23 making interdisciplinary connections
S–21 reading critically: clarifying or critiquing texts
S–8 developing intellectual perseverance

Remodelled Lesson Plan S–17

Before introducing the original lesson on the Health Department, students could reflect on the problem of egocentricity by discussing times they knowingly broke rules, weren't as careful as they knew they should be, or showed little or no concern for the legitimate rights of others. Students could discuss why they did as they did, what they were thinking at the time, and what they think about it now. **S–2**

You might then tell the students that they are going to read about one solution to the problem of people being careless or selfish in ways that can hurt other people's health. It's one of the solutions involving government. Students could then read the original lesson on the Health Department. (You may also want to mention penalties for non-compliance with public health standards.)

To probe deeper into the need for regulatory agencies, the teacher can supplement the original lesson with the following questions: Why do we need the Health Department? In what ways does it help all citizens? In what ways does it help consumers? Businessmen?

• Why do Health Department workers have to check places where food is stored, processed, sold, and served? Why don't workers at those places check health conditions? Could the Health Department workers simply ask the people who work with food whether the rules are being followed? Or their bosses? Would some people ever ignore the rules? Why?

• How do you think the people who own and work in places the Health Department checks feel about the Health Department? Why? Would they all feel that way? Why or why not? If you owned a store and Health Department workers told you some of your meat was bad and that you couldn't sell it (you had to throw it away), how might you feel? Why? What might you think? If you felt that way, how are you looking at the situation? What seems most important to you? How does that compare to how the Health person sees things? **S–25**

• Why does the government do this? Could someone else do it instead? Which would be better? Why? **S–19**

• What does this lesson tell us about government and some of the reasons we have governments? What other reasons for government do we know about? Are they like these in any ways? How could we explain all of the reasons for government that we know about?

This topic could be extended several ways:

In an extended project, the class could relate the Health Department to other ways in which government tries to protect the rights of citizens. Students could develop or practice their research skills by looking in their texts for other governmental agencies or references to government. "How could we find out where else our book talks about this? What words should we look for in the contents and index? Let's look some up. What other books could we look in? Where? How?" Small groups of students could look up a few references each and take notes to share with the class. **S–23** "From all of our sources, what things did we find out about what government does? What does this tell us about government?" **S–21**

The language arts or research aspect of this activity could be further extended by having students discuss their research processes, successes, and failures. "What did you look up? How? Did you find anything? Why do you think you didn't find what you wanted there? Where did you find what you were looking for?" **S–8**

This material could be related to science through health lessons, what germs are, what shots are for, etc. **S–23**

Students could relate science and history by finding out about past epidemics, their causes and effects, or the history of medicine (perhaps through biographies of those who contributed to major medical breakthroughs). **S–23**

Judgment is best developed, not when told what, how, and why to judge, but by repeatedly judging and then assessing those judgments.

Starting from Scratch

(3rd Grade)

by Michael Ormsby, Bennett Valley
School District, Petaluma, CA

Objectives of the remodelled lesson

The students will:
- raise and pursue root questions about law, government, leaders, and cooperation
- develop insight into their egocentricity and transfer those insights to the situation of the shipwrecked people
- begin to see the need for global understanding
- generate and assess solutions to the problems of the stranded people

Original Lesson Plan

Abstract

The text provides selections from a diary of a group of people shipwrecked on a deserted island. The entries for Days 1, 2, 5, 10, 15, 25, and 26 chronicle the difficulties the people had in working together. Day 26 ends with, "Nobody could agree last night. Today all work has stopped. What are we going to do?" The text tells students that groups need rules, that one way of making rules is to vote, and that communities often need leaders. The lesson ends with several questions on comprehension and evaluation.

Critique

The lesson doesn't allow students to discover for themselves the necessity of having rules regulating behavior for the common good. The introductory paragraphs tell the student what he or she is supposed to learn in the lesson. This makes the lesson uninteresting and not very effective.

The diary itself is very interesting and its brevity, which in other lessons in the text makes for oversimplification, raises a number of questions which require reading between the lines. The need to have rules need not be imposed on the student, but rather should be something they discover for themselves through the understanding of deeper issues: seeing other people's points of view; recognizing one's selfishness; seeing the need for global understanding.

editors' note: The text unfairly pushes two conclusions on students: the people on the island should have voted (as opposed to using consensus, for example), and that they needed a leader (as opposed to, say, having different people responsible for particular tasks). The text fails to raise the questions of whether there should be punishments for not working (mentioned in the diary), and whether jobs should have been imposed by the leader without discussion or people should have had some choice of which jobs to take. On the whole, the discussion fails to take advantage of the multitude of significant questions raised in the diary which could be used to have students begin to consider the functions of government.

218

Strategies used to remodel

S–17 questioning deeply: raising and pursuing root or significant questions
S–19 generating or assessing solutions
S–2 developing insight into egocentricity or sociocentricity
S–11 comparing analogous situations: transferring insights to new contexts
S–21 reading critically: clarifying or critiquing texts

Remodelled Lesson Plan S–17

The teacher and students read the diary part of the lesson together. Begin discussion by asking who wrote the diary and why. Then explore the specific events in the diary:

• Why did the signal group go swimming? What would have happened if a boat came along while they were swimming? Should they have gone swimming? What should they have done?

• What do you think was happening to the food (why was it missing)? What other possibilities, theft, etc.? How could they have found out for sure?

• When the food gatherers went cave exploring was it fair that other people had to go hungry? What would have been the most fair way to handle this problem? The least fair? **S–19**

Now turn the discussion to the crucial point of egocentricity. Ask students who were the most selfish or shortsighted people in the group. Explore the different roles of the people — followers, leaders, rebels, people who didn't care about anything, people who only cared about themselves, people who only cared about immediate fun. With an understanding of their egocentricity, move the students' discussion to the need for a global and long-range point of view:

• What is the responsibility of each person to themselves and to the group? How does this story relate to your own experiences? Have you been in a situation where people weren't doing what they needed to, and people were arguing about how to solve the problems? What happened? Why? **S–2** How do you think it should have been handled? What do your examples tell us about what the people on this island could have done? **S–11**

At this point, students should be able to consider the usefulness of establishing rules and who should be deciding on those rules. "What ways do you think the group could have prevented the problem of no one working together on Day 26? Are rules harder to follow if you haven't had a hand in making them? Why? Is that right?"

Have students write or describe two different scenarios for Day 35.

editors' note: To take even more advantage of the issues raised in the diary segments and the text, the lesson could be extended in several ways. Students could explore the different positions taken on the island about how to solve the problems: Why did one say, "Who asked you to be leader anyway? We're not on the ship anymore, you know."? What was the point? Do we know what this person wanted? What did each person who spoke want? Which of these ideas were the most reasonable? Least reasonable? Why?"

• Was the captain a good leader on shore? Why or why not? Why did some people agree with the captain? Why did others resent him? What kind of person would make a good leader for these people? Why? What does this tell us about the differences between good leaders and poor ones?

Students could practice generating and assessing solutions by getting into small groups and imagining themselves on the island. They would discuss what to do to survive and have a chance of being rescued. "What do we need? Who should do what? How could we prevent the kinds of problems the people had? What should we do if people don't do their jobs?" Groups could share their results and processes, along with the problems they had.

Small groups of students could define the problem. The groups could then share formulations, and explore and argue for many possible ways of looking at the problem. Taking some reasonable ways of understanding the problem, students in groups can come up with possible solutions and justifications for the solutions they prefer. *S–19*

• What does the text say was the problem? Did the group lack rules? A leader? Would voting solve their problem? Why or why not? What do you think is the problem? Why does the text explain the problem the way it does? *S–21*

• What does this story tell us about government, its purposes and its problems?

I discover what I think by expressing my thoughts in words.

City Government in East Bend

(3rd Grade)

Objectives of the remodelled lesson

The students will:
- clarify the concepts of good citizenship and good public official by contrasting opposites of each
- discuss the difficulty of voting intelligently
- distinguish relevant from irrelevant facts for choosing a candidate
- discuss what sources of information a voter should rely on
- practice clarifying and critiquing claims in their texts which confuse ideals with actual practice

Original Lesson Plan

Abstract

The students read about the mayor of East Bend. They read that she went on TV to try to convince citizens that some new plans will be good for the people of the city. The students read that she talks and listens to many different people, and has the help of city workers who are paid with tax money. The class discusses the importance of citizens and city workers working together. Students learn that mayors are elected and are asked whether or not the mayor is good at her job.

from *In Communities,* Tiegs-Adams: People and Their Heritage, 1979. by Silver Burdett & Ginn Inc. pp. 61–2.

Critique

Although a number of important concepts are introduced in this lesson, none of them are made sufficiently clear for students at this level. Since the lesson neglects to contrast 'good citizen' with 'bad citizen', many of the important details of citizenship are overlooked. Among these is intelligent voting as the basis of a free and democratic society. As early as possible, students should begin to understand the demands of citizenship in a democracy.

Students are asked if the mayor of East Bend is a good mayor without any discussion of the criteria for judging mayors. The lesson lists some of the mayor's duties, but nowhere suggests that the list is incomplete. This lesson also confuses facts with ideals by saying that city planners listen for ideas from citizens, rather than saying that *good* city planners listen to citizens and take their concerns into account.

Strategies used to remodel

S–14 clarifying and analyzing the meanings of words or phrases
S–10 refining generalizations and avoiding oversimplifications
S–31 distinguishing relevant from irrelevant facts

S–16 evaluating the credibility of sources of information
S–21 reading critically: clarifying or critiquing texts
S–27 comparing and contrasting ideals with actual practice

Remodelled Lesson Plan

To highlight the fundamental characteristics of good citizenship, the teacher might help students contrast 'good citizen' with 'bad citizen'. Say, "Since a good citizen of a city helps the city to be better, a bad citizen either doesn't help the city, or does things that hurt it." Then ask the students, "What can people do to help or hurt their city?" Possible contrasting examples include the following:

Show concern for their city.	Don't care about their city.
Work for change whenever necessary.	Don't work for needed changes. Hinder needed changes.
Have a high regard for the function that good laws serve.	Have no regard for the laws of the city.
Work to change laws that don't meet the peoples' interests.	Break laws with no attempt to change them.
Keep the city clean.	Make the city messy.
Help the city government make good decisions.	Try to get city government to make bad decisions (usually for self interest).
Try to vote for the best people for each elected position.	Don't vote, or vote without knowing or caring what is best for the city.
When voting, know what the elected position requires.	Don't understand the nature of elected offices.
Know about the candidates.	Don't know much about the candidates. **S–14**

Next, the students could focus on elections and how to decide who to vote for for mayor. Before students read, the teacher could ask them to look for what makes a mayor a good mayor. Small groups of students could share their lists, brainstorm more entries, and list opposites for each entry. The class could share all lists.

Below are some ideas that could be contrasted in the discussion. We have distinguished those which were mentioned in the text (but not contrasted) from those which were not mentioned. You may have to point out that how good a mayor is, is a matter of degree. **S–10**

In book

tells citizens plans	inaccessible, secretive
works hard	is lazy, takes long breaks, inefficient
talks to lots of different citizens, is a good listener, cares	doesn't listen or care, or cares only about friends
works with city planners and other skilled people	doesn't get help from relevant people

Not in book

makes wise appointments	gives jobs to friends, appoints wrong people
is fair and honest	is unfair, dishonest, takes bribes
uses funds efficiently	misuses or wastes funds
has authority	can't get people to listen or obey
shares the citizens' goals	doesn't share citizens' goals **S–14**

After this discussion, the students could talk about the difficulties of voting for a mayor. You might ask, "What do we need to know about the candidates to be able to decide who would make the best mayor? What facts are relevant? How can we find out what the candidates are like? What facts are irrelevant to our decision? (nice smile, good looking, kisses babies, funny) Why do you think so? **S–31** If I want you to elect me, I'll try to make myself seem good, and make the other candidates look bad. What do candidates say they will do if elected? What kinds of things will candidates not mention? What sources can we trust to give us accurate information about candidates? Why?" **S–16** The teacher could emphasize the importance of looking at the candidates' past performances, especially evidence regarding their honesty, fairness, and efficiency.

To sum up the lesson, you could ask the following questions: Is voting wisely easy or hard? What is hard about trying to be a good citizen? Or the students could review the text and write an evaluation of it. "What does the text include? Leave out? Do we know enough about this mayor to judge whether or not she is a good mayor? **S–21** Do all city planners listen to citizens? Is the claim that they do, a fact or an ideal? How could we rewrite the sentence so that it states a fact?" **S–27**

Knighthood

(3rd Grade)

by Linda M. Newton, Marin County Office of Education, San Rafael, CA

Objectives of the remodelled lesson

The students will:
- develop intellectual perseverance by learning about the Middle Ages through books, two viewings of a movie, and discussion
- raise root issues by identifying the class structure of the Middle Ages
- practice listening by watching a movie for a definite purpose and analyzing what they hear
- relate the purpose of knighthood to the necessity for protection in the Middle Ages
- transfer the insight into class distinctions to the present day and to their lives

Original Lesson Plan

Abstract

This lesson is part of a thematic unit entitled "Old Folktales at Home" and the sub-unit "The Princess and the Pea". The latter focuses on castles, chivalry, and heraldry. The task the students are to perform is as follows: List the stages of becoming a knight. Describe the responsibilities of each stage.

In class there are various library books the children may peruse. A film, *Medieval Knights*, about a boy who becomes a knight, will be viewed. The main body of information the children will need is presented in the film. It depicts two boys beginning as pages, playing jousting games and being taught by the lady of the manor. Their training in horseback-riding and tilting the quintain is emphasized. Only one of the boys becomes a knight — the one of noble birth. In advance of the film, the children are told what the task is. After viewing, the children tell what each stage is, the usual age, and the duties. The teacher records this on the board. There is a discussion which takes place as well. The thrust of the discussion is the warring aspect of knighthood. Previously, the purpose and history of castle architecture for protection have been studied. The discussion on knighthood is linked to that.

Critique

While this task is basic information (in Bloom's taxonomy, knowledge and comprehension) it doesn't begin to have the children think in any depth about the facts. More attention should be placed on the aspect of the warrior class as an offshoot of the needs of the people in the Middle Ages. This would include the idea of a class society and the education the different classes received. There are implications for our day and age with respect to socio-economics and prejudice.

Another idea that can be further developed regarding an aspect of protection — loyalty, since knights had to swear an oath of loyalty to their lords. Of all the themes mentioned here, this value is closest to the children's lives.

There is no reason why this task should have to be completed in one lesson or the film shown only once. Actually, the film is full of details and omissions supporting the concept of a class society. For example, a priest is recording the boy's history by hand and in calligraphy. Left out is who provides the food for the feast or who the lord commands. There is more to mention before viewing the film than just the task, and there is more to discuss and do afterwards that could enlarge the students' understandings of the task. The seeds for future discussions on personal actions are embedded in these concepts.

Strategies used to remodel

S-8 developing intellectual perseverance
S-17 questioning deeply: raising and pursuing root or significant questions
S-22 listening critically: the art of silent dialogue
S-16 evaluating the credibility of sources of information
S-6 developing intellectual courage
S-7 developing intellectual good faith or integrity

Remodelled Lesson Plan s-8

A day or so before viewing the film, the children will brainstorm the terms people were called during the time of castles (king, queen, prince, knight, duke, etc.). From that list it is possible to put at least some of them in order. The kind of order will have to be elicited, but it will probably be in hierarchical order. At that time, the word 'hierarchy' would be introduced. Some positions left out would be elicited by the teacher, such as, "Who grew the food or repaired items, etc.?" The terms could then be supplied by the teacher. The question of why the children didn't know the term 'serf' would be explored. (They weren't important; they weren't leaders; they aren't interesting; they didn't lead fascinating lives; etc.) This can't be left like this. The truth of their answers needs to be addressed by asking: How do you know they aren't important, etc.? What was the importance of serfs? What would the kings and queens have eaten and worn if there hadn't been serfs? How do you know about kings and queens? (There are lots of fairy tales and movies about them, etc.) The difference in the excitement level can be seen along with the idea that we hear a lot about our present leaders in the news but not about ourselves and neighbors, generally speaking. This establishes the idea of classes. **S-17**

On the day of the film, prior to viewing it, the children will be asked what they already know about knights (fighters, wear armor, etc.). Another question to tie the above lesson with the film would be: Where were they in the hierarchy? Then there would be the questions that would prepare the children for the film. "What did knights do when there wasn't a war? Would they want a war to start? Who did they fight for? How could the king be sure the knight would fight only for him?" To assist them in developing critical listening skills, the children would be told to look for the answers to these questions and for the stages in becoming a knight and their responsibilities.

After the film, the discussion could begin with checking the answers to the above questions. Regarding the last question, the children in the third grade usually do not know the word 'loyalty' and their understanding of the concept is limited. First, the part of the knight taking an oath would be looked at. It could be likened to the Pledge of Allegiance. The synonyms of loyalty and faithful are helpful: true, constant, devoted, and trustworthy. They suggest a long attachment to a person, country or cause. Of these words, 'trustworthy' would mean the most to third graders and could be built on. In any case, connecting the concept with loyalty to a friend could be made. "What do you do to show a friend or your family that you're loyal?" The children could write and share these.

Depending on the attention span of the children, the next part of the lesson could take place at this time or on another day. A chart or mind-map could be used to list the stages of knighthood. It would include: name of the stage, age, responsibilities, studies, teacher(s), and social class. These categories could be elicited from the children. Then the children could write a sentence summarizing each stage. At that point they might be ready to draw some conclusions about knighthood: What sort of people made the best knights? What else besides fighting were knights prepared for (what other jobs)? Why do you think the people of the Middle Ages needed a warrior class? What do you think about having a warrior class? **S–22**

Another day, the film might be shown again to refresh everyone's memory. The purpose of this lesson is to examine a class society. Twice before classes have been introduced and discussed. The children could be told to pay special attention to who gets to do what in the film. Afterwards, questions can be asked that help the children see this. **S–22** "In the film, who wrote the history? (priest) Who did he tell about? Why? (He knew him; he liked him) What does that tell us about writers of movies or histories? (They write about what they know and are interested in.) Why didn't a serf write the story? Why didn't the priest write about a serf?" Some of the class distinctions can be made here regarding education and separation of classes. "What might the higher classes think of the lower classes since they were uneducated and did the farming and other labor? (dumb, not able to be in charge) How do you know?" **S–16**

As these are delved into, the elements of transfer to the present can be brought in. "How is any of this like our life today? What do you think of people who do different kinds of jobs? What classes do we have? Do we have a warrior class? Do we have people who are uneducated? Have we ever? (slaves) What has happened to the children and grandchildren of slaves? What kinds of people don't you want to associate with? Should they be in a separate social class and treated differently? Why or why not?" **S–6**

Children are usually very sensitized to the value of fairness. They can now examine their own practices in being fair. They could write in their journals about how they exclude certain classmates and the effects this has on those classmates. **S–7** At another time this lesson can be used as background for discussions on Martin Luther King and Abraham Lincoln and what their lives stood for.

Problem Solving

(3rd Grade)

Objectives of the remodelled lesson

The students will:
- generate and assess solutions by applying a three step problem solving technique
- clarify the issue
- practice suspending judgment when they have insufficient information
- gather and use information to help solve problems
- evaluate proposed solutions through dialectical reasoning

Original Lesson Plan

Abstract

Students read about some of the problems caused by un-planned growth in the city of East Bend. They review five steps for solving problems, and mention possible solutions. Then they read different citizens' ideas about city problems, and see how some ideas conflict. They discuss the importance of people planning together.

The steps for problem solving are:

1. State the problem clearly.

2. Make a list of possible solutions.

3. Gather and examine information.

4. Choose the solution that seems best.

5. Test the chosen solution to find out if it really solves the problem.

from *In Communities,* Eleanor Thomas, Tiegs-Adams: People and Their Heritage, 1979. by Silver Burdett & Ginn, Inc. pp. 61–2.

Critique

This lesson is typical of the lessons on problem solving we reviewed. It provides a technique for problem solving, yet never applies it or has the students apply it to problems. At most, in any given problem solving lesson, the text or student applies two of the five steps. Students can't be expected to learn how to use a technique which they never practice in its entirety. Although learning to apply the problem solving technique to a city problem would be too difficult for children, they could use it first on problems within their experience.

Furthermore, the technique they suggest has significant problems. Although step 1 of this technique calls on students to state the problem, it fails to recognize that the first statement of a problem is seldom best. A problem cannot be stated accurately until the relevant information has been reviewed. In the above technique, information gathering is left until step 3. Stating the problem requires a process in which the problem becomes increasingly clearer in the light of accumulated information and analysis. The more completely, clearly, and accurately the problem is formulated, the more effective is the discussion of its solutions. Moreover, information gathering should include finding out the results of others' attempts to solve similar problems. No problem solving lesson we reviewed suggested this idea. Discussion of possible solutions should not precede information gathering. If we don't know what's going on or why, how can we suggest reasonable, helpful solutions? By ignoring this point, the standard approach inadvertently undermines students' insight into the need for historical background.

Also, the technique fails to mention the criteria by which solutions are to be judged, except that of "seeming to be the best". As vague and arbitrary a criterion as this, leads students to believe that they have evaluated solutions when they have not. Calling a solution "best" implies a comparison to other solutions, a comparison that presupposes criteria. Furthermore, students are asked to judge which solution is best without first considering "best for whom". Thus their method encourages students to assume one perspective, at the expense of considering others. Therefore, the technique in this lesson misses the opportunity to have students practice fairmindedness, dialectical reasoning, and the analysis of issues.

Strategies used to remodel

S–19 generating or assessing solutions
S–13 clarifying issues, conclusions, or beliefs
S–5 developing intellectual humility and suspending judgment
S–29 noting significant similarities and differences
S–26 reasoning dialectically: evaluating perspectives, interpretations, or theories

Remodelled Lesson Plan s–19

We developed an alternative set of problem solving steps, to substitute for the five-step technique outlined in the original lesson.

1. Define the Problem: Make a provisional statement of the problem. Raise questions about the details and causes of the problem. Are any concepts unclear? What kinds of facts do we need? How can we find these facts? Is anything being evaluated? If so, what are the standards we will use to evaluate? Gather and examine the information needed to settle those questions. Restate the problem more clearly in light of that information. Continue this process until you can answer questions like the following: What, exactly, is wrong? What happens in the situation? Why is this bad? What causes this to happen? Who and what are involved? How do the others involved see the problem? What other problems are related to this and how?

2. Analyze the Problem: Reflect on the final formulation of the problem and answer the following questions: What would each person involved consider necessary to solve the problem? How will we know when we've solved the problem? What further facts do we need to know to pick a solution?

3. Decide on a Solution: Find out how others have tried to solve similar problems. Brainstorm possible solutions. Compare your situation to those of others. In what ways are their situations like and unlike yours? What were the effects of their solutions? Would any of these solutions satisfy everyone involved in the problem?

If not, have students argue with each other about different solutions. They should listen and respond to arguments for incompatible solutions. In the discussion, students should point out and evaluate their own, and others' assumptions, use of concepts, and the implications and consequences of the proposed solutions. The students should listen carefully to others and modify their ideas in light of the strengths of opposing arguments. Stress the idea that this is not a contest among solutions; rather students should look together for a solution, or combination of solutions, that minimizes bad consequences and maximizes relief from the problem.

Before students attempt to apply this problem solving technique to adult problems, they should practice applying it to some of their own problems. After students have discussed a number of problems they typically encounter, the class should decide on one for problem solving practice. Below is an example of how the problem solving technique might be applied to a student problem.

Provisional statement of the problem: My brother and I fight over T.V.

Step 1) questions to define the problem: When do you fight? When do you not fight (what shows do you both like)? What happens when a fight occurs; what do you say? What do you do? What does he say? What does he do? What is the result of the fighting? How do the fights end? Why don't you like the situation? How do you think your brother sees the problem?

Reformulations will vary, depending on the answers given to these questions. Here is an example of one possible clearer formulation of the problem.

Reformulation of problem: It makes my brother and I unhappy when, on Saturday mornings and Tuesday nights, we argue, wrestle, and push each other around, hurt one another, and miss parts, or all of our favorite shows. **S–13**

Step 2) questions to analyze the problem: What do you and your brother agree is necessary to solve the problem? What do you both think a fair solution would mean? Is there anything else we need to know about the situation? Which shows are most important to each of you? Least important? What might one brother do while the other is watching his favorite show? (This lesson will require a homework assignment at this point, in order for the student to gather information. "We can't solve this problem until we have the answers to our questions.") **S–5**

Step 3) Deciding on a solution: Does anyone know of a problem similar to this one? Was it solved? How? How is that situation like this one? Unlike it? What changes in the solution are required by the differences between the situations? **S–29**

Then the class could brainstorm other possible solutions: How do you think it could be solved? (Put all solutions on the board. These may include, for instance, giving up less favorite shows to watch the most favorite, alternating each week, or getting another special privilege for giving up a favorite show.) Have the class discuss the most likely consequences of the solutions offered. The teacher may have students role-play the parts of the two brothers discussing the suggested solutions, or allow two or more students to argue for their favorite solutions. Students could form groups to argue for solutions. **S–26**

Then, the child involved can decide which solution to try first. If it works, the lesson is finished with his report to the class. If not, another solution should be tried.

Finally, sum up using the following questions: What did we do? (First, next, last?) What was important for us to keep in mind? Which parts were easy? Hard? Why? Did we solve the problem? Would this solution work for everyone?

After the class has used the problem solving steps on student problems, you could introduce the idea that cities also have problems. Have the students read the text. Ask them to describe the problem. Ask how it is like and unlike the child's problem. You may point out important similarities and differences which they missed. **S–29** Then attempt to apply the problem solving technique to this problem. You could summarize this lesson by using the same questions as the sum-up above.

Or students might write an essay in which they argue for a solution to the city problem, or in which they compare the personal problem to the city problem.

> *Teachers who can formulate and articulate what attitudes and behaviors they are trying to foster, why they are important, and how they foster them in their classrooms, are more likely to be able to create an appropriate atmosphere and to structure classroom activities that lead to good student thinking.*

An American City with a Problem
(3rd Grade)

Objectives of the remodelled lesson

The students will:
- engage in dialogical and dialectical thinking as they analyze and evaluate various arguments about a low income housing project
- clarify the basic issue and various claims made regarding the project
- use critical vocabulary while examining perspectives, assumptions, and assessing reasons
- distinguish what they know from what they don't know about the claims made and consider how they might find out, thereby practicing intellectual humility

Original Lesson Plan

Abstract

This unit focuses on a low-income housing project built in Forest Hills to move some poor people out of a New York ghetto. First, the students discuss the problem of over-crowding, learn what ghettos are, and discuss why people would want to leave them. Then the students learn about the Forest Hills plan, and discuss why Forest Hills was probably the chosen site for new housing. They discuss various forms of aid and choose which kind of aid they would prefer receiving.

Next, the students read what some residents of Forest Hills said about why they didn't want the project there. The students are asked to determine which statements are "facts" and which are "opinions". They are then asked if they agree that it was unfair that Forest Hills residents weren't consulted about the project.

The students read what some people outside Forest Hills said about the project. Students are asked if people outside Forest Hills have a right to an opinion about the project. The class discusses the needs and wants of ghetto and Forest Hills dwellers, points out conflicts, and discusses possible compromises. Students are encouraged to come to their own conclusions about the worth of the project. Then the class discusses other big city problems.

In an activity on prejudice, the teacher explains how the two parts of the word, 'pre' and 'judge' together mean "judging something or someone before you know much about him, her, or it." A student is asked to read aloud the following passage: "Many people in the ghetto are black. Almost everyone in Forest Hills is white. Those people in Forest Hills are just prejudiced against black people." Then they are asked to rewrite the last sentence without using the word 'prejudice'. In an alternative activity on prejudice, students are asked to read the same quote then make lists of two or three kinds of people or foods they are prejudiced against. The teacher encourages an open discussion of the list, in which students try to convince others that their prejudices are in error.

from *Towns and Cities*, Ronald Reed
Boyce, et al. Addison-Wesley Publishing
Co. pp. 102–113, 115.

Critique

We chose this lesson because it provides students with practice discussing a real social issue that involves arguments from more than one point of view. The empathy building exercises help students appreciate the seriousness of the problem by seeing it as those most affected might see it. Although the activities have such headings and objectives as "analyzing and evaluating arguments", they do not require students to rationally consider and judge the arguments. Instead, students are asked only to "distinguish facts from opinions", to guess who said what, and to agree or disagree with one idea.

This lesson inadvertently discourages critical analysis and evaluation by asking students to classify all statements as fact or opinion, thereby implying that facts are true (and therefore there is no room for discussion) and everything else is (arbitrary) opinion and discussion is pointless.

The text requires students to state who said what with no discussion of the possible relevance of this question. For instance, if we know that the person who said, "The government won't let criminals into the apartments" was a government official, the statement could be taken as an expression of policy. Whereas a ghetto dweller would probably not be in a position to know government intentions or procedures on this matter. Furthermore, the question misleads students into believing that they can tell who said what, when, in most cases, they can only guess.

Although the text includes a number of arguments, students discuss only one. Therefore, they are not in a strong position to evaluate the project when asked to do so. Of that argument, students are simply asked whether they agree or disagree with it, with no discussion of its worth or the justification of their reactions to it.

Students do not apply any useful tools of analysis or evaluation, such as examining assumptions or judging relevance. They do not discuss how to determine the truth or reasonableness of the various ideas presented. Nor do they discuss the relevance of the arguments to the main issue. They don't discuss the two points of view in relation to each other, and therefore they get no practice in comparing or evaluating opposing perspectives.

Finally, the text requires students to come to a conclusion regarding the housing project when, given the students lack of knowledge of the relevant facts, it should be encouraging the students to hold their conclusions tentatively.

Strategies used to remodel

S–26 reasoning dialectically: evaluating perspectives, interpretations, or theories
S–18 analyzing or evaluating arguments, interpretations, beliefs, or theories
S–30 examining or evaluating assumptions
S–33 giving reasons and evaluating evidence and alleged facts
S–13 clarifying issues, conclusions, or beliefs
S–25 reasoning dialogically: comparing perspectives, interpretations, or theories
S–5 developing intellectual humility and suspending judgment
S–35 exploring implications and consequences
S–34 recognizing contradictions
S–28 thinking precisely about thinking: using critical vocabulary
S–3 exercising fairmindedness

Remodelled Lesson Plan S-26

There are a number of ways to use the arguments given in this chapter: each student could read and note down comments to share in small groups or with the whole class, small groups could read together and share their initial ideas and perhaps answer some prepared questions, or the class as a whole could read and discuss the arguments before writing or small group discussion.

Below, we quote each argument from the original lesson and offer some discussion questions.

Ideas from Forest Hills: S-18

Argument 1: "Why did they decide to build those apartment buildings here? No one asked us if we wanted them. That's not fair!"

Questions: Is it fair to move a lot of people into a neighborhood without asking the people who already live there? How is this situation like and unlike other times people move to a new neighborhood? What does this person assume? **S-30** How do you feel when someone makes a decision that affects you, without asking what you think? If you lived in a nice area like Forest Hills and learned about the project, what would you think about it? Why? How is this argument related to the main issue? Is this a good reason to abandon the project? Why or why not? **S-33**

Argument 2: "Think of all those people moving into those big buildings! Our subways and schools will be even more crowded than they are now!"

Questions: Is this a good reason to abandon the project? Why or why not?

Argument 3: "Most crime in New York is in the ghettos. If those people move here, there will be more crime here. I think we should help poor people, but I'm afraid of them."

Questions: Is there more crime in the ghetto? Why? What does this argument assume? Are these good assumptions? **S-30** How could we find out whether crime is likely to go up? (Here, if the students do not think of it themselves, the teacher could point out that we could find out what has happened in similar cases.) **S-13** If the claim is true, does that mean that the project should be dropped? Who is this person afraid of and why? Is this a good reason to drop the project? Why or why not? **S-33**

Argument 4: "I don't believe in moving people out of the ghettos. We should spend that money to fix up the old buildings in the ghettos."

Questions: What reasons might this person give for his idea that money is better spent on other ways of helping the people living in ghettos? (Note that this issue is related to the questions students were earlier asked [see abstract] about what form of assistance they would prefer. Point out the relationship between the answer given to that question, and agreement or disagreement about this point.) How is this question related to the main issue?

Ideas From Outside Forest Hills S-25

Argument 5: "Many people in the ghetto are black. Almost everyone in Forest Hills is white. Those people in Forest Hills are just prejudiced against black people."

Questions: What does this person assume? Is it a good assumption? How could we find out if this idea is true? **S–30** Suppose we learned that the claims in arguments 1–4 were false. How would we find out whether prejudice was the reason for the Forest Hills people's response? (If they were prejudiced, they wouldn't change their conclusions in light of new evidence.) Does this argument refute 1–4? How does this argument relate to the issue? Is this a good reason to continue the project? **S–33**

Argument 6: "People in other parts of New York will feel just the same way as the people in Forest Hills. Everyone thinks the apartment buildings are a good idea. But nobody wants them in his or her neighborhood."

Questions: Is this true? Probably true? Unlikely? **S–5** What does it imply?/What follows from it? (This person may think that since no one wants the project in their area, the complaints of the Forest Hills people should be ignored.) If the claims are true, what do they mean for the project? Should it be abandoned, or should the Forest Hills people's wishes be ignored? Why? **S–35** (Discuss this argument in relation to arguments 1–4.)

Argument 7: "People in Forest Hills are afraid of black people and poor people. But most of them don't know any black people or poor people. After the apartment buildings are built, the black people and the white people will get to know each other. Then they will like each other."

Questions: What is the difference between this argument and argument 5? (The prediction that Forest Hills people will change.) What does this person assume? **S–30** How can we find out if this person is probably right? (Related cases, and studies on people of different races living near each other.) **S–13** Is this argument relevant to the issue? How? Do we have any evidence of the truth of this claim? Suppose these claims were true, why would the Forest Hills people be afraid? What assumption would they have to be making that would lead to fear, as opposed to some other emotion? **S–30**

Argument 8: "They won't let criminals into the apartment buildings. They will check everyone who wants to live there. People in Forest Hills won't have to worry about more crime because of those buildings."

Questions: Is this true? How could we know? **S–5** What argument does this contradict? (Argument 3) **S–34** How could the government know which people are criminals? What does this argument assume? **S–30** How does this argument relate to the main issue?

Argument 9: "I live in a ghetto now, but I would like to live in a place like Forest Hills. That part of New York is much prettier and safer than here. But I would be afraid to go there. Those Forest Hills people act dangerous. I'm afraid they would throw a rock through my window if I lived there."

Questions: Does this person have good reason to be afraid? Why or why not? What does this person assume? Is it a good assumption? **S–30** How does this argument relate to argument 7? To argument 4? Does either side have good reason to be afraid? Why or why not? **S–33** How does this point relate to the main issue? What does it imply for the issue? **S–35**

Tying it together S-26

Next, have the students discuss the following questions (write their answers on the board): What is the issue? Is this question clear? How could we rephrase it? What is the purpose of the project? Is the purpose worthwhile? What facts are relevant? What kinds of facts do we need to know to decide if the project would achieve its purpose? **S-28** How could someone get these facts? Can you think of any problems this project might cause? Can you think of a better project than this? **S-13** You might also ask students if there are any important ideas overlooked in the above arguments.

The students could discuss the relevance and relative importance of the different arguments: Which arguments do you think are strongest? Why? Is this project worthwhile? With which perspective do you most agree? Why? Discuss at length. If a student doesn't listen to another, that student could try to re-state the other's argument. **S-3** Encourage students to reach a compromise, or come up with a better plan.

Finally, the students could write an essay stating and defending their positions on the question: Is the Forest Hills project a good idea? Point out that assuming that you know more than you do weakens your argument. Encourage students to qualify their claims and use 'If'. **S-5**

> "Teachers need time to reflect upon and discuss ideas, they need opportunities to try out and practice new strategies, to begin to change their own attitudes and behaviors in order to change those of their students, to observe themselves and their colleagues — and then they need more time to reflect upon and internalize these concepts."
>
> *Greensboro Handbook,*
> *Greensboro Public Schools*
> *Reasoning and Writing Project*

> *One cannot develop one's fairmindedness, for example, without actually thinking fairmindedly. One cannot develop one's intellectual independence, without actually thinking independently. This is true of all the essential critical thinking traits, values, or dispositions. They are developmentally embedded in thinking itself.*

7 Remodelling Science Lessons

A critical approach to teaching science is concerned less with students accumulating undigested facts and scientific definitions and procedures, than with students learning to *think scientifically.* As children learn to think scientifically, they inevitably organize and internalize facts, learn terminology, and use scientific procedures. But they learn them deeply, because they are tied into ideas that they have thought through, and hence do not have to "re-learn" them again and again.

The biggest obstacle to science education is children's misconceptions. Although there are well-developed, defensible methods for settling many scientific questions, educators should recognize that children have intuitively developed their own ideas about the physical world. Merely presenting established methods to children does not usually affect their inner beliefs; they continue to exist in an unarticulated and therefore unchallenged form.

Rather than transferring the knowledge they learn in school to new settings, children continue to employ their pre-existing frameworks of belief. Children's own emerging egocentric conceptions about the physical world seem much more real and true to them than what they have superficially picked up in school. For example, a child was presented with evidence about current flow that was incompatible with his articulated beliefs. In response to the instructor's demonstration, the child replied, "Maybe that's the case here, but if you come home with me you'll see it's different there."[1] This child's response graphically illustrates one way children retain their own beliefs: they simply juxtapose them with a new belief.

Unless children practice expressing and defending their own beliefs, and listening critically to those of others, they will not critique or modify their own beliefs in light of school learning. "As children discover they have different solutions, different methods, different frameworks, and they try to convince each other, or at least to understand each other, they revise their understanding in many small but important ways."[2]

Elementary science materials often suffer from serious flaws which give students false and misleading ideas about science. Students are not encouraged to develop real experiments; rather, they are typically told what is true and false and given demonstrations to perform. Typical science materials present children with the finished products of science. Materials often require students to practice the skills of measuring, graphing, and counting, often for no reason but mindless drill. Such activities merely reinforce the stereotype that scientists are people who run around counting, measuring, and mixing bizarre liquids together for no recognizable reason.

Lessons also introduce scientific concepts. But students must understand scientific concepts through ordinary language and ordinary concepts. After a unit on photosynthesis, a child who was asked, "Where do plants get their food?" replied, "From water, soil, and all over." The child misunderstood what the concept 'food' means for plants and missed the crucial idea that *plants make their own food.* He was using his previous (ordinary, human) concept of 'food'. Confusion often arises when scientific concepts that have another meaning in ordinary language (such as, 'work') are not distinguished in a way that highlights how purpose affects use of language. Children need to see that each concept is correct for its purpose.

Students are rarely called upon to understand the reasons for doing their experiments or for doing them in a particular way. Students have little opportunity to come to grips with the concept of 'the controlled experiment' or understand the reasons for the particular controls used. Furthermore, standard approaches often fail to make the link between observation and conclusion explicit. Rarely do students have occasion to ask, "How did we get from *that* observation to *that* conclusion?" Scientific reasoning remains a mystery to students, whereas education in science should combat the common assumption that, "Only scientists and geniuses can understand science."

To learn from a science activity, children should understand its purpose. A critical approach to science education would allow children to ponder questions, propose solutions, and develop and conduct their own experiments. Although many of their experiments would fail, the attempt and failure provide a valuable learning experience which more accurately parallels what scientists do. When an experiment designed by children fails, those children are stimulated to amend their beliefs.

Scientific thinking is not a matter of running through a set of steps one time. Rather, it is a kind of thinking in which we continually move back and forth between questions we ask about the world and observations we make, and experiments we devise to test out various hypotheses, guesses, hunches, and models. We continually think in a hypothetical fashion: "If this idea of mine is true, then what will happen under these or those conditions? Let me see, suppose we try this. What does this result tell me? Why did this happen? If *this* is why, then *that* should happen when I ...."

We have to do a lot of critical thinking in the process, because we must ask clear and precise questions in order to devise experiments that can give us clear and precise answers. Typically the results of experiments — especially those devised by children — will be open to more than one interpretation. What one child thinks the experiment has shown often differs from what another child thinks. Here then is another opportunity to try to get children to be clear and precise in what they are saying. "Exactly how are these two interpretations different? Do they agree at all? If so, where do they agree?"

As part of learning to think scientifically, clearly, and precisely, children need opportunities to transfer ideas to new contexts. This can be linked with the scientific goal of bringing different kinds of phenomena under one scientific law, and the process of clarifying our thinking through analogies. Children should seek connections and assess explanations and models.

Finally, although scientific questions have only one correct answer, they may have a number of plausible answers of which only one is correct. It is more important for children to get into the habit of thinking scientifically than to get the correct answer through a rote process that they do not understand. The essential point is this: children should learn to do their own thinking about scientific questions from the start.

Once children give up on trying to do their own scientific thinking and start passively taking in what their textbooks tell them, the spirit of science, the scientific attitude and frame of mind, is lost. Never forget the importance of, "I can figure this out for myself! I can find some way to *test* this!" as an essential scientific stance for children in relationship to how they think about themselves as *knowers*. If they reach the point of believing that knowledge is something in books that people smarter than them figured out, then they have lost the fundamental drive that ultimately distinguishes the educated from the uneducated person.

Unfortunately, this shift commonly occurs in the thinking of most children some time during elementary school. We need to teach science, and indeed all subjects, in such a way that this shift never occurs, so that the drive to figure things out for oneself does not die, but is continually fed and supported by day to day scientific thinking.

From the outset, we must design science activities so that children cannot mindlessly perform them. We should look for opportunities that call upon children to explain or make intelligible what they are doing and why it is necessary or significant. In general, students should be asked to explain the justification for scientific claims.

Of course, all of the questions above need to be modified in the light of the grade level, the particular students, and the context. We must continually take into account precisely what questions in what form will stimulate their thinking. We want to make sure that we don't overwhelm them with questions they are not able to handle, for that will cause them to stop thinking as quickly as the straight didactic approach does.

In sum, whenever possible, children should be encouraged to express their ideas and try to convince each other to adopt them. Having to listen to their fellow students' ideas, to take those ideas seriously, and to try to find ways to test those ideas with observations and experiments are necessary experiences. Having to listen to their fellow students' objections will facilitate the process of self critique in a more fruitful way than if they are merely corrected by teachers who are typically taken as absolute authorities on "textbook" matters. Discussion with peers should be used to make reasoning from observation to conclusion explicit and help children learn how to state their own assumptions and recognize the assumptions of others.

Footnotes

1   Hugh Helm & Joseph D. Novak, "A Framework for Conceptual Change with Special Reference to Misconceptions," *Proceedings of the International Seminar on Misconceptions in Science and Mathematics,* Cornell University, Ithaca, NY, June 20–22, 1983, p. 3.

2   Jack Easley, "A Teacher Educator's Perspective on Students' and Teachers' Schemes: Or Teaching by Listening," *Proceedings of the Conference on Thinking, Harvard Graduate School of Education,* August, 1984, p. 8.

Linear Measurement

(Kindergarten)

Objectives of the remodelled lesson

The students will:
- develop confidence in their ability to understand and use systems for measuring
- discuss reasons for measuring
- discover the usefulness of standards of measurement through experience and discussing root questions

Original Lesson Plan

Abstract

The students use their hands to measure one side of a piece of paper. They then discuss why they arrived at different answers. Next, they use pencils to measure two sides of the paper. Then they use a meter-stick to measure different classroom objects, and determine which of four objects is longest and which shortest.

from *The Elementary School Science Program.*, Biological Sciences Curriculum Study. Colorado, J. B. Lippincott, Co. pp. 72–74.

Critique

The lesson covers an important point — the usefulness of having standard measuring lengths — in a concrete and vivid way. It can, however be made stronger. To better understand this point, students should further ground the experience in reality through some discussion of the purposes which measuring serves. Although the lesson gives students an experience which suggests the importance of standards of measurement, it has no *explicit* discussion of this idea. Students should discuss the potential problems arising from not using a standard.

Strategies used to remodel

S–9 developing confidence in reason
S–17 questioning deeply: raising and pursuing root or significant questions
S–1 thinking independently

Remodelled Lesson Plan s-9

As an introduction, the class could discuss the question, "Why do people measure things?" The teacher may begin by asking students to recall when they have seen people use rulers, tape measures, etc. The class could brainstorm reasons for measuring. Write these down, to be used in the later discussion. **S–17**

Then, after the students have measured with their hands and discussed the differences in their answers, they could be given a chance to suggest the usefulness of everybody using the same length. Remind students of some of the reasons for measuring they gave earlier. Ask them if the "hand method" would work well in each case. Focus their attention on cases in which lack of standards would cause problems. Ask students what problems could arise, and how they might be solved. If they don't mention that everyone could use one agreed-upon length to measure, distribute pencils (or other objects of equal length). Have the students measure and discuss whether using this would solve the problems. **S–1**

Before introducing the meter-sticks, the teacher could ask the class what problems could arise from using pencils to measure ("Would everybody know exactly what 'six pencils long' means?") When distributing the meter-sticks, mention that people all over the world use sticks that are exactly this length. Have the students compare their meter-sticks.

Before the students measure, give them a reason to want to know the lengths of objects or spaces. For example, you might say "Suppose we wanted to move these shelves over here? How could we tell if they would fit?" Or, to reinforce the importance of standards, have one student measure a space in the classroom, while others measure some outside object. ("Would the monkey-bars fit in our classroom?") **S–17**

Are Seeds Living Things?

(1ˢᵗ Grade)

by Pamela Lane-Stamm, Mattole Union
School District, Petrolia, CA

Objectives of the remodelled lesson

The students will:
- develop and conduct an experiment to answer a question
- learn the importance of the various elements to the growing process of plants
- Socratically explore the distinction between living and non-living things

Original Lesson Plan

Abstract

After reading three pages stating plants and animals are living things, students experiment to confirm that plants are living things. They put soil in a cup and put seeds in the soil. They label their cups, water the seeds and answer the questions, "Do they grow? Are they living things?"

from *Holt Science 1*, Holt, Reinhart, and
Winston Publishers, 1986, pp. 14–20.

Critique

Because the text shows pictures of the experiment being performed, including the result, children don't have an opportunity to hypothesize for themselves about what will happen. The experiment doesn't allow the children to discover what helps the seeds to grow or even if the seeds will grow. This lesson also fails to allow children to separate their observations from conclusions.

Strategies used to remodel

S-1 thinking independently
S-24 practicing Socratic discussion: clarifying and questioning beliefs, theories, or perspectives

Remodelled Lesson Plan s-1

Children should not read the text first, because it tells them what the results of their experiment will be. Children will be encouraged by the teacher to hypothesize about what will and will not grow. Ask, "Would a pencil grow? Would a leaf grow a new plant? Would a frozen pea grow? Would a dried pea grow? Would an eraser grow? A seed?" etc. Make sure the children explain why they think these things will or will not grow. **S-24**

Children can then plant the items that they think will grow and instead of planting one pot, two plants should be planted. One pot will be given soil, water, and light. The other pot will have either water, soil, or light omitted from the process. Children should chart their results on a graph and discuss what a seed needs to grow and what a seed needs to become a healthy plant. Then children may read the text and discuss if their conclusion concurs with that of the book.

editors' note: Before the experiment, the teacher could first see if students know or can guess what seeds will require to grow, perhaps letting them try their ideas first. "What do plants need to live? What do seeds need to grow? Do you have plants at home? Who takes care of them? What do they do to keep the plants alive and help them grow? What do we need to live? Can we compare that to what plants need?"

"How can you tell if something is a living thing?" (Seeds don't look like living things, or things that could live; they look more like pebbles.) **S-24**

Lesson plan remodelling as a strategy for staff and curriculum development is not a simple one-shot approach. It requires patience and commitment. But it genuinely develops the critical thinking of teachers and puts them in a position to understand and help transform the curriculum into effective teaching and learning.

Making Things Move

(1ˢᵗ Grade)

Objectives of the remodelled lesson

The students will:
- begin to develop the scientific concept 'energy' by recognizing that energy is required to make things move and develop confidence in reason by using it to analyze experiences outside of class
- think independently by forming categories of different sources of energy
- discuss significant similarities and differences among different forms of energy
- make interdisciplinary connections between science or technology and history by exploring how people lived without electricity

Original Lesson Plan

Abstract

This unit attempts to develop the concept that "energy must be used to set an object in motion or to alter its motion". Each section provides an example or two to illustrate a use of a particular form of energy (electrical, chemical, mechanical, etc.) Each example is contrasted with a human powered or living counterpart (such as, motorcycle versus bicycle).

from *Concepts in Science,* Paul F. Brandwein, et al. Harcourt Brace & World, Inc. 1980. pp. 2–8.

Critique

This lesson could be improved by having the students come up with their own examples of things that move, thereby providing a wider range of examples and fostering independent thinking. Also, in choosing their own examples, students can better integrate the scientific insight (and scientific concept) that everything requires *energy* to move or change its motion. This better enables them to use this insight outside of class. Students themselves should categorize their examples and explain why they put them in the groups they did.

Strategies used to remodel

S–1 thinking independently
S–29 noting significant similarities and differences
S–9 developing confidence in reason
S-23 making interdisciplinary connections

Remodelled Lesson Plan S-1

To initiate the process of noting similarities and differences in energy sources, begin the unit with a brainstorming session in which students mention anything they can think of that moves. Record these responses. Afterwards, go through the list encouraging students to form their own categories by asking, "Does anything else mentioned earlier have the same source of movement as this one (chemical, electrical etc.)?" (Choose any item on the list that can be grouped easily with other items.) Continue this process until as many of the items as possible have been put into categories. Ask, "How are the items in this first category different from those in the second? Third?" and so on. Have the students label the groups. Or, students could begin by collecting or drawing pictures of things that move and sorting them into categories. **S-29**

To develop the scientific concept 'energy' you could ask, "What do all of these groups have in common?" If necessary, remind students that the criteria they used for coming up with items was "anything that moves" and the criteria they used for forming categories was "things that have the same source of movement or 'energy source'." Then go back through the original lesson, asking of the examples given, "Do we already have a category of energy that this would fit, or do we need a new category? What would you call this category?"

Students could be given a homework assignment of finding examples of energy and its effects. These examples can be shared and discussed by the class. "Notice moving things. What made each move or change its motion? Was its source of energy natural or energy invented by people?" **S-9**

This lesson could be extended to relate technological advancements to history. The teacher can ask, "Do you know what kinds of energy are fairly new? Electricity is one. Not long ago, people didn't have electricity; it hadn't been invented yet. What do you think things were like then? What things didn't people have? The engines in cars is another new form of energy." Finally, have students discuss how people managed without the technologies. **S-23**

Weather Changes with the Seasons

(1ˢᵗ Grade)

by Victoria J. Martin, Cypress
Fairbanks I.S.D., Houston, TX

Objectives of the remodelled lesson

The students will:
- identify the four seasons and recognize the predictable pattern in the seasons through Socratic discussion
- think independently by categorizing pictures by season, rather than simply looking at pictures in the text
- discuss the effect of seasons on people and animals
- develop criteria for evaluating good summer clothing versus good winter clothing

Original Lesson Plan

Abstract

Students look at four pictures of the same scene during different seasons. The teacher reads a description of each season and asks "What season is it now?" The students look at more pictures and discuss them.

Critique

This lesson addresses the subject of the four seasons. It uses didactic teaching. The children just sit there and do very little interacting. More pictures and some manipulatives are needed. ***editors' note:*** Discussion of how the seasons affect people is extremely limited in the original (children play in leaves in the fall). More discussion of this point would make the concepts more real.

Strategies used to remodel

S–24 practicing Socratic discussion: clarifying and questioning beliefs, theories, or perspectives
S–1 thinking independently
S–15 developing criteria for evaluation: clarifying values and standards
S–10 refining generalizations and avoiding oversimplifications
S–33 giving reasons and evaluating evidence and alleged facts
S–34 recognizing contradictions

Remodelled Lesson Plan S–24

Divide the class into groups of 2, 3, or 4 children. Give them a seasonal picture and ask them to think about these questions and be ready to share with the class: When do you think the picture was taken? Why? How did it feel outside when this picture was taken? How do you know? Have you ever been to a place that looked like this? Where was it? When was it? Did the place always stay the same? **S–1**

Bring the class together. After discussing the pictures, you could ask them if any of the pictures seem to go together. "Why? What makes you say so? Do you agree with the way we have grouped the pictures? Why or why not? What do you think?" If grouped by season, ask them to discuss and list the seasons. If not grouped by seasons, ask them to group the pictures the way they're grouped in their texts.

Ask how seasons affect people, plants, and animals. Bring in the discussion of what farmers need to know to be successful, as in the original.

Look at the textbook and ask about how the trees look and how the people are dressed in each of the pictures. Discuss clothing used in each season. Brainstorm lists of clothing needed in each season and list on board, then discuss criteria for good summer clothes, etc. Students can discuss these criteria. "What would happen if we wore a sweater like this in the summer? Shorts in winter? Why? What do you think? Do you agree? Why? Why not?" **S–15**

Summarize and give children opportunity to supply two facts about a season. List them on the chalk board.

editors' note: The teacher could also have students compare the pictures with seasons where they live, and discuss differences in what each season is like in different places. "Do all of these spring pictures look the same? What differences are there between what spring is like here and in the picture? Why do you think that might be?" **S–10**

Have groups of students sort many pictures by season and explain their groupings, defending their views in cases of disagreement. **S–33**

To engage students in a fuller discussion of how seasons affect people, allow students to discuss how each season makes them feel, what they like and dislike about each, and how people they know feel about each. "What things do people seem to disagree about when they talk about favorite seasons? Why?" **S–34** (Students could also distinguish how the season and weather make them feel from how holidays during each season make them feel.)

The teacher might begin the discussion of how seasons affect living things by asking students to find all such references in their text and brainstorming more ideas.

Using Your Senses

(1ˢᵗ Grade)

by Victoria J. Martin, Cypress
Fairbanks I.S.D., Houston, TX

Objectives of the remodelled lesson

The students will:
- identify and explore the five senses through discussion and activities
- avoid the oversimplification in the text by noticing how we often use several senses together to perform an activity or learn about a situation
- discuss, using critical vocabulary, how our senses and our thinking can help us uncover useful information

Standard Approach

The text explains that people use their senses to hear, to see, to taste, to smell, and to feel. Students examine pictures and identify the sense being used, the part of the body used (eyes, ears, etc.), and the place or situation in which the sense is used in each picture. The "Enrichment" discusses handicapped people.

Critique

This lesson is to introduce the five senses to a first grade class. There are no manipulatives used and this is necessary to help foster retention for this age group. Questioning strategies need to be changed to foster more independent thinking. Discussion of handicapped people is not relevant at this time.

Strategies used to remodel

S–12 developing one's perspective: creating or exploring beliefs, arguments, or theories
S–33 giving reasons and evaluating evidence and alleged facts
S–10 refining generalizations and avoiding oversimplifications
S–28 thinking precisely about thinking: using critical vocabulary

Remodelled Lesson Plan S–12

Before students get out their books and read page 2, we would discuss what they know about the senses: Have you ever heard the word 'sense'? What does it mean? What kind of senses are there? How do you know?

Then ask, "How do you know your mother is cooking when you walk into the house? How might you know who is in the next room if you can't see the person? How do you know if there is salt or sugar in a measuring spoon? How do you know when a window is open without seeing it? How would you know if the traffic light changed if you weren't looking at it? Why do you think that? Do you agree? Why? Why not?"

The class could also brainstorm ideas about each sense and list them on the chalk board. "What are some different kinds of smells, tastes, and textures? What kinds of things can we tell by seeing (colors, shapes, etc.)?"

Then use the following activities with groups of four or five. Provide hands–on materials for discovering about the five senses.

• Feely box: Large shoe box with sock attached to one end. Child puts hand through sock into box, feels common object, and guesses what it is.

• Tasting jars: Ten painted baby food jars with lids with a nail hole in the lid. Q-tips can be dipped in for a taste and a guess.

• Smell Jars: Ten painted baby food jars with different scents on cotton inside.

• Sound tape: Play a tape of different sounds and provide pictures to be matched to them.

• Hidden picture cards can be used to illustrate how you can find new things if you look carefully.

For each, ask, "Which *sense* did you use here? What part of your body?" **S–33**

To summarize, children could categorize pictures into five stacks. Discuss the fact that more than one sense is used with most objects in the pictures. **S–10**

Make popcorn in an open popcorn popper while sitting on a sheet used to catch popcorn. Discuss which senses are influenced in this activity. **S–33**

editors' note: Critical thinking vocabulary can be integrated into the lesson by discussing the idea that our senses provide us with evidence for the conclusions or inferences we make. For example: If we *feel* a breeze in the room, we might *infer* that the window is open. The *evidence* for our *conclusion* that someone is cooking is the smell of food and perhaps the sounds of dishes and appliances in the kitchen. Such a discussion can also make the importance and usefulness of the senses more explicit. **S–28**

Pets

(1ˢᵗ Grade)

by Anne J. Harris, Jefferson Elementary
School, Cloverdale, CA

Objectives of the remodelled lesson

The students will:
- realize pets are some kinds of animals under the care of people
- realize there are many types of pets
- practice independent thinking
- develop intellectual good faith by discussing ways that pets are not always fun, what needs they have, the consequences of ignoring their needs, and ways to be responsible pet owners
- make interdisciplinary connections by using or setting up a bar graph showing how many students have which kinds of pets

Original Lesson Plan

Abstract

On two pages showing people with pets (bird, horse, rodent, dog), students read the following: "Animals can be pets. Pets can be fun. People take care of pets. How can we take care of pets?" The class discusses what kinds of animals can be pets, how pets can be fun and helpful, what pets need (including attention and affection).

from *Accent on Science Level 1*, Charles Merrill Publishing Co. Columbus, Ohio, 1985, pp. 58–9.

Critique

This lesson can be expanded to draw from the children's own life experiences and to use critical thinking. It uses stereotypical pets in the pictures.

editors' note: This lesson can be expanded in many ways, taking advantage of young children's natural interest in pets, to develop their knowledge of animals and the sense of responsibility emphasized in the original. The remodel offers a number of these. The lesson can also be used to teach students about bar graphs.

Strategies used to remodel

S–1 thinking independently
S–7 developing intellectual good faith or integrity
S–18 analyzing or evaluating arguments, interpretations, beliefs, or theories
S–23 making interdisciplinary connections
S–20 analyzing or evaluating actions or policies

Remodelled Lesson Plan

I would take this basic lesson on pets and add more pictures, including exotic pets. During the discussion of pets, to encourage independent thought, I would ask why people have pets. **S-1**

Prior to the start of the lesson, I would ask the children about their pets and graph the results — including a category for those who don't have pets. "How could our graph be different? Would it be different if we checked with another class? Why?" (Students could gather this data and make another graph.)

• The book says pets can be fun. In what ways are pets not fun? Are pets ever annoying or a bother? Why? What should you do about that? Is taking care of pets always fun? Why not? What would happen if a pet wasn't properly cared for? (Take each need and ask this question.) How much is this like how you would feel if you didn't get (food, affection, etc.)? **S-7**

In conclusion, the children should decide if pets are worthwhile and support their decisions. They could also decide what type of pet would be most suitable for them and why, to use the strategy of analyzing beliefs. **S-18**

editors' note: The students could be walked through the process of making the graph, thereby coming to see how it's made and discussing its usefulness. Put all of the pets and numbers on the board: "We're going to make a graph of this information so we can see it more clearly. Which category is the biggest? How many are in it? OK, so we'll make this height stand for that number. (Draw the bar and put in the number.) Now we have to mark off the rest of the numbers evenly. Now, lets take this one. Where should the top of this bar be? What number is it? OK. What label should I put for it? Now, would anyone like to make the bar for this category? ... Now. Look at the list of pets and numbers and look at the graph. If we want to know which pet is owned by the most kids and the least, which of these ways is easiest to see that? Why? Does your math book have any other kind of graph we could use?" If interest warrants, groups of students could make different kinds of graphs using the same data for comparison. **S-23**

Another direction to take this lesson would be to begin to explore zoology. "How are pets different from farm animals? Why? Wild animals? Why? How are they like them?" Students could research other animals (wild cats, foxes, pigs, etc.) and compare them to their pet counterparts: In what ways is the pet like the wild animal? Unlike it? Why? Do those differences make the wild animal a bad choice for a pet? Why or why not?

To extend the objective of developing a sense of responsibility toward pets, you might ask, "What's the difference between being a good pet owner and a bad pet owner? How do they treat their pets? Why do some people neglect or abuse pets? What effects does that have? What information do people need to know before they get a pet? Where could they get that information? What questions should they ask?" **S-20**

Students could discuss the problem of forgetting to take care of pets, and devise solutions: Why do people forget to take care of their pets? What might help people remember? Would that work for everyone? What would work for you? **S-7**

Water from the Air

(1ˢᵗ–3ʳᵈ Grades)

Objectives of the remodelled lesson

The students will:
- develop and conduct an experiment to determine where water on the outside of a glass of water comes from
- interpret the results of the experiment
- explore the implications of the experiment

Original Lesson Plan

Abstract

Students experiment to discover that the water which appears on the outside of containers of cold water comes from the air. They put food coloring in cold water and notice that the water appearing on the outside of the container is clear, not colored.

from *Discovering Science 1*, Albert Piltz, et al. Charles E. Merrill Publishing Co. 1973. pp. 82–83, T101–T102.

Critique

By presenting the experiment to the students, this lesson misses the opportunity to allow students to puzzle over how to answer the question, "Where did the water come from?" They should think about the question and figure out how to settle it. The lesson also fails to have students distinguish their observations from conclusions.

Strategies used to remodel

S–1   thinking independently
S–32 making plausible inferences, predictions, or interpretations
S–35 exploring implications and consequences

Remodelled Lesson Plan

To present the problem, rather than the solution to the problem, this lesson could begin, not with colored, but with clear ice water. Ask students to observe the container and describe what they see. Tell them that this lesson will focus on the question "Where did this water come from?" Allow discussion. "Why do you think so? How could we find out?" **S–1**

To help students develop an experiment, you might ask (allowing discussion after each question): "Why can't we tell just by looking at the water? Is the water outside just like the water inside? Could we make the water inside different in some way? How?" Have students choose one or more methods which use available materials (for instance, the water could be colored or flavored).

When students have conducted their experiments, you could ask "What do you *observe?* What can you *conclude?* Why? Is the water outside like the water inside? Where did the water come from?" **S-32** The student text could then be read and discussed as a sum up.

The class could also discuss implications of what they found out in this lesson. Possible discussion questions include the following: What have we learned about water? Air? Does all air have the same amount of water in it? What are the differences between regular water and water in the air? What effect does the water that is in the air have? What other questions could we ask? **S-35**

Despite the detail with which we have delineated the strategies, they should not be translated into mechanistic, step-by-step procedures. Keep the goal of the well-educated, fairminded critical thinker continually in mind.

Magnets

(1ˢᵗ–3ʳᵈ Grades)

by Linda Hawk, Linda Johnson, and
Loretta Jennings, Greensboro
Public Schools, Greensboro, NC

Objectives of the remodelled lesson

The students will:
- learn that a magnet has a force, either a push or a pull, through exploration and Socratic discussion
- develop confidence in their ability to reason scientifically by making, testing, and evaluating predictions
- transfer insights by applying what they have learned about magnets to other forces

Original Lesson Plan

Abstract

The students will share their knowledge of magnets through a webbing activity: organizing their ideas in a spider web shape. Next, they will use activity centers as a means for exploring many facets of magnets. Then further webbing will help students to recall and clarify their experiences in the various centers.

Critique

This lesson has several problems. It doesn't have a specific objective, it needs strategies for developing critical thinking, and it assumes that students have previous knowledge.

editors' note: Although the students may not have "school knowledge" about magnets, most have probably had some experiences with magnets. The original also had important strengths. By sharing their original beliefs, students learn from each other, make any misconceptions they have explicit (providing a better chance of correction), and can suggest their own ideas for exploration. The second webbing activity helps students develop perseverance by graphically showing them what they have learned. By allowing students to compare their original beliefs with their new beliefs, it helps students correct their original misconceptions and allows clarification and deeper processing of what they have learned.

Strategies used to remodel

S–9 developing confidence in reason
S–1 thinking independently
S–24 practicing Socratic discussion: clarifying and questioning beliefs, theories, or perspectives
S–32 making plausible inferences, predictions, or interpretations
S–12 developing one's perspective: creating or exploring beliefs, arguments, or theories
S–11 comparing analogous situations: transferring insights to new contexts

Remodelled Lesson Plan s-9

Procedure: Make magnets and materials available for exploration — all sizes, shapes, and powers of magnets and a variety of metals to test (different metals, shapes, sizes: paper clips, nails, coins, furniture, whatever). **S–1**

After students explore magnets, use Socratic questioning for observations. "What happened? What had you done? Why did you do that, did you have an idea of what might happen or were you just messing around? Why do you think that happened? Does everyone agree? Why or why not? How does that relate to what John said? How could we test that idea?" **S–24**

The teacher might then explain what took place with various magnets and why — at least enough to get across the concept of force as push or pull. (**editors' note:** You could give a lecture here if every ten minutes or so you stopped and had students pair up and share their own experiences about what you have said.)

Students' understanding of magnets can be further developed and assessed by having them think hypothetically.

• What do you think would happen if ...

You put two sphere magnets together?

You put two bar magnets together?

You put horseshoe magnets together?

You put one sphere with one bar?

You put one bar with one horseshoe? **S–32**

editors' note: For each of these questions, have students predict (and give reasons). Then several students can test each prediction. Then ask what happened and why the magnets behaved as they did. ("John, you said the two magnets pushed each other away, but Sue said they pulled together. Why don't each of you switch one of your magnets around like this and try it again?")

Ask students to pose other questions or tests, and use the same process (predict, test, discuss).

The teacher could incorporate the webbing activities from the original lesson into the remodelled lesson before the initial exploration and after discussion. Students can compare their initial ideas with what they got from the lesson. "What did you know before? Did you have any mistaken ideas? Is what we discovered compatible with this [original] belief? Why or why not?" **S–12**

Interested students could read about magnets, relating what they read with their own experiences, and later report back to the class.

If the main intention of the lesson is to introduce the scientific concept 'force', then students could brainstorm examples of force, and small groups or the class could evaluate individual items on the list, applying the scientific concept. "What other forces — physical pushes and pulls — do you know about? Which of these examples would a scientist consider a force? Why or why not?" (Disputed cases could be checked in resources.) **S–11**

Plant and Animal Products in Food .

(2ⁿᵈ Grade)

Objectives of the remodelled lesson

The students will:
- develop and discuss criteria for evaluating foods
- think fairmindedly by discussing their parents' criteria
- practice dialectical thinking by assessing reasons vegetarians and non-vegetarians give for their eating habits

Original Lesson Plan

Abstract

Students are asked to bring in empty food containers (cartons, envelopes, jars, boxes, etc.) with labels. They compare the ingredients of different brands of the same food, and divide the containers into foods which are from plants, animals, or a combination of the two. Also, they read that food provides us with the energy we need.

from *Science: Understanding Your Environment,* George G. Mallinson. Silver Burdett. 1978. p. 142.

Critique

This lesson provides the teacher with a natural place to introduce evaluation of food, but instead it focuses only on the distinction between plant and animal products. This constitutes a missed opportunity to have students develop criteria for choosing foods to eat, and apply the criteria to specific foods. The lesson also fails to discuss the differing points of view of vegetarians and meat eaters. Finally, the lesson could question students about what would happen if one didn't eat.

Strategies used to remodel

S–3 exercising fairmindedness
S–15 developing criteria for evaluation: clarifying values and standards
S–26 reasoning dialectically: evaluating perspectives, interpretations, or theories
S–24 practicing Socratic discussion: clarifying and questioning beliefs, theories, or perspectives

Remodelled Lesson Plan

After using the original lesson, the teacher could ask the students why it is important to know whether foods are made of animals, plants, or both. The class might then discuss other factors relevant to deciding which foods to choose. The teacher could ask "What are some of the things we should know about food before deciding to buy it?" List these responses. Allow room for disagreement and discussion. One student, for example, may argue that how food tastes is the most important factor; whereas another student believes that the food that is cheapest is best. If disagreement doesn't arise naturally, ask, "What do your parents think is most important when choosing food? **S-3** What do you think? What criteria do your parents use to decide? What criteria did you use? Who do you think is right? Why? Can you use both sets of standards? How?" **S-15**

Then the teacher can facilitate a dialectical discussion concerning vegetarians and non-vegetarians. The teacher can ask, "What is a vegetarian? What reasons might a vegetarian give for not eating meat or animal products? What reasons might a meat-eater give for eating meat or animal products? Which reasons make the most sense? Why?" **S-26**

Finally, ask students how we know that people require food for energy and to live. You can ask them questions such as these, "What would happen if someone were to quit eating completely? What if someone stranded on a desert island were to eat only coconuts or only fish? What does this tell about our need for food?" **S-24**

It should not be assumed that there is a universal standard for how fast teachers should proceed with the task of remodelling their lesson plans. A slow but steady evolutionary process is much more desirable than a rush job across the board.

What the Scientist Does
(2ⁿᵈ Grade)

Objectives of the remodelled lesson

The students will:
• develop and clarify their concepts of 'science'
• form categories of different things that scientists study
• clarify some scientific questions by discussing how they can be settled
• deeply question reasons for doing science

Original Lesson Plan

Abstract

We have selected introductory and concluding lessons from a unit on "What the Scientist Does." In the first lesson, students list and discuss their ideas about what scientists do. The middle lessons develop the idea that scientists observe, experiment, read, keep records, and discuss their work, in order to learn about the physical world. Each lesson has pictures of scientists engaged in scientific activities in various fields and pictures of children doing the same. The text tells the students what the scientists are doing, why, and that they can do the same. Some lessons suggest specific activities. The final lessons summarize the ideas covered and encourage students to do science.

from *Today's Basic Science 2,* John
Gabriel Navarra, et al. Harper & Row,
Publishers. 1967. pp. 6–7, T1–T3, 8–9.

Critique

This unit has several strengths: it encourages students to see themselves as scientists; it gives a fuller description of science than most texts by including reading and discussion as part of science. The material, however, is incomplete. The students do not contrast science with other disciplines, and so do not develop the distinction between science and non-science. Students are not given an opportunity to come up with a more complete list of the objects of scientific study. The unit also has no material about why people do or study science.

Strategies used to remodel

S–14 clarifying and analyzing the meanings of words or phrases
S–1 thinking independently
S–17 questioning deeply: raising and pursuing root or significant questions
S–13 clarifying issues, conclusions, or beliefs

Remodelled Lesson Plan s-14

The teacher may want to have this series of discussions at both the beginning and end of the year. The ideas covered in this lesson could also be re-introduced whenever they seem relevant to a specific discussion during the year.

You might begin by asking, "What is science? (Discuss at length.) What do scientists study? When you study science in school, what do you study about?" Have students brainstorm examples. List all responses. Then have students categorize their responses. (For instance, if one item is "frogs" and another "living things", a student may point out that the first is a specific instance of the second.) **S–1** "What do all of these categories have in common? What does that tell us about science?" You might also have students compare science to other subjects. **S–17**

The students could then select a few of the items and brainstorm questions a scientist might ask about each. List the questions. For each question ask, "How could we find out?" (If students answer, "By reading about it." you could ask, "How could we find out for ourselves? How did the people who wrote the books find out?" or similar questions.) Then have the students summarize common processes of settling scientific questions. **S–13**

Then lead a discussion about why people do science. You may want to add ideas they miss: curiosity, the need to solve specific problems, desire to improve the quality of life. Encourage extended discussion about the reasons: Are these all good reasons? Why or why not? Take some reasons one by one: Why is this a good thing? Are some of these reasons more important than others? Which ones? Why? Does anyone disagree? **S–17**

Finally, students could discuss questions like the following: What do you like about science? Why? Dislike? Why? What areas of science do you find the most interesting? What is interesting about it?

Rocks of the Earth

(2nd Grade)

Objectives of the remodelled lesson

The students will:
- practice developing and clarifying their own questions about rocks and answering them, thus engaging in intellectual perseverance
- clarify questions by discussing how scientific questions can be answered
- categorize questions by noting significant similarities and differences among questions

Original Lesson Plan

Abstract

The first lesson introduces a unit on rocks. The student page has a picture of two children by a stream in the mountains. The text draws attention to sizes and shapes of rocks. The students describe and discuss rocks they have found, compare their rocks to the picture, and discuss where rocks are found. The second lesson, which sums-up the unit, focuses on the following questions: What sizes and shapes are rocks? In what places can you find rocks? Are some rocks softer than other rocks? How can you find out which rocks are softer? Are some rocks harder than other rocks? How can you find out which rocks are harder? How can you find out if a rock is limestone? How can you make crystals? What do crystals look like? How are rocks used?

from *Discovering Science,* Albert Piltz, et al. Charles E. Merrill Publishing Co. 1973. pp. 2, 13T–T14.

Critique

The unit misses the opportunity to have students develop their own questions and reflect on how to settle them, thereby engaging in scientific reasoning. The text provides the teacher with the questions and suggests specific ways that experiments should be conducted. Students should be allowed to develop and explore their own questions, problems they are most interested in, and practice seeing how these questions guide their means of inquiry, that is, what kinds of things they need to do to answer them. This unit also misses the opportunity to have students practice classifying and discussing types of questions by comparing and contrasting the ways in which different questions are answered.

Strategies used to remodel

S–8 developing intellectual perseverance
S–1 thinking independently
S–13 clarifying issues, conclusions, or beliefs
S–29 noting significant similarities and differences

Remodelled Lesson Plan s-8

The teacher might begin the lesson by asking students, "What do you know about rocks? What would you like to find out about rocks?" **S–1**

Help students recognize how good questions are an important part of scientific inquiry by asking, "Do you know what to do to answer this question? Is the question clear? (Do you know what it means or do you need to ask further questions?) How would you find out? Do you need facts? Do you need to do an experiment? Do you need to measure or count? How should you measure? Is there any other way you can find out? Is one way better than another? Why do you think so?" **S–13** You could also record specific methods students suggest for answering questions for later discussion.

After you have completed this process for at least several of the students' questions, encourage students to think about their responses and ask, "Are any of these questions similar in the way you find out the answers? Which ones? What would you do to answer the first question mentioned? What would you do to answer the second question mentioned? How are these similar?" The teacher can begin grouping the questions on the board. **S–29**

"What are some of the kinds of things we decided that we must do to find out the answers to our questions about rocks? Were some questions harder than others? Can someone give me an example of a question they think is hard to answer? Why do you think so? Can anyone give an example of a question that is easier to answer? Why do you think so?" Conclude by mentioning that whatever problem they are trying to solve, it helps to think about what they must do to answer the questions they have.

For the rest of the unit, the students can answer the questions they find most interesting. (They may need to supplement their experiments with reading.)

Comparing Man to Animals

(2ⁿᵈ Grade)

Objectives of the remodelled lesson

The students will:
- probe the similarities and differences between people and animals
- practice scientific reasoning by clarifying and giving reasons for claims they make about animals and humans
- discuss the methods of and reasons for communication amongst humans and animals
- develop respect for and understanding of animals

Original Lesson Plan

Abstract

Students look at several pictures and notice the similarities between different animals. They review the names of the five senses, and discuss the characteristics of each animal individually. Students read about humans in their texts, then discuss the differences between humans and animals. What can humans do that animals can't? The children are assigned to make a picture collection showing activities that people do that animals can't do. Finally the importance of language is discussed. This is illustrated in a game where children try to give each other commands without talking.

from *Science: Understanding Your Environment*, George G. Mallinson. Silver Burdett. pp. 134–135.

Critique

This lesson is a missed opportunity to have students practice giving evidence in support of their beliefs, and to probe deeper into questions concerning the differences between animals and humans. Although students are asked to "share ideas about whether or not each animal has all the senses and how the senses are used" it is not clear how or if the teacher encourages them to *support* their claims with reasons. Also, this lesson emphasizes the things humans can do which animals cannot, but fails to make the point that animals don't need to do the things we do, and neglects to ask what animals can do that humans cannot (live underwater, run fast, survive outside, smell a lizard at forty paces, fly, hear better). This is a missed opportunity to develop respect and empathy for animals. Furthermore, activity 4, on communication, is not integrated with the lesson, since it is in no way related to questions about animal communication.

Strategies used to Remodel

S–29 noting significant similarities and differences
S–33 giving reasons and evaluating evidence and alleged facts
S–13 clarifying issues, conclusions, or beliefs
S–12 developing one's perspective: creating or exploring beliefs, arguments, or theories

Remodelled Lesson Plan s-29

For each student response concerning the similarities and differences between animal and human senses, ask "What makes you think so? *S–33* Did you learn it yourself or from someone else? What did you observe and conclude?" If the students say they learned it from someone else, ask, "What could you do to test this claim for yourself?" *S–13*

When discussing things humans can do that animals can't, the teacher could add questions like the following: Do you think animals would like to be able to do that? Do they need to do that? Is there something similar that they do? For example, although animals can't play all of the same games we play, do they play games of their own? Although animals can't build roads or drive cars, do you think they want to do this or need to? What can animals do that we can't? Why can't we do that? Why can some animals do that? Are there things that animals can do that you wish you could do? What? Why? *S–12*

To tie in the exercise on communication, you might add, "Do you think animals communicate? What makes you think so?" *S–33* If yes, "How do they communicate? What are the different ways humans communicate? How are these similar to or different from how animals communicate?"

The teacher could add further thought provoking questions, time and interest providing.

• What does it mean to think? Do animals think? How do you know?

• What kinds of things do animals communicate to each other? ("I'm hungry!" "I'm scared!" "Food!" "Get away!") What are some similarities and differences between what we and animals communicate? The class could also discuss how much human language dogs "understand". (Although such questions are difficult, there is no reason that children can't begin to ponder them early. This gives them valuable practice in asking further questions to clarify a problem, and distinguishing what they know from what they are unsure of.)

• Are all animals equally good or are the ones we can teach better than ones we can't? Are the ones we find useful or entertaining better than the ones we don't?

Students could research any area of animal behavior they find interesting, report the results, and the class can compare their findings to humans.

The Sun

(2ⁿᵈ–3ʳᵈ Grades)

by Gloria Jordan, Linda Jadick, Karen Aycock, and Jane Higgins, Greensboro Public Schools, Greensboro, NC

Objectives of the remodelled lesson

The students will:
- discover information about the sun through research and discussion
- engage in scientific reasoning by exploring the consequences of imagining different facts
- through fulfilling the above objectives, develop confidence in their reasoning abilities

Original Lesson Plan

Abstract

Students use encyclopedias and library books to find facts about the sun. They take notes and then put facts on a mural of the sun. The class discusses any contradictory "facts" found, and words which need clarification, and they categorize the facts.

Critique

editors' note: Although the original lesson is an improvement over the usual slavish dependence on texts, some discussion questions could be added to take students further in considering what they have learned and what it means.

Strategies used to remodel

S–9 developing confidence in reason
S–1 thinking independently
S–35 exploring implications and consequences
S–8 developing intellectual perseverance

Remodelled Lesson Plan s–9

Have the children discuss the information researched about the sun. Allow room for discussion to make assumptions explicit. Have a discussion on how to find more information on the sun. "Where else could we look to find out more? Why would that be a good place to look? What would be good to learn? How can we find it?" **S–1**

Students can engage in scientific reasoning by exploring the implications about the information found. Change the facts. For example, "If the sun were closer, what would happen to people, animals, plants? Why? If it were further away? What would happen to the water and oceans? To living things? Why?" **S–35**

"What has happened to the ozone? Why is it getting hotter and hotter?" Talk about the ozone layer, what has been done to damage it, short and long-term implications to plant and animal life on earth. **S–35**

editors' note: This lesson provides a perfect opportunity to have students deeply learn from their research. Before sending them to sources, you could have them brainstorm everything they know or think about the sun. Then tell them not to copy complete sentences from their research, only words or phrases. Reconvene the class to share their notes and reconstruct what the sources said based on their notes. Conclude with a writing assignment. By having to reconstruct what they read from sketchy notes, students more deeply process what they read; the knowledge becomes more truly theirs. **S–8**

One does not learn about critical thinking by memorizing a definition or set of distinctions.

What Will Decompose?

(2ⁿᵈ–3ʳᵈ Grades)

by Jane Davis-Seaver, Karen Marks, and Nancy Johnson, Greensboro Public Schools, Greensboro, NC

Objectives of the remodelled lesson

The students will:
- distinguish between man-made and natural objects by categorizing examples collected on a nature walk
- use the scientific process to organize information, categorize, hypothesize, test, and draw conclusions
- develop a perspective on the uses and problems of using man-made materials, by recognizing assumptions
- discuss the implications of using man-made objects, such as those made from plastic

Original Lesson Plan

Abstract

The original lesson plan is a scientific experiment to investigate what objects will decompose. The children are told that water is needed to make bacteria grow. They bury various objects, add water, and dig up each one after a specified length of time. They record the results.

Critique

We feel that a separate experiment on bacteria's need for water should precede this lesson.

This plan misses the opportunity to help children categorize and find common characteristics among natural and man-made substances through small group discussions. It does have hands–on investigation and experimentation. Its strength lies in its use of the mechanical techniques of the scientific method. We would use the original lesson plan as a part of the lesson and encourage small group discussions on such questions as these: Why do we use plastic or other man-made materials? When are these materials good to use? When are they not good to use?

Strategies used to remodel

S–12 developing one's perspective: creating or exploring beliefs, arguments, or theories
S–35 exploring implications and consequences

Remodelled Lesson Plan s-12

Rather than beginning the lesson with the experiment, start by clarifying concepts about trash by taking a nature walk to find trash, and then brainstorming ideas about the kinds of trash found. Ask what trash is decomposing and which isn't. Encourage the students to suggest categories of things that do or don't decompose, and encourage hypotheses to test. Then execute the experiment by having students choose objects from each category, make predictions regarding which objects will decompose and how quickly, and follow through on the experiment.

Following the experiment, allow for a discussion focusing on critical thinking skills. Allow for discussion on what problems have been revealed in this experiment and discussion. "What kinds of things did you predict would decompose quickly? Slowly? Not at all? What happened? Which of your predictions was verified? Which weren't? Why not? What can we say about what kinds of things decompose? Why? How are the things that decompose similar? How do they differ from those that don't decompose? Do you think that's the reason these did and those didn't? Why or why not? Can we generalize?" The class can discuss this at length, trying out generalizations, and possibly testing them with follow-up experiments.

In evaluating man-made objects, and assumptions about their use, ask if it is important to use them, and under what circumstances can natural objects be substituted. "Do we really need to make it out of plastic, or are you just assuming we do because you've always seen them that way?"

editors' note: Why do people often prefer to use man-made materials such as plastic? What problems does this cause? Where do man–made materials end up? What effects does that have?" **S-35**

Parts of a Wave

(3rd Grade)

Objectives of the remodelled lesson

The students will:
- engage in independent thinking about waves
- learn about the parts of a wave by noticing the similarities and differences in a variety of examples
- learn the standard terms and methods of measuring waves

Original Lesson Plan

Abstract

The teacher ties a rope to a post and creates a wave in the rope. The students draw a picture of the wave they observe. They read in their text that the high point of a wave is called the crest, the low point is the trough, and that the wavelength is the distance from one crest to the next.

from *The Young Scientist,* John Gabriel Navarra, et. al. Harper & Row, Publishers. 1971. pp. T63, 134.

Critique

The text suggests that the teacher create a wave with a rope for the students to observe, but this alone is not enough to foster critical thought, since all thinking is done by the text. Before using the text, the teacher should give the students a chance to discover the parts of waves for themselves, rather than simply presenting the answers to them. Furthermore, that waves are measured from crest to crest is arbitrary; students should realize this.

Strategy used to remodel

S–9 developing confidence in reason
S–29 noting significant similarities and differences

Remodelled Lesson Plan s–9

The teacher could create various waves with the rope while the students observe and draw different waves on paper. The teacher could also draw several different-looking waves on the board. Focus students' attention on the wave parts by asking questions like the following: How are these waves different? Similar? What parts do they have? How could we describe these waves? How could we distinguish them? Where could we measure them? **S–29**

Help the students see the high points, low points, and the distance between repeating patterns. (They may also mention the distance up-and-down.)

If the students don't know the standard terms, introduce them, relating each to the students' descriptions (the up-and-down length is "amplitude").

Point out that, although the wavelength could be measured from any two corresponding points (trough, crest, half-way between, etc.) it is standard practice to measure it from crest to crest.

What is remodelled today can be remodelled again. Treat no lesson plan as beyond critique and improvement.

At Work on the Earth

(3rd Grade)

Objectives of the remodelled lesson

The students will:
- distinguish the ordinary usage of 'work' from the scientific usage and discuss important similarities and differences between them
- begin to deeply understand the differences between ordinary language and technical languages

Original Lesson Plan

Abstract

Students begin the lesson by observing a picture of children pushing a raft down a river, and discussing what the children are doing. The text asks, "Would you say they are doing work?" Students say what they think 'work' means; then they are introduced to the scientific meaning of 'work'. Each child is asked to demonstrate an action that illustrates his or her understanding of the scientific concept. Other children observe and identify the force that is applied and the motion that results. Next students are asked whether water can do work, and distinguish forces used to do work (child raking leaves, a boy holding a hose still while the water moves the leaves).

from *Concepts in Science,* Paul F. Brandwein, et al. Harcourt Brace Jovanovich, Inc. 1980. pp. T8–T11.

Critique

This lesson provides an important introduction to the idea that the same word can have different meanings and that scientists, especially, have special, technical meanings for ordinary words. Unfortunately, however, this lesson fails to give students valuable practice in moving back and forth between different meanings of the same word, and recognizing and generating examples of when one, both, or neither meaning applies. Instead of moving back and forth, this lesson moves immediately to the scientific usage of the word 'work' and assumes it throughout the lesson. It doesn't explicitly develop the concept of technical language. Students need to be able to distinguish ordinary from technical concepts. To be able to think scientifically, students need to understand why scientists develop the concepts they do.

Strategies used to remodel

S–14 clarifying and analyzing the meanings of words or phrases
S–29 noting significant similarities and differences
S–17 questioning deeply: raising and pursuing root or significant questions

Remodelled Lesson Plan S-14

After the students have read their texts and done the activities, they could better develop an understanding of technical language and compare the two concepts of 'work'.

• What do you think of when you hear the word 'work'? Which of these would be examples of, or related to the scientific concept? Why do you say so? In the picture of the boy using water to push leaves, is he working in the normal sense of the word? How could we tell? Is he doing work in the scientific sense? How do we know? What is doing the work? Why do you say so?

• What's the opposite of the normal meaning of 'work'? (rest or play) Which of these is closer to the opposite of the scientific concept? Why?

• When would doing schoolwork be doing what scientists call work? Why? When would it not be work in the scientific sense? Why not?

Students can comment on what seems to be intrinsic to their ideas of work and play — what all their examples of each have in common: Does the scientific concept of 'work' apply to these cases? Which ones would the scientist call an example of work being done? For the scientist, is 'play' the opposite of 'work'? What is? **S-29**

Encourage students to see how our purposes guide how we use words by asking, "Is one of the uses of the word 'work' right and one wrong, or are both right? Why do you think so? Why do scientists have a different meaning of 'work'? Why don't they just use the ordinary meaning of the word? Should we always use 'work' the way scientists do?" **S-17**

> *Socratic questioning should be available to the teacher at all times. Questions, not answers, stimulate the mind.*

A Living System

(3ʳᵈ Grade)

Objectives of the remodelled lesson

The students will:
- engage in scientific reasoning and develop confidence in reason by formulating hypotheses about how rocks are broken into soil
- design and conduct experiments to test their hypotheses
- clarify and analyze scientific conclusions by discussing how scientists might have proven them

Original Lesson Plan

Abstract

We selected lessons from a unit on soil. In them, students are introduced to the topic, examine soil samples, and conduct experiments designed to show how rocks are broken down. Students are shown how rubbing rocks together breaks pieces off. They record contents of soil samples. They rub two pieces of sandstone together for five minutes and count the pieces. Students are told how air, water, plants, and temperature changes break rocks.

from *Concepts In Science,* Paul F. Brandwein, et al. Harcourt Brace Jovanovich, Inc. 1980. pp. T32–T34, 53–54, 56–58, 63–64.

Critique

By presenting the processes by which rocks are broken down, and the experiments which illustrate them, the lessons discourage students from struggling with the issue and developing their own hypotheses and experiments; students don't engage in scientific reasoning.

Students are told to count the pieces of rock they have broken off, yet there is no reason for learning how many pieces are broken off by five minutes of rubbing. Students shouldn't be asked to measure or count unless doing so helps settle some issue of interest. Measuring and counting, in themselves, are pointless. The idea that scientists run around counting and measuring everything in sight, for no reason, is a stereotype. Students need to learn how to use quantification as part of the process of settling questions. They need to learn to distinguish times when such activities are useful from times when they are not. Thus, this part of the lesson should be dropped.

Strategy used to remodel

S–9 developing confidence in reason
S–8 developing intellectual perseverance
S–13 clarifying issues, conclusions, or beliefs

Remodelled Lesson Plan s-9

Before students read the text which covers the ways in which rocks are broken up, they should have a chance to reason about the issue, "How are rocks broken up?" First, you might remind students that one thing they found in their soil samples was rock and ask, "Where did the little pieces of rock come from? How did big rocks get broken into pieces?" Ask them to recall partly broken, crumbling, or cracked rocks they have seen. Ask them if they know or could guess the cause. Let the students brainstorm possible answers. Make a list of their answers and allow discussion. Choose several responses and ask, "How could we find out if this breaks rocks? What could we do?" Allow discussion. The class could be split into groups, each of which can design and conduct experiments to test a hypothesis and report the results to the rest of the class. **S-8**

To summarize the lesson, the class could read and discuss the relevant passages in the text. "What are all of the things mentioned in the text that break rock into pieces? Which of these things did we test? How? Why did we do that? What happened? What did the results show? Which things mentioned in the text didn't we test for? How do you suppose scientists learned about and tested them? What might they have done? Why? What would that show?" **S-13**

A teacher committed to teaching for critical thinking must think beyond compartmentalized subject matter teaching to ends and objectives that transcend subject matter classification. To teach for critical thinking is, first of all, to create an environment that is conducive to critical thinking.

Two Concepts of 'Soil'

(3rd Grade)

Objectives of the remodelled lesson

The students will
- practice deep questioning by distinguishing the scientists' concept of 'soil' from that of the farmers
- compare the two concepts noting significant similarities and differences between their uses
- learn about reading critically by distinguishing the two concepts as they come upon them in their text and by discussing the need to figure out whether a word is used in a technical or ordinary sense

Original Lesson Plan

Abstract

Seven pages from the students' text, and one page from the teacher's edition, were selected from a unit on soil. The first page distinguishes the scientists' concept of 'soil' (all of the earth's covering is soil) from the farmers' concept (soil is the part of the land in which crops can grow). The rest of the students' pages cover the following topics: kinds of soil, makeup of soil, layers of soil, and soil conservation. The last page (from the teacher's edition) has review questions for the unit.

from *Concepts in Science,* Paul F. Brandwein, et al. Harcourt Brace Jovanovich, Inc. 1980. pp. 55, 60, 79, 81–83, 86, T41.

Critique

A basic goal of science education is to introduce students to scientific concepts, many of which have ordinary counter-parts that have related but different meanings. One major obstacle to science education, then, is the tendency to confuse scientific with ordinary concepts. Students rarely recognize the nature of scientific or technical vocabulary or its relationship to normal uses of language. The standard approach (defining the technical vocabulary then moving along) does not adequately address the problem of students' ordinary uses of language and pre-conceptions getting mixed up with technical material. After introducing the distinction between the two concepts of soil, the text simply uses the word 'soil' without saying which sense of the concept is meant, or highlighting to students the differences between technical and ordinary concepts. Scientists do not develop technical vocabulary arbitrarily. To deeply understand science and technical vocabulary, and keep them distinct from non-scientific ways of talking, students must explicitly explore how purposes determine how a word is used.

Strategies used to remodel

S–14 clarifying and analyzing the meanings of words or phrases
S–29 noting significant similarities and differences
S–17 questioning deeply: raising and pursuing root or significant questions
S–21 reading critically: clarifying or critiquing texts

Remodelled Lesson Plan s–14

When discussing the page on which the distinction between 'soil' (science) and 'soil' (farming) is made, ask students to think about the two concepts: How are the concepts similar? Different? Which concept applies in a greater number of contexts? (The teacher could draw, or, if students are familiar with them, could have students draw a simple Venn or circle-within-a-circle diagram, showing that, though all farmers' soil is scientists' soil, not all scientists soil is farmers' soil.) **S–29** Is one concept clearer than the other? Which concept is more familiar to you? Why do scientists and farmers use the same word differently? **S–17**

For the other pages, whenever the word 'soil' occurs, ask students which concept is meant. Have them explain how they know. (For instance, on page 60, the scientific concept is used. Sand is one kind of soil, but sand isn't "soil" to a farmer. On page 79 the text probably means the farmers' concept because it says "good soil", which probably means "good for growing crops".) "Would this meaning make sense in this sentence? That meaning? Why?" **S–21**

When using the review questions, again, the students could explain which concept is meant each time 'soil' occurs. **S–21**

Another way to approach this material would be to begin with a brainstorming session in which students (possibly starting with dictionaries) listed every word that comes to mind when they hear the word 'soil'. Then, after students read the definitions in their texts, they can evaluate each item on the list for its relationship to the concepts of soil in their texts: soiled clothes, dirt, sand, etc. As students read, they can distinguish the concepts as above. **S–21**

Students can use this experience with technical vocabulary to develop insight into one aspect of critical reading. "How should we read differently when a book uses special or *technical* vocabulary? What can you do when you come to a word you don't know? What can you do when you come to a word with more than one meaning? What things did we do to figure out which meaning was used?" **S–21**

School time is too precious to spend any sizeable portion of it on random facts. The world, after all, is filled with an infinite number of facts. No one can learn more than an infinitesimal portion of them. Though we need facts and information, there is no reason why we cannot gain facts as part of the process of learning how to think.

Remodelling Math Lessons

When elementary school students are asked the question, "There are 75 sheep in the field and 5 sheep dogs, how old is the shepherd?", four out of five students add, subtract, multiply, or divide to get an answer. And the more math they've had, the greater this tendency. Studies of math learning demonstrate that much of the time students don't really know what they are doing when they manipulate mathematical concepts.

As Alan Schoenfeld and others have pointed out, most students are not learning to think mathematically. They are learning to blindly follow directions, to rotely manipulate figures, to "mindlessly" do what they think they're supposed to do. The solution is to switch from formula-based instruction to problem-based instruction, making sure the problems come from real life situations and that they require mathematical thinking. Even primary grade students can begin to discover important mathematical concepts. For example, by figuring out how to answer the question, "How many paper clips would it take to make a chain from here to the principal's office?", even young children (as soon as they run out of paper clips) can begin to deeply grasp the nature of proportional thinking.

Although we have provided only two math lessons, we hope that they will help you begin to see how to help students make the connection between mathematical concepts and the real world. Remember, critical thinking in math is self-directed mathematical thinking. It is reflective, self-correcting, and based on a genuine understanding of math concepts. When students begin to learn to think mathematically, they have begun to acquire powerful tools for making sense of the world.

Bar Graph

(1ˢᵗ Grade)

by Anne J. Harris, Jefferson Elementary
School, Cloverdale, CA

Objectives of the remodelled lesson

The students will:
- participate in making a bar graph as a group and independently
- analyze and evaluate the bar graph
- discuss the values underlying their choices of television shows
- decide how important each of the values is to them and make their own bar graph to communicate this
- deeply probe the usefulness of bar graphs and when it is good to use them

Original Lesson Plan

Abstract

Students make a "shoe graph" by lining up their shoes in different categories (such as tie shoes, buckles, and slip-ons). They then "read" the "graph" and examine a bar graph in their text showing visitors to a class over a week. They answer the following questions: How many visited on Monday? Wednesday? Circle the day with the most visitors.

Critique

The sole objective of this lesson is to complete a bar graph. The assignment also asks students to interpret some of the data, but more questioning can be done here to infuse critical thinking into the lesson.

editors' note: The example of how many visitors came to class over a week is weak because it lacks purpose. To understand bar graphs, one must understand their usefulness. Therefore, students should compare different ways of presenting data, such as verbally and in a bar graph.

Strategies used to remodel

S–9 developing confidence in reason
S–1 thinking independently
S–15 developing criteria for evaluation: clarifying values and standards
S–17 questioning deeply: raising and pursuing root or significant questions

Remodelled Lesson Plan S-9

In addition to the original lesson, I would ask the students "Would the graph always work the same? How could it change? Would it be the same for our room?" Predict, then check the answer to that question by making a graph for the class. **S-1**

To foster insights into mechanical skills, I would ask the children why we would want to know this information? Where else do people use graphs? Why? **S-1**

editors' note: We suggest the class collect data that is either a topic of interest to them or a tie-in to another subject they are studying, and then translate their data into a bar graph.

One example could be to make a graph of the class' favorite TV shows. After doing the shoe bar graph in the original, the teacher could take down nominations from the class and have students count the hands for each show mentioned, while keeping a list on the board. Next, the teacher could set up the bar graph on the board, thinking aloud through the process and explaining how to mark off the scale, etc. Students could come to the board and fill in a bar. (Instead of a "show graph", this lesson could begin with a "kid graph". Students could stand in lines representing their favorite shows, notice which lines are shortest and longest, and count and record the numbers before the teacher illustrates the bar graph with the same data.)

After graphing, the students can discuss the results, read the graph, and give reasons for their choice of shows. To have students begin to see the purpose of graphing, the class could compare the list of TV shows and numbers to the graph. "Look at the list with its numbers and the bar graph. Which way of showing the data makes it easier to see which is the most popular show? Why?"

"Why is this your favorite show? Does anyone have a different reason for preferring this show? Given these reasons, why is this such a popular show? Why is this less popular?" The teacher could help the students make the values underlying their preferences explicit. **S-15**

One way to allow students (or groups of students) to produce their own bar graphs would be to have them copy this list of values and rank each value on a scale of 1 to 10. They can then take those written lists and make a bar graph showing their rankings of the values. (The same purpose could be served by having the class could poll another class, say a fifth grade class about *their* favorite shows.) The class can share and discuss the graphs.

To have the class more deeply explore the function of the graphs. "Why do we sometimes use graphs to communicate, instead of just writing our findings in words or in a table? When is a graph more helpful? When would this way be better? That way? Why?" **S-17**

Word Problems

(3rd Grade)

by Mandy Ryan and Barbara Morrow,
Greensboro Public Schools,
Greensboro, NC

Objectives of the remodelled lesson

The students will:
• clarify their understanding of math functions to solve story problems
• distinguish relevant from irrelevant information in word problems
• work independently by creating their own word problems

Standard Approach

Students read story problems and translate them into number problems in order to solve them.

Critique

The standard approach is passive in its involvement of students, requiring no independent thinking, and the students are only asked to demonstrate surface knowledge — the recall of basic facts. In addition, students get bogged down in nonessential facts.

Strategies used to remodel

S–31 distinguishing relevant from irrelevant facts
S–1 thinking independently

Remodelled Lesson Plan

The teacher will begin the lesson with a review of the four math processes: addition, subtraction, multiplication, and division. Then have students model each process. For example, the teacher could put the problem "4–1=____" on the board, and ask students for ideas on how to demonstrate this problem using their classmates. (Four students stand together, then one walks away.) Continue to do this while increasing the difficulty of the problem each time. (The teacher will also reinforce ideas with visual aids on the board.)

Then, she will elicit applications for "real life" situations and help students discriminate between the important facts in the problem and the unimportant facts. For example, "Twenty–three students came to school, two went home sick before lunch and three went to the bathroom after lunch. How many stu-

280

dents were at school at the end of the day?" The teacher should ask which facts in the situation are important to figuring out the answer and why. **S-31**

Then reverse the process by giving the students the number problem first. Ask them to create a story problem which will demonstrate the functions given. Let them do this verbally while the teacher models and reinforces the problem visually. Then have them create story problems independently. **S-1** As closure, one child will read a story problem to another while that child solves it.

"Be aware of the hidden curriculum in all schools. If teachers ask only factual questions that test memory and recall, students assume that this is the most important aspect of learning. If principals spend more time focusing on administrative concerns, discipline, or standardized test scores, teachers also assume these aspects of school are the most important."

Greensboro Handbook,
Greensboro Public Schools
Reasoning and Writing Project

"Teachers need time to reflect upon and discuss ideas, they need opportunities to try out and practice new strategies, to begin to change their own attitudes and behaviors in order to change those of their students, to observe themselves and their colleagues — and then they need more time to reflect upon and internalize these concepts."

Greensboro Handbook,
Greensboro Public Schools
Reasoning and Writing Project

Remodelling Lessons into Thematic Units

by Daniel Weil

Introduction

Before we begin a discussion of the necessity of a *thematic*, multi-cultural approach to educational curriculum design, we must first explain what we mean by a thematic approach. A thematic approach to curriculum design is a holistic approach, since it integrates the content areas that elementary teachers are responsible for teaching. A holistic or thematic approach links major concepts to the various content areas such as language arts, social studies, and science, while refining and developing skills such as reading, writing, and listening.

The Fragmented Curriculum

Teachers in the public elementary school system are required to teach a host of subjects such as reading, science, social studies, music, and mathematics. To accomplish this, many teachers are required to write lesson plans for each specific subject area indicating exactly what will be taught and how. For the most part, the curriculum has treated all these subjects as isolated pursuits of knowledge disconnected from each other. It's not unusual to consult an elementary lesson plan book and find different lesson plans written for each subject. Reading and writing is perhaps taught in the morning, using texts from which the teacher derives his or her lesson. Once this subject has been taught, students are asked to take out their math books to pursue math skills. After this, the other subject matters are addressed one-by-one with individual lesson plans for each distinct area of knowledge. Thus, the tendency is to concentrate on developing skills in various subject areas by presenting them as unique and separate areas of expertise. Through recitation and memorization of facts and details, the pursuit of the skill, say reading or writing, becomes a mechanical process done for practice in and of itself, with no correlation with concepts or understandable uses or applications. Application is either memorized or performed "outside" of a meaningful context. Problems are treated as having solutions only within the body of knowledge being learned. Sometimes the student works on art, sometimes the student studies literature. But the integration of art and literature is rarely the focus of either. The world is presented in pieces and the relevance of education to everyday life is sacrificed to the machine-like approach of an educational assembly line.

We as educators should realize that knowledge and its pursuit are not isolated. The carpenter must know geometry and the scientist must understand the social significance of that which he or she is scientifically exploring. Art is historical and literature is the culture of a society. Yet a look into the world of elementary classroom curricula would surely fail to illuminate this because the parts are rarely related to the whole. What one does in science for example, is virtually never related to society in general or discussed in social terms. This method of curriculum design, with its accompanying lesson plans for each subject area, we call a fragmented curriculum. This type of curriculum is not simply limited, but is significantly divorced from today's complex world where a variety of skills and expertise are urgently needed. We must therefore ask ourselves if the skills we are teaching actually advance conceptual understanding and critical thinking, or if they are mere servants indentured to fragmented memorization of facts and details, to routinized and regimented recitation.

We argue here for a holistic or integrated, thematic approach to curriculum and lesson plan building wherever possible, one that addresses students' need to integrate knowledge into their daily lives. After all, the problems of daily life are rarely one-dimensional. They can rarely be solved by using knowledge from only one, isolated subject area. A thematic approach to primary education calls upon all the disciplines of study to unite in a common mission — to seek to solve problems and discuss issues relevant to today's students in a climate of critical thinking and moral critique. It seeks to develop skills in concert with integrated themes, not outside of them. A curriculum such as we propose, is based on the realization that knowledge is understood through the synthesis of the parts within the whole and the whole within the parts, in the same way that individuality is understood by acknowledging the synthesis of the individual within the general society, and the society within the individual. We understand each through their relationships. Knowing the whole allows us to know the parts and vice-versa. We believe that an educated, thinking person does not merely comprehend or act upon disjointed or fragmented skills or knowledge that reduce to divorced understandings. We believe quite the contrary — that an educated, thinking person possesses knowledge drawn from many disciplines employed in concert, marshalled on a daily basis, for understanding and solving life's daily problems.

The Thematic Unit

With this in mind, we turn our attention to some possible themes which we have successfully employed within the elementary curriculum. We begin with the belief that thematic units need to be relevant to the lives of today's students. They cannot be matters of trivial pursuit but must be real life themes that illuminate conceptual understandings. For this reason, we recommend basing the themes on social study or scientific inquiries. Recently, such attempts to integrate social science and literature, or mathematics and science have been popular undertakings. Though laudable in their recognition of the need to integrate subject matters, these pursuits have not gone far enough in integrating all the subject areas under "one roof", so to speak. We argue here for a thorough and complete conceptual instructional plan, achieved through full integration of all subject areas.

An example of such a theme, and one successfully used in elementary curricula is that of the Rain Forest. Here the students are informed that they will be spending two weeks or more learning about the Rain Forest. All of the isolated skills are then plugged into this theme and used holistically to better critically understand the concept. The children use their reading skills to learn about this fascinating forest. Their writing and oral skills are employed to better understand and explore the concept. Scientific inquiry is centered around the theme in a variety of ways. Computations in mathematics are employed in connection with the theme. The uniting of what were formerly thought of as isolated or fragmented pursuits of knowledge, become employed holistically in the service of conceptual understanding. Not only is this far better suited to the pursuit of knowledge, but it also more passionately motivates and commands the attention of children.

While engaged in the study of the Rain Forest, the children are actively involved in social-scientific inquiry. They learn about the animals of the forest, the people who live there, the amazing vegetation, environmental awareness, conflicting perspectives, and the moral and social implications of current environmental practices. The inter-connectedness of these ideas is illuminated by calling on all the disciplines. Students are asked to critically look at these issues and, using all the skills they possess, discuss and evaluate conclusions and solutions. Writing is employed in scientific as well as socially relevant ways. Reading includes fiction as well as factual materials. Scientific inquiry leads to environmental awareness. The theme acts as a conceptual umbrella under which the child is busily concerned with linking various academic disciplines in the spirit of critical thinking and broad-based synthesis.

To fuel thematic instruction in the primary grades, one must use literature which addresses the theme. For example, a thematic unit about American Indians might use folktales from various tribes. These, coupled with contemporary literary selections, can become the basis for the theme. Students can read and comment on these selections through discussion and writing. When taught in the early primary grades, mathematics might be integrated through useful and relevant word problems. Mathematical calculations might also be necessary and appropriate for the upper primary grades. Cooking authentic Indian recipes is one way to have students apply mathematics within the thematic context. They could compute ingredients in mathematical terms, producing at the same time something that is authentically Indian in culture and diet. Art instruction can be centered around Indian pottery or Indian patterns. Tepee making and activities with clay can be studied relative to Indian dwellings, both past and present. Music can be integrated through study of Indian dances. Scientific inquiry can be fostered through studying the uses Indians have for various plants and herbs. These are just a sampling of ideas that point to the variety of ways the curriculum can be integrated under the rubric of the theme of American Indians. All the faculties of the student, both prior and recently acquired knowledge, can be employed in the pursuit of better understanding of American Indians and their roles both historically and presently.

The above two themes, as most themes which are scientifically and socially based, can be extended to all grade levels. American Indians or the Rain Forest are themes which are of current interest and relevance to both upper and lower primary grades. The difference in instruction would be only in the area of emphasis and the manner in which the theme was taught. For example, when teaching the theme of Africa and African-Americans, the early primary grade teacher might focus on African animals through African folktales and the likenesses and differences between African–Americans and other ethnic groups. The upper grade teacher might focus on current trends in South Africa through contemporary literature and the role of African-Americans in the struggle for Civil Rights. In either case, what is common is the theme of Africa and African-Americans. What differs is the particular emphasis and mode of presentation.

Finally, it is important to note that thematic instruction *motivates* students to learn, since it presents them with an important and broadly-based concept. When the world is presented disconnectedly, there is little motivation to learn anything but the rudimentary skills employed in the instruction, if that. However, when the curriculum is theme oriented, and integration and unity is everywhere, the student begins to see relationships and achieve understanding much more readily. There is nothing like successful learning for motivating further learning. What is more, successful teaching — which thematic teaching more readily brings about — motivates and energizes the teacher as well.

In summary, there is a pressing need for a fully integrated thematic approach in the primary grades. The advantages and benefits are many. The value of knowledge, its instruction and pursuit, are validated for both student and teacher in new and holistic ways. Education becomes importantly relevant. What is social and scientific becomes individual and personal, what is individual and personal becomes more social and scientific. Reading, writing, and mathematical skills, as well as a host of subject matter skills and principles, are no longer isolated and arbitrary pursuits of disconnected learning, but holistic instruments by which we gain true understanding. Through a thematic approach to curriculum design, critical thinking and moral insight flourish and grow. The ability to reason in connected, rather than fragmented ways, emerges and deepens. We and our children begin to feel empowered, able to act with strength, insight, and moral compassion.

The Case for a Multi-Cultural Curriculum

We have argued for a holistic, thematic approach to curriculum design. We also believe that thematic units are most effective and powerful when they are multi-cultural in both design and application. After all, not only are minorities expected to compose close to half of the public school population as early as this year, but the rapidly increasing conflict between diverse cultures in the world also intensifies the need for cultural literacy, that is, the ability to think within and appreciate more than one cultural perspective. The failure of many school districts to educate poor and minority students, though increasingly troubling, is only one dimension of the problem. Current curricula are simply not working, as suggested by numerous studies as well as the testimony of our day-to-day experience. Suffice it to say that we can no longer impose mono-ethnic, mono-cultural, and mono-historical perspectives on a multi–ethnic, multi–cultural, and multi–historical society and world. From the start, attempts to do just that were illusory, when not culturally and historically dishonest.

As we look at the faces in our classrooms, we see the changing world demographics personified. Education in the U.S., with its rich multi-cultural audience has the potential to become a truly pluralistic country, a living experiment in real educational democracy — an educational context in which the human mind, personality, and moral sensibilities are jointly celebrated. The success of this experiment requires at least adjusting curricula to rapid global changes. We must enter the 21ˢᵗ Century culturally literate. But the cultural literacy we need must be more than cultivated sociocentricity; it must be multi-dimensional at its roots. Through positive and constructive critique, we as educators can reconstruct curricula based on relevance, multi-cultural diversity, educational equity, and holistic critical thinking.

Eurocentric or mono-cultural approaches to education have clouded our picture of the real world. These approaches have not only failed, and continue to fail, they dull our awareness of how human experience is the culmination of diverse historical and social groups and processes, multi-cultural and multidimensional in origin. Up-to-date curricula must highlight social and individual phenomena within the perspective of other cultural and ethnic perspectives. Fostering an openness toward other perspectives and cultures is one of the most important aspects of critical thinking and moral critique — fairmindedness. Acknowledging that ignorance and egocentrism are at the root of bigotry and prejudice, today's multi-cultural curricula need to nurture intellectual empathy and fairmindedness. They will then be a bulwark in combating racial and ethnic intolerance, as they develop academic, personal, and social skills and understanding. Mono-lingual curricula fail to implement this essential understanding. As such, these curricula continue to promote a false sense of culture, ideas, values, and history. Broadening the curriculum to include other peoples, cultures, and belief systems creates an intellectual atmosphere where fairmindedness thrives and cooperative human relationships in a diverse ethnic and cultural world flourish.

When interviewed about school and the impact it has on their lives, low income minority students seem to have the same general complaint — they do not feel at home in the classroom. The experiences, data, interaction, and examples used in many curricula hit few, if any, responsive chords in these students. In fact, all too often, curricula have been rewritten or designed to exclude ethnic and cultural minorities. As a result, these students experience high dropout rates, many discipline problems, low self esteem, and little success within the public schools. Though this is not universally the case, it is too often the response and reality.

As teachers we must ask ourselves if we are really listening and responding to what the lives of our students are telling them and us. The multi-cultural diversity of today's classroom is the source for many messages and voices that can transform how we design and implement curricula, as well as how we teach and our students learn. We must continually monitor the voice and perspective of our students, and integrate their prior knowledge and experience to maximize the relevance of what we are teaching them. We must learn from them in order to teach them. We must think within their world, if they are to learn to think within ours.

The general argument for a multi-cultural curriculum, then, is two-fold. First, a multi-cultural curriculum addresses the issue of self esteem for minority students and newly arrived immigrants. It provides educational equity by creating educational conditions that recognize and validate the contributions of all cultures. A curriculum diverse in multi-cultural resources such as literature, music, art, and socio-historical perspectives validates the experience of the student while placing that experience into a larger context. For example, a Latino student who learns about the struggle of Martin Luther King, Jr. and the Civil Rights Movement might find his or her own experience validated and better understood within the context of that deepened conceptual understanding. The integration and active recognition of commonalties between cultures strengthens personal and social awareness about real life situations, as it empowers students.

Second, a curriculum rich in multi-cultural perspectives and activities fosters fairmindedness in students by encouraging them to see and experience issues from other cultural and ethnic perspectives. This process helps diminish social stereotyping while it nurtures tolerance, sensitivity, and intellectual empathy. It promotes cultural literacy in the best sense of the term: the ability to reason insightfully within multiple cultural perspectives. This ability is our ticket into the 21st Century and an increasingly multi-cultural society and world.

Beyond these two general arguments, the advantages of a multi-cultural curriculum can be summarized as follows:

1) It encourages educational equity by assuring equal conditions and opportunity along with democratic participation for all students.

2) It heralds and respects ethnic and cultural diversity and encourages a multi-cultural perspective and consciousness.

3) It employs a philosophy of interaction based on cooperation rather than "go-it-alone" individualism and destructive competition.

4) It is built around techniques that foster self esteem among students in an atmosphere that encourages fairmindedness and success.

5) It uses the ethnic and cultural backgrounds of both the teacher and the students as a resource to draw on for prior and present experience and knowledge.

6) It is committed to cross-cultural teaching and recognizes that one's teaching techniques and views must continually evolve and develop as multi-cultural awareness deepens.

7) It promotes the appreciation of tolerance, sensitivity, and intellectual empathy as well as multi-cultural and multi-ethnic cooperation.

8) It recognizes historical, political, and personal life as shaped by a wide range of cultures, individuals, and ethnic groups.

9) It promotes cultural literacy.

Current Trends

Currently, there is a trend underway to integrate the elementary school curriculum through the use of holistic, multi-cultural language arts units. Large companies have begun to publish literature-based language arts texts and kits. Though the effort is laudable, these program-texts have tended to oversimplify material, offer a superficial treatment of their themes, and leave little room for critical thinking and ethical and moral critique. Furthermore, although they profess a multi-cultural approach, they treat multi-cultural issues and images stereotypically, rather than fostering in-depth cultural understanding and ethnic appreciation. Although the new direction of textbook companies further testifies to the need for holistic, multi-cultural education, it leaves us much to critique and remodel.

The idea of lesson plan remodelling as presented in this handbook is specifically applicable to thematic units. Here we will present a critique and remodel of a thematic unit taken from the Harcourt/Brace/Jovanovich recently released Language Arts series entitled, "Imagination — An Odyssey Through Language".

Remodelled Thematic Unit

Objectives of the Remodelled Theme:

The students will:
- think independently by clarifying and analyzing the concepts of family relationships and friendship
- exercise fairmindedness by considering the feelings of emigrant families who have recently moved to the U.S.
- explore the feelings and underlying thoughts of how moving makes themselves and others feel
- compare the concept of family to the "social structures" of animals
- develop their own perspectives about friendships and who they would choose as friends
- develop intellectual courage when dealing with friendship and family situations that pose dilemmas
- distinguish between their ideals of friendships and family relationships and what actual practice tells them
- analyze and evaluate conflicting arguments and beliefs of literary characters
- develop critical listening by summarizing each other's viewpoints about friendships and families
- practice Socratic questioning by asking each other questions to clarify each other's viewpoints
- explore similarities and differences between families today and families before the industrial revolution

Original Thematic Unit Plan

Abstract

The series states that it "thoroughly integrates reading, writing, listening, and speaking with thinking", and that the "universal unit themes enable students to connect ideas among selections, explore positive values in depth, and share rich multi-cultural experiences." There is a teachers' edition and student books for each grade. For beginning primary grades, K–1, Story Land 1 and Story Land 2 are used and are entitled *Happy Times!* For purposes of this critique and remodelling process, we will concentrate on these particular books with this grade level in mind.

Within the body of the books are various themes, all of which entail an average time frame of two weeks. One theme, and the focus of our remodel, entitled "Hello Friends", concerns itself with the concept or theme of "building positive relationships with family members and friends". The unit contains three reading selections and two picture books. These are designed to form the basis or foundation for the theme. The skill objectives of the theme are indicated as Writing/Thinking, Reading/Thinking, Speaking/Thinking, and Listening/Thinking. Various learning strategies are suggested, and the series offers suggestions on how to tie the lessons to the child's own experiences. To help teachers foster critical thinking among their students, the authors provide two categories of questions designed to enhance discussion: **Thought Questions** and, **Memory Questions**.

They attribute three general characteristics to **Thought Questions:** 1) "They ask for new ideas and new ways to use ideas or opinions", 2) "They may have many good answers", and 3) "They have answers that come from your thoughts". The authors define the variety of "Thought questions" by using "key words and phrases" such as "What ____?" questions (for example, "Imagine the best friend you can have. What would he or she be like?"), "What _____ if ____?" questions. ("What would the world be like if people had no friends?"), or "How do you feel about ____?" questions ("How do you feel about your best friend? Give reasons.").

Memory Questions are also defined as having three general attributes: 1) "They ask for facts and details", 2) "They have only one correct answer", and 3) "They have answers that ask you to recall information." Once again, the authors formally define the variety of "Memory Questions" by using "key words and phrases". For example, they suggest there are "Who ___?", "Which one ___?", "Where___?", "When ___?", "What ___?" , and "How many ___?" questions. For example, "Who are four of your friends?", "Which one have you known the longest?", "Where did you meet your friend?", "When do you have the best times with your friend?", "How many friends do you have?", "What did your friend do yesterday?"

In "Hello Friends", students are asked questions that encourage them to view friendship and family relationships positively. Through stories that use animals as their characters, children are encouraged to think about how it feels to leave home, go to school, and make friends. Friendship is often portrayed through animal stories and students are asked to think about what friends do. They are asked to discuss how their friends are the same as and different from themselves. In a picture story about story-time in a classroom, students are asked to compare and contrast what they do in school and what other children do in school. In another picture story about a birthday, children are asked questions such as, "What are different family members doing to make the party fun?" and "How do you think the boy feels about his birthday party?"

Memory and thought questions guide the discussions within the teachers' text. It is suggested that the teacher use a variety of language techniques to reinforce language arts. These skills are all to be developed in accordance with the theme and in fact focus on reiterating the concepts presented within it. Various activities are suggested to engage the students in skills such as the writing process, including pre-writing, writing, and editing techniques. For example, in one activity, students are encouraged to make a booklet showing activities done with family, with friends, and by oneself. The listening process objectives call for students to listen to a story about friends and then draw a picture of the friends they heard about in the story. For oral language, a suggested objective is to retell a story about friends or family through an activity using puppets. And finally, for the reading process, the objective indicated is to read about building relationships with friends and family and then convey the story to another student in the class.

Science and social studies are incorporated into the theme only in the section entitled, "Think and Extend" which appears at the end of each selection. Here, students are asked, for example, to identify big and small animals. It's recommended that they cut pictures of animals from magazines and classify them accordingly. For social studies, it's recommended that the students learn about different people who work at the school and their jobs. It's suggested that they engage in a language experience activity with the teacher, dictating the names of some of the people at the school and the various jobs they perform.

Critique

Although there are some positive aspects to this thematic unit on building relationships between family members and friends, there is much that could be improved. The unit fails to take advantage of the wealth of available multi-cultural literature relevant to the theme. Although there is an attempt to picture multi-cultural children in some of the stories, the actual content of the stories is completely devoid of multi-cultural content and expression. The family is depicted in the selections as a nuclear unit and thereby portrays Eurocentric views of what an American family should be. Students are never exposed to friendships as they exist in other cultures so as to see the similarities, differences, and universal themes. The reading selections fail to take into account the different perspectives that children from varying cultural backgrounds face at home and elsewhere. The literature selected here neither validates cultural identity and experience, nor places this identity and experience in a larger context. Cross-cultural friendships are never addressed, encouraged, or even recognized in the literature. For the theme to offer literal and expressive meaning to various cultural backgrounds and interests of today's students, it should include literature that welcomes and recognizes ethnic and multi-cultural diversity, as it enhances self-expression and self esteem for all students. To develop fairmindedness, children need to be exposed to a rich mixture of literature that seeks to build their concept of themselves both as individuals and as citizens of the world.

Another weakness with the reading selections is their lack of conflict. The literature choices are devoid of struggle, emotion, and passion. There is nothing to figure out, no controversy to discuss, and thus nothing to challenge the mind. Language arts literature needs to deal with some form of conflict and to arouse at least some passion. Here, we are never confronted with the need for problem solving within the theme. Friendships never experience problems and families never deviate from the portrait painted by the readings. Friendships and family are treated generically and superficially as if they were concepts existing outside of cultural reality. As a result, the readings fail to serve as a model for facing real-life situations in a world which grows rapidly more complex each day. Good literature, thematically connected with critical discussion, should foster imaginative writing and study of real personal and social experience.

The unit assumes that family and friends are important, but the student is never encouraged to explore why or to question the validity of this assumption. Consequently, the various activities and objectives do little to promote critical thinking about the theme.

We maintain that skills are by-products of the whole act of "making sense" of experience. They develop naturally when fostered within the context of critical and relevant learning. There is no need to practice the skills in isolation. Here, however, the skills taught serve as vehicles for recitation and recall only. The listening objectives, reading objectives, and speaking and writing objectives have all been decided by the authors. Children are encouraged and rewarded for using these skills to portray family and friendship as they have learned them: devoid of conflict, Eurocentric, and inherently good.

In this way, the skills developed are merely relevant to theme conformity, not to critical inquiry. Students recall and draw pictures of friends they learned about in a story or retell a story using puppets. They are encouraged to retell stories to each other or write about things friends do. These activities and approaches to understanding human relationships impose a false picture on reality, disconnected from actual experience. This is especially true of new immigrant families. For many of them, friendships have been destroyed and lost through war, death, and relocation. Too often the family has been broken and forced to live apart by external socio-economic pressures beyond their control. Many children bring this experience with them into the classroom. The selections offered here foster an image of family relationships and friendships that are simply not universal to all cultures; furthermore, they are less and less relevant in today's rapidly changing world.

Finally, it must be pointed out that although an attempt is made to delineate memory or "recall questions" and critical thinking questions, the "thought questions" provided do not go far enough in promoting real critical thinking and ethical exploration. Because the ethical standards have been established by the author, the students do not have the opportunity to really think things through on their own. The subtle but influential standards for "acceptable answers" fosters thinking within ethnocentric perspectives. This method is in fact harmful because it presents "pseudo-critical thinking" as authentic critical thinking.

Strategies used to remodel

S–23 making interdisciplinary connections
S–1 thinking independently
S–14 clarifying and analyzing the meanings of words or phrases
S–3 exercising fairmindedness
S–4 exploring thoughts underlying feelings and feelings underlying thoughts
S–11 comparing analogous situations: transferring insights to new contexts
S–12 developing one's perspective: creating or exploring beliefs, arguments, or theories
S–14 clarifying and analyzing the meanings of words or phrases
S–6 developing intellectual courage
S–10 refining generalizations and avoiding oversimplifications
S–27 comparing and contrasting ideals with actual practice
S–18 analyzing or evaluating arguments, interpretations, beliefs, or theories
S–19 generating or assessing solutions
S–22 listening critically: the art of silent dialogue
S–24 practicing Socratic discussion: clarifying and questioning beliefs, theories, or perspectives
S–28 thinking precisely about thinking: using critical vocabulary
S–29 noting significant similarities and differences

The Remodelled Thematic Unit S-23

The original theme of friendship and family relationships is ideal for early primary grades. In fact, the theme can be remodelled to work well anywhere in the K–6 curriculum. It can be extended in important and stimulating ways well beyond the two weeks allotted.

First, it's possible to base the theme on new multi-cultural literature selections. The choice of literature is important because it lays the foundation for the entire unit. The teachers should work with the students when selecting the literature. This discussion will provide an important springboard for the rest of the unit. Because the unit is student/teacher composed, it will be more relevant to the students' lives and will be more motivating.

Since the cultural backgrounds of teachers and pupils should determine what literature to employ, it is hard to recommend specific literature for the unit. There is a great deal of multi-cultural children's literature, both contemporary and traditional. One idea for the unit is folktales from other countries. Folktales are rich in cultural content, historically enlightening, amusing, and motivating for students of all ages. Furthermore, they are conflict based and ethically concerned. They are especially delightful in the early grades for they introduce children to varied cultures and nationalities through animals from the host countries. This provides an excellent and motivating objective for scientific inquiry alongside the theme. Many of these tales are available on filmstrips and videos. Many African and Native-American folktales, for example, have interesting and exciting tales that discuss friendship and family relationships in amusing and provocative ways. Because the conflicts are value-based, they invite critical thinking and moral critique on all levels. Students can begin to appreciate friendships and family relationships as they relate to diverse cultures and ethnic groups.

To begin the unit, the students could engage in independent thinking by discussing the concepts that they will later read about in the folk tales. The teacher could start by asking, "What is a family?", allowing the children to make use of and see the value in the knowledge they already have about family life. Students should be encouraged to explore different kinds of families, that is, the extended family as found in different parts of the world and the nuclear family generally associated with U.S. or European cultures. "Who do you think of as members of your family? How many people do you need for a family?" The class could conduct a poll of the students to see how many family members each student had living at home. They could then develop math skills by learning how to graph and analyze the results. Afterwards, they could discuss the results of the graph in groups. *S-1* "Some of us have large families and others have small families. What do you think are the benefits of a large family? What's good about a small family? What do families do? What is important to you about your family?" Have the students look at the families they have known and ask, "What is different about some of the families you have seen?

What is a homeless family? How would their lives be different from yours? What special problems would they face?" **S–14**

Next you can read a folktale, or perhaps a few different folktales, to the class and discuss how the families in these stories are similar to and different from their own families. This opens the discussion about families from different parts of the country, and can lead to a discussion about families that have immigrated to the U.S. This will help children learn to enter sympathetically into perspectives that differ from their own. "What is different about the families you know that have come here from a different country? How do people from other countries feel when they must leave friends and loved ones to come to the U.S.? Have you ever had to move away and make new friends? How did it feel?" These situations can be role-played in innovative and imaginative ways. **S–3** "What were you thinking when (what might you think if) you moved away? How would this effect how you would feel? Would everyone think the same way about the situation? What else might someone think about moving? How would they feel?" **S–4**

If the students read a story about families that uses animal characters, a scientific discussion about the characteristics of the animals and the resemblance of their "social structure" (families, herds, packs, etc.) to families could be probed to further illuminate the concept of family. Older students might do an independent research project by investigating the family structure of a particular animal, writing a short essay, and presenting their findings to the class. You might want to show films or videos that address the family structure of animals. "Does this animal belong to a group? What is the group called? Are the members of the group related by blood, or do they group together for another reason? What is the role of the different animals in the group?" **S–11**

Next you can ask the children to explore the concept of friendship. "What is a friend? What do you associate with friendship? What do you think of when you think of an enemy? What qualities do you look for in friends? Can somebody be your friend even if he or she has a different color skin or speaks a different language? What if your friend isn't accepted because of the color of his or her skin, should you still be friends? Why or why not? **S–12** Is everybody in your family a friend? Can friends ever be like family? Have you ever wished someone wasn't your friend? If so, why?" **S–14**

Students should be encouraged to discuss dilemmas involving friendship and family relationships and seek solutions to these dilemmas. These dilemmas can be actual or student created. They could also be introduced through literature selections. In all cases, the dilemmas should challenge the notions of friendship and family relationships. This should not be done in a negative way, but in a way that fosters controversy and discussion about these themes. One example might be: What if your friends told you to steal something from a store or they wouldn't be your friends anymore? Would you do it? Explain. Should we do everything our friends tell us to do, even if we think it is wrong? Why? Can we always trust our friends? **S–6**

You could also ask students if they think they should always listen to family members. "When is it not appropriate to listen to your mom or dad? Are moms and dads always right? Why or why not? *S-10* What if another family member asked you to do something that didn't seem right? What could you do? Are family relationships and friendships perfect? Why or why not? How could they be made better? What could be done to improve them? Can you think of a time when you weren't a good friend? Why did you feel and act that way?" *S-27*

Conflicting points of view can arise in stories or in created dramatizations of real life episodes. Here students can be asked to consider the characters' conflicting points of view, evaluate all sides of the argument, give reasons to support their conclusions about the strengths and weaknesses of the solution offered, and offer other possible solutions. For example, if students were discussing "Cinderella", the teacher could ask: Why did the step sisters think that Cinderella should do all the work? Do you think these were good reasons? How do you think Cinderella felt about doing all the work? What do you think about her reasons? Why did the sisters not want Cinderella to go to the ball? Can you think of a solution that would help them to get along better? *S-18*

Problems often arise on the playground and can be incorporated into a "conflict-resolution" activity. This might be a special time of the day or week when students deal specifically with conflicts and student relationships. During this time, they could be encouraged to fairmindedly consider each other's viewpoints and explore solutions to their problems. *S-19*

To promote critical listening skills, students should be in an environment where respect is given to what other students say. The teacher can ask students to summarize verbally or through a writing exercise (in the case of older students) what another student has to say about friendship and family relationships. *S-22* The teacher should encourage student formulated questions during discussions which elicit information from the student who is talking, as a way of laying the foundation for the development of Socratic questioning techniques. *S-24*

The teacher should also help the children to develop critical vocabulary, by using it in discussions and by reformulating student questions to include it. When reading literature, the students can be asked to *infer* what might happen next. "What *evidence* or *reasons* do you have to support this *inference* or *conclusion?*" For example, if reading "The Boy Who Cried Wolf", the teacher might ask, "What are the *implications* or *consequences* of the boy's actions? What do you think is going to happen the next time he cries 'Wolf'? What can we *infer* or *tell* about lying in this story? Does lying have *implications* for a friendship? Does lying have a negative effect on friendship? Why?" *S-28*

Rather than concentrating the curriculum and activities on jobs and personnel at the school, as recommended in the original thematic lesson plan, the focus could be on jobs that family members and their friends have. This best integrates the focus of study with the overall theme. The students could also discuss the contributions they make to the family by recognizing the chores that they do as being important to the functioning of the household. This holistic approach helps to show complex relationships family and friends have to the outside world and the roles they must adopt inside and outside the family. It extends the relevance of the theme both personally and socially, as children are invited to share various details about their lives.

This section could also be extended, with older students particularly, to include discussion about the structure of families before technological development and the industrial revolution. Students should discover the changing role of the family. "What kinds of things did families have to do before, that they don't do now?" This could be centered around the idea of the farming family that worked together at home, rather than away from home. "To what extent do families still have to work together? How have the jobs or responsibilities of family members changed? How did families use to spend much of their time? How did they get their food? How did they wash their clothes and dishes? How has working and going to school outside of the home changed the structure of the family?" It could also be mentioned that in some countries the families still work closely together in the home, depending on the work of each member to contribute to the overall goods they need. **S–29**

Infusing critical thinking into the thematic unit often leads to the remodelling of objectives for proposed activities. For example, the objectives of the "listening/thinking" skills might be to actively engage students in a discussion of a story that the teacher read aloud. The objective should be to personalize it, or make it pertinent to their lives, not to simply retell the story by drawing pictures of the characters. "Writing/thinking" activities might have as their objective the creation of a class "Big Book", born out of class discussions which involve all the children. This "Big Book" could be about the students' conception of friendships and family relationships and how these conceptions manifest themselves in the students' immediate lives. The "reading/thinking" activities could then have as their objectives students reading the "Big Book" either individually, in pairs, or as a whole group with the teacher. Rather than having oral language activities be the retelling of a story with puppets, students could dramatize real-life friendships and family relationships. Dilemmas concerning having to make choices involving friends and families could be role played.

What we are proposing here is this: rather than using and developing skills to reiterate and repeat the theme, students could be encouraged to use them actively and to critically participate in the theme. In this way, the theme becomes socially and personally accessible. In a word, it becomes relevant.

Cooperative learning strategies should be incorporated throughout many of the discussions and activities. These strategies encourage positive relationships and help build an atmosphere of mutual respect, while building skills of cooperation.

Summary

We can no longer afford to treat subject areas as isolated pursuits of disconnected knowledge. Instead we must proceed holistically, understanding that subjects interrelate, working to help students build a unity of skills as they construct knowledge of the whole. We have argued here for a thematic, multi-cultural approach to curriculum design and classroom learning. The foundation for this approach is a multi-cultural social studies or scientifically based language arts program that is couched within relevant situations that face today's students.

This developmentally appropriate curriculum, with its hands-on study, its multi-cultural awareness, and it's emphasis on reason and values, can move teaching and learning toward comprehension, critical thinking, and ethical critique. Listening, reading, and writing about the content of the thematically chosen literature, draws the reader into the world of the past, present, and future. Integrating language with all subject areas across the curriculum, making it an effective part of the content theme, incorporates reading, writing, listening, and speaking processes in the service of comprehension, cultural literacy, and critical thought. This should be the goal of today's curriculum. Language shapes verbal thinking. We use it to create meaning in our lives. A classroom where clear and precise language use is heralded, is a classroom where critical thinking, cultural recognition, and moral critique is celebrated.

> *If we simply present the teacher with pre-packaged finished lesson plans, designed by the critical thinking of someone else, someone who used a process that is not clearly understood by the teacher, then a major opportunity for the teacher to develop her own critical thinking skills, insights, and motivations will have been lost.*

> **We can never become fairminded unless we learn how to enter sympathetically into the thinking of others, to reason from their perspective and eventually to try seeing things as they see them.**

Thinking Critically About Teaching: From Didactic to Critical Teaching

John Dewey once asked a class he visited, "What would you find if you dug a hole in the earth?" Getting no response, he repeated the question: again he obtained nothing but silence. The teacher chided Dr. Dewey, "You're asking the wrong question." Turning to the class, she asked, "What is the state of the center of the earth?" The class replied in unison, "Igneous fusion."

To begin to teach critical thinking one must critique present educational practices and the beliefs underlying them and develop a new conception of knowledge and learning. Educators must ask themselves crucial questions about the nature of knowledge, learning, and the human mind. Educators should reflect on their own thought processes, their own experiences of learning, misunderstanding, confusion, and insight. They should recall and analyze their successes and failures when attempting to teach. They should examine the conceptions and assumptions implicit in their educational practices and self-consciously develop their own theories of education through analysis, evaluation, and reconstruction of their understanding of education and what it means to learn.

Most instructional practice in most academic institutions around the world presupposes a didactic theory of knowledge, learning, and literacy ill-suited to the development of critical minds and persons. After a superficial exposure to reading, writing, and arithmetic, schooling is typically fragmented thereafter into more or less technical domains, each with a large technical vocabulary and an extensive content or propositional base. Students memorize and reiterate domain-specific details. Teachers lecture and drill. Active integration of the students' daily non-academic experiences is rare. Little time is spent stimulating student questions. Students are expected to "receive" the knowledge "given" them. Students are not typically encouraged to doubt what they are told in the classroom or what is written in their texts. Students' personal points of view or philosophies of life are considered largely irrelevant to education. Classrooms with teachers talking and students listening are the rule. Ninety percent of teacher questions require no more thought than recall. Dense and typically speedy coverage of content is typically followed by content-specific testing. Interdisciplinary synthesis is ordinarily viewed as a personal responsibility of the student and is not routinely tested. Technical specialization is considered the natural goal of schooling and is correlated with getting a job. Few multi-logical issues or problems are discussed or assigned and even fewer teachers know how to conduct such discussions or assess student participation in them. Students are rarely expected to engage in dialogical or dialectical reasoning, and few teachers are proficient analysts of such reasoning. Knowledge is viewed as verified intra-disciplinary propositions and well-supported intra-disciplinary theories. There is little or no discussion of the nature of prejudice or bias, little or no discussion of metacognition, and little or no discussion of what a disciplined, self-directed mind or self-directed thought requires. The student is expected to develop into a literate, educated person through years of what is essentially content memorization and ritual performance.

The dominant pattern of academic instruction and learning is based on an uncritical theory of knowledge, learning, and literacy that is coming under increasing critique by theorists and researchers. Those who operate on the didactic theory in their instruction rarely formulate it explicitly. Some would deny that they hold it, even though their practice implies it. In any case, it is with the theory implicit in practice that we are concerned.

To illustrate, consider this letter from a teacher with a Master's degree in physics and mathematics, with 20 years of high school teaching experience in physics:

> After I started teaching, I realized that I had learned physics by rote and that I really did not understand all I knew about physics. My thinking students asked me questions for which I always had the standard textbook answers, but for the first time it made me start thinking for myself, and I realized that these canned answers were not justified by my own thinking and only confused my students who were showing some ability to think for themselves. To achieve my academic goals I had to memorize the thoughts of others, but I had never learned or been encouraged to learn to think for myself.

The extent and nature of "coverage" for most grade levels and subjects implies that bits and pieces of knowledge are easily attained, without any significant consideration of the basis for that knowledge. Speed coverage of content ignores the need of students to seriously consider content before accepting it. Most of us have experienced the difference between "intellectual" or merely verbal "knowledge" and true understanding — "Aha! So *that's* what that means!" Most teaching and most texts, designed to achieve the former kind of knowledge rather than the latter, are, in this sense, unrealistic. Students rarely grapple with content. As a result, standard practice tends to foster intellectual arrogance in students, particularly in those who have retentive memories and can repeat back what they have heard or read. Pretending to know is encouraged. Much standardized testing, which frames problems isolated from their real-life contexts and provides directions and hints regarding their correct solution, validates this pretense.

This has led Alan Schoenfeld, for example, to conclude that "most instruction in mathematics is, in a very real sense, deceptive and possibly fraudulent." In "Some Thoughts on Problem-Solving Research and Mathematics Education", (Mathematical Problem Solving: Issues in Research, Frank K. Lester and Joe Garofalo, editors, © 1982 Franklin Institute Press), he cites a number of examples, including the following:

> Much instruction on how to solve word problems is based on the "key word" algorithm, where the student makes his choice of the appropriate arithmetic operation by looking for syntactic cues in the problem statement. For example, the word 'left' in the problem "John had eight apples. He gave three to Mary. How many does John have left?" ... serves to tell the students that subtraction is the appropriate operation to perform. (p. 27)

> In a widely used elementary text book series, 97 percent of the problems "solved" by the key-word method would yield (serendipitously?) the correct answer.
>
> Students are drilled in the key-word algorithm so well that they will use subtraction, for example, in almost any problem containing the word 'left'. In the study from which this conclusion was drawn, problems were constructed in which the appropriate operations were addition, multiplication, and division. Each used the word 'left' conspicuously in its statement and a large percentage of the students subtracted. In fact, the situation was so extreme that many students chose to subtract in a problem that began "Mr. Left ..." (p. 27)
>
> I taught a problem-solving course for junior and senior mathematics majors at Berkeley in 1976. These students had already seen some remarkably sophisticated mathematics. Linear algebra and differential equations were old hat. Topology, Fourier transforms, and measure theory were familiar to some. I gave them a straightforward theorem from plane geometry (required when I was in the tenth grade). Only two of eight students made any progress on it, some of them by using arc length integrals to measure the circumference of a circle. (Schoenfeld, 1979). Out of the context of normal course work these students could not do elementary mathematics. (pp. 28–29)
>
> In sum, all too often we focus on a narrow collection of well-defined tasks and train students to execute those tasks in a routine, if not algorithmic fashion. Then we test the students on tasks that are very close to the ones they have been taught. If they succeed on those problems we and they congratulate each other on the fact that they have learned some powerful mathematical techniques. In fact, they may be able to use such techniques mechanically while lacking some rudimentary thinking skills. To allow them and ourselves to believe that they "understand" the mathematics is deceptive and fraudulent. (p. 29)

This approach to learning in math is too often paralleled in the other subject areas. Grammar texts, for example, present skills and distinctions, then drill students in their use. Thus, students, not genuinely understanding the material, do not spontaneously recognize situations calling for the skills and distinctions covered. Such "knowledge" is generally useless to them. They fail to grasp the uses of, the reasoning behind, and the meaning of the knowledge presented to them. In the rush to keep up, they turn their minds off. Since they are not expected to make sense of the bits they take in, they cease expecting what they learn, hear, read, or do to make sense to them.

Most teachers made it through their college classes mainly by "learning the standard textbook answers" and were neither given an opportunity nor encouraged to determine whether what the text or the professor said was "justified by their own thinking".

Predictable results follow. Students, on the whole, do not learn how to work by or think for themselves. They do not learn how to gather, analyze, synthesize, and assess information. They do not learn how to recognize and define problems for themselves. They do not learn how to analyze the diverse logic of the questions and problems they face and hence how to adjust their thinking to those problems. They do not learn how to enter sympathetically into the thinking of others, nor how to deal rationally with conflicting points of view. They do not learn to become critical readers, writers, speakers, or listeners. They do not learn to use their native languages clearly, precisely, or persuasively. They do not, therefore, become "literate" in the proper sense of the word. Neither do they gain much in the way of genuine knowledge, since, for the most part, they could not explain the basis for what they believe. They would be hard pressed to explain, for example, which of their beliefs were based on rational assent and which on simple conformity to what they have been told. They have little sense as to how they might critically analyze their own experience or identify national or group bias in their own thinking. They are much more apt to learn on the basis of irrational than rational modes of thought. They lack the traits of mind of a genuinely educated person: intellectual humility, courage, integrity, perseverance, and confidence in reason.

If this is a reasonable characterization of a broad scholastic effect, then instruction based on a didactic theory of knowledge, learning, and literacy is the fundamental determining cause. Administrators and teachers need to explicitly grasp the differences between instruction based on two very different sets of assumptions, the first deeply buried in the hearts and minds of most educators, parents, and administrators; the second emerging only now as the research base for a critical theory progressively expands. We express the basic difference as follows: "Knowledge can be 'given' to one who, upon receiving it, knows it", compared to, "Knowledge must be created and, in a sense, rediscovered by each knower."

Only if we see the contrast between these views clearly, will we be empowered to move from the former conception to the latter. Now let us set out the two opposing theories systematically in terms of specific contrasting assumptions and practices.

Two Conflicting Theories of Knowledge, Learning, and Literacy: The Didactic and the Critical

The Scholastically Dominant Theory of Knowledge, Learning and Literacy assumes:

1) That the fundamental need of students is to be taught more or less directly *what* to think, not *how* to think. (That students will learn *how* to think if only they know *what* to think.) • Thus, students are *given* or told details, definitions, explanation, rules, guidelines, and reasons to learn.

2) That knowledge is independent of the thinking that generates, organizes, and applies it. • Thus, students are said to know when they can repeat what has been covered. Students are given the finished products of others' thoughts.

3) That educated, literate people are fundamentally repositories of content analogous to an encyclopedia or a data bank, directly comparing situations in the world with "facts" that they carry about fully formed as a result of an absorptive process. That an educated, literate person is fundamentally a true believer, that is, a possessor of truth, and therefore claims much knowledge. • Thus, texts, assignments, lectures, discussions, and tests are detail-oriented and content-dense.

The Emerging Critical Theory of Knowledge, Learning, and Literacy assumes:

1) That the fundamental need of students is to be taught *how*, not *what*, to think. • Thus, significant content should be taught by raising live issues that stimulate students to gather, analyze and assess that content.

2) That all knowledge or content is generated, organized, applied, analyzed, synthesized, and assessed by thinking; that gaining knowledge is unintelligible without engagement in such thinking. (It is *not* assumed that one can think without something, some content, to think about.) • Thus, students should be given opportunities to puzzle their way through to knowledge and explore its justification, as part of the process of learning.

3) That an educated, literate person is fundamentally a repository of strategies, principles, concepts, and insights embedded in processes of thought rather than atomic facts. Experiences analyzed and organized by critical thought, not facts picked up one-by-one, characterize the educated person. Much of what is "known" is constructed by the thinker *as needed* from context to context, not *prefabricated* in sets of true statements about the world. That an educated, literate person is fundamentally a seeker and questioner rather than a true believer, and is therefore cautious in claiming knowledge. • Thus, classroom activities should consist of questions and problems for students to discuss and discover how to solve. Teachers should model insightful consideration of questions and problems, and facilitate fruitful discussions.

4) That knowledge, truth, and understanding can be transmitted from one person to another by verbal statements in the form of lectures or didactic writing. • Thus, for example, social studies texts present principles of geography and historical explanations. Questions at the end of the chapter are framed in identical language and can be answered by repeating the texts. "The correct answer" is often in bold type or otherwise emphasized.

4) That knowledge and truth can rarely, and insight never, be transmitted from one person to another by the transmitter's verbal statements alone. That one person cannot directly give another what he or she has learned; one can only facilitate the conditions under which people learn for themselves by figuring out or thinking things through. • Thus, students offer their own ideas, and explore ideas given in the texts, providing their own examples and reasons. Students come to conclusions by practicing reasoning historically, geographically, scientifically, etc.

5) That students do not need to be taught skills of listening in order to learn from others; they only need to learn to pay attention, which requires self-discipline or will power. Students should therefore be able to listen on command by the teacher. • Thus, students are told to listen carefully and are tested on their abilities to remember and to follow directions.

5) That students need to be taught how to listen critically, an active and skilled process that can be learned by degrees with various levels of proficiency. Learning what others mean by what they say requires questioning, trying on, and testing; hence, engaging in public or private debates with them. • Thus, teachers would continually model active critical listening, asking probing and insightful questions of the speaker.

6) That the basic skills of reading and writing can be taught without emphasis on higher-order critical thinking skills. • Thus, reading texts provide comprehension questions requiring recall of random details. Occasionally, "main point," "plot," and "theme" lessons cover these concepts. Literal comprehension is distinguished from "extras" such as inferring, evaluating, and thinking beyond. Only after basic literal comprehension has been established is the deeper meaning probed.

6) That the basic skills of reading and writing are inferential skills that require critical thinking, that students who cannot read and write critically are defective readers and writers, and that critical reading and writing involve dialogical processes in which probing critical questions are raised and answered. (What is the fundamental issue? What reasons, what evidence is relevant? Is this authority credible? Are these reasons adequate? Is this evidence accurate and sufficient? Does this contradict that? Does this conclusion follow? Should another point of view be considered?) • Thus, teachers should routinely require students to *explain* what they have read, to reconstruct the ideas, and to evaluate written material. Students should construct and compare interpretations, reasoning their way to the most plausible interpretations. Discussion moves back and forth between what was said and what it means.

7) That students who have no questions typically are learning well, while students with many questions are experiencing difficulty in learning; that doubt and questioning weaken belief.

7) That students who have no questions typically are not learning, while those who have pointed and specific questions are. Doubt and questioning, by deepening understanding, strengthen belief by putting it on more solid ground. • Thus, teachers can evaluate their teaching by asking themselves: Are my students asking better questions — insightful questions, questions which extend and apply what they have learned? ("Is that why...?" Does this mean that ...?" "Then what if ...?")

8) That quiet classes with little student talk are typically reflective of students learning, while classes with much student talk are typically disadvantaged in learning.

8) That quiet classes with little student talk are typically classes with little learning, while student talk, focused on live issues, is a sign of learning (provided students learn dialogical and dialectical skills).

9) That knowledge and truth can typically be learned best by being broken down into elements and the elements into subelements, each taught sequentially and atomistically. Knowledge is additive. • Thus, texts provide basic definitions and masses of details, but have little back-and-forth movement between them. They break knowledge into pieces, each of which is to be mastered one-by-one: subjects arc taught separately. Each aspect is further broken down: each part of speech is covered separately; social studies texts are organized chronologically, geographically, etc.

9) That knowledge and truth are heavily systemic and holistic and can be learned only by continual synthesis, movement back and forth between wholes and parts, tentative graspings of a whole guiding us in understanding its parts, periodic focus on the parts (in relation to each other) shedding light upon the whole, and that the *wholes* that we learn have important relations to other wholes as well as to their own parts and hence need to be frequently canvassed in learning any whole. (This assumption implies that we cannot achieve in-depth learning in any given domain of knowledge unless we grasp its relation to *other* domains of knowledge.) • Thus, education should be organized around issues, problems, and basic concepts which are pursued and explored through all relevant subjects. Teachers should routinely require students to relate knowledge from various fields. Students should compare analogous events or situations, propose examples, and apply new concepts to other situations.

10) That people can gain significant knowledge without seeking or valuing it, and hence that education can take place without a significant transformation of values for the learner. • Thus, for example, texts tend to inform students of the importance of studying the subject or topic covered, rather than proving it by showing its immediate usefulness.

10) That people gain only the knowledge that they seek and value. All other learning is superficial and transitory. All genuine education transforms the basic values of the person educated, resulting in persons becoming life-long learners and rational persons. • Thus, instruction poses problems meaningful to students, requiring them to use the tools of each academic domain.

11) That understanding the mind and how it functions, its epistemological health and pathology, are not important or necessary parts of learning. To learn the basic subject matter of the schools, one need not focus on such matters, except perhaps with certain disadvantaged learners.

11) That understanding the mind and how it functions, its health and pathology, are important, are necessary parts of learning. To learn the basic subject matter of the schools in depth requires that we see how we as thinkers and learners process that subject matter.

12) That ignorance is a vacuum or simple lack, and that student prejudices, biases, misconceptions, and ignorance are automatically replaced by the knowledge given them. • Thus, little if any attention is given to students' beliefs. Material is presented from the point of view of the authority, the one who knows.

12) That prejudices, biases, and misconceptions are built up through actively constructed inferences embedded in experience and must be broken down through a similar process, hence, that students must reason their way out of them. • Thus, students need many opportunities to express their views, however biased and prejudiced, in a nonthreatening environment, to argue their way

out of their internalized misconceptions. Teachers should cultivate in themselves a genuine curiosity about how students look at things, why they think as they do, and the structure of students' thought. The educational process starts where the students are, and walks them through to insight.

13) That students need not understand the rational ground or deeper logic of what they learn in order to absorb knowledge. Extensive but superficial learning can later be deepened. • Thus, for example, historical and scientific explanations are presented to students as given, not as having been reasoned to. In language arts, skills and distinctions are rarely explicitly linked to such basic concepts as 'good writing' or 'clear expression'.

13) That rational assent is essential for all genuine learning; that an in-depth understanding of basic concepts and principles is essential for rational assent to non-foundational concepts and facts. That in-depth understanding of root concepts and principles should organize learning within and across subject matter domains. • Thus, students are encouraged to discover how the details relate to basic concepts. Details are traced back to the foundational purposes, concepts, and insights.

14) That it is more important to cover a great deal of knowledge or information superficially than a small amount in depth. That only after the facts are understood, can students discuss their meaning; that higher order thinking can and should only be practiced by students who have "mastered" the material. That thought-provoking discussions are for the gifted and advanced, only.

14) That it is more important to cover a small amount of knowledge or information in-depth (deeply probing its foundation, meaning, and worth) than a great deal of knowledge superficially. That the "slowest," as well as the brightest, students can and must probe the significance and justification of what they learn.

15) That the roles of teacher and learner are distinct and should not be blurred.

15) That we learn best by teaching or explaining to others what we know. Students need many opportunities to teach what they know and formulate their understandings in different ways, and to respond to diverse questions from other learners.

16) That the teacher should correct the learners' ignorance by telling them what they don't know and correcting their mistakes.

16) That students need to learn to distinguish for themselves what they know from what they don't know. Students should recognize that they do not genuinely know or comprehend what they have merely memorized. Self-directed learning requires recognition of ignorance. • Thus, teachers respond to mistakes and confusion by probing with questions, allowing students to correct themselves and each other. Teachers routinely allow students the opportunity to supply their own ideas on a subject before reading their texts.

17) That the teacher has the fundamental responsibility for student learning. • Thus, teachers and texts provide knowledge, questions, and drill.

17) That students should have increasing responsibility for their own learning. Students should see that only they can learn for themselves and actively and willingly engage themselves in the process. • Thus, the teacher provides opportunities for students to decide what they need to know and helps them develop strategies for finding or figuring it out.

18) That students will automatically transfer what they learn in didactically taught courses to relevant real-life situations. • Thus, for example, students are told to perform a given skill on a given group of items. The text will *tell* students when, how, and why to use that skill.

18) That most of what students memorize in didactically taught courses is either forgotten or inert, and that the most significant transfer requires in-depth learning which focuses on experiences meaningful to the student. Transfer must be directly taught.

19) That the personal experience of the student has no essential role to play in education.

19) That the personal experience of the student is essential to all schooling at all levels and in all subjects, that it is a crucial part of the content to be processed (applied, analyzed, synthesized, and assessed) by the students.

20) That students who can correctly answer questions, provide definitions, and apply formulae while taking tests have proven their knowledge or understanding of those details. Since the didactic approach tends to assume, for example, that knowing a word is knowing its definition (and an example), didactic instruction tends to overemphasize definitions. By merely supplementing definitions with assignments that say "Which of these twelve items are X?", students do not come to see the usefulness of the concept and fail to use it spontaneously when appropriate.

20) That students can often provide correct answers, repeat definitions, and apply formulae while yet not understanding those questions, definitions, or formulae. That proof of knowledge and understanding are found in the students' ability to explain in their own words, with examples, the meaning and significance of the knowledge, why it is so, to *spontaneously* use it when appropriate.

21) That learning is essentially a private monological process in which learners can proceed more or less directly to established truth, under the guidance of an expert in such truth. The authoritative answers that teachers have are the fundamental standards for assessing students' learning.

21) That learning is essentially a public, communal dialogical and dialectical process in which learners can only proceed indirectly to truth, with much zigging and zagging, backtracking, misconception, self-contradiction, and frustration along the way. Not authoritative answers, but authoritative standards are the criteria for engagement in the communal, dialogical process of enquiry.

Common Problems with Texts

When one examines textbooks from the perspective of the critical theory of knowledge, one is in a better position to restructure how one uses them. The single biggest problem, from this perspective, is that texts, primarily presupposing a didactic view of knowledge, are not designed to allow students to process or integrate what they "cover".

The object behind many lesson plans seems to be to expose students to a wide variety of unassessed "facts," on the assumption that, since this constitutes new information for them, it is good in itself. We, however, feel that school time is too precious to spend any sizeable portion of it covering *random* facts. The world, after all, is filled with an infinite number of facts. No one can learn more than an infinitesimal portion of them. Random fact-collecting is therefore pointless. True, we need facts and information, but there is no reason why we cannot gain facts *as part of the process* of learning how to think, as part of broader cognitive-affective objectives. Problem-solving or exploring basic ideas or issues are effective ways to find and use facts and to discover why facts interest us in the first place. We ought not to overburden students' minds with facts that they cannot put to use in their thinking. If we don't comprehend the relevance and significance of facts, we tend to forget them rather quickly. We encourage the reader therefore to develop a skeptical eye for lesson plans, activities, and questions that fall into the category of trivial pursuit or "fact-for-fact's sake". Keep a wastebasket handy.

Often, though the lesson as a whole covers significant material, parts of it are trivial. The student's text provides insignificant details, and the teacher's edition suggests trivial activities which interrupt discussion of significant material. As a rule, texts fail to properly distinguish the trivial from the significant. Useless details and basic concepts receive equal time. End-of-chapter review questions especially confuse major with minor points. Structuring instruction around basic ideas and issues highlights crucial details.

Beyond the lessons and activities that need to be abandoned for their triviality, there are also lesson plans and activities that drill students — reading or filling out graphs, time-lines, and charts, generalizing, categorizing, researching, experimenting, problem-solving, and comparing. Such lessons turn skills of thought and crucial insights into mechanical procedures, or vague slogans. Students practice the skills for practice itself, seldom in a context in which the skill promotes understanding; thus, students fail to learn when to apply this or that procedure and so need to be told when to use it. The application of the skill is often merely memorized (and so easily forgotten), rather than understood. Students look for "indicator words", verbal cues, and shortcuts, rather than recognizing the logic of situations requiring use of the skill. Thus they can use the skill *only on request,* that is, when given directions to do so. They do not learn to recognize contexts in which the skill is needed. Students read maps, charts, graphs, etc., at the most basic level, rattling off facts; they do not discuss the meaning, significance, or implications of what they find. They copy charts and graphs, or formats for them, fill in graphs and time-lines, but do not then *use* them as helpful displays to organize information. The purposes of skills, the contexts within which they are needed, and the reasons for applying them in certain ways, should be discussed or discovered by students. Students should interpret the details they find and then explore their implications or significance.

This integration should be viewed, not as slowing down, but as deepening the understanding of the material. We should view the critical thinking that students practice as providing them with powerful concepts which they can use in a host of circumstances thereafter, and as laying the foundation for the "I-can-figure-things-out-for-myself" attitude essential for education. Standard practice and testing methods, whenever possible, should be replaced with those requiring skill, insight, and information. They should be presented to students with minimal direction given beforehand and minimal guidance given only when students are hopelessly bogged down.

Standard Treatment of Critical Thinking, Reasoning, and Argumentation

Finally, we recommend that the teacher keep an eye out for texts, questions, and activities that claim to emphasize or teach critical thinking, logic, reasoning, or argumentation. Often what is taught, or the way it is taught, discourages clear and fairminded thought.

Texts generally lack an integrated theory of critical thinking or the critical person. Lessons fail to clarify the relationship of specific critical skills and insights to the concept of the critical thinker. Critical thinking should not be conceived merely as a set of discrete skills and ideas, but should be unified and grounded in a consistent, complete, and accurate theory of thought and reason. This theory should be related to the practical problem of deciding what to believe, question, or reject, understood in terms of the distinction between the reasonable and the unreasonable person. Particular distinctions and insights should be connected to that theory, and specific skills should be placed within it. A unified conception of reasoning includes a unified conception of poor reasoning. Thus, each flaw in reasoning should be understood in terms of the underlying principles of good reasoning such as consistency, completeness, clarity, and relevance, as well as being tied into a well developed conception of why we reason poorly and why we are often influenced by poor reasoning.

The following problems are among the most common:

- Instruction in critical thinking should be integrated into the rest of the subjects whenever useful, rather than appearing occasionally in separate lessons. Instead of consistently using such terms as conclusion, inference, assumption, interpretation, and reasons whenever they are applicable, texts often restrict their use to too narrow contexts. Aspects of critical thinking are generally tacked on — taught in separate lessons and taught as drill, rather than brought in whenever relevant. Lacking a complete and explicit theory of reasoning and the rational person, text writers limit the use of critical skills and insights, failing to bring them in when interpretation, exploration, organization, analysis, synthesis, or evaluation are discussed or most needed.

- Some texts give checklists for evaluating reasoning. They rarely mention looking at or evaluating the argument as a whole. Students are asked to spot strengths and weaknesses in arguments but are given little guidance in figuring out how the points add up. Critical thinking lessons in texts have an overall lack of context when discussing arguments or conclusions. They use snippets rather than complete arguments, and ignore the larger context of the issue itself. Texts often seem to assume that students' final conclusions can be based solely on the analysis and evaluation of one argument. Critical insight should lead to clearer and richer understanding, more rationally informed beliefs about the issue — not merely a critique of a particular argument.

- A common misconception found in texts is the problem of vagueness. Texts typically misunderstand the nature of the problem. Usually texts mistakenly claim that some words are "vague" because "people have their own definitions". The cure is to provide your own definition. We, on the other hand, claim that words themselves are not vague. Sentences are vague (in some contexts). A particular word or phrase within a vague statement may be the culprit requiring clarification *in the context of that issue* — the word itself is not vague in and of itself (nor are the words making up the phrase) but only in some contexts. Definitions, since they are worded abstractly, rarely usefully clarify a word used vaguely. We recommend discussions like those mentioned in the strategy "clarifying and analyzing the meanings of words or phrases" and "clarifying issues, conclusions, or beliefs".

• Many texts emphasize micro-skills. Yet they seldom attempt to teach critical vocabulary to students. Perhaps this is fortunate, since they often misuse the vocabulary of critical thinking or logic. Many texts use the words 'infer' or 'conclude' when requiring students to recall, describe, or guess. Micro-skills (like many other skills) are treated as independent items, rather than as tools which assist understanding. "Analysis of arguments" too often consists of "separating fact from opinion" or simply agreeing or disagreeing, rather than clarifying or evaluating arguments.

• Teachers' notes often suggest debates. Yet traditional debate, with its emphasis on winning and lack of emphasis on rationality or fairminded understanding of the opposition, with its formal structure and artificial limits, rarely provides for the serious, honest, fairminded analysis and evaluation of ideas and arguments we want to foster. If afterward students merely vote on the issue, they need not rationally evaluate the views or justify their evaluations. Ultimately, such activities may encourage treatment of questions calling for reasoned judgment as though they were questions of preference. Debates can be useful if students are required to sympathetically consider both sides of an issue, not just defend their side, and to assess arguments for their rational persuasiveness rather than for mere cleverness.

• Many texts tend to simply ask students to agree or disagree with conclusions. They fail to require that students show they understand or have rationally evaluated what they agree or disagree with. Discussion is limited. Micro-skills are rarely practiced or orchestrated in these contexts which most require them. Argument evaluation is further oversimplified, since only two choices are presented: agreement or disagreement. Students are not asked "To what extent do you agree with this claim, or with what part of it?"

"Fact/Opinion," "Emotive Language," Value, and Bias

By far, the most all-pervasive, confused, and distorted ideas about critical thinking are found in the manner in which students are encouraged to "distinguish fact from opinion," and in the treatment of "emotive language", values, and bias. Texts generally set up or presuppose a false dichotomy with facts, rationality, and critical thinking on one side and values, emotions, opinions, bias, and irrationality on the other.

Texts give one or more of the following explanations of "the fact/opinion distinction": Facts are true; can be proven; are the most reliable source of information. Opinions are what someone thinks is true; are not necessarily true for everyone; are disputed; are judgments. Opinions are not necessarily either right or wrong. Often opinion is treated as equivalent to bias; *any* writing which expresses opinion, feeling, or judgment is labeled biased.

Among our criticisms of the uses of "the fact/opinion distinction" are the following: *1)* Students are usually asked to judge the truth of claims they are not in a position to know; *2)* the way the distinction is drawn in examples and exercises promotes uncritical thought, for example, the distinction often unhelpfully lumps together significantly different types of claims; *3)* often neither category is presented so as to allow for rational assessment. (Facts are presented as true, and therefore need no debate; opinions are just opinions, so there is no "truth of the matter". Texts generally speak of exchanging opinions, but rarely of assessing them.)

When asked to make this "distinction", students are typically given two or more statements. They are asked to read them and determine into which of the two categories each fits. Since the statements lack context, their truth or *reasonableness* typically cannot be rationally judged. Hence, as a rule, students are forced to make their judgments on a superficial basis. In place of some reasoned assessment, students are given "indicators of fact". For example, statements judged to be facts are those which contain numbers, or observations, or are phrased in "neutral" language. Statements judged to be opinions are those which contain such expressions as, 'I think', 'good', 'worst', 'should', 'I like', or any evaluative term.

Since facts are defined as true, in effect, texts typically teach students to accept any statement with numbers, descriptions, etc., in it. Fact/opinion exercises typically teach students that every statement that "sounds like a fact" is *true* and *should be accepted*. Claims which seem factual are not open to question. Students are rarely in a position to know whether or not the claim is true, but, since they need only look at the form of the statement and not its content, they can "get the right answers" to the exercises.

Students are often told that history is fact. (The evaluations and interpretations that appear in students' history books are forgotten.) Thus, if they read that a certain condition caused a historical event, they are in effect encouraged to believe it is fact and therefore true. But causes of historical events must be reasoned to. They are not written on the events for all to see. The interpretation, inextricably part of any historical account, is ignored.

This "distinction" between fact and opinion has no single, clear purpose. Sometimes text writers seem to intend to teach students to distinguish acceptable from questionable claims, and at other times, statements which are empirically verifiable from those which are not (that is, whether evidence or observation alone verifies the claim). In effect, many texts confuse these two distinctions by shifting from one to the other. Given the way texts usually teach the distinction, the claim, "I think there are four chairs in that room", would be categorized as opinion, since it begins with "I think", (an opinion indicator) and, since the speaker is unsure, the claim cannot be counted as true. Yet, by the second sense of the distinction, the claim is factual — that is, we need only look in the room and count chairs to verify it. It requires no interpretation, analysis, evaluation, judgment; it expresses no preference.

Texts virtually never address claims that are certainly true, but are not empirical, for example: "Murder is wrong." or "A diet of potato chips and ice cream is bad for you." Students following the "indicator word" method of drawing the distinction, are forced to call these claims opinion. They are then forced to say that, although they agree with them, they may not be true for everybody; the opposite opinion is just as valid; no objective support can be marshalled for them or objective criteria or standards used to evaluate them. Students who look at the contents of the claims would call them "facts", because they are unquestionably true. These students would miss the distinction between these claims and claims that can be tested by experiment or observation.

The distinction between fact and opinion is often drawn in such other guises as the distinction between accurate and biased or slanted accounts, news and editorials, history and historical fiction, knowledge and information, and belief and value. Thus, on the criterion above, a passage, selection, article or book which contains nothing but "facts" could not possibly be biased or untrustworthy. Yet in reality, a "purely factual" account could well be biased. What the writer claims as facts could simply be false, or without basis — that is, I could simply say it without verifying it. (When I claim that there are four chairs in that room, I may have pulled that number out of the sky.) Crucial facts which could influence one's interpretation of the given facts could have been left out. Interpretations or inferences can be implied.

The distinction, as typically covered, lumps together too many completely different kinds of statements. Among the "opinions" we found were the following: "I detest that TV show." "Youth is not just a time, it is an age." "Jon is my best student." "Most children in Gail's class do not like her." Thus, expressions of preference, evocative statements, evaluations, and descriptions of people's attitudes are put in the same category, given the same status.

Many of the distinctions covered in a confused way could be covered so as to foster critical thinking. Unfortunately, as texts are presently written, this end is seldom achieved. We recommend that students distinguish acceptable from questionable claims and evidence from interpretation, and that the teacher use the applications such as those given in the strategy "clarifying issues, conclusions, or beliefs".

Texts often seem to assume that evaluation and emotion are antithetical to reason, always irrational or a-rational; that all beliefs, except belief in facts, are irrational or mere whims. Values (like emotions) are "just there"; they cannot be analyzed, clarified, assessed, or restructured. Judging another's opinions amounts to checking them against your own, rather than openmindedly considering their support. Evaluative terms are often described as "emotive language" and are linked to the concepts of opinion and bias. Students are cautioned to look out for such terms and to not allow their beliefs to be influenced by them. We recommend these points be replaced with the more pertinent distinction of *rationally justified* use of evaluative terms from *unjustified* use, or *supported* from *unsupported* use of evaluative language, and that students analyze and assess values and discuss standards or criteria. Students can then share their views regarding the status of such claims and the significance of their disagreements. Students should be encouraged, not to abandon evaluative language, but to use it appropriately, when its use is justified; not to discount it, but to assess it. They should learn to analyze terms and determine what kinds of facts are required to back them up; set reasonable standards and apply them fairmindedly.

Texts are correct in distinguishing communications that attempt to influence belief from other kinds of writing and speech (as a basic distinction of critical thinking), but then they fall. They lump together what should be made separate: attempts to persuade, convince, or influence *by reason*, from other attempts to influence (such as by force, repetition, or irrelevant association). Not all appeals to emotion are equivalent; they can be relevant or irrelevant, well-supported or unsupported.

According to texts, bias occurs when a writer or speaker expresses a feeling on a topic. However developed the explanations of bias are, students' practice invariably consists of examining single sentences and underlining words that "show bias", that is, "emotive" or evaluative words. Students do not evaluate passages for bias. Students do not distinguish contexts in which writers' conclusions and evaluations are appropriately expressed from when they are not, or when the feelings or opinions have rational grounds from when they reflect mere whim, impression, or prejudice, or when evaluations are *supported* from when they are merely *asserted.* Nor do students discuss *how* they should take bias into consideration — for example, by considering other views. The practical effect of the standard approach is to teach students to notice when someone uses evaluative terms, and then measure that use against their own beliefs. We suggest that instead, students consider questions like the following: What is wrong with bias? Why? How can I detect it? How does that fit in with the ideal of the fairminded critical thinker? What should I do when I realize the author is biased? What does the text mean by warning me against being "unduly influenced" by bias?

"Be aware of the hidden curriculum in all schools. If teachers ask only factual questions that test memory and recall, students assume that this is the most important aspect of learning. If principals spend more time focusing on administrative concerns, discipline, or standardized test scores, teachers also assume these aspects of school are the most important." *Greensboro Handbook*

Remodelling the Curriculum

Curricula can play a significant role in school life. Directed by a district's curriculum, instruction must meet the educational goals and objectives stated in the curriculum. It is crucial, therefore, that its articulation and interpretation are compatible with critical thinking. A curriculum heavily loaded with detail, for example, may restrict the teacher's freedom to emphasize critical thinking by requiring large amounts of information to be covered quickly and superficially. Curriculum may also draw attention away from critical thinking by emphasizing goals, activities, and instruction contrary to critical thought or by being linked to tests that focus on recall. Some curricula mention critical thinking in vague, superficial, or narrow ways, creating confusion and mis-instruction. One of the most significant problems is the neglect of the essential role of critical thinking in the student's acquisition of knowledge. Rarely is the concept of knowledge analyzed. Instead, articulation assumes that all educators know what knowledge is and how it differs from opinion, belief, or prejudice. Any attempt to make critical thinking a significant part of the educational life of students must involve a restructuring of the curriculum, making explicit the philosophy of knowledge and learning that underlay its writing and direct its implementation. This chapter offers suggestions for analyzing, evaluating, and remodelling curricula to emphasize education based on principles of critical thought, coherently integrated into a rich philosophy of education.

Curriculum: What is it?

Written curricula can and do appear in a variety of forms. The *Oxford English Dictionary* defines curriculum as: "A course; specifically a regular course of study or training, as at a school or university." Some curricula written in this narrow sense list the particular courses students are to study, detailing the content of these courses, and perhaps even including course outlines. Curricula of this type are often restrictive and often rely heavily on a memorization/recall method of instruction, severely limiting teacher freedom, creativity, and individuality.

Most curricula are more complete than this, broader in scope, addressing much more than content and outline. Generally, curricula are best thought of as a conception, written or presupposed in practice, of what to teach and how to teach it. More complete curricula contain, therefore, all or most of the following elements, each of which is a possible source of problems: philosophy, goals, standards, curriculum and instructional objectives, assessment, and instructional examples. Let us first consider each element in order, from general to specific.

Philosophy: A theory or logical analysis of the principles underlying education, knowledge, teaching, and learning, including assumptions about educational purposes and practices intended to influence or direct all subsequent curriculum formulations and applications.

Commentary: There are two major problems to watch out for here: 1) either the philosophy articulated is too vaguely expressed to be more than a set of empty platitudes, or 2) it is so narrowly expressed that it forces many teachers to accede to an approach that they do not and should not accept. The philosophy should provide a defensible analysis of the principles underlying education, knowledge, teaching, and learning which is open to alternative teaching styles, respects the individual differences between teachers, and is sufficiently clear and specific to have clear-cut implications for teaching and learning.

Goals: Usually an abstract statement of expected student attainment as a result of education.

Commentary: Goals should be written as unambiguously as possible. For critical thinking to be a significant element in the whole, some articulation of it must be visible throughout the goal statements.

Standards: A broad statement of expected student achievement on completion of a year's study within a specific subject area.

Commentary: If critical thinking is to play a significant role in instruction, then critical thinking standards must be explicit throughout. This is virtually never done.

Curriculum Objectives: A more specific statement of learning achievement shown by the student in any subject after completing the unit of study.

Instructional Objectives: Descriptions of minimal student achievement that should be demonstrated at the completion of one or more lessons.

Commentary: In both curriculum and instructional objectives, care must be taken not to imply lower order behavioral responses as the goal. These objectives should focus on the depth of student understanding, not, for example, on their ability merely to reproduce "correct" responses on recall oriented tests and assignments.

Assessment: Description of how student progress toward these goals, standards, and objectives is to be assessed; often used to assess teacher efficacy; rarely expressed, but implied by the Instructional Objectives.

Commentary: Again, care must be taken not to put the emphasis on lower order and multiple choice testing.

Instructional Examples: Curriculum may end with examples of instruction appropriate to the attainment of these goals, standards, and objectives.

Commentary: If the curriculum contains model instructional examples, they should explicitly display methods that encourage independent and critical thought.

The Importance of Philosophy of Education to Curriculum Construction

All curricula reflect some philosophy of education; however, often this philosophy is not expressed, but uncritically assumed. Whether expressed or assumed, some philosophy is, *without exception*, the basis of any formulation of educational purposes, goals, and objectives. It determines, one way or another, the nature of educational practice. It is clear that most curriculum writers do not consider the statement of philosophy to be a significant element, since they are often satisfied with a vague, platitudinous treatment. Some curricula include under "Philosophy" statements that are not, properly speaking, definitive of a philosophical perspective. In these cases, what is called "philosophy" is nothing more than a broad and general educational objective. Failure to make assumed philosophy explicit often leads to the development of curricula based on unacceptable or questionable educational assumptions which would be rejected if openly stated.

Sometimes the expressed philosophy is inconsistent with the methods of instruction or assessment. In these cases, the goals are often vaguely defined, obscuring the contradiction between curriculum objectives, instructional examples, and philosophy. For example, an educational "Philosophy" might emphasize the importance of autonomous and critical thought, while assessment focuses on testing which requires only recall and robotic practice of skills. Curriculum needs, then, an articulated theory of education, knowledge, teaching, and learning that guides all subsequent articulations of goals, objectives, and instructional examples. At the same time, the philosophy should not rule out alternative teaching styles, except those incompatible with independence of thought and other fundamental educational values (truth, fairmindedness, empathy, rationality, self-criticism).

Knowing and Thinking: A Model Philosophical Statement

Of fundamental and critical importance in any discussion of educational philosophy is the conception of knowledge and learning guiding the formulation of the curriculum. Since we can roughly understand curriculum as a course of study which has knowledge as its objective, those involved in both curriculum development and teaching should be clear about their answers to such questions as these: "What is knowledge? How do humans acquire knowledge? How are students best taught so they acquire genuine knowledge?" These questions may seem to have obvious answers or to be irrelevant to practical problems of instruction, but they are not. Indeed, one fundamental obstacle to educational reform is a set of misconceptions about knowledge embedded in teaching practice.

One persistent unexpressed misconception is that knowledge consists of bits and pieces of information to be implanted in the student's mind by the teacher and materials. Knowledge is unwittingly considered to be a thing that can be put into students' heads as some object might be put into their hands. Didactic instruction becomes dominant, and instruction is reduced to giving students information (principles, values, facts, etc.) to accept as true and commit to memory. Memorization and recall then become the fundamental modes of thought, and students study to reproduce the "correct answers" given to them by the teacher or text. Curriculum based on this misconception of knowledge confuses the mere appearance of knowledge with genuine knowledge. A parrot or tape recorder, let us not forget, is not a knower. Many who verbally reject rote learning unwittingly continue to encourage it simply because they fail to examine the philosophy underlying their instruction. Some practitioners also unknowingly undermine whatever

315

effort they exert to break out of this mold by continually assessing student progress in ways that encourage memorization and recall rather than depth of understanding.

A particularly significant misconception in this model is that if one has the "stuff" of knowledge, one will automatically reason well. The power of reasoning, in this view, naturally follows the acquisition of information, and need not, indeed cannot, precede or accompany it. Students are expected to get the information first, and then through it, start to think. Unfortunately, because of the amount of information taken to be essential, the time for thought is put off later and later. Furthermore, students who passively and uncritically accept information, do not go on to think critically once they learn to parrot it. The habits of learning they established in getting information transfer to subsequent learning. Information parrots become parrots of thinking.

Content dense curricula often create fragmented and un-engaging instruction. Subjects become isolated units having little or no relation to each other, and are often defined in terms of a long list of fragmented specifics. Students rarely see how parts relate to the whole, or to their lives outside school. As a result, both teacher and student come to think of knowledge as bits of information grouped under the general heading of one or another subject. Under the heading "science," for example, are many subheadings: biology, astronomy, physiology, chemistry, physics, geology, and so on, with each subheading containing the bits of information that constitute that field.

The conception of knowledge and learning presupposed in the didactic paradigm of memorization and recall is deceptive. It produces the illusion and confidence of knowledge without the substance, without the comprehension and understanding essential to any valid claim to knowledge. Remember, though people claim to know many things, a claim to know does not, in and of itself, certify actual knowledge. To claim knowledge is to imply not only that the thing claimed is true, but also that the knower understands the claim and the reasons for making it. The strength of one's conviction does not attest to its truth. There is often conviction in prejudice, certitude in gossip, rumor, and hearsay, confidence in unjustified authority, and blind faith in tradition. Students must grasp the difference between belief and knowledge. Blind memorization blurs that distinction.

Consider how a person moves from believing a rumor to ascertaining its truth, from believing the claim of some authority to verifying, and thus knowing, its truth. This shift from believing to knowing requires the active engagement of thought; it requires looking for and assessing reasons for and against. The person who has moved from belief to knowledge understands the claim and the reason for it. This person can justify it. Knowledge exists only in minds that have comprehended and justified it through thought. Knowledge is something we must think our way to, not something we can simply be given. Knowledge is produced by thought, analyzed by thought, comprehended by thought, organized by thought, evaluated, refined, maintained, and transformed by thought. Knowledge can be acquired *only* through thought. The educational philosophy underlying educational goals, standards, and objectives should be based on an accurate and full conception of the dependence of knowledge on thought.

This conception of knowledge, that it exists only in and through critical thought, should pervade the whole of the curriculum. All of the disciplines — mathematics, chemistry, biology, geography, sociology, history, philosophy, literature, composition, and so on — are modes of thought. Remember, we *know* mathematics, not to the extent that we can recite mathematical formulas and apply them upon request, but only to the extent that we can *think mathematically*. We know science, not to the extent that we can recall information from our science textbooks and have gone through a series of actions described in a lab manual, but only to the extent that we can *think scientifically*. We understand sociology, history, and philosophy only to the extent that we can think sociologically, historically, and philosophically. We understand and can truly hold such values as freedom of speech and thought, tolerance for honest differences and plurality, and civic responsibility only to the extent that we have honestly examined the reasons for them and the practical consequences of holding them. When we teach courses in such a way that students pass without thinking their way into the knowledge that these subjects make possible, students leave without any more knowledge than they had initially. When we sacrifice thought to gain coverage, make no mistake, we *sacrifice knowledge at the same time.* The issue is not "Shall we sacrifice knowledge to spend time on thought?", but "Shall we continue to sacrifice both knowledge and thought for the mere appearance of learning, for inert, confused learning?"

As an illustrative example, consider history. In history classes, students expect to be given names, events, dates, places, and explanations to repeat on papers and tests. Teachers typically tell students what events occurred, their causes, their results, and their significance. When asked, students can say that understanding the past is important to understanding the present, but they do not take this seriously. They see no useful application of what they study in history classes, and so are frequently bored. History seems to them a dull drudgery, with no real purpose or significance, except to those who need to know it: teachers.

Consider history taught as a mode of thought. Viewed from the paradigm of a critical education, blindly memorized content ceases to be the focal point. The *logic* of historical thought — that is, learning to think historically *by* thinking historically — becomes the focal point. Students learn the content of history, in other words, while learning to think historically. They learn by experience that history is not a simple recounting of past events, but also an interpretation of these events from a point of view. In recognizing that each historian writes from a point of view, students can begin to identify and thus assess the points of view leading to various interpretations and propose their own interpretations based on alternative points of view. They can learn that historical accounts are not necessarily a matter of simple "true or false". The student of history has to assess the gain and loss of alternative conflicting accounts. To begin to recognize this fundamental logic of historical thought, students could explore the significance of their own personal history and the relationship of their past to their present. They could begin to see that their past and the way they interpret it significantly influences their perception of their present and anticipation of their future. Understanding their own interpretations and constructions of personal history becomes an important tool for understanding the present. From here it is a short step to recognizing the importance of cultural, national, and world history in understanding the present, as well as understanding the news as a mode of historical thinking. They learn, in short, to think historically. They not only gain historical information and insights, but also acquire skills, abilities, and values.

Knowledge, Skills, and Values: The Philosophical Statement Continued

Knowledge is a tool we use for many purposes: to explain, illuminate, answer, clarify, settle, solve, inform, perform, and accomplish. Divorced from its use, from the skills entailed by getting and using it, knowledge is empty. Indeed, one does not really know something if one does not understand its verification or purpose. To come to know anything, then, requires one to acquire the skills embodied in it. Schooling based on a didactic, lecture-drill-test, paradigm assumes that in giving students bits of information, they have, or will get, the skills embodied in the knowledge.

317

This is much too optimistic, for students frequently see no sense to, nor use for, the information they accumulate. Furthermore, not learning information in the context of its use, they have no sense of how to use it. This lack cannot be made up for by mere reiteration of those uses.

Also entailed by knowledge is the notion of value. No one learns what they do not in some sense value. Knowledge has value because of its use. We value what it allows us to accomplish. Consider, for example, the things that students *do* value, how quickly they learn these things, how much they know about them, and how well they retain and use what they really come to know. A list would include sports, both professional and personal (skate-boarding, bicycling, etc.), music, television and movies, cars, fashions and styles, arcade games, and so on. Taking any one of these, say skate-boarding, it is easy to see the connection between knowledge, skills, and values. Students who value skate-boarding spend much time and energy learning the differences between available wheels, trucks, and boards, the advantages and disadvantages of each, the kind of riding best suited to each, and how well these components work together. They then use this knowledge to assemble a board adequate to the kind of riding they prefer. Difficulties do not dampen their enthusiasm to learn. Contrast this with someone who does not value skate-boarding, but who must, for some reason, learn the same information about wheels, trucks, and boards. Although we can, with some difficulty, get the uninterested student to memorize some of the same information as the interested student, the difference in the level of understanding and retention between the two is large. We could say that those who simply memorize the information do not really know about skate-boarding, but have only transitory — and typically confused — information. They do not value the information they have about skate-boarding because they do not value skate-boarding. They ineptly apply it. They confuse it. They distort it. They forget it.

Many skills and values gained by learning a body of knowledge have application beyond that body of knowledge. Many skills and values can be transferred to a wide variety of domains of thought. An education emphasizing critical thinking fosters transfer by stimulating students to use their own thinking to come to conclusions and solutions, to defend positions on issues, to consider a wide variety of points of view, to analyze concepts, theories, and explanations, to clarify issues and conclusions, to evaluate the credibility of authorities, to raise and pursue root questions, to solve non-routine problems, to try out ideas in new contexts, to explore interdisciplinary connections, to evaluate arguments, interpretations, and beliefs, to generate novel ideas, to question and discuss each other's views, to compare perspectives and theories, to compare ideals with actual practice, to examine assumptions, to distinguish relevant from irrelevant facts, to assess evidence, to explore implications and consequences, and to come to terms with contradictions, paradoxes, and inconsistencies. These intellectual skills and abilities cut across traditional disciplinary boundaries. They apply equally well to science as to language, to mathematics as to social studies, and have relevance to and significance in non-academic spheres of student life as well. To gain knowledge through critical thinking is to empower the student as a thinker, learner, and doer.

A Moment For Reflection

At this point, we recommend that the readers spend a few minutes reviewing the last two sections with the following question in mind: *"How does this expression of philosophy of education compare to those I have read in the curriculum statements I have seen?"* Most importantly, compare the above philosophy of education, the interrelation of knowledge, critical thinking, and values, to the sketchy objectives that often pass for a philosophy of education in standard curriculum.

Curriculum: Formulations and Reformulations

The problem with most of the goals and objectives of many curricula is that they are deeply vague and ambiguous. Lacking specificity, they are subject to many, even conflicting, interpretations and implementations. Ambiguous goals and objectives are often interpreted in ways that result in lecture and testing for retention of information, rather than in ways that emphasize principles of critical thought.

Another problem is that, although many of these goals and objectives complement each other, curricula present them as though they were separate and disconnected. A serious attempt to achieve any of the major goals involves linking goals with the other goals complementary to them. Otherwise, the result is superficial coverage of multiple topics. If nothing else, combining multiple but complementary goals and objectives saves time. Fortunately, whenever we approach our objectives deeply, we accomplish multiple goals simultaneously. By moving from the surface to depth, students learn more content skills, and see their value. They learn more, not because they "cover" more, but because they forget less and are able to *generate* more, that is, they see the implications of what they learn. This emphasis on depth of learning is sometimes called "high content".

A Model Case

What follows are examples of suggestions for curriculum development taken from the *Cooperative County Course of Study: Guide to a Balanced, Comprehensive, Curriculum, 1984–1987*, assembled and published by the California County Superintendents Association and the California State Steering Committee for Curriculum Development and Publications. (Published by Office of the Alameda Superintendent of Schools, California, 1984. Kay Pacheco, project director.) This document provides some excellent suggestions for curriculum development and some well thought-out examples of instructional techniques. However, it lacks an over-arching philosophy of education and creates an unwitting vacillation between didactic and critical modes of instruction. At times it emphasizes rote learning, at others, deeper, more critical discussion of the material. There are also ambiguities and vaguenesses in it, contributing to potential confusion regarding the goals and objectives. Examples below illustrate how these problems can lead to confusion in instruction. A remodelled curriculum that eliminates much of the vagueness and ambiguity of the original follows each cited example. Questions and comments follow, to elucidate the kinds of problems inherent in the original curriculum. This serves as a model for the kind of questioning that could be done when evaluating curricula. We do not comment on all of the objectives listed under the goals.

English Language Arts/Reading

This section is divided into six areas, each with a goal for the area, several objectives for reaching that goal, and sample learner behaviors corresponding to the various grade levels. The six areas and their stated goals are:

(Original Curriculum)
Listening and Speaking: To develop listening and speaking skill.
Reading: Develop reading skill.
Writing: Develop writing skill.

Vocabulary/Grammar: Develop appropriate use of words.

Literature, Media, and Subjects: Respond critically and creatively to appropriate literature, media, and subjects.

Study and Locational Skills: Use study and locational skills for independent living.

Under the first goal are five objectives students are to reach to have accomplished the goal. Contained in parentheses for each objective are the learner behaviors for students at the secondary school level.

Original Curriculum

Goal 1: To develop listening and speaking skills

Objectives:	*Learner Behaviors:*
1.1 To express facts and information received from listening.	Rates the value of information gained from each member of a panel.
1.2 To express personal and imaginative responses from listening.	Critiques the effectiveness of a media presentation.
1.3 To present ideas and information orally for various settings and purposes.	Uses facts and challenges opinions in a debate.
1.4 To gather information by listening and questioning.	Interviews and researches a person and writes an article.
1.5 To develop interpersonal communication skills.	Understands the rules and procedures of formal groups, such as parliamentary procedure.

These goals are very vague, ambiguous, and, if not further explained, superficial. Each can, and will, be construed in any number of ways, based on the teacher's background, operant educational philosophy, and past practice.

Several questions come to mind regarding both the goal and objectives stated in the original curriculum. For example, Objective 1.1 of the original refers to the gathering of facts, and the accompanying "Learner Behaviors" speaks of rating those facts. What *exactly* do both of these mean? Should any statement claimed to be factual be taken as factual? Not at all. How, then, is fact to be distinguished from purported fact? Do all facts stated in a conversation have relevance to the issue under discussion? Not necessarily, but how is relevance to be decided? Is there a difference between facts and conclusions drawn from the facts? Quite, but how are the two distinguishable? Is a conclusion drawn from facts always a reasonable or justifiable conclusion? No, not always, but how are conclusions to be assessed? By the agreement or disagreement with students' own beliefs, prejudices, and preferences? We hope not. By the strength of the conviction of the speaker? Never. By the charismatic persuasiveness or forceful personality of the speaker? By no means. Curriculum that does not address these questions, or that ambiguously mentions them, is very likely to lead to instruction that confuses facts with purported facts, that fails to distinguish facts from conclusions, and that promotes an unreasonable acceptance or rejection of conclusions drawn from facts.

Consider how this goal and its objectives might be reworded to explicitly emphasize critical thinking. We can do so by remembering that knowledge must be actively constructed, not passively acquired, and by understanding in what sense active listening is a mode of critical thinking.

Reading, writing, and listening presuppose a range of similar skills, abilities, and values. Passive, uncritical reading, writing, speaking, and listening have common failings. They fail to recognize the problems for thought that each ability involves. In each case, for example, we need to organize ideas, consider logical relationships, reflect upon experiences, and use imagination. If I am speaking to you, I have to decide what to say and how to say it. To do this, I need to clarify my own thoughts, provide elaborations and illustrations, give reasons and explanations, and consider implications and consequences. I need to evaluate and rank my ideas, emphasizing the main points and ordering the rest. I need to anticipate questions or problems you might have. I need to consider your point of view and background. I even need to assess your interest in what I am saying to determine how long or how far to pursue a line of thought.

If I am listening to you, I need to be prepared to raise questions to you or to myself as I actively attempt to make sense of what you are saying. These questions reflect critical thinking skills, and might include the following:

> What is she getting at?
> What is her purpose?
> Do I need any further elaboration of any point made?
> Do I see how the various points fit together?
> How does what she is saying fit into my experience?
> Do I understand why she is saying what she is saying?
> Do I follow the implications?
> Do I agree or disagree?
> Should I pursue or drop the conversation?
> Should I take this seriously or let it go in one ear and out the other?

Remodelled Curriculum

Goal 1.0: To develop critical listening and speaking skills

Objectives	**Learner Behaviors:**
1.1 In listening, to distinguish between a fact and a purported fact, between facts and conclusions; to critically assess conclusions. In speaking, to use facts and conclusions drawn from facts, using critical thinking principles whenever appropriate.	Questions the facts and conclusions drawn from the facts given by members of a panel, or in debate; indicates the basis for questioning.
1.2 To express well thought-out responses from listening, using critical thinking principles whenever appropriate.	Students insightfully discuss the degree to which a situation comedy realistically approaches the problems of everyday life, asking themselves: What is the problem, how is it approached and handled, how would this problem be handled in real life?
1.3 To distinguish between opinions and judgments of varying strengths, as in a rationally defensible opinion and an irrational or indefensible opinion, using critical thinking principles whenever appropriate.	Uses facts and defensible opinions to challenge less defensible opinions in class discussion or debate. Demonstrates reasoned judgment by supporting things said with good reasons.

The remodelled curriculum makes it clearer that a listener is not a passive receptor of information, but participates in the conversation, striving to understand and to clarify, to question, probe, and test, to grapple with ideas and claims. Not only do students better understand the topic discussed and retain the information, they also acquire valuable intellectual skills. As students use these skills, they better appreciate their value, making it more likely that they continue to use them in other contexts. Speaking, also, ceases to be concerned with confidence only, but is seen as a primary method of expressing one's thoughts, ideas, and beliefs to another. Students not only recognize the importance of knowing how to express oneself *intelligibly* (grammar, syntax, vocabulary, etc.), but also *intelligently,* appreciating the connection between thought and language, that the thought itself is as important as its expression. Indeed, if one's thoughts are unclear, vague, contradictory, or confused, the expression of them will likewise be unclear, etc. Students should know how to formulate, assess, and express their thoughts and ideas clearly and accurately. This is more clearly the focus of the remodelled curriculum than the original.

History/Social Studies

The History/Social Science curriculum in the *Cooperative County Course of Study* is superficial and vague, creating potential misunderstanding and mis-learning. Critical thinking standards are not explicit in either the Instructional Objectives or Learner Behaviors. Lower order behavioral responses and a superficial understanding of history and social science are inadvertently encouraged.

The problem with vaguely stated objectives and Learner Behaviors is their likely interpretation, given the dominant mode of instruction in today's schooling. The didactic paradigm of instruction is still the operant paradigm in most instructional settings. Teachers who were themselves didactically taught are likely to teach didactically. This tendency can be reduced only by bringing principles of critical thought to the fore in philosophical statements, subject-matter curriculum, and instructional examples.

Selected objectives and Learner Behaviors from the first goal are reproduced below. Comments follow, as well as a remodelled goal, objectives, and behaviors.

Original Curriculum

Goal 1.0: To acquire knowledge drawn from history, social science, and the humanities

Objectives	**Learner Behaviors**
1.1 To understand the past and present of American, Western, and non-Western civilizations.	Recommends solutions to contemporary economic problems based on the historic ideas, traditions, and institutions of the United States.
1.3 To know the democratic functions of local, state, and national government.	Lists the positive and negative aspects of a specific lobby, and supports one group by citing appropriate facts and figures.
1.4 To know the historical development of issues and concerns of major cultures.	Compares the United States position on disarmament to the U.S.S.R. position as related to political, geographic, and economic factors.

Objective 1.1 is very vague. It is given some specificity in the Learner Behavior which focuses on ideas, traditions, and institutions of the American past. However, the Learner Behavior is intended only as one example of what could be done with the objective. In what other ways are we to "understand the past"? This is not clear. It is susceptible to many and divergent interpretations, increasing the potential for shallow coverage.

The words 'to understand' in objectives 1.1, and 'to know' in objectives 1.3 and 1.4, are also vague and ambiguous. Is there a difference between knowing and understanding? We do not think there is. However, how might these two phrases be interpreted given the dominant mode of instruction in schools? In Bloom's taxonomy, 'knowledge' is synonymous with recall. Objective 1.3 might be interpreted something like this: "To be able to list the different branches and departments of government, and to describe the structure and purpose of each." Little more than memorization is required to fulfill this objective. The learner behavior becomes, literally, *listing* "positive and negative aspects of a specific lobby". This same criticism applies to Objective 1.4 and its accompanying Learner Behavior. A comparison of the Soviet and American position on disarmament may likewise become a list: "We think this, they think that." Simple lists do not require any understanding of the historical development of the positions, the assumptions underlying them, or the implications following from them. The list itself might not be fair, since citizens of the U.S. tend to think of their weapons as *defensive,* and Soviet weapons as *offensive.* Neither is any assessment of the two positions likely to be fair, without significant sympathetic role-playing of the Soviet point of view.

An important objective not included anywhere in this curriculum is insight into the notion that history is written from a point of view. The U.S. has a history, but accounts of this history vary with the point of view of the writer. A history of the U.S. written from the perspective of white male settlers will be very different from one reflecting the perspective of Native Americans, African-Americans, women, immigrants, or the British. Not only should students read historical accounts, they should also be sensitive to differences in perspective, be able to identify the perspective from which any historical report is written, assess this perspective, and, if necessary, rewrite it more objectively.

Remodelled Curriculum

Goal 1.0: To understand the meaning and significance of history, social science, and the humanities, and to acquire information drawn from them

Objectives	Learner Behaviors
1.1 To learn to think historically; to understand that historical accounts are interpretations of events; and to see how the past has shaped the present and how the present is shaping the future.	Rewrites historical accounts from a perspective other than the one from which it was written; assesses differing perspectives, and looks for relevant information that might have been left out of an account.
1.2 To understand the democratic functions of and purposes for the various branches and departments of local, state, and national government.	To defend, in writing or orally, the necessity of a branch or department of local, state, or national government to preserving democracy and individual rights; to argue against the necessity of one.
1.3 To understand the historical development of major issues and concerns of major cultures.	Compares, contrasts, and evaluates the United States and Soviet positions on disarmament, historically, politically, geographically, and economically, retaining a sensitivity to their tendency to favor the position of their own country.

Science

The science curriculum in the *Cooperative County Course of Study* is generally well done. The section reproduced below is representative of the rest of the science curriculum. At times, it tends to waiver between didactic and critical modes of instruction, but does, overall, emphasize and promote independent, critical thought. Students devise experiments to test for various results, and do not merely follow step-by-step instruction on how to set up and conduct tests. They use precise terminology and data in expressing experimental conclusions. They locate, examine, and assess contradictions and discrepancies, and defend a conclusion. They formulate principles about the interdependence of organisms and the implications for survival. The emphasis is on original work, discovery, application, and critical evaluation. Students apply what they learn. They learn to think scientifically, and so better learn science.

Original Curriculum

Goal 2.0: To develop and apply rational and creative thinking processes

Objectives	*Learner Behaviors:*
2.1 To develop the ability to organize and generate data.	Organizes data on the basis of a continuous variable and uses an accepted classification system to order or identify objects or phenomena.
2.2 To develop the ability to apply and evaluate data and generate theories.	Examines data from different sources for discrepancies and contradictions and defends a conclusion.
2.3 To use data-gathering and theory building processes in problem solving.	Tests a hypothesis by designing an experiment, collecting and recording data, and applies the results to an appropriate theory.
2.4 To demonstrate scientific information through the use of models, diagrams, and displays.	Conducts an original experiment to answer one unresolved scientific question.

Although these objectives and learner behaviors are desirable, there are some potential problems with this section. The science curriculum seems to assume a philosophy of knowledge and learning different from the rest of the curriculum. In the science curriculum the philosophy is more critical than didactic, emphasizing the connection between knowledge, skills, and value. It tends to encourage student discovery, application of knowledge, precision in method and terminology, evaluation of information, and original experimentation. This philosophy, however, is not explicit. Although it may have been assumed by the writers of this section, the possibility for didactic implementation is increased by the failure to explicitly state it.

This, however, is not the only problem with this section. The *Cooperative County Course of Study* science curriculum also has a lengthy list of content to be covered. How are teachers likely to cover this content given the dominant, unexpressed philosophy of education? Given that this dominant philosophy is didactic, instruction may tend toward the easier and quicker lecture-memorization approach. Content may be seen as an end in itself, that students having these bits of information know science. Although a more defensible and better philosophy may be assumed in the science curriculum, failure to state it explicitly may result in instruction contrary to it.

Conclusion

Curriculum can provide continuity, consistency, and focus in teaching. There must be, for example, some consistency in instruction and content between different sections of the same subject and level. Curriculum provides this consistency. Students must also be similarly prepared to move from one grade level to the next, one grade picking up where the last ended. This continuity is also provided by the curriculum. All too often, however, the focus is blurred. Curricula are often vaguely and ambiguously written, with heavy emphasis on the specification of content to be covered. One significant reason for this is the absence of a clear and defensible philosophy of education.

The philosophy of education must be explicitly stated to avoid several problems. First, it must be explicit to ensure that the conception of knowledge and learning guiding curriculum development is reasonable and realistic. If we believe that knowledge is best conceived as bits of information, and that learning is the ability to reiterate these bits of information, then we should state it openly. If, on the other hand, deficiencies of the didactic conception are verbally acknowledged, the implications of this admission should be followed up. The philosophy of knowledge, learning, and teaching must be in harmony with practice.

Second, the relation between knowledge, skills, and values must be explicit to ensure that conflicting conceptions of knowledge and learning do not creep in. Interestingly, in the *Cooperative County Course of Study*, discovery, application, precision, and critical evaluation have heaviest emphasis in the science curriculum. But, independent, critical thought is equally valuable and necessary in all subject areas. There appear to be two conceptions of knowledge and learning in this curriculum. The first is more didactic, and tacitly implied in all curriculum areas but science. The second is richer, and appears principally in the science section. Lacking explicit articulation, this conflict or contradiction is ignored. Remember, educational practice arises from some conception of knowledge, teaching, and learning. The dominant mode of instruction today is, as it has been for generations, didactic. Research has refuted this superficial approach, but we have not yet broken down the habits that instantiate it. We must now begin to write curricula so that we come to terms with a conception of knowledge, teaching, and learning that takes full cognizance of the intrinsically "thought-filled" nature of each.

> *The highest development of intelligence and conscience creates a natural marriage between the two. Each is distinctly limited without the other. Each requires special attention in the light of the other.*

> School time is too precious to spend any sizeable portion of it on random facts. The world, after all, is filled with an infinite number of facts. No one can learn more than an infinitesimal portion of them. Though we need facts and information, there is no reason why we cannot gain facts as part of the process of learning how to think.

Remodelling: A Foundation for Staff Development

The basic idea behind lesson plan remodelling as a strategy for staff development in critical thinking is simple. Every practicing teacher works daily with lesson plans of one kind or another. To remodel lesson plans is to critique one or more lesson plans and to formulate one or more new lesson plans based on that critical process. It is well done when the remodeller understands the strategies and principles used in producing the critique and remodel, when the strategies are well-thought-out, and when the remodel clearly follows from the critique. The idea behind our particular approach to staff development in lesson plan remodelling is also simple. A group of teachers or a staff development leader with a reasonable number of exemplary remodels and explanatory principles can design practice sessions that enable teachers to begin to develop new teaching skills as a result of experience in lesson remodelling.

When teachers have clearly contrasting "befores" and "afters", lucid and specific critiques, a set of principles clearly explained and illustrated, and a coherent unifying concept, they can increase their own skills in this process. One learns how to remodel lesson plans to incorporate critical thinking only through practice. The more one does it the better one gets, especially when one has examples of the process to serve as models.

Of course, a lesson remodelling strategy for critical thinking in-service is not tied to any particular handbook of examples, but it is easy to see the advantages of having such a handbook, assuming it is well-executed. Some teachers lack a clear concept of critical thinking. Some stereotype it as negative, judgmental thinking. Some have only vague notions, such as "good thinking", or "logical thinking", with little sense of how such ideals are achieved. Others think of it simply in terms of a laundry list of atomistic skills and so cannot see how these skills need to be orchestrated or integrated, or how they can be misused. Teachers rarely have a clear sense of the relationship between the component micro-skills, the basic, general concept of critical thinking, and the obstacles to using it fully.

It is theoretically possible but, practically speaking, unlikely that most teachers will sort this out for themselves as a task in abstract theorizing. In the first place, most teachers have little patience with abstract theory and little experience in developing it. In the second place, few school districts could give them the time to do so, even if they were qualified and motivated enough themselves. But sorting out the basic concept is not the only problem. Someone must also break down that concept into "principles", translate the "principles" to applications, and implement them in specific lessons.

On the other hand, if we simply give teachers prepackaged, finished lesson plans designed by someone else, using a process unclear to them, then we have lost a major opportunity for the teachers to develop their own critical thinking skills, insights, and motivations. Furthermore, teachers who cannot use basic critical thinking principles to critique and remodel their own lesson plans probably won't be able to implement someone else's effectively. Providing teachers with the scaffolding for carrying out the process for themselves and examples of its use opens the door for continuing development of critical skills and insights. It begins a process which gives the teacher more and more expertise and success in critiquing and remodelling the day-to-day practice of teaching.

Lesson plan remodelling can become a powerful tool in critical thinking staff development for other reasons as well. It is action-oriented and puts an immediate emphasis on close examination and critical assessment of what is taught on a day-to-day basis. It makes the problem of critical thinking infusion more manageable by paring it down to the critique of particular lesson plans and the progressive infusion of particular principles. Lesson plan remodelling is developmental in that, over time, more and more lesson plans are remodelled, and what has been remodelled can be remodelled again; more strategies can be systematically infused as the teacher masters them. It provides a means of cooperative learning for teachers. Its results can be collected and shared, at both the site and district levels, so teachers can learn from and be encouraged by what other teachers do. The dissemination of plausible remodels provides recognition for motivated teachers. Lesson plan remodelling forges a unity between staff development, curriculum development, and student development. It avoids recipe solutions to critical thinking instruction. And, finally, properly conceptualized and implemented, it unites cognitive and affective goals and integrates the curriculum.

Of course, the remodelling approach is no panacea. It will not work for the deeply complacent or cynical, or for those who do not put a high value on students' learning to think for themselves. It will not work for those who lack a strong command of critical thinking skills and self-esteem. It will not work for those who are "burned out" or have given up on change. Finally, it will not work for those who want a quick and easy solution based on recipes and formulas. The remodelling approach is a long-term solution that transforms teaching by degrees as teachers' critical insights and skills develop and mature. Teachers who can develop the art of critiquing their lesson plans and using their critiques to remodel them more and more effectively, will progressively *1)* refine and develop their own critical thinking skills and insights; *2)* re-shape the actual or "living" curriculum (what is in fact taught); and *3)* develop their teaching skills.

The approach to lesson remodelling developed by the Center for Critical Thinking and Moral Critique depends on the publication of handbooks such as this one which illustrate the remodelling process, unifying well-thought-out critical thinking theory with practical application. They explain critical thinking by translating general theory into specific teaching strategies. The strategies are multiple, allowing teachers to infuse more strategies as they understand more dimensions of critical thought. This is especially important since the skill at, and insight into, critical thought varies.

This approach, it should be noted, respects the autonomy and professionality of teachers. They choose which strategies to use in a particular situation and control the rate and style of integration. It is a flexible approach, maximizing the teacher's creativity and insight. The teacher can apply the strategies to any kind of material: textbook lessons, the teacher's own lessons or units, discussion outside of formal lessons, etc.

In teaching for critical thinking in the strong sense, we are committed to teaching in such a way that children, as soon and as completely as possible, learn to become responsible for their own thinking. This requires them to learn how to take command of their thinking, which requires them to learn how to notice and think about their own thinking, and the thinking of others. Consequently, we help children talk about their thinking in order to be mindful and directive in it. We want them to study their own minds and how they operate. We want them to gain tools by which they can probe deeply into and take command of their own mental processes. Finally, we want them to gain this mentally skilled self-control to become more honest with themselves and more fair to others, not only to "do better" in school. We want them to develop mental skills and processes in an ethically responsible way. This is not a "good-boy/bad-boy" approach to thinking, for people must think their own way to the ethical insights that underlie fairmindedness. We are careful not to judge the content of the students' thinking. Rather, we facilitate a process whereby the students' own insights can be developed.

The global objectives of critical thinking-based instruction are intimately linked to specific objectives. Precisely because we want students to learn how to think for themselves in an ethically responsible way we use the strategies we do: we help them gain insight into their tendency to think in narrowly self-serving ways (egocentricity); encourage them to empathize with the perspectives of others; to suspend or withhold judgment when they lack sufficient evidence to justify making a judgment; to clarify issues and concepts; to evaluate sources, solutions, and actions; to notice when they make assumptions, how they make inferences and where they use, or ought to use, evidence; to consider the implications of their ideas; to identify contradictions or inconsistencies in their thinking; to consider the qualifications or lack of qualifications in their generalizations; and do all of these things in encouraging, supportive, non-judgmental ways. The same principles of education hold for staff development.

Beginning to Infuse Critical Thinking

Let us now consider how to incorporate these general understandings into in-service design. Learning the art of lesson plan remodelling can be separated into five tasks. Each can be the focus of some stage of in-service activity:

1) *Clarifying the global concept* — How is the fairminded critical thinker unlike the self-serving critical thinker and the uncritical thinker? What is it to think critically? Why think critically?

2) *Understanding component principles* underlying the component critical thinking values, processes, and skills — What are the basic values that (strong sense) critical thinking presupposes? What are the micro-skills of critical thinking? What are its macro-processes? What do critical thinkers do? Why? What do they avoid doing? Why?

3) *Seeing ways to use the various component strategies in the classroom* — When can each aspect of critical thought be fostered? When is each most needed? Which contexts most require each dimension? What questions or activities foster it?

4) *Getting experience in lesson plan critique* — What are the strengths and weaknesses of this lesson? What critical principles, concepts, or strategies apply to it? What important concepts, insights, and issues underlie this lesson? Are they adequately emphasized and explained? What use would the well-educated person make of this material? Will that usefulness be clear to the students? Will this material, presented in this way, make sense and seem justified to the students?

5) *Getting experience in lesson plan remodelling* — How can I take full advantage of the strengths of this lesson? How can this material best be used to foster critical insights? Which questions or activities should I drop, use, alter, or expand upon? What should I add to it? How can I best promote genuine and deep understanding of this material?

Let us emphasize at the outset that these goals or understandings are interrelated and that achieving any or all of them is a matter of degree. We therefore warn against trying to achieve "complete" understanding of any one of them before proceeding to the others. Furthermore, we emphasize that understanding should be viewed practically or pragmatically. One does not learn about critical thinking by memorizing a definition or set of distinctions. The teacher's mind must be actively engaged at each point in the process — concepts, principles, applications, critiques, and remodels. At each level, "hands-on" activities should immediately follow any introduction of explanatory or illustrative material. When, for example, teachers read a handbook formulation of one of the principles, they should then have a chance to brainstorm applications of it, or an opportunity to formulate another principle. When they read the critique of one lesson plan, they should have an opportunity to remodel it or to critique another. When they read a complete remodel set — original lesson plan, critique, and remodel — they should have a chance to critique their own, individually or in groups. This back-and-forth movement between example and practice should characterize the staff development process overall. These practice sessions should not be rushed, and the products of that practice should be collected and shared with the group as a whole. Teachers need to see that they are fruitfully engaged in this process; dissemination of its products demonstrates this fruitfulness. Staff development participants should understand that initial practice is not the same as final product, that what is remodelled today by critical thought can be re-remodelled tomorrow and improved progressively thereafter as experience, skills, and insights grow.

Teachers should be asked early on to formulate what critical thinking means to them. You can examine some teacher formulations in the chapter, "What Critical Thinking Means to Me". However, do not spend too much time on the general formulations of what critical thinking is before moving to particular principles and strategies. The reason for this is simple. People tend to have trouble assimilating general concepts unless they are clarified through concrete examples. Furthermore, we want teachers to develop an operational view of critical thinking, to understand it as particular intellectual behaviors derivative of basic insights, commitments, and principles. Critical thinking is not a set of high-sounding platitudes, but a very real and practical way to think things out and to act upon that thought. Therefore, we want teachers to make realistic translations from the general to the specific as soon as possible and to periodically revise their formulations of the global concept in light of their work on the details. Teachers should move back and forth between general formulations of critical thinking and specific strategies in specific lessons. We want teachers to see how acceptance of the general concept of critical thinking translates into clear and practical critical thinking teaching and learning strategies, and to use those strategies to help students develop as rational and fairminded thinkers.

For this reason, all the various strategies explained in the handbook are couched in terms of behaviors. The principles express and describe a variety of behaviors of the "ideal" critical thinker; they become applications to lessons when teachers canvass their lesson plans for places where each can be fostered. The practice we recommend helps guard against teachers using these strategies as recipes or formulas, since good judgment is always required to apply them.

Some Staff Development Design Possibilities

1) Clarifying the global concept

After a brief exposition or explanation of the global concept of critical thinking, teachers might be asked to reflect individually (for, say, 10 minutes) on people they have known who are basically uncritical thinkers, those who are basically selfish critical thinkers, and those who are basically fairminded critical thinkers. After they have had time to think of meaningful personal examples, divide them into small groups to share and discuss their reflections.

Or one could have them think of dimensions of their own lives in which they are most uncritical, selfishly critical, and fairminded, and provide specific examples of each.

2) Understanding component teaching strategies that parallel the component critical thinking values, processes, and skills

Each teacher could choose one strategy to read and think about for approximately 10 minutes and then explain it to another teacher, without reading from the handbook. The other teacher can ask questions about the strategy. Once one has finished explaining his or her strategy, roles are reversed. Following this, pairs could link up with other pairs and explain their strategies to each other. At the end, each teacher should have a basic understanding of four strategies.

3) Seeing how the various component strategies can be used in classroom settings

Teachers could reflect for about 10 minutes on how the strategies that they chose might be used in a number of classroom activities or assignments. They could then share their examples with other teachers.

4) Getting experience in lesson plan critique

Teachers can bring one lesson, activity, or assignment to the in-service session. This lesson, or one provided by the in-service leader, can be used to practice critique. Critiques can then be shared, evaluated, and improved.

5) Getting experience in lesson plan remodelling

Teachers can then remodel the lessons which they have critiqued and share, evaluate, and revise the results.

Other in-service activities include the following:

- Copy a remodel, eliminating strategy references. Groups of teachers could mark strategies on it; share, discuss, and defend their versions. Remember, ours is not "the right answer". In cases where participants disagree with, or do not understand why we cited the strategies we did, they could try to figure out why.

- Over the course of a year, the whole group can work on at least one remodel for each participant.

- Participants could each choose several strategies and explain their interrelationships, mention cases in which they are equivalent, or how they could be used together. (For example, refining generalizations could be seen as evaluating the assumption that all x's are y's.)

- To become more reflective about their teaching, teachers could keep a teaching log or journal, making entries as often as possible, using prompts such as these: What was the best question I asked today? Why? What was the most effective strategy I used today? Was it appropriate? Why or why not? What could I do to improve that strategy? What did I actively do today to help create the atmosphere that will help students to become critical thinkers? How and why was it effective? What is the best evidence of clear, precise, accurate reasoning I saw in a student today? What factors contributed to that reasoning? Did the other students realize the clarity of the idea? Why or why not? What was the most glaring evidence of irrationality or poor thinking I saw today in a student? What factors contributed to that reasoning? How could I (and did I) help the student to clarify his or her own thoughts? (From *The Greensboro Plan*)

The processes we have described thus far presuppose motivation on the part of the teacher to implement changes. Unfortunately, many teachers lack this motivation. We must address this directly. This can be done by focusing attention on the insights that underlie each strategy. We need to foster discussion of them so that it becomes clear to teachers not only *that* critical thinking requires this or that kind of activity but *why*, that is, what desirable consequences it brings about. If, for example, teachers do not see why thinking for themselves is important for the well-being and success of their students, they will not take the trouble to implement activities that foster it, even if they know what these activities are.

To meet this motivational need, we have formulated "principles" to suggest important insights. For example, consider the brief introduction which is provided in the Strategy chapter for the strategy "exercising fairmindedness":

Principle: To think critically about issues, we must be able to consider the strengths and weaknesses of opposing points of view; to imaginatively put ourselves in the place of others in order to genuinely understand them; to overcome our egocentric tendency to identify truth with our immediate perceptions or long-standing thought or belief. This trait correlates with the ability to reconstruct accurately the viewpoints and reasoning of others and to reason from premises, assumptions, and ideas other than our own. This trait also correlates with the willingness to remember occasions when we were wrong in the past, despite an intense conviction that we were right, and the ability to imagine our being similarly deceived in a case at hand. Critical thinkers realize the unfairness of judging unfamiliar ideas until they fully understand them.

The world consists of many societies and peoples with many different points of view and ways of thinking. To develop as reasonable persons, we need to enter into and think within the frameworks and ideas of different peoples and societies. We cannot truly understand the world if we think about it only from *one* viewpoint, as North Americans, as Italians, or as Soviets.

Furthermore, critical thinkers recognize that their behavior affects others, and so consider their behavior from the perspective of those others.

Teachers reflecting on this principle in the light of their own experience should be able to give their own reasons why fairmindedness is important. They might reflect upon the personal problems and frustrations they faced when others — spouses or friends, for example — did not or would not empathically enter their point of view. Or they might reflect on their frustration as children when their parents, siblings, or schoolmates did not take their point of view seriously. Through examples of this sort, constructed by the teachers themselves, insight into the need for an intellectual sense of justice can be developed.

Once teachers have the insight, they are ready to discuss the variety of ways that students can practice thinking fairmindedly. As always, we want to be quite specific here, so that teachers understand the kinds of behaviors they are fostering. The handbooks provide a start in the application section following the principle. For more of our examples, one can look up one or more remodelled lesson plans in which the strategy was used, referenced under each. Remember, it is more important for teachers to think up their own examples and applications than to rely on the handbook examples, which are intended as illustrative only.

Lesson plan remodelling as a strategy for staff and curriculum development is not a simple, one-shot approach. It requires patience and commitment. But it genuinely develops the critical thinking of teachers and puts them in a position to understand and help structure the inner workings of the curriculum. While doing so, it builds confidence, self-respect, and professionality. With such an approach, enthusiasm for critical thinking strategies will grow over time. It deserves serious consideration as the main thrust of a staff development program. If a staff becomes proficient at critiquing and remodelling lesson plans, it can, by redirecting the focus of its energy, critique and "remodel" any other aspect of school life and activity. In this way, the staff can become increasingly less dependent on direction or supervision from above and increasingly more activated by self-direction from within. Responsible, constructive critical thinking, developed through lesson plan remodelling, promotes this transformation.

Besides devising in-service days that help teachers develop skills in remodelling their lessons, it is important to orchestrate a process that facilitates critical thinking infusion on a long-term, evolutionary basis. As you consider the "big picture", remember the following principles:

✔ *Involve the widest possible spectrum of people* in discussing, articulating, and implementing the effort to infuse critical thinking. This includes teachers, administrators, board members, and parents.

✔ *Provide incentives to those who move forward in the implementation process.* Focus attention on those who make special efforts. Do not embarrass or draw attention to those who do not.

✔ *Recognize that many small changes are often necessary before larger changes can take place.*

✔ *Do not rush implementation.* A slow but steady progress with continual monitoring and adjusting of efforts is best. Provide for refocusing on the long-term goal and on ways of making the progress visible and explicit.

✔ *Work continually to institutionalize the changes made* as the understanding of critical thinking grows, making sure that the goals and strategies being used are deeply embedded in school-wide and district-wide statements and articulations. Foster discussion on how progress in critical thinking instruction can be made permanent and continuous.

✔ *Honor individual differences among teachers.* Maximize the opportunities for teachers to pursue critical thinking strategies in keeping with their own educational philosophy. Enforcing conformity is incompatible with the spirit of critical thinking.

It's especially important to have a sound long-term plan for staff development in critical thinking. The plan of the Greensboro City Schools is especially noteworthy for many reasons. *1)* It does not compromise depth and quality for short-term attractiveness. *2)* It allows for individual variations between teachers at different stages of their development as critical thinkers. *3)* It provides a range of incentives to teachers. *4)* It can be used with a variety of staff development strategies. *5)* It is based on a broad philosophical grasp of the nature of education, integrated into realistic pedagogy. *6)* It is long-term, providing for evolution over an extended period of time. Infusing critical thinking into the curriculum cannot be done overnight. It takes a commitment that evolves over years. The Greensboro plan is in tune with this inescapable truth.

Consider these features of the Greensboro plan for infusing reasoning and writing into instruction:

A good staff development program should be realistic in its assessment of time. Teachers need time to reflect upon and discuss ideas, they need opportunities to try out and practice new strategies, to begin to change their own attitudes and behaviors in order to change those of their students, to observe themselves and their colleagues — and then they need more time to reflect upon and internalize concepts.

Furthermore, we think that teachers need to see *modeled* the teacher attitudes and behaviors that we want them to take back to the classroom. We ask teachers to participate in Socratic discussion, we ask teachers to write, and we employ the discovery method in our workshops. We do *not* imply that we have "the answer" to the problem of how to get students to think, and we seldom lecture.

In planning and giving workshops, we follow these basic guidelines. Workshop leaders:

1. model for teachers the behaviors they wish them to learn and internalize. These teaching behaviors include getting the participants actively involved, calling upon and using prior experiences and knowledge of the participants, and letting the participants process and deal with ideas rather than just lecturing to them.

2. use the discovery method, allowing teachers to explore and to internalize ideas and giving time for discussion, dissension, and elaboration.

3. include writing in their plans — we internalize what we can process in our own words.

Here is what Greensboro said about the remodelling approach:

After studying and analyzing a number of approaches and materials, this nucleus recommends Richard Paul's approach to infusing critical thinking into the school curriculum (which has a number of advantages).

1. It avoids the pitfalls of pre-packaged materials, which often give directions which the teacher follows without understanding why or even what the process is that she or he is following. Pre-packaged materials thus do not provide an opportunity for the teacher to gain knowledge in how to teach for and about thinking, nor do they provide opportunity for the teacher to gain insight and reflection into his or her own teaching.

2. It does not ask teachers to develop a new curriculum or a continuum of skills, both of which are time-consuming and of questionable productivity. The major factor in the productivity of a curriculum guide is how it is used, and too many guides traditionally remain on the shelf, unused by the teacher.

3. It is practical and manageable. Teachers do not need to feel overwhelmed in their attempts to change an entire curriculum, nor does it need impractical expenditures on materials or adoption of new textbooks. Rather, the teacher is able to exercise his or her professional judgment in deciding where, when, at what rate, and how his or her lesson plans can be infused with more critical thinking.

4. It infuses critical thinking into the curriculum rather than treating is as a separate subject, an "add on" to an already crowded curriculum.

5. It recognizes the complexity of the thinking process, and rather than merely listing discreet skills, it focuses on both affective strategies and cognitive strategies.

This focus on affective and cognitive strategies may seem confusing at first, but the distinction is quite valid. Paul's approach recognizes that a major part of good thinking is a person's affective (or emotional) approach, in other words, attitudes or dispositions. Although a student may become very skilled in specific skills, such as making an inference or examining assumptions, he or she will not be a good thinker without displaying affective strategies such as exercising independent judgment and fairmindedness or suspending judgment until sufficient evidence has been collected. Likewise, Paul also emphasizes such behavior and attitudes as intellectual humility, perseverance, and faith in reason, all of which are necessary for good thinking.

Paul's approach also gives specific ways to remodel lesson plans so that the teacher can stress these affective and cognitive skills. Thirty-one specific strategies are examined and numerous examples of how to remodel lesson plans using these strategies are presented. These concrete suggestions range from ways to engage students in Socratic dialogue to how to restructure questions asked to students.

A critical factor in this approach is the way that a teacher presents material, asks questions, and provides opportunities for students to take more and more responsibility on themselves for thinking and learning. The teacher's aim is to create an environment that fosters and nurtures student thinking.

This nucleus recommends that this approach be disseminated through the faculty in two ways. First, a series of workshops will familiarize teachers with the handbooks. Secondly, nucleus teachers will work with small numbers of teachers (two or three) using peer collaboration, coaching, and cooperation to remodel and infuse critical thinking into lesson plans.

Since no two districts are alike, just as no two teachers are alike, any plan must be adjusted to the particular needs of a particular district. Nevertheless, all teachers assess their lessons in some fashion or other, and getting into the habit of using critical thought to assess their instruction cannot but improve it. The key is to find an on-going process to encourage and reward such instructional critique.

The Greensboro Plan: A Sample Staff Development Plan

by Janet L. Williamson

Greensboro, North Carolina is a city of medium size nestled in the rolling hills of the Piedmont, near the Appalachian Mountains. The school system enrolls approximately 21,000 students and employs 1,389 classroom teachers. Students in the Greensboro city schools come from diverse economic and balanced racial backgrounds. Forty-six percent of the students are White. Fifty-four per cent of the student population is minority; 52% is Black and 2% is Asian, Hispanic, or Native American. Every socio-economic range from the upper middle class to those who live below the poverty line is well-represented in the city schools. However, almost 28% of the student population has a family income low enough for them to receive either free or discounted lunches. Although our school system is a relatively small one, Greensboro has recently implemented a program that is beginning successfully to infuse critical thinking and writing skills into the K-12 curriculum.

The Reasoning and Writing Project, which was proposed by Associate Superintendent, Dr. Sammie Parrish, began in the spring of 1986, when the school board approved the project and affirmed as a priority the infusion of thinking and writing into the K-12 curriculum. Dr. Parrish hired two facilitators, Kim V. DeVaney, who had experience as an elementary school teacher and director of computer education and myself, Janet L. Williamson, a high school English teacher, who had recently returned from a leave of absence during which I completed my doctorate with a special emphasis on critical thinking.

Kim and I are teachers on special assignment, relieved of our regular classroom duties in order to facilitate the project. We stress this fact: we are facilitators, not directors; we are teachers, not administrators. The project is primarily teacher directed and implemented. In fact, this tenet of teacher empowerment is one of the major principles of the project, as is the strong emphasis on and commitment to a philosophical and theoretical basis of the program.

We began the program with some basic beliefs and ideas. We combined reasoning and writing because we think that there is an interdependence between the two processes and that writing is an excellent tool for making ideas clear and explicit. We also believe that no simple or quick solu-

335

tions would bring about a meaningful change in the complex set of human attitudes and behaviors that comprise thinking. Accordingly, we began the project at two demonstration sites where we could slowly develop a strategic plan for the program. A small group of fourteen volunteers formed the nucleus with whom we primarily worked during the first semester of the project.

Even though I had studied under Dr. Robert H. Ennis, worked as a research assistant with the Illinois Critical Thinking Project, and written my dissertation on infusing critical thinking skills into an English curriculum, we did not develop our theoretical approach to the program quickly or easily. I was aware that if this project were going to be truly teacher-directed, my role would be to guide the nucleus teachers in reading widely and diversely about critical thinking, in considering how to infuse thinking instruction into the curriculum, and in becoming familiar with and comparing different approaches to critical thinking. My role would not be, however, to dictate the philosophy or strategies of the program.

This first stage in implementing a critical thinking program, where teachers read, study, and gather information, is absolutely vital. It is not necessary, of course, for a facilitator to have a graduate degree specializing in critical thinking in order to institute a sound program, but it is necessary for at least a small group of people to become educated, in the strongest sense of the word, about critical thinking and to develop a consistent and sound theory or philosophy based on that knowledge — by reading (and rereading), questioning, developing a common vocabulary of critical thinking terms and the knowledge of how to use them, taking university or college courses in thinking, seeking out local consultants such as professors, and attending seminars and conferences.

In the beginning stages of our program, we found out that the importance of a consistent and sound theoretical basis is not empty educational jargon. We found inconsistencies in our stated beliefs and our interactions with our students and in our administrators' stated beliefs and their interaction with teachers. For example, as teachers we sometimes proclaim that we want independent thinkers and then give students only activity sheets to practice their "thinking skills;" we declare that we want good problem solving and decision-making to transfer into all aspects of life and then tend to avoid controversial or "sensitive" topics; we bemoan the lack of student thinking and then structure our classrooms so the "guessing what is in the teacher's mind" is the prevailing rule. We also noted a tendency of some principals to espouse the idea that teachers are professionals and then declare that their faculty prefer structured activities rather than dealing with theory or complex ideas. Although most administrators state that learning to process information is more important than memorizing it, a few have acted as if the emphasis on critical thinking is "just a fad." One of the biggest contradictions we have encountered has been the opinion of both teachers and administrators that "we're already doing a good job of this (teaching for thinking)," yet they also say that students are not good thinkers.

While recognizing these contradictions is important, it does not in and of itself solve the problem. In the spirit of peer coaching and collegiality, we are trying to establish an atmosphere that will allow us to point out such contradictions to each other. As our theories and concepts become more internalized and completely understood, such contradictions in thought and action become less frequent. In all truthfulness, however, such contradictions still plague us and probably will for quite a while.

We encountered, however, other problems that proved easier to solve. I vastly underestimated the amount of time that we would need for an introductory workshop, and our first workshops failed to give teachers the background they needed; we now structure our workshops for days, not hours. There was an initial suggestion from the central office that we use *Tactics for Thinking*. as a basis, or at least a starting point, for our program. To the credit of central office administration, although they may have questioned whether we should use an already existing program, they certainly did not mandate that we use any particular approach. As we collected evaluations of our program from our teachers, neighboring school systems, and outside consultants, however, there seemed to be a general consensus that developing our own program, rather than adopting a pre-packaged one, has been the correct choice.

Finally, teachers became confused with the array of materials, activities, and approaches. They questioned the value of developing and internalizing a concept of critical thinking and asked for specifics — activities they could use immediately in the classroom. This problem, however, worked itself out as teachers reflected on the complexity of critical thinking and how it can be fostered. We began to note and collect instances such as the following: a high school instructor, after participating in a workshop that stressed how a teacher can use Socratic questioning in the classroom, commented that students who had previously been giving unsatisfactory answers were now beginning to give insightful and creative ones. Not only had she discovered that the quality of the student's response is in part determined by the quality of the teacher's questions, she was finding new and innovative ways to question her students. Another teacher, after having seen how the slowest reading group in her fourth grade class responded to questions that asked them to think and reflect, commented that she couldn't believe how responsive and expressive the children were. I can think of no nucleus teacher who would now advocate focusing on classroom activities rather than on a consistent and reflective approach to critical thinking.

As the nucleus teachers read and studied the field, they outlined and wrote the tenets that underscore the program. These tenets include the belief that real and lasting change takes place, not by writing a new curriculum guide, having teachers attend a one day inspirational workshop at the beginning of each new year, adopting new textbooks that emphasize more skills, or buying pre-packaged programs and activity books for thinking. Rather, change takes place when attitudes and priorities are carefully and reflectively reconsidered, when an atmosphere is established that encourages independent thinking for both teachers and students, and when we recognize the complex interdependence between thinking and writing.

The nucleus teachers at the two demonstration schools decided that change in the teaching of thinking skills can best take place by remodelling lesson plans, not by creating new ones, and they wrote a position paper adopting Richard Paul's *Critical Thinking Handbook*. This approach, they wrote, is practical and manageable. It allows the teacher to exercise professional judgment and provides opportunity for teachers to gain insight into their own teaching. In addition, it recognizes the complexity of the thinking process and does not merely list discrete skills.

The primary-level teachers decided to focus upon language development as the basis for critical thinking. Their rationale was that language is the basis for both thinking and writing, that students must master language sufficiently to be able to use it as a tool in thinking and writing, and that this emphasis is underdeveloped in many early classrooms. This group of teachers worked on increasing teacher knowledge and awareness of language development as well as developing and collecting materials, techniques and ideas for bulletin boards for classroom use.

By second semester, the project had expanded to two high schools. This year, the second year of the program, we have expanded to sixteen new schools, including all six middle schools. Kim and I have conducted workshops for all new nucleus teachers as well as for interested central office and school-based administrators. Also, this year, at three of the four original demonstration sites, workshops have been conducted or planned that are led by the original nucleus teachers for their colleagues.

It is certainly to the credit of the school board and the central administration that we have had an adequate budget on which to operate. As I have mentioned, Kim and I are full-time facilitators of the program. Substitutes have been hired to cover classes when teachers worked on the project during school hours. We were able to send teachers to conferences led by Richard Paul and we were able to bring in Professor Paul for a very successful two-day workshop.

Our teachers work individually and in pairs, and in small and large groups at various times during the day. A number of teachers have video-taped themselves and their classes in action, providing an opportunity to view and reflect on ways that they and their colleagues could infuse more thinking opportunities into the curriculum.

Essentially, we have worked on three facets in the program: 1) workshops that provide baseline information, 2) follow-up that includes demonstration teaching by facilitators, individual study, collegial sharing of ideas, peer coaching, individual and group remodelling of lesson plans, teachers writing about their experiences both for their personal learning and for publication, team planning of lessons, peer observation, and 3) dissemination of materials in our growing professional library.

We are expanding slowly and only on a volunteer basis. Currently, we have approximately seventy nucleus teachers working in twenty schools. By the end of next year, 1988-1989, we plan to have a nucleus group in each of the schools in the system. Plans for the future should include two factions: ways for the nucleus groups to continue to expand their professional growth and knowledge of critical thinking and an expansion of the program to include more teachers. We plan to continue to build on the essential strengths of the program — the empowerment of teachers to make decisions, the thorough theoretical underpinnings of the program, and the slow and deliberate design and implementation plan.

Our teachers generally seem enthusiastic and committed. In anonymous written evaluations of the program, they have given it overwhelming support. One teacher stated:

> It is the most worthwhile project the central office has ever offered ....Because
> * it wasn't forced on me.
> * it wasn't touted as the greatest thing since sliced bread.
> * it was not a one-shot deal that was supposed to make everything all better.
> * it was not already conceived and planned down to the last minute by someone who had never been in a classroom or who hadn't been in one for X years.
> It was, instead,
> * led by professionals who were still very close to the classroom.
> * designed by us.
> * a volunteer group of classroom teachers who had time to reflect and read and talk after each session, and who had continuing support and information from the leaders, not just orders and instructions.

Short Range and Long Range Goals

Developing and sustaining a good critical thinking program is a long-range enterprise that takes a number of years. Accordingly, we have developed both long-range and short-range goals. Truthfully, we began the program with some confusion and hesitancy about our goals; we developed many of these goals as the program progressed and we continue to redefine our priorities.

Short range goals include:
* Staff development and workshops for all teachers, for school based administrators, and for central office administrators.
* Development of a professional library with materials and resources which teachers have identified as useful.

- Adoption of an elementary writing process model which can be used by all teachers.
- Adoption of a secondary writing model which can be used by teachers in all disciplines.
- Establishment of demonstration schools and demonstration classrooms.
- Development and encouragement of peer observations and peer coaching.
- Establishment of a network for communicating and sharing with other school systems.
- Adoption of instruments that encourage self-reflection and analysis of teaching.
- Adoption of processes and instruments for evaluating the project.
- Growth in knowledge and mastery of a number of programs and approaches to critical thinking as well as an expanded, common vocabulary of critical thinking terms.
- Participation of teachers in a number of experiences of remodelling lessons and sharing these remodelled lessons with colleagues.

Long range goals include:
- Development of a concept of critical thinking that allows for individual perceptions as well as for the differences between technical thinking and thinking dialectically.
- Development of ways to help students transfer good thinking from discipline to discipline and from school work to out-of-school experiences.
- Development of insight into our own thinking, including our biases and a consideration of contradictions in our espoused objectives and our behavior.
- Development of a supportive atmosphere that fosters good thinking for teacher, administrators, and students.

> *In teaching for critical thinking in the strong sense, we are committed to teaching in such a way that children learn as soon and as completely as possible how to become responsible for their own thinking.*

> **When the powerful tools of critical thinking are used merely at the service of egocentrism, sociocentrism, or ethnocentrism, then genuine communication and discussion end, and people relate to one another in fundamentally manipulative, even if intellectual, ways.**

14 What Critical Thinking Means to Me: The Views of Teachers

Critical thinking is a process through which one solves problems and makes decisions. It is a process that can be improved through practice, though never perfected. It involves self-discipline and structure. Sometimes it can make your head hurt, but sometimes it comes naturally. I believe for critical thinking to be its most successful, it must be intertwined with creative thinking.

Kathryn Haines
Grade 5

Thinking critically gives me an organized way of questioning what I hear and read in a manner that goes beyond the surface or literal thought. It assists me in structuring my own thoughts such that I gain greater insight into how I feel and appreciation for the thoughts of others, even those with which I disagree. It further enables me to be less judgmental in a negative way and to be more willing to take risks.

Patricia Wiseman
Grade 3

Critical thinking is being able *and* willing to examine all sides of an issue or topic, having first clarified it; supporting or refuting it with either facts or reasoned judgment; and in this light, exploring the consequences or effects of any decision or action it is possible to take.

Kim V. DeVaney
Facilitator, WATTS

All of us think, but critical thinking has to do with becoming more aware of *how* we think and finding ways to facilitate clear, reasoned, logical, and better-informed thinking. Only when our thoughts are backed with reason and logic, and are based on a process of careful examination of ideas and evidence, do they become critical and lead us in the direction of finding what is true. In order to do this, it seems of major importance to maintain an open-minded willingness to look at other points of view. In addition, we can utilize various skills which will enable us to become more proficient at thinking for ourselves.

Nancy Johnson
Kindergarten

Critical thinking is a necessary access to a happy and full life. It provides me the opportunity to analyze and evaluate my thoughts, beliefs, ideas, reasons, and feelings as well as those of other individuals. Utilizing this process, it helps me to understand and respect others as total persons. It helps me in instructing my students and in my personal life. Critical thinking extends beyond the classroom setting and has proven to be valid in life other than the school world.

Veronica Richmond
Grade 6

Critical thinking is the ability to analyze and evaluate feelings and ideas in an independent, fairminded, rational manner. If action is needed on these feelings or ideas, this evaluation motivates meaningfully positive and useful actions. Applying critical thinking to everyday situations and classroom situations is much like Christian growth. If we habitually evaluate our feelings and ideas based on a reasonable criteria, we will become less likely to be easily offended and more likely to promote a positive approach as a solution to a problem. Critical thinking, like Christian growth, promotes confidence, creativity, and personal growth.

Carolyn Tarpley
Middle School
Reading

Critical thinking is a blend of many things, of which I shall discuss three: independent thinking; clear thinking; and organized Socratic questioning.

As for the first characteristic mentioned above, a critical thinker is an independent thinker. He doesn't just accept something as true or believe it because he was taught it as a child. He analyzes it, breaking it down into its elements; he checks on the author of the information and delves into his or her background; he questions the material and evaluates it; and then he makes up his own mind about its validity. In other words, he thinks independently.

A second criterion of critical thinking is clarity. If a person is not a clear thinker, he can't be a critical thinker. I can't say that I agree or disagree with you if I can't understand you. A critical thinker has to get very particular, because people are inclined to throw words around. For example, they misuse the word 'selfish.' A person might say: "You're selfish, but *I'm* motivated!" A selfish person is one who systematically *ignores* the rights of others and pursues his own desires. An unselfish one is a person who systematically *considers* the rights of others while he pursues his own desires. Thus, clarity is important. We have to be clear about the meanings of words.

The most important aspect of critical thinking is its spirit of Socratic questioning. However, it is important to have the questioning organized in one's mind and to know in general the underlying goals of the discussion. If you want students to retain the content of your lesson, you must organize it and help them to see that ideas are connected. Some ideas are derived from basic ideas. We need to help students to organize their thinking around basic ideas and to question. To be a good questioner, you must be a wonderer — wonder aloud about meaning and truth. For example, "I wonder what Jack means." "I wonder what this word means?" "I wonder if anyone can think of an example?" "Does this make sense?" "I wonder how true that is?" "Can anyone think of an experience when that was true?" The critical thinker must have the ability to probe deeply, to get down to basic ideas, to get beneath the mere appearance of things. We need to get into the very spirit,

342

the "wonderment" of the situation being discussed. The students need to feel, "My teacher really wonders; and really wants to know what we think." We should wonder aloud. A good way to stimulate thinking is to use a variety of types of questions. We can ask questions to get the students to elaborate, to explain, to give reasons, to cite evidence, to identify their points of view, to focus on central ideas, and to raise problems. Socratic questioning is certainly vital to critical thinking.

Thus, critical thinking is a blend of many characteristics, especially independent thinking, clear thinking, and Socratic questioning. We all need to strive to be better critical thinkers.

Holly Touchstone
Middle School
Language Arts

Critical thinking is wondering about that which is not obvious, questioning in a precise manner to find the essence of truth, and evaluating with an open mind.

As a middle school teacher, critical thinking is a way to find out from where my students are coming (a way of being withit). Because of this "withitness" produced by bringing critical thinking into the classroom, student motivation will be produced. This motivation fed by fostering critical thinking will produce a more productive thinker in society.

Thus, for me, critical thinking is a spirit I can infuse into society by teaching my students to wonder, question, and evaluate in search of truth while keeping an open mind.

Malinda McCuiston
Middle School
Language Arts, Reading

Critical thinking means thinking clearly about issues, problems, or ideas, and questioning or emphasizing those that are important to the "thinker." As a teacher, I hope to develop Socratic questioning so that my students will feel comfortable discussing why they believe their thoughts to be valid. I hope that they will develop language skills to communicate with others and that they will be open to ideas and beliefs of others.

Jessie Smith
Grade 1

The spirit of critical thinking is a concept that truly excites me. I feel the strategies of critical thinking, implemented appropriately in my classroom, can enable me to become a more effective teacher. By combining this thinking process with my sometimes overused emotions and intuitive power, I can critically examine issues in my classroom as well as in my personal life. I feel it is of grave importance for us as educators to provide a variety of opportunities for our students to think critically by drawing conclusions, clarifying ideas, evaluating assumptions, drawing inferences, and giving reasons and examples to support ideas. Also, Socratic dialogue is an effective means of enabling the students to discover ideas, contradictions, implications, etc., instead of being told answers and ideas given by the teacher. Critical thinking is an excellent tool for the teacher to help the students learn how to think rather than just what to think. Hopefully critical thinking will help me be a more effective teacher as well as excite my students.

Beth Sands
Middle School
Language Arts

Critical thinking is what education should be. It is the way I wish I had been taught. Although I left school with a wealth of facts, I had never learned how to connect them or to use them. I loved learning but thought that being learned meant amassing data. No one ever

343

taught me how to contrast and compare, analyze and dissect. I believed that all teachers knew everything, all printed material was true and authority was always right. It took me years to undo the habits of "good behavior" in school. I want to save my students the wasted time, the frustration, the doubts that I encountered during and after my school years. And teaching and using critical thinking is the way to do that.

Nancy Poueymirou
High School
Language Arts

For me, critical thinking is a combination of learning and applying a data base of learning to evaluate and interrelate concepts from diverse academic disciplines. Critical thinking is understanding that knowledge, wisdom, and education are not divided into math, science, English, etc. It is the fairness of tolerance combined with a strong sense of ethics and morals. It is the fun of feeling your mind expand as you accomplish intellectual challenges that attain your own standards. It is the zest of life.

Joan Simons
High School
Biology

Both as teacher and individual, I find critical thinking skills essential elements of a full and enjoyable life. With the ability to think critically, one can both appreciate and cope with all aspects of life and learning. When dealing with problems, from the most mundane to the most complex, the ability to think critically eliminates confusion, dispels irrational emotion, and enables one to arrive at an appropriate conclusion. At the same time, as we ponder the beauty and creativity of our environment, we are free to "wonder" and enjoy the complexity around us, rather than be perplexed or intimidated by it, because we have the mental capability to understand it. To live is to be ever curious, ever learning, ever investigating. Critical thinking enables us to do this more fully and pleasurably.

Mary Lou Holoman
High School
Language Arts

A critical thinker never loses the joy of learning, never experiences the sadness of not caring or not wondering about the world. The essence of the truly educated person is that of being able to question, inquire, doubt, conclude, innovate. And beyond that, to spread that enthusiasm to those around him, obscuring the lines that divide teacher and student, enabling them to travel together, each learning from the other.

Jane Davis-Seaver
Grade 3

Critical thinking is a means of focusing energy to learn. The learning may be academic (proscribed by an institutional curriculum or self-directed) or non-academic (determined by emotional need). It provides a systematic organization for gathering information, analyzing that information, and evaluating it to reach reasonable, acceptable conclusions for yourself.

Blair Stetson
Elementary
Academically Gifted

Critical thinking is the ability to reason in a clear and unbiased way. It is necessary to consider concepts or problems from another's point of view and under varying circumstances in order to make reasoned judgments. Awareness of one's own reasoning processes enables one to become a more fairminded and objective thinker.

Karen Marks
Elementary
Academically Gifted

Critical thinking is questioning, analyzing, and making thoughtful judgments about questions, ideas, issues or concepts. It refines thoughts to more specific or definite meanings. The critical thinker must be an active listener who does not simply accept what he/she hears or reads on face value without questioning, but looks for deeper meaning. Critical thinking also involves evaluating the ideas explored or problems addressed and better prepares a student to be able to think about the world around him or her.

Becky Hampton
Grade 6

Critical thinking has given me a broader means of evaluating my daily lesson plans. It has helped me better understand the thinking principles of each student I teach. It has also enabled me to practice strategies in lesson planning and to become a more effective classroom teacher.

Pearl Norris Booker
Grade 2

Critical thinking provides me the opportunity to broaden the thinking process of my students. It can be used to have the students reason and think about different ideas of a problem or a given situation.

Portia Staton
Grade 3

Critical thinking is a process that takes all the ideas, questions and problems that we are faced with each day and enables us to come up with solutions. It is the process by which we are able to search for evidence that support already existing answers, or better yet, to come up with new solutions to problems. Through critical thinking, one begins to realize that many times there is more than one solution whereupon decisions can be made. To me, critical thinking has helped and will continue to help me understand myself and the world around me.

Debbie Wall
Grade 4

Critical thinking is a skill that involves the expansion of thoughts and the art of questioning. This skill must be developed over a period of time. It is a way of organizing your thoughts in a logical sequence. Knowledge is gained through this process.

Carolyn Smith
Grade 5

Critical thinking is questioning, analyzing and evaluating oral or written ideas. A critical thinker is disciplined, self-directed, and rational in problem solving. Reaching conclusions of your own rather than accepting everything as it is presented, is internalizing critical thinking.

Denise Clark
Grade 2

To think critically, one must analyze and probe concepts or ideas through reasoning. It makes one an *active* reasoner, not a *passive* accepter of ideas (or facts). It turns one into a doer, an evaluater, or re-evaluater. Critical thinking occurs everywhere, is applicable everywhere and while it can be tedious, need not be, because as one thinks critically, new ideas are formed, conclusions are drawn, new knowledge is acquired.

Janell Prester
Grade 3

Critical thinking means to think through and analyze a concept or idea. You are able to back up your reasoning and think through an idea in a manner which allows an over-all focus. If a person is a critical thinker, a yes-no answer is too brief. An answer to a problem or idea must have an explanation and reasoning backing it.

Donna Phillips
Grade 4

Critical thinking is a tool that teachers can use to offer a new dimension of education to their students: that of thinking about, questioning and exploring the concepts in the curriculum. When critical thinking is an integral part of the teaching-learning process, children learn to apply thinking skills throughout the curriculum as well as in their daily lives. Socratic dialogue fosters critical thinking and motivates the teacher and learner to share and analyze experiences and knowledge. Critical thinking involves the child in the learning process and makes education more meaningful to the individual, thus facilitating learning.

Andrea Allen
Grade 1

The most important part of critical thinking, to me, is *discovery*. We discover a deeper level of thinking. We discover the reasons for ideas instead of just accepting ideas. We are motivated by action, interaction, and involvement. We discover we have the ability to expand our thoughts to include all aspects and perspectives of our beliefs.

Mandy Ryan
Grade 5

Critical thinking, to me, is the process of analyzing new and old information to arrive at solutions. It's the process of learning to question information that you may have taken for granted. It's being independent. Critical thinking is letting people think for themselves and make judgments for themselves.

Leigh Ledet
Grade 4

Critical thinking is the process of taking the knowledge you have gained through past experience or education and re-evaluating conclusions on a certain situation or problem. Because students must evaluate the reasons for their beliefs, they become actively involved in learning through the teacher's use of Socratic questioning. Allowing students to clarify their reasons through the writing process further stimulates the students to become critical thinkers. The ultimate goal for students to understand in using critical thinking is to become active thinkers for themselves.

Robin Thompson
Middle School
Language Arts

Critical thinking, to me, is to be open-ended in my thoughts. It is like opening a door which leads to many other doors through which ideas may evolve, move about, change, and come to rest. It is like a breath of freshness in which one can gain new insight over long-established opinions. It stimulates and generates endless new possibilities.

Eutha M. Godfrey
Grades 2-3

Critical thinking is thinking that demonstrates an extension of an idea or concern beyond the obvious. A critical thinker's values are significant to his learning.

Frances Jackson
Grade 2

To me, critical thinking means independence. It gives me a tool which lets me explore my own mind extending beyond basic recall to a higher level of reasoning. I then feel more in touch with myself and my own inner feelings. This results in my becoming a better decision-maker.

Jean Edwards
Grade 5

Critical thinking is the process of working your mind through different channels. It is the process of thinking logically. Critical thinking is analyzing your thoughts through questions. It is the process of seeing that your ideas and concepts may not be the same as another's. It is opening your mind to those who have different views and looking at their views.

Cathy L. Smith
Grade 3

Critical thinking is to question in-depth at every possible angle or point of view, to look at someone else's point of view without making hasty judgments. Critical thinking is to logically and fairly re-orient your own personal point of view, if necessary. To think critically, you are self-directed in your thinking process, as well as disciplined.

Mary Duke
Grade 1

Critical thinking is the vehicle by which I encourage students to become active participants in the learning process. I allow more time for and become more aware of the need for students to express ideas verbally and in written form to clarify ideas in their own minds. I recognize the importance of developing skills for analyzing and evaluating. Ultimately, once students become comfortable using critical thinking skills, they assume greater responsibility for their learning.

Dora McGill
Grade 6

Critical thinking is clear, precise thinking. I believe that all human actions and expressions, in some way involve thinking. For example, I believe that feelings, emotions and intuitions are much the results of earlier thought (reactions) to stimuli. I think that this, in one way, explains the variations of emotional responses in some people to similar stimuli. Thus, I believe that critical thinking not only has the potential to clarify new and former conscious thoughts but also to effect/change likely (future) emotive and intuitive reactions/responses.

More concrete and less theoretical outcomes of critical thinking may be more relevant to me as an educator. Better questioning skills on the part of the students and the teacher are an obvious outcome. There seem to be several positive outcomes of better questioning: more opportunity for in-depth understanding of content, a natural (built-in) process for accessing the effectiveness of lessons, and more opportunity for student participation, self-assessment, and direction are three apparent outcomes. There are, of course, many other outcomes of developing better questioning skills, and from the other skills of critical thinking.

I simply believe that critical thinking improves the overall integrity of the individual and the collective group, class, school, community, etc.

Richard Tuck
High School
Art

I perceive critical thinking in teaching as a tool for my learning. As I attempt to develop the critical thinker, I will become more aware of the students' thoughts, values, and needs. I must learn from what students offer, and develop acceptance and sensitivity to the individual. The knowledge I gain from the student will determine what I utilize as strategies or principles of critical thinking.

> Loretta Jennings
> Grade 1

Critical thinking is the ability to look at a problem or issue with a spirit of openmindedness and to take that problem and analyze or evaluate it based on the facts or good "educated" hypotheses. Critical thinking is being flexible enough to suspend one's bias towards an issue in order to study all sides to formulate an opinion or evaluation.

> Mark Moore
> Grade 4

Critical thinking to me involves mental conversations and dialogues with myself. I try first to establish the facts. Then I try to search for criteria to examine my "facts." The next question is whether or not there are distortions and irrelevancies. I have to examine whether I have a personal bias which has led me to select only certain facts and leave others out.

I then try to mentally list facts and arguments on both sides of a question and, finally, draw logical questions and conclusions.

> Barbara Neller
> Middle School
> Social Studies

Critical thinking is a systematic, logical approach to life in which an individual, using this method, truly learns and understands a concept rather than imitates or mimics. Knowledge and intellectual growth are achieved by a variety of strategies which include examining a variety of viewpoints, making assumptions based on viable evidence and forming well thought out conclusions.

> Jane S. Thorne
> High School
> Math

Critical thinking allows students to become active participants in their learning. Socratic dialogue stimulates communication between teacher and students, thus creating an atmosphere where everyone is encouraged to become risk-takers. A teacher needs to become a model of critical thinking for the students. Through this interaction, content can be analyzed, synthesized, and evaluated with thinking.

> Carol Thanos
> Grade 6

Critical thinking is the complex process of exploring an issue, concept, term or experience which requires verbal as well as non-verbal involvement from the participant. It involves listing ideas related to the subject, so that the person involved could objectively examine the relationship of the ideas thought of. It demands the person involved in the process to investigate the certain issue, concept, or process from varied vantage points, in order that intuitions, assumptions, and conclusions are presented with reasoned opinions or experienced evidences. Critical thinking is a task that involves the participant's in-depth assessment of his or her body of knowledge, experience and emotions on the subject in question.

> Ariel Collins
> High School
> Language Arts

Critical thinking is thinking that is clear, fairminded, and directed. It is not sloppy or self-serving thinking, but deep and probing thought aimed at finding the truth. It is skillful thinking aimed at genuine understanding, not superficial head-shaking. It is *the* tool used by and descriptive of an educated person whose mantra would be "veritas."

Helen Cook
Middle School
Science

Critical thinking is a process of questioning and seeking truth and clarity. It is a continual endeavor as one is constantly exposed to new knowledge which must be reconciled with prior conclusions. As one's body of knowledge grows, it is all the more important to be able to critically consider and determine *what is truth.*

Critical thinking demands certain prerequisites: openmindedness, willingness to withhold snap judgments, commitment to explore new ideas. The development of such qualities empowers me to participate in the various facets of critical thinking, e.g., clarifying ideas, engaging in Socratic discussions. These skills are not nearly so difficult as achieving the mind-set which must precede them. Only a *commitment* to question and persevere and honestly pursue truth will supply the impetus necessary to delve beneath the surface of issues and concepts. Yet this predisposition is difficult to achieve, because it necessitates taking risks, making mistakes, being wrong and being corrected — activities very threatening to our safe ego boundaries.

Only in transcending these ego boundaries does growth occur and genuine learning transpire. Critical thinking is comprised of a sense of wonderment, daring and determination. It is undergirded by a value of truth and personal growth. It is the continual learning process of the individual.

Deborah Norton
High School
Social Studies

The definition of critical thinking that I now hold is one that explains some things that I have felt for some time. I am convinced that everything that I know, that is a part of my education, I have figured out or found for myself. I have had close to twenty years of formal, didactic education, but I could tell you very little about anything that was presented to me in lecture through all those classes, except perhaps some trivia. In college, I did my real learning through the writing that I did, either from research or from contemplation. I have felt that this was true, but a lot of my own teaching has continued to be didactic and students have learned to be very accepting and non-questioning and to *expect* to be told what the right answer is, what someone else has decided the right answer is. I hope that I can change that now. I now feel that it is imperative that my students learn to be critical thinkers, and I hope that I can model that belief and, through all my activities in class, lead them in that direction. We all need to be open-minded, to realize that there are often many sides to a problem, many points of view and that there are strategies and techniques for analyzing, making decisions, and making learning our own. I want to be, and I want my students to be, questioning, open-minded, fairminded, synthesizing individuals — in other words, critical thinkers.

Liza Burton
High School
Language Arts

Logical thinking to gain insights. It is stimulating thinking, questioning and exploring ideas, values, beliefs, and truths. It is making judgments, developing a sense of fairmindedness and long-term learning.

Sandra Hunter
Atkins

Critical thinking is a process which an individual can use to obtain information, analyze what is said, critique (think about it) and then determine it's truth. Critical thinking is a higher form of decision making. The process allows a person to continually delve, probe, ask, re-ask, question, and re-question other's views. Critical thinking is a thought process that is usable in many facets of life.

Rosa L. Jones
Mineral Springs Elementary
Assistant Principal

In my opinion, critical thinking means breaking issues into fractionated parts which will be dealt with through critical eyes accordingly. Critical thinking also means not taking ideas and opinions for what they are and accepting them, but challenging each and every aspect of the given idea or opinion.

Lizzie Morrison
Hill

Critical thinking means looking carefully at the world around you and analyzing what is observed in order to make decisions when choosing the best course of action for your next goal. It is important to use when interacting with others around you (friends, relatives, co-workers) if you want to have a satisfying relationship with them.

As a teacher, I would like to help students see the importance of thinking critically by using critical thinking strategies on a regular basis in the classroom. The content area being taught, then, would thus be used in more than one way: to help students learn to analyze those facts in light of their own experiences, and to apply thinking skills in their own lives.

Carol Tirrell
Old Richmond Elementary
Reading Coordinator

Critical thinking is thinking at a deeper level because you are analyzing your thoughts with the objective of improving how you hande life's challenges.

Janice Tomlinson
Whitaker
Reading Coordinator

Critical thinking means being able to critique or evaluate reasons that are given to me, making sure that I remain openminded and fairminded.

Robyn G. Martin
Southwest Elementary
1st Grade

To me critical thinking means considering a viewpoint (thought or action) from many angles, analyzing and evaluating its strengths and weaknesses within the framework of the values of critical thinking.

I have learned through this workshop to evaluate reasons, "to think about my thinking in order to make my thinking more clear, precise, accurate, and fair." I have learned to control bias and to think before I form an opinion, thereby looking at all aspects of an issue and evaluate the reasons for the issue.

> Ollie Hutchens
> Assistant Principal
> Sedge Garden Elementary

Critical thinking is a way of interpreting, classifying, and using the abundance of information and experiences that we are confronted with. A person must sort relevant and non-relevant information. Then, he must synthesize this new information with previous knowledge, thus enriching or altering his existing knowledge base. Finally, he must use this altered knowledge base when dealing with new situations.

> Connie Prevatte
> Easton
> Reading Coordinator

Critical thinking is your brain shifting gears as needed to evaluate evidence, read between the lines, see other's points of view, etc. It is knowing when to sift through information and when to emphasize certain facts over others. It is knowing when to look at the surface and when to go beyond and question deeply. Critical thinkers know when to generalize to transfer knowledge to other areas.

> Myrna Wheeler
> Mineral Springs

Critical thinking is the ability to reasonably explore all aspects before making judgments. It's the ability to look beyond the obvious when exploring ideas. Open minds are more apt to be critical thinkers. Looking at information and carefully pulling out the relevant applies to the critical thinker. Patience in relation to conclusions is crucial as not to rush our opinions and ideas.

> Karen Ranson
> Children's Center

I believe that critical thinking is a process of interpreting, analyzing, and applying information that an individual is exposed to. The learner begins to look at information trying to evaluate it using information gained through past experience. He tries to see how it can be applied to other situations. He begins to question his beliefs, as well as the beliefs of others, and then alters his own thinking as he experiences more. He must try to filter out information and experiences that do not have a direct bearing on the situation at hand.

> Bobby Stern
> Hall-Woodward School
> 2-3rd Grade

Critical Thinking is the process of being able to take basic concepts and problems and apply them to every day problems in math.

> Liz Clark
> Paisley Middle School
> Math

Critical Thinking is evaluating information and basing thoughts and actions on those evaluations.

> Rena Hill
> Kernersville

Critical thinking is a rational way of thinking about things and acting upon them.

Dorothy Williams
Grade 5

Critical thinking is the process by which one takes power over their own learning.. Instead of being a passive recipient of information, the student makes judgements as to what she thinks is relevant. The student uses her own knowledge base to draw comparisons, and if new insights occur, they are tested against what is known to see if the insight is still viable. Critical thinkers are involved.

The implications for the classroom – We as teachers often pre-digest information by classifying, throwing out irrelevant data, isolating particular tasks to attain specific goals in the shortest amount of time possible. We do not give the student the time to collect data, decide what is relevant, discuss, analyze, and reach their own conclusions. Students are expected to come to the same destination point without having made the journey. The challenge for the teacher, who believes in the value of critical thinking, is to make the time for learning despite pressures to cover pages in texts. As one educational reformer has stated, "Teaching less is more." We need to teach for knowledge that will be internalized rather than information that is only held in short term memory until the test is completed.

Karen Marks
Academically Gifted

Critical thinking, in the broadest sense, is the individual pursuit of a responsible existence – the *search* for a path – to act instead of react. In learning, it is also the search, the questioning and the way that broadens our minds, not just the answer. As we explore critical thinking and identify it for ourselves, we find that the questions far out-number the answers and that the path goes in every direction!

Terry Edwards
Kindergarten

Critical thinking is the ability to analyze and critique information. It is the ability to evaluate objectively one's own thinking and then question the outcome. It is reflective thinking.

Pam Lowry
Middle School
Social Studies

Critical thinking includes: listening, questioning, analyzing, comparing, contrasting, restating, trying ideas in new and different ways – this is in part what it means to think critically. A critical thinker is one who does not accept ideas or information without checking – going to other sources— experimenting, questioning, asking for examples of information – one who tries to remember that they may bring to a new learning situation fears, prejudice, and bias and who tries to keep those old ideas at bay in order to at least consider new possibilities.

Linda Denmark
Grade 1

A good critical thinker uses skills, dispositions, and content in different ways depending upon the context. Skills – the ability to use them, the willingness to do so, and the perception of when and how to use them – are important, but not, I think, the most crucial element. Skills are usually testable and can be isolated – comparing and contrasting, recognizing an assumption – and they can be used either critically or non-critically. One can think in a "weak" sense using only skills.

Dispositions or attitudes are, to me, the basis of "strong" sense critical thinking. The willingness to listen — *really* listen to another point of view – fairmindedness, and moving away from egocentricity are more difficult to accomplish and internalize than learning thinking skills. The triangle needs all three aspects – but dispositions should be heavily emphasized because they are more difficult to internalize.

Finally, one cannot think critically in isolation; one must have content to think about. It may well be that certain skills, such as observing, vary from context to context. In other words, observing in science and observing closely in reading literature may be different; they may be "domain specific". In practical terms, I think this means we infuse critical thinking into *all* aspects of the curriculum. It is not an "ad on" or a series of worksheets and activities.

Jan Williamson
Facilitator, WATTS

Critical thinking seems to be, in essence, taking charge of one's thoughts and thinking for oneself rather than just accepting at face value what "seems to be". It is facilitated by practiced interpreting, and looking at different points of view. With knowledge becoming quickly obsolete, the notion of "becoming educated" by gaining knowledge must be replaced by the concept of an educated person as one who is proficient as a thinker, a seeker, a questioner.

Nancy Johnson
Kindergarten

I have been asked to describe critical thinking several times before, but I am not sure that I can yet give a definition. Critical thinking is, in a way, a state of mind – an open state of mind in which "teacher" and "student", or perhaps, I should say, participants, enter into research and dialogical discussion to try to understand and assimilate various points of view. Critical thinkers try to see issues from different points of view and are constantly modifying their own conceptions and looking deeper and in various directions. This philosophy calls for very little "right answer" type of teaching and encourages students to probe, to question, to try new things, and not to be afraid of making mistakes. In my classes, I encourage students to learn from each other, to enter into discussions with students with differing points of view and differing backgrounds. I believe that small group learning is among the best ways to learn.

Liza Burton
High School
English

Critical thinking is asking provocative questions, wanting to consider answers and possibilities, an atmosphere of openness and possibility of humor. It is also paradoxical thinking – being able to hold ambiguity, but also being hard-nosed, careful, thorough, detailed. Critical thinking is analysis, synthesis, and evaluation – seeing relationships, analysis, new terms, thinking about thinking, being aware of one's process, organizing, finding a variety of solutions.

Nancy Osborne
High School
English

Critical thinking is the ability to suspend one's judgment until all sides of the issue are studied. One must verify the facts in order to render a judgment.

Mark Moore
Academically Gifted

353

Critical thinking actively involves the learner in the thinking and learning process. Students don't truly learn by the following method: teacher lecture, student absorption, student regurgitation. Students learn by "hands on", active participation. Critical thinking activities allow students to participate actively, freely discuss their ideas, ask questions, and gain ownership of the information covered in lessons.

> Dale Russell
> Grade 2

Critical thinking is the process in which acquired knowledge is applied to new problems/situations in order to devise new solutions. By applying knowledge to solve new problems, higher order thinking takes place, and often creative thinking is implemented into the process. Creative thinking means going beyond standard ways of thinking and becoming limitless in creating solutions. By using critical and creative thinking, one is more flexible in accepting new knowledge because of the opportunity to "bounce things (ideas) around" in one's mind more. The use of Socratic dialogue and questioning, as well as writing, are essential tools in the implementation of both critical and creative thinking processes.

> Robin Thompson
> Middle School
> Sixth Grade

Critical thinking means: As a teacher, to become a questioner so that students learn for themselves. To have students doubt and question what I say – to interact on each other's ideas – not to just memorize. To be able to start the lesson with questioning that opens the students' minds – that causes them to want to know why it is important to know certain information. To see the value of experiences and the value of what they are studying, to enjoy class and not want to miss for fear of losing out on information they want to learn.

> Sheila May
> High School
> Business

What does critical thinking mean to me? Critical thinking is the ability to put new information into an old framework. No information is independent. It can be linked to something. Can you identify the thing or things that this new information relates to, and why? For example, can you fit the idea of a mathematical variable into a number line, or anything, for that matter? Does it help your idea of a number line or does it confuse you and why? Can you use this tool and why or why not?

> Bob Fish
> High School
> Mathematics

Critical thinking is an active process of learning and decision making. Critical thinking should be utilized not only in the classroom but in all aspects of life. In critical thinking the thinker takes knowledge that he knows and uses it to question, evaluate, compare, contrast, etc. in order to solve a problem. The critical thinker should be willing to question and ask why. Critical thinkers will more readily internalize solutions/decisions because of their active participation.

> Becky Berry
> Jefferson

Critical thinking is autonomous thinking: thinking for oneself, thinking independently. It is also the ability to analyze, to make things better, clearer. As a teacher I can encourage my students to brainstorm or argue ideas among themselves. They can exercise independent judgement in the classroom. I need to help them assemble information, analyze, synthesize, formulate and draw conclusions whenever possible.

> Jeannene Caesar
> Bolton Elementary
> 3rd Grade

I am a firm believer that we are raising children who tend to be passive and lazy "thinkers". I use the term "thinker" loosely because we as adults have reduced our decision making to Chicken Sandwich or Hamburger? Marriage or Singleness? Any thought processes that involve more time are too much of an effort. What can we expect of our young ones when we model inappropriate behaviors?

Critical thinking involves getting your feet wet. Explore all the sides of issues. Do not stick to what is convenient and easy. You are not looking for argumentation, you are looking for educational awareness.

> Lynn Anton
> Vienna Elementary
> 4th Grade

For me, critical thinking means being intentional. I think about my thoughts and expression of my thoughts (written, oral, artistic, or nonverbal) in such a way that my behavior results in an expanded view of the world and clearer understanding of my role in the world.

> Terry Jones
> Walkertown

In the classroom, critical thinking is discovery. It is each student discovering meaning for himself. As this is done, he internalizes the information so that it can be applied in his life. The strategies and techniques that a teacher employs facilitate the critical thinking of their students.

> Carolyn McKinney
> Kernersville

Critical thinking is the increased ability to question, weigh, and analyze information which we receive and must process.

> Peggy M. Davis
> Brunson Elementary

Critical thinking is a method used to gather, process, and/or disseminate information. It is a necessary process that can be used as a consumer, patient, spouse, friend, and citizen.

> Valerie Clark
> Speas Elementary School
> Assistant Principal

Critical thinking involves discussion which takes time. It cannot be rushed. It involves asking questions which foster more questions. A simple yes/no answer is not sufficient in critical thinking. One must wonder why the answer to a question is correct. The true answer must always be explained further and sought through by analyzing and searching continuously.

> Yvonne M. Woodward
> Middle School
> Language Arts

Critical thinking is thinking more deeply. It involves reasoning logically and analyzing, organizing, examining and questioning information to attain several possible answers rather than focusing on finding just the correct answers! Because we live in an information-saturated era, it is imperative that each student's educational experience provide opportunities to practice and develop the ability to think critically.

> Jean Botzis
> Middle School
> Social Studies

Critical thinking involves probing one's own ideas (or one suggested by others) beyond the initial expression of that idea. By asking questions about ideas, one digs deeper into an issue, opinion, or statement, and begins to expand those thoughts. Critical thinking gives clarity to ideas and opens the mind to new avenues. Searching and questioning in the classroom allows for the sharing of individual thoughts. Expressing these thoughts often helps students form new ideas, or expand on thoughts that take on new meaning. An example might be to look at a special topic, for instance: "What it means to live under a democratic form of government." Encourage students to share how they feel about the "pros and cons" of this subject. Being able to listen to the thoughts of others and respond to them in kind, can broaden one's scope.

Critical thinking causes students to actively form their own concepts. Asking "discovery" questions causes students to "think" of an answer. This method adds self-confidence as one begins to form real ideas in one's mind. Critical thinking can be taught by questioning others for the purpose of bringing out ideas.

> Alice Newell
> Grade 3

Critical thinking is a process which allows one to question the validity as well as the understanding of information obtained. It enables one to establish a point of view upon which to analyze information received. It also encourages one to develop and utilize one's own thought processes in any given situation.

> Yvonne Hunt
> Middle School
> Reading

Critical thinking is an analyzing process in which the brain begins to encourage one to question, comprehend, and digest a situation, thought, or idea. Critical thinking is a skill to be learned, developed and practiced. After practicing critical thinking, it becomes more automatic and natural. Critical thinking can be fostered through writing, discussing, and constructive arguing.

> Donna Rickard
> Middle School
> Mathematics

Questioning is the first word that comes to mind when I think of critical thinking. As I question or my students question we analyze the material which we are discussing in such a way as to determine its usefulness to us. We need to be able to weed out or through material to determine what is important. We need to be able to determine how what we have learned can be applied to other similar situations. For example, will learning "Word Perfect", the way we are learning it, be of value to students in two or three years? That word processing program will be out of date by then. Will the students be able to take what they know and fairly easily transfer this knowledge to another word processing program?

Critical thinking is not accepting what someone says as gospel but analyzing, critiquing, questioning, synthesizing that information to determine if it is reasonable for them.

Gayle Nelson
High School
Business

Critical thinking is a process in which we consider all alternatives, use logic, consider different viewpoints, erase prejudice, and listen actively.

Mary Mayer
Brunson
School Counselor

Critical thinking is the ability to question, evaluate, connect things, analyze, select, pattern, make judgements about information in the broadest sense and to take risks so that universal issues implicit in school content and in life are internalized in a manner that results in greater effort in living for the greatest good.

Jane Pfefferkorn
Cultural Arts Specialist

Critical thinking for me is a process of examining and restructuring information in a way that has meaning and can be of use. This process is one by which the essence of meaning can be derived, hence, clarity is either gained or increased. The process involves critical listening and questioning in order to arrive at the desired goal. Critical thinking goes across the curriculum where education is concerned and enhances the quality of life when implemented outside the classroom.

Minnie Hewitt
Reading Coordinator
Forest Park School

Critical thinking is empowering students to be responsible for their own learning. Critical thinking is a process leading students to think in new ways, think about how they think, and take an active role in learning. Critical thinking uses stratagem which make students draw on their experiences, examine their values, and come to conclusions. Critical thinking is an active activity stretching the person to his limits and desiring to go further.

Lib Raymer
Forest Park
5th Grade

Critical thinking is using strategies of thinking to enable one to make life decisions in such a way that one feels competent and confident after the decisions are made.

Brenda Furches
Northwest Middle

To me, critical thinking means approaching a problem or a question logically, considering the various components or consequences of a solution or decision before arriving at one. It means not making snap judgments, but carefully and thoughtfully weighing facts and implications before taking action.

Since critical thinking applies to both personal life and to our concern today, I'd like to briefly consider both. In my personal life, critical thinking allows me to exercise patience in dealing with other people, and to make careful decisions about how I spend my time and money. At school, I would try to teach critical thinking for this reason also – to help students better deal with other people – to be aware of the consequences of their behavior before they act. Obviously, the need for critical thinking as related to academics must be realized, too. But for the middle schools, I see the more immediate recovery in inter-personal relationships.

Nancy Reid
Northwest Middle

Critical thinking is taking the information you have experienced, and applying it to questions, techniques, and reasonings to solve everyday life situations and problems that arise.

E. Hodges
Philo Middle School

What is critical thinking? It is the ability to think at a higher level; the ability to discriminate between knowledge known and not known, so that known knowledge can be reinterpreted in different frameworks. For example, Einstein, Darwin, and Newton originated world-changing theories by discrimination of knowledge and reinterpretation of it.

Joan C. Simons
High School
Biology

Critical thinking is an on-going process of expanding one's mind into the awareness of why and how we react to events in our life. When we go through our days with little critical thought, we are reacting to events in patterns of habit, like robots. Humans have highly developed minds with which to think. Critical thinking allows us the possibility of controlling our reactions instead of following pre-programmed reactions without thought. When a person is faced with a new situation where there is no set pattern of old reactions, he is forced to think critically about the situation. We as humans need to apply the critical on-going thinking not only to new situations, but also to old patterned reactions. Critical thinking will improve our relationship to the entire realm of our existence when applied, because it will involve us with new events and restructure old events and patterns. Every facet of our lives will be touched: emotional, physical, and mental.

Barbara Lampley
Grade 1

Regarding a Definition of Critical Thinking

Many people who feel that they don't know what critical thinking is, or means, request a definition. When they realize there is no *one* definition of critical thinking given by all theorists, many people feel frustrated and confused. "Even the experts can't agree about what they're talking about. How can I teach it if *I* don't know what it is, and no one else can tell me?" This reaction, though understandable, is somewhat mistaken. Although theorists provide a variety of definitions, they do not necessarily reject each others' definitions. They feel that their own definitions most usefully convey the basic concept, highlighting what they take to be its most crucial aspects, but they do not necessarily hold that other definitions are "wrong" or worthless. Novices, on the other hand, often get caught up in the wording of definitions and do not probe into them to see how compatible their meanings are. The various proposed definitions, when examined, are in fact much more similar than they are different.

Furthermore, because of the complexity of critical thinking, its relationship to an unlimited number of behaviors in an unlimited number of situations, its conceptual interdependence with other concepts (such as the critical person, the reasonable person, the critical society, a critical theory of knowledge, learning, literacy, and rationality, not to mention the opposites of these concepts), it is important not to put too much weight on any one definition. A variety of useful definitions have been formulated by distinguished theoreticians, and we should value these diverse formulations as helping to make important features of critical thought more apparent.

Harvey Siegel, for example, has defined critical thinking as "thinking appropriately moved by reasons". This definition helps us remember that our minds are often *inappropriately* moved by forces other than reason: by desires, fears, social rewards and punishments, etc. It points out the connection between critical thinking and the classic philosophical ideal of rationality. Yet, clearly, the ideal of rationality is itself open to multiple explications. Similar points can be made about Robert Ennis' and Matthew Lipman's definitions.

Robert Ennis defines critical thinking as "rational reflective thinking concerned with what to do or believe." This definition usefully calls attention to the wide role that critical thinking plays in everyday life, for, since all behavior is based on what we believe, all human action is based upon what we in some sense *decide* to do. However, like Siegel's definition, it assumes that the reader has a clear concept of rationality and of the conditions under which a decision can be said to be a "reflective" one. There is also a possible ambiguity in Ennis' use of 'reflective'. As a person internalizes critical standards — sensitivity to reasons, evidence, relevance, consistency, and so forth — the application of these standards to action becomes more automatic, less a matter of conscious effort and, hence, less a matter of overt "reflection" (assuming that Ennis means to imply by 'reflection' a special consciousness or deliberateness).

Matthew Lipman defines critical thinking as "skillful, responsible thinking that is conducive to judgment because it relies on criteria, is self-correcting, and is sensitive to context." This definition is useful insofar as one has a clear sense of the difference between responsible and irresponsible thinking, as well as what to encompass in the appropriate self-correction of thought, the appropriate use of criteria, and appropriate sensitivity to context. Of course, it would not be difficult to find instances of thinking that were self-correcting, used criteria, and responded to context *in one sense* but nevertheless were *uncritical* in some other sense. For example, one's particular criteria might be uncritically chosen or the manner of responding to context might be critically deficient in a variety of ways.

We make these points not to underestimate the usefulness of these definitions but to point out limitations in the process of definition itself when dealing with a complex concept such as critical thinking. Rather than working solely with one definition of critical thinking, it is more desirable to retain a host of definitions, and this for two reasons: 1) in order to maintain insight into the various dimensions of critical thinking that alternative definitions highlight, and 2) to help oneself escape the limitations of any given definition. In this spirit, we will present a number of definitions which we have formulated. Before reading these definitions, you might review the array of teachers' formulations in the chapter "What Critical Thinking Means to Me". You will find that virtually all the teachers' definitions are compatible with each other, even though they are all formulated individually. Or consider the following list of definitions.

Critical Thinking is:

a) skilled thinking which meets epistemological demands irrespective of the vested interests or ideological commitments of the thinker;

b) skilled thinking characterized by empathy into diverse opposing points of view and devotion to truth as against self-interest;

c) skilled thinking that is consistent in the application of intellectual standards, holding oneself to the same rigorous standards of evidence and proof to which one holds one's antagonists;

d) skilled thinking that demonstrates the commitment to entertain all viewpoints sympathetically and to assess them with the same intellectual standards, without reference to one's own feelings or vested interests, or the feelings or vested interests of one's friends, community or nation;

e) the art of thinking about your thinking while you're thinking so as to make your thinking more clear, precise, accurate, relevant, consistent, and fair;

f) the art of constructive skepticism;

g) the art of identifying and removing bias, prejudice, and one-sidedness of thought;

h)   the art of self-directed, in-depth, rational learning;

i)   thinking that rationally certifies what we know and makes clear wherein we are ignorant;

j)   the art of thinking for one's self with clarity, accuracy, insight, commitment, and fairness.

A Definition of Critical Thinking

We can now give a definition of critical thinking that helps tie together what has been said so far, a definition that highlights three crucial dimensions of critical thought:

1) the perfections of thought
2) the elements of thought
3) the domains of thought

The Definition:

Critical thinking is disciplined, self-directed thinking which exemplifies the perfections of thinking appropriate to a particular mode or domain of thought. It comes in two forms. If disciplined to serve the interests of a particular individual or group, to the exclusion of other relevant persons and groups, it is sophistic or *weak sense critical thinking*. If disciplined to take into account the interests of diverse persons or groups, it is fairminded or *strong sense critical thinking*.

Critical thinkers use their command of the elements of thought to adjust their thinking to the logical demands of a type or mode of thought. As they come to habitually think critically in the strong sense, they develop special traits of mind: intellectual humility, intellectual courage, intellectual perseverance, intellectual integrity, and confidence in reason. Sophistic or weak sense critical thinkers develop these traits only narrowly in accordance with egocentric and sociocentric commitments.

Now we shall explain what we mean by the *perfections* and *imperfections* of thought, the *elements* of thought, the *domains* of thought, and *traits of mind*. In each case we will comment briefly on the significance of these dimensions. We will then relate these dimensions to the process of helping students to come to terms, not only with the logic of their own thought, but with the logic of the disciplines they study, as well.

The Perfections and Imperfections of Thought

clarity _____ vs _____ unclarity

precision _____ vs _____ imprecision

specificity _____ vs _____ vagueness

accuracy _____ vs _____ inaccuracy

relevance _____ vs _____ irrelevance

consistency _____ vs _____ inconsistency

logical _____ vs _____ illogical

depth _____ vs _____ superficiality

completeness _____ vs _____ incompleteness

significance _____ vs _____ triviality

fairness _____ vs _____ bias or one-sidedness

adequacy (for purpose) _____ vs _____ inadequacy

Each of the above are general canons for thought; they represent legitimate concerns irrespective of the discipline or domain of thought. To develop one's mind and discipline one's thinking with respect to these standards requires extensive practice and long-term cultivation. Of course achieving these standards is a relative matter and often they have to be adjusted to a particular domain of thought. Being *precise* while doing mathematics is not the same as being precise while writing a poem or describing an experience. Furthermore, there is one perfection of thought that may be periodically incompatible with the others, and that is *adequacy to purpose.*

Because the social world is often irrational and unjust, because people are often manipulated to act against their interests, because skilled thought is often used to serve vested interest, those whose main purpose is to forward their selfish interests, often skillfully violate the common standards for good thinking. Successful propaganda, successful political debate, successful defense of a group's interests, successful deception of one's enemy often requires the violation or selective application of many of the above standards. The perfecting of one's thought as an instrument for success in a world based on power and advantage differs from the perfecting of one's thought for the apprehension and defense of fair-minded truth. To develop one's critical thinking skills merely to the level of adequacy for social success is to develop those skills in a lower or *weaker* sense.

It is important to underscore the commonality of this weaker sense of critical thinking for it is dominant in the everyday world. Virtually all social groups disapprove of members who make the case for their competitors or enemies, however justified that case may be. Skillful thinking is commonly a tool in the struggle for power and advantage, not an angelic force that transcends this struggle. It is only when the struggle becomes mutually destructive and it becomes advantageous for all to go beyond the onesidedness of each social group, that a social ground can be laid for fairmindedness of thought. No society yet in existence cultivates fairness of thought generally in its citizens.

The Elements of Thought

Both sophistic and fairminded critical thinking are skilled in comparison with uncritical thinking. The uncritical thinker is often unclear, imprecise, vague, illogical, unreflective, superficial, inconsistent, inaccurate, or trivial. To avoid these imperfections requires some command of the elements of thought. These include an understanding of and an ability to formulate, analyze, and assess:

1) The problem or question at issue
2) The purpose or goal of the thinking
3) The frame of reference or points of view involved
4) Assumptions made
5) Central concepts and ideas involved
6) Principles or theories used
7) Evidence, data, or reasons advanced
8) Interpretations and claims made
9) Inferences, reasoning, and lines of formulated thought
10) Implications and consequences which follow

Focusing on the nature and interrelationships of the elements of thought illuminates the logic of any particular instance of reasoning or of any domain of knowledge. For example, *at least one question is at issue in every instance of reasoning.* Can the student identify and precisely express those problems or questions, distinguishing the differences between them?

All human reasoning is oriented to serve some purpose or goal. Can students clearly express their purpose or goal and adjust their thinking to serve it? Can students analyze and critique their purpose or goal? Do students recognize the point of view or frame of reference in which they are thinking? Do they consider alternative points of view?

All reasoning must start somewhere and proceed in some direction. Can students identify what they are assuming or taking for granted in their reasoning? Can they follow out the implications and consequences of their reasoning? Can they identify contradictions in their thought?

All reasoning uses some ideas or concepts and not others. Can students identify and analyze the most fundamental concepts in their reasoning? Can they determine, for example, whether they are using a term in keeping with established usage or modifying that usage?

Most reasoning relies on principles or theories to make sense of what one is reasoning about. Can students identify the principles or theories they are using? Can they clarify them, question them, consider alternatives, apply them precisely?

Most reasoning is based on some experiences, evidence, or data which are interpreted and used as the basis of inferences. Can students identify the experiences, evidence, or data they are using or basing their reasoning upon? Can they identify their inferences? Can they rationally argue in favor of their inferences? Can they formulate and consider possible objections to their inferences?

Finally, as we have already emphasized, *all disciplines have a logic.* Can students discuss the logic of the disciplines they are studying? Can they identify their fundamental goals or purposes? The kind of questions they attempt to answer? Their basic concepts or ideas? Their basic assumptions? Their basic theories or principles? The sort of data, evidence, or experiences they focus upon? Whether there is fundamentally one or multiple conflicting schools of thought within the discipline? When students cannot answer these questions about a subject field, they cannot think critically within it. They have no idea how to begin to compare one field to any other, nor therefore how to correct or qualify the results of one field in light of the results of another.

Traits of Mind

There are, we believe, at least seven interdependent traits of mind we need to cultivate if we want students to become critical thinkers in the strong sense. They are:

a) *Intellectual Humility:* Awareness of the limits of one's knowledge, including sensitivity to circumstances in which one's native egocentrism is likely to function self-deceptively; sensitivity to bias and prejudice in, and limitations of one's viewpoint.

b) *Intellectual Courage:* The willingness to face and assess fairly ideas, beliefs, or viewpoints to which one has not given a serious hearing, regardless of one's strong negative reactions to them.

c) *Intellectual Empathy:* Recognizing the need to imaginatively put oneself in the place of others to genuinely understand them.

d) *Intellectual Good Faith (Integrity):* Recognition of the need to be true to one's own thinking, to be consistent in the intellectual standards one applies, to hold oneself to the same rigorous standards of evidence and proof to which one holds one's antagonists.

e) *Intellectual Perseverance:* Willingness to pursue intellectual insights and truths despite difficulties, obstacles, and frustrations.

f) *Faith in Reason:* Confidence that in the long run one's own higher interests and those of humankind at large will be served best by giving the freest play to reason, by encouraging people to come to their own conclusions by developing their own rational faculties.

g) *Intellectual Sense of Justice:* Willingness to entertain all viewpoints sympathetically and to assess them with the same intellectual standards, without reference to one's own feelings or vested interests, or the feelings or vested interests of one's friends, community, or nation.

These intellectual traits are interdependent. Each is best developed while developing the others as well. Consider intellectual humility. To become aware of the limits of our knowledge, we need the *courage* to face our own prejudices and ignorance. To discover our own prejudices, we must *empathize* with and reason within points of view we are hostile toward. To do so, we must typically *persevere* over a period of time, for reasoning within a point of view against which we are biased is difficult. We will not make that effort unless we have the *faith in reason* to believe we will not be deceived by whatever is false or misleading in the opposing viewpoint, and an *intellectual sense of justice*. We must recognize an intellectual *responsibility* to be fair to views we oppose. We must feel *obliged* to hear them in their strongest form to ensure that we are not condemning them out of ignorance or bias on our part. At this point we come full circle back to where we began: the need for *intellectual humility*.

These traits are applicable to *all* domains or modes of knowledge, not merely to some. Like the perfections and elements of thought, with which they are intimately intertwined, they are universally relevant. Of course, those reasoning to achieve selfish ends often betray intellectual standards to gain success. Schooling today neglects this deep-seated problem of selfish thought. Though most students enter and leave school as essentially uncritical thinkers, some develop a range of critical thinking skills to advance selfish ends. Yet the difference between selfish and fairminded thought rarely becomes a significant issue in instruction. Before going further, therefore, something more should be said about the nature of selfish thought.

Selfish Critical Thinking, Prejudice, and Human Desire

Human action is grounded in human motives and human motives are typically grounded in human desire and perceived interest. Getting what we want and what advances our prestige, wealth, and power naturally structures and shapes how we understand the situations and circumstances of our daily lives. We routinely categorize, make assumptions, interpret, and infer from within a viewpoint which we use to advance our personal ends and desires. We are, in a word, naturally prejudiced in our own favor. We reflexively and spontaneously gravitate to the slant on things that justifies or gratifies our desires. It is not enough to be taught to be ethical, honest, kind, generous, thoughtful, concerned with others, and respectful of human rights. The human mind easily construes situations so it can conceive of selfish desire as self-defense, cruelty as discipline, domination as love, intolerance as conviction, evil as good.

The mere conscious will to do good does not remove prejudices which shape our perceptions or eliminate the on-going drive to form them. To minimize our egocentric drives, we must develop critical thinking in a special direction. We need, not only intellectual skills, but intellectual character as well. Indeed we must develop and refine our intellectual skills *as* we develop and refine our intellectual character, to embed the skills in our character and shape our character through the skills.

People not only *can*, but often *do* create the illusion of moral character in a variety of ways. For instance we systematically confuse group mores with universal moral standards. When people act in accordance with the injunctions and taboos of their groups they naturally feel righteous. They receive much praise in moral terms. They may even be treated as moral leaders, if they act in a striking or moving fashion. For this reason, people often cannot distinguish moral from religious conformity or demagoguery from genuine moral integrity.

Genuine moral integrity requires intellectual character, for *bona fide* moral decisions require thoughtful discrimination between what is ethically justified and what is merely socially approved. Group norms are typically articulated in the language of morality and a socialized person inwardly experiences shame or guilt for violating a social taboo. In other words, what we

364

often take to be the inner voice of conscience is merely the internalized voice of social authority — the voice of our mother and father, our teachers and other "superiors" speaking within us.

Another common way we systematically create the illusion of morality is through egocentrically structured self-deception, the shaping and justification of self-serving perceptions and viewpoints. When engaged in such spontaneous thought we systematically confuse our viewpoint with reality itself. We do not experience ourselves as selecting among a range of possible perceptions; quite the contrary, it seems to us that we are simply observing things as they are. What is really egocentric intellectual arrogance we experience as righteous moral judgment. This leads us to see those who disagree with us as fools, dissemblers, or worse.

Since our inner voice tells us our motives are pure and we see things as they really are, those who set themselves against us, or threaten to impede our plans, seem the manifestation of evil. If they use violence to advance their ends, we experience their action as aggressive, as blind to human rights and simple justice. But if we use it, it is justifiable self-defense, restoring law and order, protecting right and justice.

Self-announced prejudice almost never exists. Prejudice almost always exists in obscured, rationalized, socially validated, functional forms. It enables people to sleep peacefully at night even while flagrantly abusing the rights of others. It enables people to get more of what they want, or to get it more easily. It is often sanctioned with a superabundance of pomp and ceremony. It often appears as the very will of God. Unless we recognize these powerful tendencies toward selfish thought in our social institutions, in what appear to be lofty actions, we will not face squarely the problem of education.

Education, properly conceived, cultivates knowledge through higher order thinking, a process which simultaneously cultivates traits of mind intrinsic to the standards and values presupposed by fairmindedness. Unless we take the tendency toward selfish thinking seriously, we are apt to contribute to students' critical thinking only in the narrow-minded sense.

The Spirit of Critical Thinking

To tie all of the above together, consider how the concept of critical thinking can be unpacked. The term 'critical', as we use it, does not mean thinking which is negative or finds fault, but rather thinking which evaluates reasons and brings thought and action in line with our evaluations, our best sense of what is true. The ideal of the critical thinker could be roughly expressed in the phrase 'reasonable person'. Our use of the term 'critical' is intended to highlight the intellectual *autonomy* of the critical thinker. That is, as a critical thinker, I do not simply accept conclusions (uncritically). I evaluate or critique reasons. My critique enables me to distinguish poor from strong reasoning. To do so to the greatest extent possible, I make use of a number of identifiable and learnable skills. I analyze and evaluate reasons and evidence; make assumptions explicit and evaluate them; reject unwarranted inferences or "leaps of logic"; use the best and most complete evidence available to me; make relevant distinctions; clarify; avoid inconsistency and contradiction; reconcile apparent contradictions; and distinguish what I know from what I merely suspect to be true.

The uncritical thinker, on the other hand, doesn't reflect on or evaluate reasons for a particular set of beliefs. By simply agreeing or disagreeing, the uncritical thinker accepts or rejects conclusions, often without understanding them, and often on the basis of egocentric attachment or unassessed desire. Lacking skills to analyze and evaluate, this person allows irrelevant reasons to influence conclusions, doesn't notice assumptions and therefore fails to evaluate them, accepts any inference that "sounds good"; is unconcerned with the strength and completeness of evidence, can't sort out ideas, confuses different concepts, is an unclear thinker, is oblivious to contradictions, and feels certain, even when not in a position to know. The classic uncritical thinker says, "I've made up my mind! Don't confuse me with the facts." Yet, critical thinking is more than evaluation of simple lines of thought.

As I evaluate beliefs by evaluating the evidence or reasoning that supports them (that is, the "arguments" for them), I notice certain things. I learn that sometimes I must go beyond evaluating small lines of reasoning. To understand an issue, I may have to think about it for a long time, weigh many reasons, and clarify basic ideas. I see that evaluating a particular line of thought often forces me to re-evaluate another. A conclusion about one case forces me to come to a certain conclusion about another. I find that often my evaluation of someone's thinking pivots around the meaning of a concept, which I must clarify. Such clarification affects my understanding of other issues. I notice previously hidden relationships between beliefs about different issues. I see that some beliefs and ideas are more fundamental than others. As I think my way through my beliefs, I find I must orchestrate the skills I have learned into a longer series of moves. As I strive for consistency and understanding, I discover opposing sets of basic assumptions which underlie those conclusions. I find that, to make my beliefs reasonable, I must evaluate not individual beliefs but, rather, large sets of beliefs. Analysis of an issue requires more work, a more extended process, than that required for a short line of reasoning. I must learn to use my skills, not in separate little moves but together, coordinated into a long sequence of thought.

Sometimes, two apparently equally strong arguments or lines of reasoning about the same issue come to contradictory conclusions. That is, when I listen to one side, the case seems strong. Yet when I listen to the other side, that case seems equally strong. Since they contradict each other, they cannot both be right. Sometimes it seems that the two sides are talking about different situations or speaking different languages, even living in different "worlds". I find that the skills which enable me to evaluate a short bit of reasoning do not offer much help here.

Suppose I decide to question two people who hold contradictory conclusions on an issue. They may use concepts or terms differently, disagree about what terms apply to what situations and what inferences can then be made, or state the issue differently. I may find that the differences in their conclusions rest, not so much on a particular piece of evidence or on one inference, as much as on vastly different perspectives, different ways of seeing the world, or different conceptions of such basic ideas as, say, human nature. As their conclusions arise from different perspectives, each, to the other, seems deluded, prejudiced, or naive. How am I to decide who is right? My evaluations of their inferences, uses of terms, evidence, etc. also depend on perspective. In a sense, I discover that *I have a perspective*.

I could simply agree with the one whose overall perspective is most like my own. But how do I know I'm right? If I'm sincerely interested in evaluating beliefs, should I not also consider things from other perspectives?

As I reflect on this discovery, I may also realize that my perspective has changed. Perhaps I recall learning a new idea or even a system of thought that changed the way I see myself and the world around me in fundamental ways, which even changed my life. I may remember how pervasive this change was — how I began to interpret a whole range of situations differently, continually used a new word, concept, or phrase, paid attention to previously ignored facts. I realize that I now have a new choice regarding the issue under scrutiny.

I could simply accept the view that most closely resembles my own. But I realize that I cannot reasonably reject the other perspective unless I understand it. To do so would be to say, "I don't know what you think, but whatever it is, it's false." The other perspective, however strange it seems to me now, may have something both important and true, which I have overlooked and without which my understanding is incomplete. Thinking along these lines, I open my mind to the possibility of change of perspective. I make sure that I don't subtly ignore or dismiss these new ideas; I realize I can make my point of view richer, so it encompasses more. As I think within another perspective, I begin to see ways in which it is right. It points out complicating factors I had previously ignored, makes useful distinctions I had missed, offers plausible interpretations of events I had never considered, and so on. I become able to move between various perspectives, freed from the limitations of my earlier thought.

One of the most important stages in my development as a thinker, then, is a clear recognition that I have a perspective, one that I must work on and change as I learn and grow. To do this, I can't be inflexibly attached to any particular beliefs. I strive for a consistent "big picture". I approach other perspectives differently. I ask how I can reconcile the points of view. I use principles and insights flexibly and do not approach analysis as a mechanical, "step one, step two" process. I pursue new ideas in depth, trying to understand the perspectives from which they come. I am willing to say, "This view sounds new and different; I don't yet understand it. There's more to this idea than I realized; I can't just dismiss it."

Looked at another way, suppose I'm rethinking my stand on an issue. I re-examine my evidence. Yet, I cannot evaluate my evidence for its completeness unless I consider evidence cited by those who disagree with me. Similarly, I find I can discover my basic assumptions by considering alternative assumptions, alternative perspectives. I can examine my own interpretation of situations and principles by considering alternative interpretations. I learn to use fairmindedness to clarify, enhance, and improve my perspective.

A narrowminded critical thinker, lacking this insight, says not, "This is how *I* see it," but, "This is how *it is.*" While working on pieces of reasoning, separate arguments, and individual beliefs, this person tends to overlook the development of perspective as such. Such thinking consists of separate or fragmented ideas and the examination of beliefs one at a time without appreciation for connections between them. While conscious and reflective about particular conclusions, this type of thinker is unreflective about his or her own point of view, how it affects his or her evaluations of reasoning, and how it is limited. When confronted with alternative perspectives or points of view, this person assesses them by their degree of agreement with his or her own view. Such an individual is given to sweeping acceptance or sweeping rejection of points of view and is tyrannized by the words he or she uses. Rather than trying to understand why others think as they do, such people dismiss new ideas, assuming the objectivity and correctness of their own beliefs and responses.

As I strive to think fairmindedly, I discover resistance to questioning my beliefs and considering those of others. I find a conflict between my desire to be fairminded and my desire to feel sure of what I think. It sometimes seems a lot easier to avoid the confusion, frustration, and embarrassment that I feel when re-assessing my beliefs. Simply trying to ignore these feelings doesn't make them go away. I realize that unless I directly address these obstacles to fairminded critical thought, I tend to seek its appearance rather than its reality, that I tend to accept rhetoric rather than fact, that without noticing it, I hide my own hypocrisy, even from myself.

By contrast, the critical thinker who lacks this insight, though a good arguer, is not a truly reasonable person. Giving good-sounding reasons, this person can find and explain flaws in opposing views and has well-thought-out ideas, but this thinker never subjects his or her own ideas to scrutiny. Though giving lip service to fairmindedness and describing views opposed to his or her own, this thinker doesn't truly understand or seriously consider them. One who often uses reasoning to get his or her way, cover up hidden motives, or make others look stupid or deluded is merely using skills to reinforce his or her own views and desires, without subjecting them to scrutiny. Such people are not truly reasonable. By cutting themselves off from honestly assessing their own perspectives or seriously considering other perspectives, these people are not using their mental capacities to their fullest extent.

To sum up, the fully reasonable person, the kind of critical thinker we want to foster, contrasts with at least two other kinds of thinkers. The first kind has few intellectual skills of any kind and tends to be naive, easily confused, manipulated, and controlled, and therefore easily defeated or taken in. The second has skills, but only of a restricted type, which enable pursuit of narrow, selfish interests and effective manipulation of the naive and unsuspecting. The first we call "uncritical thinkers" and the second "weak sense", or selfish, critical thinkers. What we aim at, therefore, are "strong sense" critical thinkers, those who use the fullest powers of their minds in the service of sincere, fairminded understanding and evaluation of their beliefs.

> *One does not learn about critical thinking by memorizing a definition or set of distinctions.*

Glossary: An Educator's Guide to Critical Thinking Terms and Concepts

accurate: Free from errors, mistakes, or distortion. *Correct* connotes little more than absence of error; *accurate* implies a positive exercise of one to obtain conformity with fact or truth; *exact* stresses perfect conformity to fact, truth, or some standard; *precise* suggests minute accuracy of detail. Accuracy is an important goal in critical thinking, though it is almost always a matter of degree. It is also important to recognize that making mistakes is an essential part of learning and that it is far better that students make their own mistakes, than that they parrot the thinking of the text or teacher. It should also be recognized that some distortion usually results whenever we think within a point of view or frame of reference. Students should think with this awareness in mind, with some sense of the limitations of their own, the text's, the teacher's, the subject's perspective. See *perfections of thought.*

ambiguous: A sentence having two or more possible meanings. Sensitivity to ambiguity and vagueness in writing and speech is essential to good thinking. *A continual effort to be clear and precise in language usage is fundamental to education.* Ambiguity is a problem more of sentences than of individual words. Furthermore, not every sentence that can be construed in more than one way is problematic and deserving of analysis. Many sentences are clearly intended one way; any other construal is obviously absurd and not meant. For example, "Make me a sandwich." is never seriously intended to request metamorphic change. It is a poor example for teaching genuine insight into critical thinking. For an example of a problematic ambiguity, consider the statement, "Welfare is corrupt." Among the possible meanings of this sentence are the following: Those who administer welfare programs take bribes to administer welfare policy unfairly; Welfare policies are written in such a way that much of the money goes to people who don't deserve it rather than to those who do; A government that gives money to people who haven't earned it

369

corrupts both the giver and the recipient. If two people are arguing about whether or not welfare is corrupt, but interpret the claim differently, they can make little or no progress; they aren't arguing about the same point. Evidence and considerations relevant to one interpretation may be irrelevant to others.

analyze: To break up a whole into its parts, to examine in detail so as to determine the nature of, to look more deeply into an issue or situation. *All learning presupposes some analysis of what we are learning,* if only by categorizing or labelling things in one way rather than another. Students should continually be asked to analyze their ideas, claims, experiences, interpretations, judgments, and theories and those they hear and read. See *elements of thought.*

argue: There are two meanings of this word that need to be distinguished: *1)* to argue in the sense of *to fight* or to emotionally disagree; and *2)* to give reasons for or against a proposal or proposition. In emphasizing critical thinking, we continually try to get our students to move from the first sense of the word to the second; that is, we try to get them to see the importance of *giving reasons* to support their views without getting their egos involved in what they are saying. This is a fundamental problem in human life. To argue in the critical thinking sense is to use logic and reason, and to bring forth facts to support or refute a point. It is done in a spirit of cooperation and good will.

argument: A reason or reasons offered for or against something, the offering of such reasons. This term refers to a discussion in which there is disagreement and suggests the use of logic and bringing forth of facts to support or refute a point. See *argue.*

to assume: To take for granted or to presuppose. Critical thinkers can and do make their assumptions explicit, assess them, and correct them. Assumptions can vary from the mundane to the problematic: I heard a scratch at the door. I got up to let the cat in. I *assumed* that only the cat makes that noise, and that he makes it only when he wants to be let in. Someone speaks gruffly to me. I feel guilty and hurt. I assume he is angry *at me,* that he is only angry at me when I do something bad, and that if he's angry at me, he dislikes me. *Notice that people often equate making assumptions with making false assumptions.* When people say, "Don't assume", this is what they mean. In fact, we cannot avoid making assumptions and some are justifiable. (For instance, we have assumed that people who buy this book can read English.) Rather than saying "Never assume", we say, "Be aware of and careful about the assumptions you make, and be ready to examine and critique them." See *assumption, elements of thought.*

assumption: A statement accepted or supposed as true without proof or demonstration; an unstated premise or belief. *All human thought and experience is based on assumptions.* Our thought must begin with something we take to be true in a particular context. We are typically unaware of what we assume and therefore rarely question our assumptions. Much of what is wrong with human thought can be found in the uncritical or unexamined assumptions that underlie it. For example, we often experience the world in such a way as to assume that we are observing things just as they are, as though we were seeing the world without the filter of a point of view. People we disagree with, of course, we recognize as *having a point of view.* One of the key dispositions of critical thinking is the on-going sense that as humans we always think within a perspective, that we virtually never experience things totally and absolutistically. There is a connection, therefore, between thinking so as to be *aware of our assumptions* and being *intellectually humble.*

authority: *1)* The power or supposed right to give commands, enforce obedience, take action, or make final decisions. *2)* A person with much knowledge and expertise in a field, hence reliable. Critical thinkers recognize that ultimate authority rests with reason and evidence, since it is only on the assumption that purported experts have the backing of reason and evidence that they rightfully gain authority. Much instruction discourages critical thinking by encouraging students to believe that whatever the text or teacher says is true. As a result, students do not learn how to assess authority. See *knowledge.*

bias: A mental leaning or inclination. We must clearly distinguish two different senses of the word 'bias'. One is neutral, the other negative. In the neutral sense we are referring simply to the fact that, *because of one's point of view, one notices some things rather than others,* emphasizes some points rather than others, and thinks in one direction rather than others. This is not in itself a criticism because *thinking within a point of view is unavoidable.* In the negative sense, we are implying *blindness or irrational resistance to weaknesses within one's own point of view* or to the strength or insight within a point of view one opposes. Fairminded critical thinkers try to be aware of their bias (in sense one) and try hard to avoid bias (in sense two). Many people confuse these two senses. Many confuse bias with emotion or with evaluation, perceiving any expression of emotion or any use of evaluative words to be biased (sense two). Evaluative words that can be justified by reason and evidence are not biased in the negative sense. See *criteria, evaluation, judgment, opinion.*

clarify: To make easier to understand, to free from confusion or ambiguity, to remove obscurities. *Clarity* is a fundamental perfection of thought and *clarification* a fundamental aim in critical thinking. Students often do not see why it is important to write and speak clearly, why it is important to *say what you mean and mean what you say.* The key to clarification is *concrete, specific* examples. See *accurate, ambiguous, logic of language, vague.*

concept: An idea or thought, especially a generalized idea of a thing or of a class of things. Humans think within concepts or ideas. *We can never achieve command over our thoughts unless we learn how to achieve command over our concepts or ideas.* Thus we must learn how to identify the concepts or ideas we are using, contrast them with alternative concepts or ideas, and clarify what we include and exclude by means of them. For example, most people say they believe strongly in democracy, but few can clarify with examples what that word does and does not imply. *Most people confuse the meaning of words with cultural associations,* with the result that 'democracy' means to people whatever *we* do in running *our* government — any country that is different is undemocratic. We must distinguish the concepts implicit in the English language from the psychological associations surrounding that concept in a given social group or culture. The failure to develop this ability is a major cause of uncritical thought and selfish critical thought. See *logic of language.*

conclude/conclusion: To decide by reasoning, to infer, to deduce; the last step in a reasoning process; a judgment, decision, or belief formed after investigation or reasoning. All beliefs, decisions, or actions are based on human thought, but rarely as the result of conscious reasoning or deliberation. *All that we believe is,* one way or another, *based on conclusions* that we have come to during our lifetime. Yet, we rarely monitor our thought processes, we don't critically assess the conclusions we come to, to determine whether we have sufficient grounds or reasons for accepting them. People seldom recognize when they have come to a conclusion. They confuse their conclusions with evidence, and so cannot assess the reasoning that took them from evidence to conclusion. Recognizing that *human life is inferential,* that we continually come to conclusions about ourselves and the things and persons around us, is essential to thinking critically and reflectively.

consistency: To think, act, or speak in agreement with what has already been thought, done, or expressed; to have intellectual or moral integrity. Human life and thought is filled with inconsistency, hypocrisy, and contradiction. We often say one thing and do another, judge ourselves and our friends by one standard and our antagonists by another, lean over backwards to justify what we want or negate what does not serve our interests. Similarly, we often confuse desires with needs, treating our desires as equivalent to needs, putting what we want above the basic needs of others. *Logical and moral consistency are fundamental values of fairminded critical thinking.* Social conditioning and native egocentrism often obscure social contradictions, inconsistency, and hypocrisy. See *personal contradiction, social contradiction, intellectual integrity, human nature.*

contradict/contradiction: To assert the opposite of; to be contrary to, go against; a statement in opposition to another; a condition in which things tend to be contrary to each other; inconsistency; discrepancy; a person or thing containing or composed of contradictory elements. See *personal contradiction, social contradiction.*

criterion (criteria, pl): A standard, rule, or test by which something can be judged or measured. Human life, thought, and action are based on human values. The standards by which we determine whether those values are achieved in any situation represent criteria. Critical thinking depends upon making explicit the standards or criteria for rational or justifiable thinking and behavior. See *evaluation.*

critical listening: A mode of monitoring how we are listening so as to maximize our accurate understanding of what another person is saying. By understanding the logic of human communication — that *everything spoken expresses point of view,* uses some ideas and not others, has implications, etc. — critical thinkers can listen so as to enter sympathetically and analytically into the perspective of others. See *critical speaking, critical reading, critical writing, elements of thought, intellectual empathy.*

critical person: One who has mastered a range of intellectual skills and abilities. If that person generally uses those skills to advance his or her own selfish interests, that person is a critical thinker only in a weak or qualified sense. If that person generally uses those skills fairmindedly, entering empathically into the points of view of others, he or she is a critical thinker in the strong or fullest sense. See *critical thinking.*

critical reading: *Critical reading is an active, intellectually engaged process* in which the reader participates in an inner dialogue with the writer. Most people read uncritically and so miss some part of what is expressed while distorting other parts. A critical reader realizes the way in which *reading, by its very nature, means entering into a point of view other*

372

than our own, the point of view of the writer. A critical reader actively looks for assumptions, key concepts and ideas, reasons and justifications, supporting examples, parallel experiences, implications and consequences, and any other structural features of the written text, to interpret and assess it accurately and fairly. See *elements of thought.*

critical society: A society which rewards adherence to the values of critical thinking and hence *does not use indoctrination and inculcation as basic modes of learning* (rewards reflective questioning, intellectual independence, and reasoned dissent). Socrates is not the only thinker to imagine a society in which independent critical thought became embodied in the concrete day-to-day lives of individuals; William Graham Sumner, North America's distinguished anthropologist, explicitly formulated the ideal:

> The critical habit of thought, if usual in a society, will pervade all its mores, because it is a way of taking up the problems of life. Men educated in it cannot be stampeded by stump orators and are never deceived by dithyrambic oratory. They are slow to believe. They can hold things as possible or probable in all degrees, without certainty and without pain. They can wait for evidence and weigh evidence, uninfluenced by the emphasis or confidence with which assertions are made on one side or the other. They can resist appeals to their dearest prejudices and all kinds of cajolery. Education in the critical faculty is the only education of which it can be truly said that it makes good citizens. (*Folkways,* 1906)

Until critical habits of thought pervade our society, however, there will be a tendency for schools as social institutions to transmit the prevailing world view more or less uncritically, to transmit it as reality, not as a picture of reality. Education for critical thinking, then, requires that the school or classroom become a microcosm of a critical society. See *didactic instruction, dialogical instruction, intellectual virtues, knowledge.*

critical thinking: *1)* Disciplined, self-directed thinking which exemplifies the perfections of thinking appropriate to a particular mode or domain of thinking. *2)* Thinking that displays mastery of intellectual skills and abilities. *3)* The art of thinking about your thinking while you are thinking in order to make your thinking better: more clear, more accurate, or more defensible. Critical thinking can be distinguished into two forms: "selfish" or "sophistic", on the one hand, and "fairminded", on the other. In thinking critically we use our command of the elements of thinking to adjust our thinking successfully to the logical demands of a type or mode of thinking. See *critical person, critical society, critical reading, critical listening, critical writing, perfections of thought, elements of thought, domains of thought, intellectual virtues.*

critical writing: To express ourselves in language requires that we arrange our ideas in some relationships to each other. When accuracy and truth are at issue, then we must understand what our thesis is, how we can support it, how we can elaborate it to make it intelligible to others, what objections can be raised to it from other points of view, what the limitations are to our point of view, and so forth. *Disciplined writing requires disciplined thinking; disciplined thinking is achieved through disciplined writing.* See *critical listening, critical reading, logic of language.*

critique: An objective judging, analysis, or evaluation of something. The purpose of critique is the same as the purpose of critical thinking: to appreciate strengths as well as weaknesses, virtues as well as failings. *Critical thinkers critique in order to redesign, remodel, and make better.*

cultural association: Undisciplined thinking often reflects associations, personal and cultural, absorbed or uncritically formed. If a person who was cruel to me as a child had a particular tone of voice, I may find myself disliking a person who has the same tone of voice. Media advertising juxtaposes and joins logically unrelated things to influence our buying habits. Raised in a particular country or within a particular group within it, we form any number of mental links which, if they remain unexamined, unduly influence our thinking. See *concept, critical society.*

cultural assumption: Unassessed (often implicit) belief adopted by virtue of upbringing in a society. Raised in a society, we unconsciously take on its point of view, values, beliefs, and practices. At the root of each of these are many kinds of assumptions. Not knowing that we perceive, conceive, think, and experience within assumptions we have taken in, we take ourselves to be perceiving "things as they are", not "things as they appear from a cultural vantage point". Becoming aware of our cultural assumptions so that we might critically examine them is a crucial dimension of critical thinking. It is, however, a dimension almost totally absent from schooling. Lip service to this ideal is common enough; a realistic emphasis is virtually unheard of. See *ethnocentricity, prejudice, social contradiction.*

data: Facts, figures, or information from which conclusions can be inferred, or upon which interpretations or theories can be based. As critical thinkers we must make certain to distinguish hard data from the inferences or conclusions we draw from them.

dialectical thinking: Dialogical thinking (thinking within more than one perspective) conducted to test the strengths and weaknesses of opposing points of view. (Court trials and debates are, in a sense, dialectical.) When thinking dialectically, reasoners pit two or more opposing points of view in competition with each other, developing each by providing support, raising objections, countering those objections, raising further objections, and so on. Dialectical thinking or discussion can be conducted so as to "win" by defeating the positions one disagrees with — using critical insight to support one's own view and point out flaws in other views (associated with critical thinking in the restricted or weak sense), or fairmindedly, by conceding points that don't stand up to critique, trying to integrate or incorporate strong points found in other views, and using critical insight to develop a fuller and more accurate view (associated with critical thinking in the fuller or strong sense). See *monological problems.*

dialogical instruction: Instruction that fosters dialogical or dialectic thinking. Thus, when considering a question, the class brings all relevant subjects to bear and considers the perspectives of groups whose views are not canvassed in their texts — for example, "What did King George think of the *Declaration of Independence*, the Revolutionary War, the Continental Congress, Jefferson and Washington, etc.?" or, "How would an economist analyze this situation? A historian? A psychologist? A geographer?" See *critical society, didactic instruction, higher order learning, lower order learning, Socratic questioning, knowledge.*

dialogical thinking: Thinking that involves a dialogue or extended exchange between different points of view or frames of reference. Students learn best in dialogical situations, in circumstances in which they continually express their views to others and try to fit other's views into their own. See *Socratic questioning, monological thinking, multilogical thinking, dialectical thinking.*

didactic instruction: Teaching by telling. In didactic instruction, the teacher directly tells the student what to believe and think about a subject. The student's task is to remember what the teacher said and reproduce it on demand. In its most common form, this mode of teaching falsely assumes that one can directly give a person knowledge without that person having to think his or her way to it. It falsely assumes that knowledge can be separated from understanding and justification. It confuses the ability to *state* a principle with *understanding* it, the ability to *supply* a definition with *knowing* a new word, and the act of *saying* that something is important with *recognizing* its importance. See *critical society, knowledge.*

domains of thought: Thinking can be oriented or structured with different issues or purposes in view. *Thinking varies in accordance with purpose and issue.* Critical thinkers learn to discipline their thinking to take into account the nature of the issue or domain. We see this most clearly when we consider the difference between issues and thinking within different academic disciplines or subject areas. Hence, mathematical thinking is quite different from, say, historical thinking. Mathematics and history, we can say then, represent different domains of thought. See the *logic of questions.*

egocentricity: A tendency to view everything in relationship to oneself; to confuse immediate perception (how things *seem*) with reality. One's desires, values, and beliefs (seeming to be self-evidently correct or superior to those of others) are often uncritically used as the norm of all judgment and experience. Egocentricity is one of the fundamental impediments to critical thinking. As one learns to think critically in a strong sense, one learns to become more rational, and less egocentric. See *human nature, strong sense critical thinker, ethnocentrism, sociocentrism, personal contradiction.*

elements of thought: All thought has a universal set of elements, each of which can be monitored for possible problems: Are we clear about our *purpose or goal?* about the *problem or question at issue?* about our *point of view or frame of reference?* about our *assumptions?* about the *claims* we are making? about the *reasons or evidence* upon which we are basing our claims? about our *inferences and line of reasoning?* about the *implications and consequences* that follow from our reasoning? Critical thinkers develop skills of identifying and assessing these elements in their thinking and in the thinking of others.

emotion: A feeling aroused to the point of awareness, often a strong feeling or state of excitement. When our egocentric emotions or feelings get involved, when we are excited by infantile anger, fear, jealousy, etc., our objectivity often decreases. Critical thinkers need to be able to monitor their egocentric feelings and use their rational passions to reason themselves into feelings appropriate to the situation as it really is, rather than to how it seems to their infantile ego. Emotions and feelings themselves are not irrational; however, it is common for people to feel strongly when their ego is stimulated.

375

One way to understand the goal of strong sense critical thinking is as the attempt to develop rational feelings and emotions at the expense of irrational, egocentric ones. See *rational passions, intellectual virtues.*

empirical: Relying or based on experiment, observation, or experience rather than on theory or meaning. *It is important to continually distinguish those considerations based on experiment, observation, or experience from those based on the meaning of a word or concept or the implications of a theory.* One common form of uncritical or selfish critical thinking involves distorting facts or experience in order to preserve a preconceived meaning or theory. For example, a conservative may distort the facts that support a liberal perspective to prevent empirical evidence from counting against a theory of the world that he or she holds rigidly. Indeed, within all perspectives and belief systems many will distort the facts before they will admit to a weakness in their favorite theory or belief. See *data, fact, evidence.*

empirical implication: That which follows from a situation or fact, not due to the logic of language, but from experience or scientific law. The redness of the coil on the stove empirically implies dangerous heat.

ethnocentricity: A tendency to view one's own race or culture as central, based on the deep-seated belief that one's own group is superior to all others. Ethnocentrism is a form of egocentrism extended from the self to the group. Much uncritical or selfish critical thinking is either egocentric or ethnocentric in nature. ('Ethnocentrism' and 'sociocentrism' are used synonymously, for the most part, though 'sociocentricity' is broader, relating to *any* group, including, for example, sociocentricity regarding one's profession.) The "cure" for ethnocentrism or sociocentrism is empathic thought within the perspective of opposing groups and cultures. Such empathic thought is rarely cultivated in the societies and schools of today. Instead, many people develop an empty rhetoric of tolerance, saying that others have different beliefs and ways, but without seriously considering those beliefs and ways, what they mean to those others, and their reasons for maintaining them.

evaluation: To judge or determine the worth or quality of. *Evaluation has a logic and should be carefully distinguished from mere subjective preference.* The elements of its logic may be put in the form of questions which may be asked whenever an evaluation is to be carried out: *1)* Are we clear about *what precisely we are evaluating?; 2)* Are we clear about *our purpose?* Is our purpose legitimate?; *3)* Given our purpose, what are the *relevant criteria or standards* for evaluation?; *4)* Do we have *sufficient information* about that which we are evaluating? Is that *information relevant to the purpose?;* and *5)* Have we *applied our criteria accurately and fairly to the facts* as we know them? Uncritical thinkers often treat evaluation as mere preference or treat their evaluative judgments as direct observations not admitting of error.

evidence: The data on which a judgment or conclusion might be based or by which proof or probability might be established. Critical thinkers distinguish the evidence or raw data upon which they base their interpretations or conclusions from the inferences and assumptions that connect data to conclusions. Uncritical thinkers treat their conclusions as something given to them in experience, as something they directly observe in the world. As a result, they find it difficult to see why anyone might disagree with their conclusions. After all, the truth of their views is, they believe, right there for everyone to see! Such people find it difficult or even impossible to describe the evidence or experience without coloring that description with their interpretation.

explicit: Clearly stated and leaving nothing implied; *explicit* is applied to that which is so clearly stated or distinctly set forth that there should be no doubt as to the meaning; *exact and precise* in this connection both suggest that which is strictly defined, accurately stated, or made unmistakably clear; *definite* implies precise limitations as to the nature, character, meaning, etc. of something; *specific* implies the pointing up of details or the particularizing of references. Critical thinking often requires the ability to be explicit, exact, definite, and specific. Most students cannot make what is *implicit* in their thinking *explicit*. This deficiency hampers their ability to monitor and assess their thinking.

fact: What actually happened, what is true; verifiable by empirical means; distinguished from interpretation, inference, judgment, or conclusion; the raw data. There are distinct senses of the word 'factual': "True" (as opposed to "claimed to be true"); and "empirical" (as opposed to conceptual or evaluative). You may make many "factual claims" in one sense, that is, claims which can be verified or disproven by observation or empirical study, but I must evaluate those claims to determine if they are true. People often confuse these two senses, even to the point of accepting as true, statements which merely "seem factual", for example, "29.23 % of Americans suffer from depression." Before I accept this as true, I should assess it. I should ask such questions as "How do you know? How *could* this be known? Did you merely ask people if they were depressed and extrapolate those results? How exactly did you arrive at this figure?" Purported facts should be assessed for their accuracy, completeness, and relevance to the issue. Sources of purported facts should be assessed for their qualifications, track records, and impartiality. Education which stresses retention and repetition of factual claims stunts students' desire and ability to assess alleged facts, leaving them open to manipulation. Activities in which students are asked to "distinguish fact from opinion" often confuse these two senses. They encourage students to *accept as true* statements which merely "look like" facts. See *intellectual humility, knowledge.*

fair: Treating both or all sides alike without reference to one's own feelings or interests; *just* implies adherence to a standard of rightness or lawfulness without reference to one's own inclinations; *impartial* and *unbiased* both imply freedom from prejudice for or against any side; *dispassionate* implies the absence of passion or strong emotion, hence, connotes cool, disinterested judgment; *objective* implies a viewing of persons or things without reference to oneself, one's interests, etc.

faith: *1)* Unquestioning belief in anything. *2)* Confidence, trust, or reliance. A critical thinker does not accept faith in the first sense, for every belief is reached on the basis of some thinking, which may or may not be justified. Even in religion one believes in one religion rather than another, and in doing so implies that there are good reasons for accepting one rather than another. A Christian, for example, believes that there are good reasons for not being an atheist, and Christians often attempt to persuade non-Christians to change their beliefs. In some sense, then, everyone has confidence in the capacity of his or her own mind to judge rightly on the basis of good reasons, and does not believe simply on the basis of blind faith.

fallacy/fallacious: An error in reasoning; flaw or defect in argument; an argument which doesn't conform to rules of good reasoning (especially one that appears to be sound). Containing or based on a fallacy; deceptive in appearance or meaning; misleading; delusive.

higher order learning: Learning through exploring the foundations, justification, implications, and value of a fact, principle, skill, or concept. *Learning so as to deeply understand.* One can learn in keeping with the rational capacities of the human mind or in keeping with its irrational propensities, cultivating the capacity of the human mind to discipline and direct its thought through commitment to intellectual standards, or one can learn through mere association. Education for critical thought produces higher order learning by helping students actively think their way to conclusions; discuss their thinking with other students and the teacher; entertain a variety of points of view; analyze concepts, theories, and explanations in their own terms; actively question the meaning and implications of what they learn; compare what they learn to what they have experienced; take what they read and write seriously; solve non-routine problems; examine assumptions; and gather and assess evidence. Students should learn each subject by engaging in thought within that subject. They should learn history by thinking historically, mathematics by thinking mathematically, etc. See *dialogical instruction, lower order learning, critical society, knowledge, principle, domains of thought.*

human nature: The common qualities of all human beings. People have both a primary and a secondary nature. Our primary nature is spontaneous, egocentric, and strongly prone to irrational belief formation. It is the basis for our instinctual thought. People need no training to believe what they want to believe: what serves their immediate interests, what preserves their sense of personal comfort and righteousness, what minimizes their sense of inconsistency, and what presupposes their own correctness. People need no special training to believe what those around them believe: what their parents and friends believe, what is taught to them by religious and school authorities, what is repeated often by the media, and what is commonly believed in the nation in which they are raised. People need no training to think that those who disagree with them are wrong and probably prejudiced. People need no training to assume that their own most fundamental beliefs are self-evidently true or easily justified by evidence. People naturally and spontaneously identify with their own beliefs. They experience most disagreement as personal attack. The resulting defensiveness interferes with their capacity to empathize with or enter into other points of view.

On the other hand, *people need extensive and systematic practice to develop their secondary nature, their implicit capacity to function as rational persons.* They need extensive and systematic practice to recognize the tendencies they have to form irrational beliefs. They need extensive practice to develop a dislike of inconsistency, a love of clarity, a passion to seek reasons and evidence and to be fair to points of view other than their own. People need extensive practice to recognize that they indeed have a point of view, that they live inferentially, that they do not have a direct pipeline to reality, that it is perfectly possible to have an overwhelming inner sense of the correctness of one's views and still be wrong. See *intellectual virtues.*

idea: Anything existing in the mind as an object of knowledge or thought; *concept* refers to generalized idea of a class of objects, based on knowledge of particular instances of the class;

conception, often equivalent to concept, specifically refers to something conceived in the mind or imagined; *thought* refers to any idea, whether or not expressed, that occurs to the mind in reasoning or contemplation; *notion* implies vagueness or incomplete intention; *impression* also implies vagueness of an idea provoked by some external stimulus. Critical thinkers are aware of what ideas they are using in their thinking, where those ideas came from, and how to assess them. See *clarify, concept, logic, logic of language.*

imply/implication: A claim or truth which follows from other claims or truths. One of the most important skills of critical thinking is the ability to distinguish between what is actually implied by a statement or situation from what may be carelessly inferred by people. Critical thinkers try to *monitor their inferences to keep them in line with what is actually implied* by what they know. When speaking, critical thinkers *try to use words that imply only what they can legitimately justify.* They recognize that there are established word usages which generate established implications. To say of an act that it is murder, for example, is to imply that it is intentional and unjustified. See *clarify, precision, logic of language, critical listening, critical reading, elements of thought.*

infer/inference: An inference is a step of the mind, an intellectual act by which one concludes that something is so in light of something else's being so, or seeming to be so. If you come at me with a knife in your hand, I would probably infer that you mean to do me harm. Inferences can be strong or weak, justified or unjustified. Inferences are based upon assumptions. See *imply/implication.*

insight: The ability to see and clearly and deeply understand the inner nature of things. Instruction for critical thinking fosters insight rather than mere performance; it cultivates the achievement of deeper knowledge and understanding through insight. *Thinking one's way into and through a subject leads to insights* as one synthesizes what one is learning, relating one subject to other subjects and all subjects to personal experience. Rarely is insight formulated as a goal in present curricula and texts. See *dialogical instruction, higher order learning, lower order learning, didactic instruction, intellectual humility.*

intellectual autonomy: Having rational control of ones beliefs, values, and inferences. The ideal of critical thinking is to learn to think for oneself, to gain command over one's thought processes. Intellectual autonomy does not entail willfulness, stubbornness, or rebellion. It entails a commitment to analyzing and evaluating beliefs on the basis of reason and evidence, to question when it is rational to question, to believe when it is rational to believe, and to conform when it is rational to conform. See *know, knowledge.*

(intellectual) confidence or faith in reason: Confidence that in the long run *one's own higher interests and those of humankind at large will best be served by giving the freest play to reason* — by encouraging people to come to their own conclusions through a process of developing their own rational faculties; faith that (with proper encouragement and cultivation) people can learn to think for themselves, form rational viewpoints, draw reasonable conclusions, think coherently and logically, persuade each other by reason, and become reasonable, despite the deep-seated obstacles in the native character of the human mind and in society. Confidence in reason is developed through experiences in which one reasons one's way to insight, solves problems through reason, uses reason to persuade, is persuaded by reason. Confidence in reason is undermined when one is expected to perform tasks without understanding why, to repeat statements without having verified or justified them, to accept beliefs on the sole basis of authority or social pressure.

intellectual courage: The willingness to face and fairly assess ideas, beliefs, or viewpoints to which we have not given a serious hearing, regardless of our strong negative reactions to them. This courage arises from the recognition that *ideas considered dangerous or absurd are sometimes rationally justified* (in whole or in part), and that *conclusions or beliefs espoused by those around us or inculcated in us are sometimes false or misleading*. To determine for ourselves which is which, we must not passively and uncritically "accept" what we have "learned". Intellectual courage comes into play here, because inevitably we will come to see some truth in some ideas considered dangerous and absurd and some distortion or falsity in some ideas strongly held in our social group. It takes courage to be true to our own thinking in such circumstances. Examining cherished beliefs is difficult, and the penalties for non-conformity are often severe.

intellectual empathy: Understanding the need to imaginatively put oneself in the place of others to genuinely understand them. We must recognize our egocentric tendency to identify truth with our immediate perceptions or longstanding beliefs. Intellectual empathy correlates with the ability to accurately reconstruct the viewpoints and reasoning of others and to *reason from premises, assumptions, and ideas other than our own*. This trait also requires that we remember occasions when we were wrong, despite an intense conviction that we were right, and consider that we might be similarly deceived in a case at hand.

intellectual humility: Awareness of the limits of one's knowledge, including sensitivity to circumstances in which one's native egocentrism is likely to function self-deceptively; sensitivity to bias and prejudice in, and limitations of one's viewpoint. Intellectual humility is based on the recognition that *no one should claim more than he or she actually knows*. It does not imply spinelessness or submissiveness. It implies the lack of intellectual pretentiousness, boastfulness, or conceit, combined with insight into the strengths or weaknesses of the logical foundations of one's beliefs.

intellectual integrity: Recognition of the need to be true to one's own thinking, to be consistent in the intellectual standards one applies, to hold oneself to the same rigorous standards of evidence and proof to which one holds one's antagonists, to practice what one advocates for others, and to honestly admit discrepancies and inconsistencies in one's own thought and action. This trait develops best in a supportive atmosphere in which people feel secure and free enough to honestly acknowledge their inconsistencies, and can develop and share realistic ways of ameliorating them. It requires honest acknowledgment of the difficulties of achieving greater consistency.

intellectual perseverance: Willingness and consciousness of the need to pursue intellectual insights and truths despite difficulties, obstacles, and frustrations; firm adherence to rational principles despite irrational opposition of others; a sense of the need to struggle with confusion and unsettled questions over an extended period of time in order to achieve deeper understanding or insight. This trait is undermined when teachers and others continually provide the answers, do students' thinking for them or substitute easy tricks, algorithms, and short cuts for careful, independent thought.

intellectual sense of justice: Willingness and consciousness of the need to entertain all viewpoints sympathetically and to assess them with the same intellectual standards, without reference to one's own feelings or vested interests, or the feelings or vested interests of one's friends, community, or nation; implies adherence to intellectual standards without reference to one's own advantage or the advantage of one's group.

intellectual virtues: The traits of mind and character necessary for right action and thinking; the traits of mind and character essential for fairminded rationality; the traits that distinguish the narrowminded, self-serving critical thinker from the openminded, truth-seeking critical thinker. These *intellectual traits are interdependent.* Each is best developed while developing the others as well. They cannot be imposed from without; they must be cultivated by encouragement and example. People can come to deeply understand and accept these principles by analyzing their experiences of them: learning from an unfamiliar perspective, discovering you don't know as much as you thought, and so on. They include: intellectual sense of justice, intellectual perseverance, intellectual integrity, intellectual humility, intellectual empathy, intellectual courage, (intellectual) confidence in reason, and intellectual autonomy.

interpret/interpretation: To give one's own conception of, to place in the context of one's own experience, perspective, point of view, or philosophy. Interpretations should be distinguished from the facts, the evidence, the situation. (I may interpret someone's silence as an expression of hostility toward me. Such an interpretation may or may not be correct. I may have projected my patterns of motivation and behavior onto that person, or I may have accurately noticed this pattern in the other.) The best interpretations take the most evidence into account. Critical thinkers recognize their interpretations, distinguish them from evidence, consider alternative interpretations, and reconsider their interpretations in the light of new evidence. *All learning involves personal interpretation, since whatever we learn we must integrate into our own thinking and action.* What we learn must be given a meaning by us, must be meaningful to us, and hence involves interpretive acts on our part. Didactic instruction, in attempting to directly implant knowledge in students' minds, typically ignores the role of personal interpretation in learning.

intuition: The direct knowing or learning of something without the conscious use of reasoning. We sometimes seem to know or learn things without recognizing how we came to that knowledge. When this occurs, we experience an inner sense that what we believe is true. The problem is that sometimes we are correct (and have genuinely experienced an intuition) and sometimes we are incorrect (having fallen victim to one of our prejudices). A critical thinker does not blindly accept that what he or she thinks or believes but cannot account for is necessarily true. A critical thinker realizes how easily we confuse intuitions and prejudices. Critical thinkers may follow their inner sense that something is so, but only with a healthy sense of intellectual humility.

There is a second sense of 'intuition' that is important for critical thinking, and that is the meaning suggested in the following sentence: "To develop your critical thinking abilities, it is important to develop your critical thinking *intuitions*." This sense of the word is connected to the fact that we can learn concepts at various levels of depth. If we learn nothing more than an abstract definition for a word and do not learn how to apply it effectively in a wide variety of situations, one might say that we end up with no *intuitive* basis for applying it. We lack the insight into how, when, and why it applies. Helping students to develop critical thinking intuitions is helping them gain the practical insights necessary for a ready and swift application of concepts to cases in a large array of circumstances. We want critical thinking to be "intuitive" to our students, ready and available for immediate translation into their everyday thought and experience.

irrational/irrationality: 1) Lacking the power to reason. 2) Contrary to reason or logic. 3) Senseless, absurd. Uncritical thinkers have failed to develop the ability or power to reason well. Their beliefs and practices, then, are often contrary to reason and logic, and are sometimes senseless or absurd. It is important to recognize, however, that in societies with irrational beliefs and practices, it is not clear whether challenging those beliefs and practices — and therefore possibly endangering oneself — is rational or irrational. Furthermore, suppose one's vested interests are best advanced by adopting beliefs and practices that are contrary to reason. Is it then rational to follow reason and negate one's vested interests or follow one's interests and ignore reason? These very real dilemmas of everyday life represent on-going problems for critical thinkers. Selfish critical thinkers, of course, face no dilemma here because of their consistent commitment to advance their narrow vested interests. Fairminded critical thinkers make these decisions self-consciously and honestly assess the results.

irrational learning: All rational learning presupposes rational assent. And, though we sometimes forget it, not all learning is automatically or even commonly rational. *Much that we learn in everyday life is quite distinctively irrational.* It is quite possible — and indeed the bulk of human learning is unfortunately of this character — *to come to believe any number of things without knowing how or why.* It is quite possible, in other words, to believe for irrational reasons: because those around us believe, because we are rewarded for believing, because we are afraid to disbelieve, because our vested interest is served by belief, because we are more comfortable with belief, or because we have ego identified ourselves, our image, or our personal being with belief. In all of these cases, our beliefs are without rational grounding, without good reason and evidence, without the foundation a rational person demands. We become rational, on the other hand, to the extent that our beliefs and actions are grounded in good reasons and evidence; to the extent that we recognize and critique our own irrationality; to the extent that we are not moved by bad reasons and a multiplicity of irrational motives, fears, and desires; to the extent that we have cultivated a passion for clarity, accuracy, and fairmindedness. These global skills, passions, and dispositions, integrated into behavior and thought, characterize the rational, the educated, and the critical person. See *higher and lower order learning, knowledge, didactic instruction.*

judgment: 1) The act of judging or deciding. 2) Understanding and good sense. A person has good judgment when they typically judge and decide on the basis of understanding and good sense. Whenever we form a belief or opinion, make a decision, or act, we do so on the basis of implicit or explicit judgments. All thought presupposes making judgments concerning what is so and what is not so, what is true and what is not. To cultivate people's ability to think critically is to foster their judgment, to help them to develop the habit of judging on the basis of reason, evidence, logic, and good sense. Good judgment is developed, not by merely learning about principles of good judgment, but by frequent practice judging and assessing judgments.

justify/justification: The act of showing a belief, opinion, action, or policy to be in accord with reason and evidence, to be ethically acceptable, or both. Education should foster reasonability in students. This requires that both teachers and students develop the disposition to ask for and give justifications for beliefs, opinions, actions, and policies. Asking for a justification should not, then, be viewed as an insult or attack, but rather as a normal act of a rational person. Didactic modes of teaching that do not encourage students to question the justification for what is asserted fail to develop a thoughtful environment conducive to education.

know: To have a clear perception or understanding of, to be sure of, to have a firm mental grasp of; *information* applies to data that are gathered in any way, as by reading, observation, hearsay, etc. and does not necessarily connote validity; *knowledge* applies to any body of facts gathered by study, observation, etc. and to the ideas inferred from these facts, and connotes an *understanding* of what is known. Critical thinkers need to distinguish knowledge from opinion and belief. See *knowledge*.

knowledge: The act of having a clear and justifiable grasp of what is so or of how to do something. Knowledge is based on understanding or skill, which in turn are based on thought, study, and experience. 'Thoughtless knowledge' is a contradiction. 'Blind knowledge' is a contradiction. 'Unjustifiable knowledge' is a contradiction. Knowledge implies justifiable belief or skilled action. Hence, when students blindly memorize and are tested for recall, they are not being tested for knowledge. *Knowledge is continually confused with recall in present-day schooling.* This confusion is a deep-seated impediment to the integration of critical thinking into schooling. *Genuine knowledge is inseparable from thinking minds.* We often wrongly talk of knowledge as though it could be divorced from thinking, as though it could be gathered up by one person and given to another in the form of a collection of sentences to remember. When we talk in this way, we forget that *knowledge*, by its very nature, *depends on thought*. Knowledge is produced by thought, analyzed by thought, comprehended by thought, organized, evaluated, maintained, and transformed by thought. Knowledge can be *acquired only* through thought. Knowledge exists, properly speaking, only in minds that have comprehended and justified it through thought. Knowledge is not to be confused with belief nor with symbolic representation of belief. Humans easily and frequently believe things that are false or believe things to be true without knowing them to be so. A book contains knowledge only in a derivative sense, only because minds can thoughtfully read it and through that process gain knowledge.

logic: *1)* Correct reasoning or the study of correct reasoning and its foundations. *2)* The relationships between propositions (supports, assumes, implies, contradicts, counts against, is relevant to, ...). *3)* The system of principles, concepts, and assumptions that underlie any discipline, activity, or practice. *4)* The set of rational considerations that bear upon the truth or justification of any belief or set of beliefs. *5)* The set of rational considerations that bear upon the settlement of any question or set of questions. The word 'logic' covers a range of related concerns all bearing upon the question of rational justification and explanation. *All human thought and behavior is to some extent based on logic* rather than instinct. Humans try to figure things out using ideas, meanings, and thought. Such intellectual behavior inevitably involves "logic" or considerations of a logical sort: some sense of what is relevant and irrelevant, of what supports and what counts against a belief, of what we should and should not assume, of what we should and should not claim, of what we do and do not know, of what is and is not implied, of what does and does not contradict, of what we should or should not do or believe. *Concepts have a logic* in that we can investigate the conditions under which they do and do not apply, of what is relevant or irrelevant to them, of what they do or don't imply, etc. *Questions have a logic* in that we can investigate the conditions under which they can be settled. *Disciplines have a logic* in that they have purposes and a set of logical structures that bear upon those purposes: assumptions, concepts, issues, data, theories, claims, implications, consequences, etc. The concept of logic is a seminal notion in critical thinking. Unfortunately, it takes a considerable length of time before most people become comfortable with its multiple uses. In part, this is due to people's failure to monitor their own thinking in keeping with the standards of reason and logic. This is not to deny, of course, that logic is involved in all human thinking. It is rather to say that the logic we use is often implicit, unexpressed, and sometimes contradictory. See *knowledge, higher and lower order learning, the logic of a discipline, the logic of language, the logic of questions.*

the logic of a discipline: The notion that every technical term has logical relationships with other technical terms, that some terms are logically more basic than others, and that every discipline relies on concepts, assumptions, and theories, makes claims, gives reasons and evidence, avoids contradictions and inconsistencies, has implications and consequences, etc. Though all students study disciplines, most are ignorant of the logic of the disciplines they study. This severely limits their ability to grasp the discipline as a whole, to think independently within it, to compare and contrast it with other disciplines, and to apply it outside the context of academic assignments. Typically now, students do not look for seminal terms as they study an area. They do not strive to translate technical terms into analogies and ordinary words they understand or distinguish technical from ordinary uses of terms. They do not look for the basic assumptions of the disciplines they study. Indeed, on the whole, they do not know what assumptions are nor why it is important to examine them. What they have in their heads exists like so many BB's in a bag. Whether one thought supports or follows from another, whether one thought elaborates another, exemplifies, presupposes, or contradicts another, are matters students have not learned to think about. They have not learned to use thought to understand thought, which is another way of saying that they have not learned how to use thought to gain knowledge. *Instruction for critical thinking cultivates the students' ability to make explicit the logic of what they study.* This emphasis gives depth and breath to study and learning. It lies at the heart of the differences between lower order and higher order learning. See *knowledge.*

the logic of language: For a language to exist and be learnable by persons from a variety of cultures, it is necessary that *words have definite uses and defined concepts that transcend* *particular cultures.* The English language, for example, is learned by many peoples of the world unfamiliar with English or North American cultures. Critical thinkers must learn to use their native language with precision, in keeping with educated usage. Unfortunately, many students do not understand the significant relationship between precision in language usage and precision in thought. Consider, for example, how most students relate to their native language. If one questions them about the meanings of words, their account is typically incoherent. They often say that people have their own meanings for all the words they use, not noticing that, were this true, we could not understand each other. Students speak and write in vague sentences because they have no rational criteria for choosing words — they simply write whatever words pop into their heads. They do not realize that every language has a highly refined logic one must learn in order to express oneself precisely. They do not realize that even words similar in meaning typically have different implications. Consider, for example, the words explain, expound, explicate, elucidate, interpret, and construe. *Explain* implies the process of making clear and intelligible something not understood or known. *Expound* implies a systematic and thorough explanation, often by an expert. *Explicate* implies a scholarly analysis developed in detail. *Elucidate* implies a shedding of light upon by clear and specific illustration or explanation. *Interpret* implies the bringing out of meanings not immediately apparent. *Construe* implies a particular interpretation of something whose meaning is ambiguous. See *clarify, concept.*

the logic of questions: The range of rational considerations that bear upon the settlement of a given question or group of questions. A critical thinker is adept at analyzing questions to determine what, precisely, a question asks and how to go about rationally settling it. A critical thinker recognizes that different kinds of questions often call for different modes of thinking, different kinds of considerations, and different procedures and techniques. Uncritical thinkers often confuse distinct questions and use considerations irrelevant to an issue while ignoring relevant ones.

lower order learning: Learning by rote memorization, association, and drill. There are a variety of forms of lower order learning in the schools which we can identify by understanding the relative *lack of logic informing them.* Paradigmatically, lower order learning is learning by sheer association or rote. Hence students come to think of history class, for example, as a place where you hear names, dates, places, events, and outcomes; where you try to remember them and state them on tests. Math comes to be thought of as numbers, symbols, and formulas — mysterious things you mechanically manipulate as the teacher told you in order to get the right answer. Literature is often thought of as uninteresting stories to remember along with what the teacher said is important about them. Consequently, students leave with a jumble of undigested fragments, scraps left over after they have forgotten most of what they stored in their short-term memories for tests. Virtually never do they grasp the logic of what they learn. Rarely do they relate what they learn to their own experience or critique each by means of the other. Rarely do they try to test what they learn in everyday life. Rarely do they ask "Why is this so? How does this relate to what I already know? How does this relate to what I am learning in other classes?" To put the point in a nutshell, very few students think of what they are learning as worthy of being arranged logically in their minds or have the slightest idea of how to do so. See *didactic instruction, monological and multilogical problems and thinking.*

monological (one-dimensional) problems: Problems that can be solved by reasoning exclusively within one point of view or frame of reference. For example, consider the following problems: *1)* Ten full crates of walnuts weigh 410 pounds, whereas an empty crate weighs 10 pounds. How much do the walnuts alone weigh?; and *2)* In how many days of the week does the third letter of the day's name immediately follow the first letter of the day's name in the alphabet? I call these problems and the means by which they are solved "monological". They are settled within one frame of reference with a definite set of logical moves. When the right set of moves is performed, the problem is settled. The answer or solution proposed can be shown by standards implicit in the frame of reference to be the "right" answer or solution. *Most important human problems are multilogical rather than monological,* nonatomic problems inextricably joined to other problems, with some conceptual messiness to them and very often with important values lurking in the background. When the problems have an empirical dimension, that dimension tends to have a controversial scope. In multilogical problems, it is often arguable how some facts should be considered and interpreted, and how their significance should be determined. When they have a conceptual dimension, there tend to be arguably different ways to pin the concepts down. Though life presents us with predominantly multilogical problems, schooling today over-emphasizes monological problems. Worse, and more frequently, present instructional practices treat multilogical problems as though they were monological. The posing of multilogical problems, and their consideration from multiple points of view, play an important role in the cultivation of critical thinking and higher order learning.

monological (one-dimensional) thinking: Thinking that is conducted exclusively within one point of view or frame of reference: figuring our how much this $67.49 pair of shoes with a 25% discount will cost me; learning what signing this contract obliges me to do; finding out when Kennedy was elected President. A person can think monologically whether or not the question is genuinely monological. (For example, if one considers the question, "Who caused the Civil War?" only from a Northerner's perspective, one is thinking monologically about a multilogical question.) The strong sense critical thinker avoids monological thinking when the question is multi-logical. Moreover, higher order learning requires multi-logical thought, even when the problem is monological (for example, learning a concept in chemistry), since students must explore and assess their original beliefs to develop insight into new ideas.

multilogical (multi-dimensional) problems: Problems that can be analyzed and approached from more than one, often from conflicting, points of view or frames of reference. For example, many ecological problems have a variety of dimensions to them: historical, social, economic, biological, chemical, moral, political, etc. A person comfortable thinking about multilogical problems is comfortable thinking within multiple perspectives, in engaging in dialogical and dialectical thinking, in practicing intellectual empathy, in thinking across disciplines and domains. See *monological problems, the logic of questions, the logic of disciplines, intellectual empathy, dialogical instruction.*

multilogical thinking: Thinking that sympathetically enters, considers, and reasons within multiple points of view. See *multilogical problems, dialectical thinking, dialogical instruction.*

national bias: Prejudice in favor of one's country, it's beliefs, traditions, practices, image, and world view; a form of sociocentrism or ethnocentrism. It is natural, if not inevitable, for people to be favorably disposed toward the beliefs, traditions, practices, and world view within which they were raised. Unfortunately, this favorable inclination commonly becomes a form of prejudice: a more or less rigid, irrational ego-identification which significantly distorts one's view of one's own nation and the world at large. It is manifested in a tendency to mindlessly take the side of one's own government, to uncritically accept governmental accounts of the nature of disputes with other nations, to uncritically exaggerate the virtues of one's own nation while playing down the virtues of "enemy" nations. National bias is reflected in the press and media coverage of every nation of the world. Events are included or excluded according to what appears significant within the dominant world view of the nation, and are shaped into stories to validate that view. Though constructed to fit into a particular view of the world, the stories in the news are presented as neutral, objective accounts, and uncritically accepted as such because people tend to uncritically assume that their own view of things is the way things really are. To become responsible critically thinking citizens and fairminded people, students must practice identifying national bias in the news and in their texts, and to broaden their perspective beyond that of uncritical nationalism. See *ethnocentrism, sociocentrism, bias, prejudice, world view, intellectual empathy, critical society, dialogical instruction, knowledge.*

opinion: A belief, typically one open to dispute. Sheer unreasoned opinion should be distinguished from reasoned judgment — beliefs formed on the basis of careful reasoning. See *evaluation, judgment, justify, know, knowledge, reasoned judgment.*

the perfections of thought: Thinking, as an attempt to understand the world as it is, has a natural excellence or fitness to it. This excellence is manifest in its *clarity, precision, specificity, accuracy, relevance, consistency, logicalness, depth, completeness, significance, fairness, and adequacy.* These perfections are general canons for thought; they represent legitimate concerns irrespective of the discipline or domain of thought. To develop one's mind and discipline one's thinking with respect to these standards *requires extensive practice and long-term cultivation.* Of course, achieving these standards is a relative matter and varies somewhat among domains of thought. Being *precise* while doing mathematics is not the same as being precise while writing a poem, describing an experience, or explaining a historical event. Furthermore, one perfection of thought may be periodically incompatible with the others: adequacy to purpose. Time and resources sufficient to thoroughly analyze a question or problem is all too often an unaffordable luxury. Also, since the social world is often irrational and unjust, because people are often manipulated to act against their interests, and because skilled thought often serves vested interest, thought adequate to these manipulative purposes may require *skilled violation of the common standards for good thinking.* Skilled propaganda, skilled political debate, skilled defense of a group's interests, skilled deception of one's enemy may require the violation or selective application of any of the above standards. Perfecting one's thought as an instrument for success in a world based on power and advantage differs from perfecting one's thought for the apprehension and defense of fairminded truth. *To develop one's critical thinking skills merely to the level of adequacy for social success is to develop those skills in a lower or <u>weaker</u> sense.*

personal contradiction: An inconsistency in one's personal life, wherein one says one thing and does another, or uses a double standard, judging oneself and one's friends by an easier standard than that used for people one doesn't like; typically a form of hypocrisy accompanied by self-deception. Most personal contradictions remain unconscious. People too often ignore the difficulty of becoming intellectually and morally consistent, preferring instead to merely admonish others. Personal contradictions are more likely to be discovered, analyzed, and reduced in an atmosphere in which they can be openly admitted and realistically considered without excessive penalty. See *egocentricity, intellectual integrity.*

perspective (point of view): Human thought is relational and selective. It is impossible to understand any person, event, or phenomenon from every vantage point simultaneously. Our purposes often control how we see things. Critical thinking requires that this fact be taken into account when analyzing and assessing thinking. This is not to say that human thought is incapable of truth and objectivity, but only that human truth, objectivity, and insight is virtually always limited and partial, virtually never total and absolute. The hard sciences are themselves a good example of this point, since qualitative realities are systematically ignored in favor of quantifiable realities.

precision: The quality of being accurate, definite, and exact. The standards and modes of precision vary according to subject and context. See *the logic of language, elements of thought.*

prejudice: A judgment, belief, opinion, point of view — favorable or unfavorable — formed before the facts are known, resistant to evidence and reason, or in disregard of facts which contradict it. Self-announced prejudice is rare. Prejudice almost always exists in obscured, rationalized, socially validated, functional forms. It enables people to sleep peacefully at night even while flagrantly abusing the rights of others. It enables people to get more of what they want, or to get it more easily. It is often sanctioned with a superabundance of pomp and self-righteousness. Unless we recognize these powerful tendencies toward selfish thought in our social institutions, even in what appear to be lofty actions and moralistic rhetoric, we will not face squarely the problem of prejudice in human thought and action. Uncritical and selfishly critical thought are often prejudiced. Most instruction in schools today, because students do not think their way to what they accept as true, tends to give students prejudices rather than knowledge. For example, partly as a result of schooling, people often accept as authorities those who liberally sprinkle their statements with numbers and intellectual-sounding language, however irrational or unjust their positions. This prejudice toward psuedo-authority impedes rational assessment. See *insight, knowledge.*

premise: A proposition upon which an argument is based or from which a conclusion is drawn. A starting point of reasoning. For example, one might say, in commenting on someone's reasoning, "You seem to be reasoning from the premise that everyone is selfish in everything they do. *Do* you hold this belief?"

principle: A fundamental truth, law, doctrine, value, or commitment, upon which others are based. Rules, which are more specific, and often superficial and arbitrary, are based on principles. Rules are more algorithmic; they needn't be understood to be followed. Principles must be understood to be appropriately applied or followed. Principles go to the heart of the matter. Critical thinking is dependent on principles, not rules and procedures. Critical thinking is principled, not procedural, thinking. Principles cannot be truly grasped through didactic instruction; they must be practiced and applied to be internalized. See *higher order learning, lower order learning, judgment.*

problem: A question, matter, situation, or person that is perplexing or difficult to figure out, handle, or resolve. Problems, like questions, can be divided into many types. Each has a (particular) logic. See *logic of questions, monological problems, multilogical problems.*

problem-solving: Whenever a problem cannot be solved formulaically or robotically, critical thinking is required: first, to determine the nature and dimensions of the problem, and then, in the light of the first, to determine the considerations, points of view, concepts, theories, data, and reasoning relevant to its solution. Extensive practice in independent problem-solving is essential to developing critical thought. Problem-solving is rarely best approached procedurally or as a series of rigidly followed steps. For example, problem-solving schemas typically begin, "State the problem." Rarely can problems be precisely and fairly stated prior to analysis, gathering of evidence, and dialogical or dialectical thought wherein several provisional descriptions of the problem are proposed, assessed, and revised.

proof (prove): Evidence or reasoning so strong or certain as to demonstrate the truth or acceptability of a conclusion beyond a reasonable doubt. How strong evidence or reasoning have to be to demonstrate what they purport to prove varies from context to context, depending on the significance of the conclusion or the seriousness of the implications following from it. See *domain of thought.*

rational/rationality: That which conforms to principles of good reasoning, is sensible, shows good judgment, is consistent, logical, complete, and relevant. Rationality is a summary term like 'virtue' or 'goodness'. It is manifested in an unlimited number of ways and depends on a host of principles. There is some ambiguity in it, depending on whether one considers only the logicalness and effectiveness by which one pursues one's ends, or whether it includes the assessment of ends themselves. There is also ambiguity in whether one considers selfish ends to be rational, even when they conflict with what is just. Does a rational person have to be just or only skilled in pursuing his or her interests? Is it rational to be rational in an irrational world? See *perfections of thought, irrational/irrationality, logic, intellectual virtues, weak sense critical thinking, strong sense critical thinking.*

rational emotions/passions: R. S. Peters has explained the significance of the affective side of reason and critical thought in his defense of the necessity of "rational passions":

> There is, for instance, the hatred of contradictions and inconsistencies, together with the love of clarity and hatred of confusion without which words could not be held to relatively constant meanings and testable rules and generalizations stated. A reasonable man cannot, without some special explanation, slap his sides with delight or express indifference if he is told that what he says is confused, incoherent, and perhaps riddled with contradictions.
> Reason is the antithesis of arbitrariness. In its operation it is supported by the appropriate passions which are mainly negative in character — the hatred of irrelevance, special pleading, and arbitrary fiat. The more developed emotion of indignation is aroused when some excess of arbitrariness is perpetuated in a situation where people's interests and claims are at stake. The positive side of this is the passion for fairness and impartial consideration of claims ....
> A man who is prepared to reason must feel strongly that he must follow the arguments and decide things in terms of where they lead. He must have a sense of the giveness of the impersonality of such considerations. In so far as thoughts about persons enter his head they should be tinged with the respect which is due to another who, like himself, may have a point of view which is worth considering, who may have a glimmering of the truth which has so far eluded himself. A person who proceeds in this way, who is influenced by such passions, is what we call a reasonable man.

rational self: Our character and nature to the extent that we seek to base our beliefs and actions on good reasoning and evidence. Who we are, what our true character is, or our predominant qualities are, is always somewhat or even greatly different from who we *think* we are. Human egocentrism and accompanying self-deception often stand in the way of our gaining more insight into ourselves. We can develop a rational self, become a person who gains significant insight into what our true character is, only by reducing our egocentrism and self-deception. Critical thinking is essential to this process.

rational society: See *critical society.*

reasoned judgment: Any belief or conclusion reached on the basis of careful thought and reflection, distinguished from mere or unreasoned opinion on the one hand, and from sheer fact on the other. Few people have a clear sense of which of their beliefs are based on reasoned judgment and which on mere opinion. Moral or ethical questions, for example, are questions requiring reasoned judgment. One way of conceiving of subject-matter education is as developing students' ability to engage in reasoned judgment in accordance with the standards of each subject.

reasoning: The mental processes of those who reason; especially the drawing of conclusions or inferences from observations, facts, or hypotheses; the evidence or arguments used in this procedure. A critical thinker tries to develop the capacity to transform thought into reasoning at will, or rather, the ability to make his or her inferences explicit, along with the assumptions or premises upon which those inferences are based. Reasoning is a form of explicit inferring, usually involving multiple steps. When students write a persuasive paper, for example, we want them to be clear about their reasoning.

reciprocity: The act of entering empathically into the point of view or line of reasoning of others; learning to think as others do and by that means sympathetically assessing that thinking. (Reciprocity requires creative imagination as well as intellectual skill and a commitment to fairmindedness.)

relevant: Bearing upon or relating to the matter at hand; *relevant* implies close logical relationship with, and importance to, the matter under consideration; *germane* implies such close natural connection as to be highly appropriate or fit; *pertinent* implies an immediate and direct bearing on the matter at hand (a pertinent suggestion); *apposite* applies to that which is both relevant and happily suitable or appropriate; *applicable* refers to that which can be brought to bear upon a particular matter or problem. Students often have problems sticking to an issue and distinguishing information that bears upon a problem from information that does not. Merely reminding students to limit themselves to relevant considerations fails to solve this problem. The usual way of teaching students the term 'relevant' is to mention only clear-cut cases of relevance and irrelevance. Consequently, students do not learn that not everything that *seems* relevant is, or that some things which *do not seem* relevant are. Sensitivity to (ability to judge) relevance can only be developed with continual practice — practice distinguishing relevant from irrelevant data, evaluating or judging relevance, arguing for and against the relevance of facts and considerations.

self-deception: Deceiving one's self about one's true motivations, character, identity, etc. One possible definition of the human species is "The Self-Deceiving Animal". Self-deception

390

is a fundamental problem in human life and the cause of much human suffering. Overcoming self-deception through self-critical thinking is a fundamental goal of strong sense critical thinking. See *egocentric, rational self, personal contradiction, social contradiction, intellectual virtues.*

social contradiction: An inconsistency between what a society preaches and what it practices. In every society there is some degree of inconsistency between its image of itself and its actual character. Social contradiction typically correlates with human self-deception on the social or cultural level. Critical thinking is essential for the recognition of inconsistencies, and recognition is essential for reform and eventual integrity.

sociocentricity: The assumption that one's own social group is inherently and self-evidently superior to all others. When a group or society sees itself as superior, and so considers its views as correct or as the only reasonable or justifiable views, and all its actions as justified, there is a tendency to presuppose this superiority in all of its thinking and thus, to think closedmindedly. All dissent and doubt are considered disloyal and rejected without consideration. Few people recognize the sociocentric nature of much of their thought.

Socratic questioning: A mode of questioning that deeply probes the meaning, justification, or logical strength of a claim, position, or line of reasoning. Socratic questioning can be carried out in a variety of ways and adapted to many levels of ability and understanding. See *elements of thought, dialogical instruction, knowledge.*

specify/specific: To mention, describe, or define in detail; limiting or limited; specifying or specified; precise; definite. Student thinking, speech, and writing tend to be vague, abstract, and ambiguous rather than specific, concrete, and clear. Learning how to state one's views specifically is essential to learning how to think clearly, precisely, and accurately. See *perfections of thought.*

strong sense critical thinker: One who is predominantly characterized by the following traits: *1)* an ability to question deeply one's own framework of thought; *2)* an ability to reconstruct sympathetically and imaginatively the strongest versions of points of view and frameworks of thought opposed to one's own; and *3)* an ability to reason dialectically (multilogically) in such a way as to determine when one's own point of view is at its weakest and when an opposing point of view is at its strongest. Strong sense critical thinkers are not routinely blinded by their own points of view. They know they have points of view and therefore recognize on what framework of assumptions and ideas their own thinking is based. They realize the necessity of putting their own assumptions and ideas to the test of the strongest objections that can be leveled against them. Teaching for critical thinking in the strong sense is teaching so that students explicate, understand, and critique their own deepest prejudices, biases, and misconceptions, thereby discovering and contesting their own egocentric and sociocentric tendencies. Only if we contest our inevitable egocentric and sociocentric habits of thought, can we hope to think in a genuinely rational fashion. Only dialogical thinking about basic issues that genuinely matter to the individual provides the kind of practice and skill essential to strong sense critical thinking.

Students need to develop all critical thinking skills in dialogical settings to achieve ethically rational development, that is, genuine fairmindedness. If critical thinking is taught simply as atomic skills separate from the empathic practice of entering into points of view that students are fearful of or hostile toward, they will simply find additional means of rationalizing prejudices and preconceptions, or convincing people that their point of view is the correct one. They will be transformed from vulgar to sophisticated (but not to strong sense) critical thinkers.

teach: The basic inclusive word for the imparting of knowledge or skills. It usually connotes some individual attention to the learner; *instruct* implies systematized teaching, usually in some particular subject; *educate* stresses the development of latent faculties and powers by formal, systematic teaching, especially in institutions of higher learning; *train* implies the development of a particular faculty or skill or instruction toward a particular occupation, as by methodical discipline, exercise, etc. See *knowledge.*

theory: A systematic statement of principles involved in a subject; a formulation of apparent relationships or underlying principles of certain observed phenomena which has been verified to some degree. Often without realizing it, we form theories that help us make sense of the people, events, and problems in our lives. Critical thinkers put their theories to the test of experience and give due consideration to the theories of others. Critical thinkers do not take their theories to be facts.

think: The general word meaning to exercise the mental faculties so as to form ideas, arrive at conclusions, etc.; *reason* implies a logical sequence of thought, starting with what is known or assumed and advancing to a definite conclusion through the inferences drawn; *reflect* implies a turning of one's thoughts back on a subject and connotes deep or quiet continued thought; *speculate* implies a reasoning on the basis of incomplete or uncertain evidence and therefore stresses the conjectural character of the opinions formed; *deliberate* implies careful and thorough consideration of a matter in order to arrive at a conclusion. Though everyone thinks, few people think critically. We don't need instruction to think; we think spontaneously. We need instruction to learn how to discipline and direct our thinking on the basis of sound intellectual standards. See *elements of thought, perfections of thought.*

truth: Conformity to knowledge, fact, actuality, or logic: a statement proven to be or accepted as true, not false or erroneous. Most people uncritically assume their views to be correct and true. Most people, in other words, assume themselves to possess the truth. Critical thinking is essential to avoid this, if for no other reason.

uncritical person: One who has not developed intellectual skills (naive, conformist, easily manipulated, dogmatic, easily confused, unclear, closedminded, narrowminded, careless in word choice, inconsistent, unable to distinguish evidence from interpretation). Uncriticalness is a fundamental problem in human life, for when we are uncritical we nevertheless think of ourselves as critical. The first step in becoming a critical thinker consists in recognizing that we are uncritical. Teaching for insight into uncriticalness is an important part of teaching for criticalness.

vague: Not clearly, precisely, or definitely expressed or stated; not sharp, certain, or precise in thought, feeling, or expression. Vagueness of thought and expression is a major obstacle to the development of critical thinking. We cannot begin to test our beliefs until we recognize clearly what they are. We cannot disagree with what someone says until we are clear about what they mean. Students need much practice in transforming vague thoughts into clear ones. See *ambiguous, clarify, concept, logic, logic of questions, logic of language.*

verbal implication: That which follows, according to the logic of the language. If I say, for example, that someone used flattery on me, I *imply* that the compliments were insincere and given only to make me feel positively toward that person, to manipulate me against my reason or interest for some end. *See imply, infer, empirical implication, elements of thought.*

weak sense critical thinkers: 1) Those who do not hold themselves or those with whom they ego-identify to the same intellectual standards to which they hold "opponents". 2) Those who have not learned how to reason empathically within points of view or frames of reference with which they disagree. 3) Those who tend to think monologically. 4) Those who do not genuinely accept, though they may verbally espouse, the values of critical thinking. 5) Those who use the intellectual skills of critical thinking selectively and self-deceptively to foster and serve their vested interests (at the expense of truth); able to identify flaws in the reasoning of others and refute them; able to shore up their own beliefs with reasons.

world view: All human action takes place within a way of looking at and interpreting the world. As schooling now stands, very little is done to help students to grasp how they are viewing the world and how those views determine the character of their experience, their interpretations, their conclusions about events and persons, etc. In teaching for critical thinking in a strong sense, we make the discovery of one's own world view and the experience of other people's world views a fundamental priority. See *bias, interpret.*

Recommended Readings in Critical Thinking

The General Case for Critical Thinking

Bailin, Sharon. *Achieving Extraordinary Ends: An Essay of Creativity.* Kluwer-Academic Publishers, Norwell, MA, 1988.

Baron, Joan and Robert Sternberg. *Teaching Thinking Skills: Theory and Practice.* W. H. Freeman Co., New York, NY, 1987.

Blair, J. Anthony and Ralph H. Johnson, eds. *Informal Logic (First International Symposium).* Edgepress, Point Reyes, CA, 1980.

Glaser, Edward M. *An Experiment in the Development of Critical Thinking.* AMS Press, New York, NY, reprint of 1941 edition.

Mill, John Stuart. *On Liberty.* AHM Publishing Corp., Arlington Heights, IL., 1947.

Resnick, Lauren. *Education and Learning to Think.* National Academy Press, Washington, D.C., 1987.

Scheffler, Israel. *Reason and Teaching.* Hackett Publishing, Indianapolis, IN, 1973.

Siegel, Harvey. *Educating Reason: Rationality, Critical Thinking, & Education.* Routledge Chapman & Hall, Inc., New York, NY, 1988.

Sumner, William G. *Folkways.* Ayer Co., Publishing, Salem, NH, 1979.

Toulmin, Stephen E. *The Uses of Argument.* Cambridge University Press, New York, NY, 1958.

Critical Thinking Pedagogy

Brookfield, Stephen D. *Developing Critical Thinkers.* Jossey-Bass, San Francisco, CA, 1987.

Costa, Arthur L. *Developing Minds: A Resource Book for Teaching Thinking.* A.S.C.D., Alexandria, VA, 1985.

D'Angelo, Edward. *The Teaching of Critical Thinking.* B. R. Grüner, N. V., Amsterdam, 1971.

Goodlad, John. *A Place Called School.* McGraw-Hill, New York, 1984.

Lipman, Matthew. *Ethical Inquiry.* Institute for the Advancement of Philosophy for Children, Upper Montclair, N.J., 1977.

Lipman, Matthew. *Harry Stottlemeier's Discovery.* Institute for the Advancement of Philosophy for Children, Upper Montclair, N.J., 1982.

Lipman, Matthew. *Lisa.* Institute for the Advancement of Philosophy for Children, Upper Montclair, N.J., 1976.

Lipman, Matthew. *Mark.* Institute for the Advancement of Philosophy for Children, Upper Monclair, N.J., 1980.

Lipman, Matthew, Ann M. Sharp, and Frederick S. Oscanyan. *Philosophical Inquiry.* University Press of America, Lanham, Maryland, 1979.

Lipman, Matthew, and Ann M. Sharp. *Philosophy in the Classroom.* 2nd edition, Temple University Press, Philadelphia, PA, 1980.

Lipman, Matthew. *Social Inquiry.* Institute for the Advancement of Philosophy for Children, Upper Montclair, N.J., 1980.

Meyers, Chet. *Teaching Students to Think Critically: A Guide for Faculty in all Disciplines.* Jossey-Bass, San Francisco, CA, 1986.

Paul, Richard W., et al. *Critical Thinking Handbook: K–3. A Guide to Remodelling Lesson Plans in Language Arts, Social Studies, and Science.* The Center for Critical Thinking and Moral Critique, Rohnert Park, CA, 1987.

Paul, Richard W., et al. *Critical Thinking Handbook: 4th–6th. A Guide to Remodelling Lesson Plans in Language Arts, Social Studies, and Science.* The Center for Critical Thinking and Moral Critique, Rohnert Park, CA, 1987.

Paul, Richard W., et al. *Critical Thinking Handbook: 6th–9th A Guide to Remodelling Lesson Plans in Language Arts, Social Studies, and Science.* The Center for Critical Thinking and Moral Critique, Rohnert Park, CA, 1989.

Paul, Richard W., et al. *Critical Thinking Handbook: High School. A Guide for Redesigning Instruction.* The Center for Critical Thinking and Moral Critique, Rohnert Park, CA, 1989.

Raths, Louis. *Teaching for Thinking: Theories, Strategies, and Activities for the Classroom*. 2nd edition, Teachers College Press, New York, NY, 1986.

Ruggiero, Vincent. *Thinking Across the Curriculum*. Harper & Row, New York, NY, 1988.

Ruggiero, Vincent. *Art of Thinking*. 2nd edition, Harper & Row, New York, NY, 1988.

Sizer, Theodore R. *Horace's Compormise: The Dilemma of the American High School*. Houghton Mifflin, Boston, 1984.

College Textbooks (Not Focused on a Specific Discipline)

Barker, Evelyn M. *Everyday Reasoning*. Prentice-Hall, Englewood Cliffs, NJ, 1981.

Barry, Vincent E., and Joel Rudinow. *Invitation to Critical Thinking*. 2nd edition, Holt, Rinehart & Winston, New York, NY, 1990.

Brown, Neil and Stuart Keely. *Asking the Right Questions: A Guide to Critical Thinking*. 2nd edition, Prentice-Hall, Englewood Cliffs, NJ, 1986.

Capaldi, Nicholas. *The Art of Deception*. 2nd edition, Prometheus Books, Buffalo, New York, 1979.

Cederblom, Jerry. *Critical Reasoning*. 2nd edition, Wadsworth Publishing Co., Belmont, CA, 1986.

Chaffee, John. *Thinking Critically*. 2nd edition, Houghton Mifflin, Boston, MA, 1988.

Damer, T. Edward. *Attacking Faulty Reasoning*. 2nd edition, Wadsworth Publishing Co., Belmont, CA, 1987.

Engel, Morris. *Analyzing Informal Fallacies*. Prentice-Hall, Englewood Cliffs, NJ, 1980.

Engel, Morris. *With Good Reason: An Introduction to Informal Fallacies*. 3rd edition, St. Martin's Press, New York, NY, 1986.

Fahnestock, Jeanne and Marie Secor. *Rhetoric of Argument*. McGraw-Hill Book Co., New York, NY, 1982.

Fisher, Alec. *The Logic of Real Arguments*. Cambridge University Press, New York, NY, 1988.

Govier, Trudy. *A Practical Study of Argument*. 2nd edition, Wadsworth Publishing Co., Belmont, CA, 1988.

Hitchcock, David. *Critical Thinking: A Guide to Evaluating Information*. Methuan Publications, Toronto, Canada, 1983.

Hoagland, John. *Critical Thinking*. Vale Press, Newport News, VA, 1984.

Johnson, Ralph H. and J. A. Blair. *Logical Self-Defense*. 2nd edition, McGraw-Hill, New York, NY, 1983.

Kahane, Howard. *Logic and Contemporary Rhetoric*. 5th edition, Wadsworth Publishing Co., Belmont, CA, 1988.

Meiland, Jack W. *College Thinking: How to Get the Best Out of College*. New American Library, New York, NY, 1981.

Michalos, Alex C. *Improving Your Reasoning*. Prentice-Hall, Englewood Cliffs, NJ, 1986.

Miller, Robert K. *Informed Argument*. 2nd edition, Harcourt, Brace, Jovanovich, San Diego, CA, 1989.

Missimer, Connie. *Good Arguments: An Introduction to Critical Thinking*. 2nd edition, Prentice-Hall, Englewood Cliffs, NJ, 1986.

Moore, Brooke N. *Critical Thinking: Evaluating Claims and Arguments in Everyday Life*. 2nd edition, Mayfield Publishing Co., Palo Alto, CA, 1989.

Moore, Edgar. *Creative and Critical Reasoning*. 2nd edition, Houghton Mifflin, Boston, MA, 1984.

Nickerson, Raymond S. *Reflections on Reasoning*. L. Erlbaum, Assoc., Hillsdale, NJ, 1986.

Ruggiero, Vincent. *Moral Imperative*. Mayfield Publishing, Palo Alto, CA, 1984.

Scriven, Michael. *Reasoning*. McGraw-Hill Book Co., New York, NY, 1976.

Seech, Zachary. *Logic in Everyday Life: Practical Reasoning Skills*. Wadsworth Publishing Co., Belmont, CA, 1988.

Shor, Ira. *Critical Teaching & Everyday Life*. University of Chicago Press, Chicago, IL, 1987.

Toulmin, Stephen E., Richard Rieke, and Alan Janik. *An Introduction to Reasoning*. Macmillan Publishing Co., New York, NY, 1979.

Weddle, Perry. *Argument: A Guide to Critical Thinking*. McGraw-Hill, New York, NY, 1978.

Wilson, John. *Thinking with Concepts*. 4th edition, Cambridge University Press, New York, NY, 1987.

Science and Critical Thinking

Giere, Ronald N. *Understanding Scientific Reasoning*. Holt, Rinehart, and Winston, New York, NY, 1979. (Out of print.)

Radner, Daisie and Radner, Michael. *Science and Unreason*. Wadsworth, Publishing Co., Belmont, CA, 1982.

Mathematics and Critical Thinking

Schoenfeld, Alan. *Mathematical Problem Solving*. Academic Press, Orlando, FL, 1985.

Language Arts and Critical Thinking

Adler, Mortimer. *How to Read a Book*. Simon and Schuster, New York, NY, 1972.

Horton, Susan. *Thinking Through Writing*. Johns Hopkins, Baltimore, MD, 1982.

Kytle, Ray. *Clear Thinking for Composition*. 5th edition, McGraw-Hill Book Co., New York, NY, 1987.

Mayfield, Marlys. *Thinking for Yourself: Developing Critical Thinking Skills Through Writing*. Wadsworth Publishing Co., Belmont, CA, 1987.

Rosenberg, Vivian. *Reading, Writing, and Thinking: Critical Connections*. McGraw-Hill Book Co., New York, NY, 1989.

Scull, Sharon. *Critical Reading and Writing for Advanced ESL Students*. Prentice-Hall, Englewood Cliffs, NJ, 1987.

Critical Thinking and the Media

Lazere, Donald. *American Media & Mass Culture*. University of California Press, Berkeley, CA, 1987.

Also of Interest

Baker, Paul J., and Louis Anderson. *Social Problems: A Critical Thinking Approach*. Wadsworth Publishing Co., Belmont, CA, 1987.

Bloom, Benjamin. *Taxonomy of Educational Objectives*. David McKay Co., Inc., New York, 1956.

Goffman, Erving. *Presentation of Self in Everyday Life*. Doubleday & Co., New York, NY, 1959.

Lappé, Francis Moore. *Rediscovering America's Values*. Ballantine Books, New York, NY, 1989.

Siegel, Harvey. *Relativism Refuted*. Kluwer-Academic Publishers, Norwell, MA, 1987.

Tavris, Carol. *Anger: The Misunderstood Emotion*. Simon & Schuster, New York, NY, 1987.

Wilson, Barrie. *The Anatomy of Argument*. University Press of America, Lanham, Maryland, 1980.

Critical Thinking Resources

from the
Foundation for Critical Thinking

 Grade Level Handbooks

 Hundreds of audio and video tapes by distinguished educators

 Annual Conferences

 A Critical Thinking Clearing House

 The Latest Theory and Research

 Staff Development

Critical Thinking Strategies

What every teacher needs to know!

What do I do when . . .

. . . *my students do not learn how to work by, or think for, themselves?*

. . . *they don't know how to reason well enough to master a subject?*

How do I . . .

. . . *teach "content" when my students don't read, write, speak, or listen critically?*

Solution!

✔ *How-to-do-it handbooks help you the teacher, alone or with others, to use critical thinking as a powerful tool for teaching and learning.*

✔ *Devised and designed by one of the best known and respected authorities on critical thinking, Richard Paul.*

✔ *Acclaimed by teachers and leading educators, such as Art Costa, Sandra Black, Bob Swartz.*

Critical Thinking Strategies

Handbooks K-3, 4-6, 6-9, High School

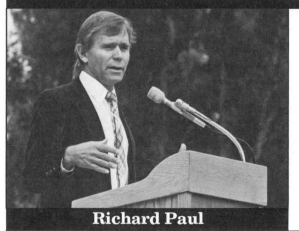
For more information: **(707) 664-2940**   ☛ *Please see Order Form on page 409*

Richard Paul has written over forty articles on critical thinking in the last five years, yet ready access to them has been hampered by the variety of publications in which they have appeared. This anthology collects together the major essays of Richard Paul on critical thinking, including a number of important unpublished ones. As a collection, it makes a powerful case for critical thinking as essential not only for academic but for political, social, and personal life as well. Paul inevitably canvases critical thinking from a broad perspective. He views it historically, socially, psychologically, ethically, philosophically, and pedagogically. While seeing clearly its universal application across domains of knowledge and learning, he also sees the need for working out the details of that universality in specific contexts and domains. Bringing his major papers together enables the reader to grasp something of the breadth and depth of the

role thinking plays in human life and knowledge, and of why reform of education grounded in critical thinking is essential to the future of humankind. It enables the reader to see why critical thinking must be cultivated from the earliest years of children's lives and why this must be understood as a long term commitment.

Paul's writings on critical thinking model the processes that all thinking must undergo as it develops. They overlap and criss-cross each other in many different ways. Reflective readers will find themselves coming at the same ground from a number of different vantage points.

As the table of contents indicates, this volume includes essays and papers that integrate the theory and practice of critical thinking and critical thinking instruction. It will be of special interest, therefore, to educators concerned with classroom practice.

Critical Thinking
Table of Contents

☞ *Please see Order Form on page 409*

Critical Thinking Audio & Video Catalog

☛ *Please see Order Form on page **409***

With many distinguished educators:

Richard Paul

Carol Tavris

David Perkins

Robert Ennis

☛ *Please see* Order Form *on page **409***

The Best of Theory and Practice

Art Costa

Dianne Romain

John Chaffee

Vincent Ryan Ruggiero

☛ *Please see* Order Form *on page* **409**

From Kindergarten through Graduate School

Jan Talbot

Ralph Johnson

J. Anthony Blair

Linda Phillips

☛ *Please see Order Form on page 409*

Critical Thinking Forum
on VHS Tape!

❑

from the
Center for Critical Thinking and Moral Critique
a series of eight Resource Programs produced for PBS Adult Learning Service

Part I: Why Critical Thinking?

Critical Thinking and the Human Emotions — Most instruction is designed without an adequate understanding of the profound role of human emotions and passions in learning. In this program, Carol Tavris, distinguished social psychologist and author of *Anger: The Misunderstood Emotions,* engages in a lively discussion on the relation of disciplined thought to emotions and passions. Many of the traditional views of reason and emotion are critiqued in this session, and the implications for education emerge vividly.

Critical Thinking and Mathematical Problem Solving — Surely it's not possible to pass a math class without doing much disciplined thinking. Not so! argues Alan Schoenfeld, distinguished math educator from the University of California. Most students do not learn to think mathematically precisely because of the domination of didactic lecture, standard algorithmic practice and one-dimensional testing that characterizes most math classes. When independent critical thinking is the heart of class activity, Schoenfeld says, genuine mathematical thinking emerges for the first time.

Infusing Critical Thinking into Community College Instruction — For critical thinking to become a significant force in student learning, it is essential that it permeate instruction across the disciplines. Unfortunately, students do not arrive on campus with developed critical thinking abilities and most professors are up in the air as to how they can cover essential content and also foster critical thinking. In this program, faculty development leaders from five diverse community colleges discuss their strategies for making critical thinking central to instruction.

Infusing Critical Thinking into Instruction at Four Year Colleges and Universities — Though four year colleges and universities tend to draw students with higher test scores and grade point averages than those entering community colleges, it does not follow that those students have developed critical thinking skills and abilities adequate to university learning. Five faculty development leaders from diverse colleges and universities discuss the problem of infusing critical thinking into instruction.

☛ *Please see Order Form on page 409*

Critical Thinking Forum
on VHS Tape!

❑

from the

Center for Critical Thinking and Moral Critique
a series of eight Resource Programs produced for PBS Adult Learning Service

Part II: How to Infuse Critical Thinking K–12

Critical Thinking: The Thinking that Masters the Content — This program investigates why traditional didactic instruction inevitably fails and why critical thinking is essential to in-depth learning. Three dimensions of thought are emphasized: 1) fine-textured thinking such as identifying evidence and reasons, probing for assumptions, drawing careful conclusions, and noticing inconsistencies; 2) skills such as reasoning within multiple points of view and reading, writing, speaking, and listening critically; and 3) affective skills so students develop traits such as fairmindedness, intellectual courage, humility, and persistence.

Transforming Critical Thinking Principles into Teaching Strategies — Critical thinking is based not on rules but on principles that can be learned by any willing teacher and transformed into a variety of teaching and learning strategies. In this program, a variety of grade-levels and subject matter illustrations are used to illustrate how critical thinking principles that are integrated into modes of teaching become modes of learning as well.

Remodelling Lessons and Redesigning Instruction to Infuse Critical Thinking — In this program, the teacher becomes the focus as Richard Paul explains how, by learning to think critically about their own instruction, teachers can remodel their lessons and redesign their instruction. Virtually every traditional lesson or unit can be remodelled in a variety of ways to infuse critical thinking. When it is, passive students become actively engaged. The teacher's monologue becomes a classroom dialogue. And content becomes something understood, mastered, and used — not just something memorized today and forgotten tomorrow.

The Greensboro Plan: Long-Term Critical Thinking Staff Development in an Urban Multi-Racial School District — In its third year of a long-term staff development program to infuse critical thinking, two teachers become full-time classroom consultants to encourage teachers to think critically about their own instruction. The aim is to remodel lessons and redesign instruction in order to infuse reasoning, writing, and critical thinking pervasively. Slowly but progressively, a new atmosphere is developing that encourages independent thinking for both teachers and students. This volunteer program, growing in support from both teachers and administrators, is a model for districts willing to work for long-term, substantial, educational reform.

☛ *Please see Order Form on page 409*

Annual Conference
on
Critical Thinking

Every year in the first week of August, the Center hosts the oldest and largest critical thinking conference. Each year the conference has over 100 presenters, nearly 300 sessions, and over 1,000 registrants. The conference is designed to meet the needs and concerns of the widest variety of educational levels. Practitioners, administrators, professors, and theoreticians regularly attend the conference. Many registrants have responsibilities for curriculum design and inservice training or particular subject matter concerns: math, science, language arts, social studies, humanities, fine arts, …. Others are principally concerned with assessment issues, remediation, or preservice education. Still others want information about the relation of critical thinking to citizenship, to vocational or professional education, or to personal development. Some are eager to explore the relation of critical thinking to the classic ideals of the liberally educated person and the free society or to world-wide social, economic, and moral issues. The conference discussions and dialogues that result from bringing together such a large number of committed critical thinkers with such a broad background of concerns are not only truly exciting but also rich in practical pay-offs.

PLEASE SEND ME MORE INFORMATION ON THE CENTER'S ANNUAL CONFERENCES ON CRITICAL THINKING:

NAME: _____

ADDRESS: _____

_____

_____

_____

SPECIAL INTERESTS (GRADE LEVELS, SUBJECT, ETC.)

_____

_____

_____

_____

_____

_____

Order Form

Please send me free information on:

The Annual Critical Thinking Conference ....☐

The Audio & Video Tape Collection ....☐

Other (Specify) _____ ☐

I would like to order the following:

Books

Critical Thinking:What Every Person Needs to Survive
  in a Rapidly Changing World (700 pp.)..☐ $19.95 _____

Critical Thinking Handbook: K–3 (322 pp.) ....☐ $18.00 _____

Critical Thinking Handbook: 4–6 (316 pp.) ....☐ $18.00 _____

Critical Thinking Handbook: 6–9 (320 pp.) ....☐ $18.00 _____

Critical Thinking Handbook: High School (416 pp.) ....☐ $18.00 _____

The Greensboro Plan for Critical Thinking Staff Development (212 pp.) ....☐ $8.95 _____

Discount Available for Bulk Orders

VHS Tapes

Critical Thinking Forum 1990: Parts I and II ....☐ $650 _____
All eight programs delivered as available in Spring/Fall 1990

Part I: Why Critical Thinking?..☐ $375 _____
Four programs delivered as available in Spring 1990

Part II: How to Infuse Critical Thinking K–12 ....☐ $375 _____
Four programs delivered as available in Fall 1990

Purchase by Individual Program *(please check those you wish to order)*

Critical Thinking and the Human Emotions ....☐ $125 _____

Critical Thinking and Mathematical Problem Solving ....☐ $125 _____

Infusing Critical Thinking into Community College Instruction ....☐ $125 _____

Infusing Critical Thinking into Instruction at Four Year Colleges/Universities ....☐ $125 _____

Critical Thinking: The Thinking that Masters the Content ....☐ $125 _____

Transforming Critical Thinking Principles into Teaching Strategies ....☐ $125 _____

Remodeling Lessons & Redesigning Instruction to Infuse Critical Thinking ....☐ $125 _____

The Greensboro Plan: Long Term Critical Thinking Staff Development ....☐ $125 _____

Shipping: $3.50 for the first tape or book, $1.00 for each additional item

  Foreign Orders: $7.50 for the first tape or book, $2.00 for each additional item   Shipping $ _____

California orders 6.25% tax $ _____

Total $ _____

Make Check or Purchase Order Payable to: Foundation for Critical Thinking *(U.S. currency only)*

Send order to: Center for Critical Thinking and Moral Critique
           Sonoma State University, Rohnert Park, CA 94928   (707)664-2940

Ship to:

Name: _____

Address: _____

_____ Phone: _____

Help Us "Remodel" this Handbook

In the spirit of good critical thinking, we want your assessment of this handbook and ideas for its improvement. Your ideas might be rewarded with a scholarship to the next International Conference on Critical Thinking!

Evaluation:

Here's what I found most useful about the handbook:

_____

_____

_____

_____

This is what I think is in need of change:

_____

_____

_____

_____

Here are my ideas for improving the handbook:

_____

_____

_____

Send evaluation to: Center For Critical Thinking; Sonoma State University; Rohnert Park, CA 94928.